THE
U.S. LEGAL SYSTEM

Volume 2

Jury Duty–Witnesses, Expert
Appendices
Indexes

Edited by
Timothy L. Hall
University of Mississippi Law School

SALEM PRESS, INC.
Pasadena, California   Hackensack, New Jersey

∞ The paper used in these volumes conforms to the American National Standard for Permanence of Paper for Printed Library Materials, Z39.48-1992 (R1997).

Parts of this publication previously appeared in *American Justice* (1996), *Magill's Legal Guide* (1999), and *Encyclopedia of the U.S. Supreme Court* (2000), all copyrighted by Salem Press, Inc. New material has been added.

Library of Congress Cataloging-in-Publication Data
The U.S. legal system / editor, Timothy L. Hall.
    p. cm. — (Magill's choice)
Includes bibliographical references and indexes.
    ISBN 1-58765-189-0 (set : alk. paper) — ISBN 1-58765-190-4 (v. 1 : alk. paper) — ISBN 1-58765-191-2 (v. 2 : alk. paper)
    1. Law—United States—Popular works. 2. Justice, Administration of—United States—Popular works.   I. Title: US legal system. II. Title: United States legal system.   III. Hall, Timothy L., 1955-IV. Series
    KF387.U15 2004
    349.73—dc22

                            2003027174

First Printing

PRINTED IN THE UNITED STATES OF AMERICA

Contents

CONTENTS

THE U.S. LEGAL SYSTEM

Jury duty

Duty to serve on a jury, which accompanies the constitutional right to be tried by a jury, that is every citizen's right and responsibility

The right to a trial by jury is guaranteed in the U.S. Constitution by the Sixth Amendment for criminal cases and the Seventh Amendment for civil cases. Alongside this right is the duty of citizens to serve when summoned and selected as members of a jury. Indeed, failure to appear for jury duty when summoned is considered contempt of court, which may be punishable by fine or imprisonment.

Although many persons might consider jury duty to be a burden, it is in fact a direct way in which citizens can participate in the legal system. In some states, citizens may have the opportunity to decide on some laws by referendum. Typically, however, they elect representatives who govern on their behalf. By contrast, jury duty gives the direct power of decision making to those who serve on juries. As Alexis de Tocqueville, the Frenchman who chronicled American life in the early 1800's, wrote in his book *Democracy in America*, "The jury system as it is understood in America . . . [is] as direct . . . a consequence of the sovereignty of the people as universal suffrage." Consequently, service on a jury is as much a right as it is a responsibility.

Selecting Juries

The process of selecting juries begins with the creation of a pool from which prospective jurors can be summoned. The responsibility for creating jury pools is vested in local jury commissioners or court administrators, who have source lists at their disposal from which to draw potential jurors. In the federal court system and in all state courts voter registration lists are used for this purpose. However, in order to ensure that jury pools represent a cross section of the population, many courts supplement voter lists with other source lists such as lists of licensed drivers and taxpayers, census rolls, or telephone directories. Some states require that at least one of these lists be used in addition to voter lists.

Once a master list of potential jurors has been compiled, the next step is to determine whether those on the list are qualified to

MANDATORY SOURCE LISTS USED TO SUMMON POTENTIAL JURORS

State	Types of Lists Used
Alabama	voter registration
Alaska	voter registration; permanent fund distribution applicants
Arizona	voter registration
Arkansas	voter registration
California	voter registration
Colorado	voter registration
Connecticut	voter registration
Delaware	voter registration
District of Columbia	voter registration
Florida	voter registration
Georgia	voter registration
Hawaii	voter registration
Idaho	voter registration
Illinois	voter registration; drivers license
Indiana	voter registration
Iowa	voter registration; motor vehicle registration
Kansas	voter registration; drivers license; census rolls
Kentucky	voter registration; drivers license
Louisiana	voter registration; drivers license
Maine	voter registration
Maryland	voter registration
Massachusetts	voter registration
Michigan	voter registration
Minnesota	voter registration; drivers license
Mississippi	voter registration

serve as jurors. In general, persons must be at least eighteen years of age, citizens of the United States, and residents of the district in which the court sits in order to serve as jurors, and they must be capable of speaking and understanding the English language. Usually, the process of qualifying potential jurors is accomplished

State	Types of Lists Used
Missouri	voter registration; drivers license
Montana	voter registration
Nebraska	voter registration
Nevada	voter registration
New Hampshire	voter registration; drivers license; state I.D. card
New Jersey	voter registration; drivers license
New Mexico	voter registration
New York	voter registration
North Carolina	voter registration
North Dakota	voter registration; drivers license
Ohio	voter registration; drivers license
Oklahoma	voter registration; drivers license
Oregon	voter registration
Pennsylvania	voter registration
Rhode Island	voter registration; drivers license; state I.D. card
South Carolina	voter registration; drivers license; state I.D. card
South Dakota	voter registration; drivers license
Tennessee	voter registration; drivers license; state income tax rolls
Texas	voter registration; drivers license; state income tax rolls
Utah	voter registration
Vermont	voter registration
Virginia	voter registration; drivers license; state and local tax rolls
Washington	voter registration
West Virginia	voter registration; drivers license; state income tax rolls
Wisconsin	voter registration
Wyoming	voter registration

by mailing a form containing a list of questions to determine whether persons meet the requirements established by law. The jury commissioner or court administrator then reviews the returned questionnaires to decide if the persons qualify. Those who are not qualified to serve are removed from the jury pool. Those who meet the qualifications determined by law remain in the jury pool and are summoned periodically at random for jury duty. The U.S. Supreme Court has required that persons from the master list be randomly selected as a means of ensuring fairness and avoiding the exclusion of certain groups from the jury pool.

Once persons have received a summons for jury duty, they may be exempted or excused from service under certain circumstances. In both the federal and state court systems, for example, persons in active military service may be exempted from jury duty. Public officials and public safety officers are exempt from federal jury duty. In some states, full-time students, senior citizens over a certain age, and persons employed in certain occupations, such as clergy, physicians, or attorneys, may be exempt.

When jury duty presents an undue hardship or an extreme inconvenience, persons may seek excusal or temporary deferment from service. For example, ill persons or persons suffering from incapacitation might request a medical hardship excusal, whereas the sole owners of businesses or seasonal employees who must forgo earning income during jury duty might seek excusal on the grounds of economic hardship. Such persons may be required to furnish proof of their inability to serve as jurors.

Term of Service and Pay

The time during which persons summoned for jury duty may serve ranges from as long as a month in some places to as short as one day. During their term of service, jurors may be considered for and actually serve on several juries or may not serve on any jury. Some courts have adopted the "one day/one trial" system of jury duty. In such courts, jurors serve for the shorter of either one day or, if selected, one trial. Once the day is over, persons who have not been selected to serve on a jury are dismissed and have completed their service. If they have been selected for a jury, they are dismissed after the conclusion of the trial and are deemed to have completed their service.

For their services, jurors receive a modest compensation. In the federal court system, for example, jurors are paid forty dollars per day plus an additional ten dollars per day if they serve more than thirty days. Jurors may also be compensated for mileage or transportation costs, parking, and other expenses. The federal courts pay jurors a travel allowance of thirty-one cents per mile. Most

JUROR FEES IN STATE AND FEDERAL COURTS IN 2003

Jurisdiction	Juror Fees per Day	Jurisdiction	Juror Fees per Day
Federal	$40-50	Missouri	$6
Alabama	10	Montana	12-25
Alaska	(12.50)	Nebraska	35
Arizona	0-12	Nevada	9-30
Arkansas	5-20	New Hampshire	(10)
California	0-15	New Jersey	5-40
Colorado	0-50	New Mexico	5.15/hour
Connecticut	0-50	New York	0-40
Delaware	0-20	North Carolina	0-30
District of Columbia	0-30	North Dakota	25
Florida	0-30	Ohio	10-40
Georgia	5*	Oklahoma	12.50
Hawaii	30	Oregon	10
Idaho	(10)	Pennsylvania	9-25
Illinois	4*	Rhode Island	15
Indiana	15-40	South Carolina	10
Iowa	10	South Dakota	10-50
Kansas	10	Tennessee	10
Kentucky	12.50	Texas	6-30*
Louisiana	12	Utah	18.50-49
Maine	10	Vermont	30
Maryland	15*	Virginia	30
Massachusetts	0-50	Washington	10*
Michigan	(7.50)	West Virginia	40
Minnesota	30	Wisconsin	(8)*
Mississippi	15	Wyoming	30-50

Source: U.S. Department of Justice, Bureau of Justice Statistics, *Sourcebook of Criminal Justice Statistics Online.*

Note: The data in this table have been simplified to show the broad range of jury fees paid by different federal and state jurisdictions. All jurisdictions pay at least some money to persons who are actually sworn in on jury panels, but many pay nothing or reduced fees to persons who are merely waiting to be empaneled, and some jurisdictions base their rates of payment on how many days jurors serve. For example, Arizona pays nothing for the first day and $12 for each subsequent day. The numbers in the table above indicate the minimum and maximum rates paid by each jurisdiction, as of June, 2003. Fees that vary by county within their states are marked with asterisks (*). Fees that are half-day rates are enclosed within parentheses, as in the case of Alaska. New Mexico is alone in paying jurors by the hour.

state courts have similar compensation systems but may pay more or less than the federal courts.

Employers may not dismiss, threaten to dismiss, or decrease the seniority or benefits of any employee who is absent because of jury duty. Although employers are not required by state or federal law to pay jurors their regular salary or wages during an employee's term of jury duty, it is common for employment contracts to stipulate that jurors will be paid for at least part of their jury duty. Jurors without such a provision in their employment contracts may suffer financial hardship and may seek to be excused.

The *Voir Dire* Process

Panels of prospective jurors are considered for service on a particular jury trial through a process known as *voir dire*, a French term meaning "to speak truthfully." During this process, prospective jurors are interviewed or questioned by the attorneys representing each party in a case. Through their questions, the attorneys seek to determine whether prospective jurors can be impartial and objective decision makers.

If the attorneys conclude that prospective jurors are unable to fairly hear and decide the dispute, the attorneys may challenge for cause the seating of the jurors. The attorneys may also make peremptory challenges to prospective jurors, which allows them to exclude jurors without stating a specific reason. Jurors may not be excluded on the basis of race, ethnicity, or gender, and the number of peremptory challenges allowed in each case varies depending on the court and the nature of the case. If prospective jurors are not challenged by either attorney, they are seated on the jury to decide the case.

The Role of the Juror

The members of a jury are sworn to decide cases fairly and impartially. Thus, jurors' primary responsibility is to listen and watch carefully and attentively as the case is litigated. The judge advises the jurors that they may not discuss the case with each other or with anyone else until all of the evidence has been admitted, the attorneys have given their closing arguments, and the judge has instructed the jury as to the law. At that point, the jury retires in private to deliberate and reach a verdict. Using the law as provided to them by the judge in charge of jury instructions, the jurors are required to decide if the evidence presented warrants one verdict or another. Once the jury has rendered a verdict, the jurors' responsibility has been fulfilled and the case is over pending an appeal by the losing party.

—Kurt M. Saunders

Suggested Readings

Sources of information on jury selection and the nature and function of juries include Randolph N. Jonakait, *The American Jury System* (New Haven, Conn.: Yale University Press, 2003); Rita J. Simon's *The Jury: Its Role in American Society* (Lexington, Mass.: Lexington Books, 1980); and John Guinther's *The Jury in America* (New York: Facts on File, 1988). For further discussion of the jury as a part of the democratic process see Jeffery Abramson's *We, the Jury: The Jury System and the Ideal of Democracy* (New York: Basic Books, 1994). Randall Kennedy's *Race, Crime, and the Law* (New York: Pantheon Books, 1997) discusses the role of race and bias in jury selection and deliberations. Additional critical perspectives on juries and jury decision making can be found in Stephen J. Adler's *The Jury: Trial and Error in the American Courtroom* (New York: Times Books, 1994), Paula DiPerna's *Juries on Trial: Faces of American Justice* (New York: Dembner Books, 1984), and Valerie P. Hans and Neil Vidmar's *Judging the Jury* (New York: Plenum Press, 1986). Two books on the actual workings of juries are *Punitive Damages: How Juries Decide*, edited by Cass R. Sunstein et al. (Chicago: University of Chicago Press, 2002), and Stephen D. Easton, *How to Win Jury Trials: Building Credibility with Judges and Jurors* (Philadelphia: American Law Institute-American Bar Association Committee on Continuing Professional Education, 1998).

See also Adversary system; Grand juries; Judges; Juries; Jury nullification; Jury sequestration; Trials.

JURY NULLIFICATION

*Acquittal of a criminal defendant by a jury because the jury either
thinks the law is unjust or believes that the defendant or the crime
is commendable*

Jury nullification can be a significant restriction on the government's power to prosecute crimes successfully against the community's will. Under the American system of justice, three questions must be answered before a person can be convicted of a
crime: What are the facts, what was the defendant's moral intent,
and what is the law? The jury decides the first two under definitions of the law which are presented to it by the judge. "Jury nullification" takes place when the jury ignores (or nullifies) the law
and acquits the defendant in spite of the judge's instructions. Under the constitutional provision forbidding "double jeopardy,"
the defendant cannot be tried again.

Historically, before juries could exercise this power, two great
issues had to be settled. The first was whether judges have the
power to punish jurors for bringing in the "wrong" verdict. A precedent was established in England in 1670, in what is generally referred to as Bushel's case. Bushel was one of twelve jurors who refused to convict William Penn (later to became governor of the
American colony of Pennsylvania) of fomenting a riot. Penn had
been preaching a Quaker sermon in public at a time when the
Quakers were being persecuted. After the jurors refused to
change their verdict, the judge fined them forty marks apiece.
They refused to pay and were committed to Newgate Prison.
Eventually they were released on bail, and when England's high
court finally decided the case a year later, it was held that no jury
can be punished for its verdict.

The second issue was whether juries could return "general verdicts" or only "special verdicts." A special verdict results when
the jury is only allowed to answer specific questions of fact. A
general verdict determines whether the accused is guilty or innocent. To render a general verdict, juries must judge the application
of the facts to the law. In North America, the move from special to
general verdicts was largely the result of unpopular prosecutions
brought against printers by royal governors in the eighteenth century. At the trial of John Peter Zenger for seditious libel, Zenger's

attorney argued that the jury had the power to decide whether Zenger was truly guilty of seditious libel. The prosecution argued that the jury could decide only whether Zenger had published the articles at issue in the case. Zenger was acquitted when the jury brought in the general verdict of "not guilty."

It is the general verdict that allows jury nullification. Juries may decide to disobey the judge's instructions if they believe either that the law is unjust or that the defendant's act was admirable or justified in some way. Prosecutors have no recourse, because acquittal is final in the American judicial system. During the nineteenth century, there was a substantial free jury movement in the United States, led by the radical American essayist Lysander Spooner. Although the movement subsided, many still argue that judges should inform jurors that they may "nullify" the law if they think it unjust. Regardless of whether juries are formally notified of this power, there are undoubtedly cases in which nullification takes place. For example, it is sometimes suggested that African American jurors are prone to acquit African American defendants, particularly on less serious charges, because they believe that there is considerable official harassment of blacks. It is difficult to tell with any certainty how common this practice may be.

See also Acquittal; Adversary system; Judges; Judicial review; Juries; Jury duty; Perjury; Trials; Verdicts.

JURY SEQUESTRATION

Isolation of jurors from the public during a trial in order to prevent them from being improperly influenced by news reports, family members, friends, or other sources of information

A paramount concern for judges during jury trials is ensuring that jurors' decisions are based on properly presented evidence. In controversial cases there are fears that jurors' exposure to news reports or opinionated acquaintances will improperly affect jury deliberations and the verdict. In such cases judges may order the jury to be sequestered in order to shield jurors from improper sources of information. Because jurors must live together in a hotel away from their friends and family, jury sequestration imposes significant costs on the personal lives of jurors. Sequestration also generates significant expenses for the court, which must pay for the jurors' food and lodging throughout the course of the trial.

Sequestration may occur in cases involving highly publicized crimes or well-known defendants. Sequestration may be particularly appropriate when the news media informs the public about information and evidence that is not admissible in court. For example, if the police found a bloody weapon in the defendant's home but that weapon could not be presented at trial because it was found during an illegal search, the judge may sequester the jury to prevent the jurors from reading about the weapon in the newspapers.

Because of the cost and inconvenience of jury sequestration, judges rarely order it. Judges must often make a decision about sequestration at the beginning of a trial. If sequestration is possible, judges may ask potential jurors during jury selection if sequestration would create special hardships that would make it exceptionally unfair or difficult for them to serve. For example, the mother of a young child may be excused from jury duty if the judge agrees that sequestration would pose an exceptional hardship for the mother and child.

When jurors are sequestered, bailiffs must monitor their contact with the outside world. In some situations, bailiffs cut out and destroy all newspaper articles about the trial before the newspapers are given to the jurors. Bailiffs also monitor television programs watched by jurors to make sure that they do not watch news stories about the trial. Judges also instruct jurors on the importance of their responsibilities and warn them to avoid all news reports and conversations about the trial. If the bailiffs or other jurors inform the judge that a specific juror has read prohibited newspaper articles, talked about the case with outsiders, or otherwise undertaken forbidden behavior, the judge may dismiss the juror from the case and seat an alternate. In major cases, alternate jurors are sequestered along with the regular jurors and hear the same evidence presented in court, even if they are not ultimately permitted to participate in deliberating the verdict.

—*Christopher E. Smith*

See also Bailiffs; Change of venue; Evidence, rules of; Juries; Jury duty; Trial publicity; Trials; Witnesses.

JUSTICE DEPARTMENT, U.S.

Cabinet-level department that serves as a link between the court system and the executive branch of the federal government; it brings suit against violators of federal law and defends the U.S. government against claims brought by persons, organizations, and local and state governments

American political thought traditionally divides the functions of a law-based society's government into three categories: the making of laws, the adjudication of laws, and the execution of laws. In the United States the three functions are carried out by separate branches of the federal government. Law execution is the primary responsibility of the executive branch, headed by the president. Because the functions and responsibilities overlap, the executive branch is limited in part by the judicial branch, which interprets the law and establishes guilt. The Department of Justice is the agency of the federal government which represents the executive branch in litigation connected with the enforcement of federal laws. This arrangement at once ensures both that the agencies charged with enforcing the law have a strong legal advocate and that a separation of powers is maintained between the judicial and executive branches. It is this balance of protecting the executive's power to enforce the law (through the Department of Justice) and protecting the public interest against possible abuses of power by the executive (through the courts and the Congress) which distinguishes American justice from that of most other governmental systems.

Organization

The U.S. Department of Justice was established in 1870. The attorney general, already an established position within the president's cabinet since 1789, was placed at the head of the new department. The attorney general is appointed by the president and confirmed by the Senate, as are the deputy attorney general, associate attorney general, solicitor general, inspector general, various assistant attorneys general, various bureau directors, and other political positions within the Department of Justice. In the mid-1990's, the department employed almost 100,000 persons. Attorneys, of which there are several thousand, are hired directly by the applicable division. Justice Department attorneys, Federal Bureau of Investigation (FBI) special agents, and other professional positions are not under the federal civil service.

As the chief law enforcement officer of the federal government, the attorney general advises the president and other executive officials on legal affairs and represents the United States in legal matters generally. As head of the Justice Department, the attorney general oversees what amounts to an enormous law office whose sole client is the United States government. The Justice Department is organized into six litigation divisions, which correspond to its six basic areas of responsibility: ensuring the enforcement of criminal law, antitrust statutes, civil rights, environmental law, and tax law, and defending the U.S. government against civil claims.

Criminal Law

The Criminal Division of the Justice Department is charged with the drafting and enforcement of virtually all federal criminal laws. Unlike the state and local authorities, the federal government is specifically charged by the U.S. Constitution with criminal jurisdiction over only counterfeiting and piracies and other felonies committed on the high seas. The criminal code of the United States nevertheless has expanded beyond that modest mandate to include a variety of laws justified under the constitutional authority to make laws deemed "necessary and proper for carrying into execution" the broad powers granted to it. By the mid-1990's the U.S. criminal code comprised an extensive and complex mosaic of about a thousand general criminal statutes (excluding statutes specifically within the jurisdiction of the other Justice Department divisions).

The Criminal Division was established with a general governmental reorganization under President Franklin D. Roosevelt in 1933. The scope of its authority is wide. Separate sections within the Criminal Division enforce laws on child exploitation and obscenity, money laundering, narcotics, internal security, and other areas. The largest component of the Criminal Division is the Fraud Section, which focuses in particular upon fraud which crosses district and national boundaries, which involves financial and insurance institutions, and which concerns government programs and procurement.

Although separate from the Criminal Division, an Office of Professional Responsibility ensures the continued ethical standards of employees within the Justice Department itself and investigates alleged criminal or ethical misconduct. The office reports directly to the attorney general. The existence of such an office highlights the strict ethical standards which the Justice Department must unequivocally maintain.

Antitrust Division

Economic fairness is a fundamental aspect of American justice. The free enterprise principles that undergird the country's economic philosophy necessarily permit market forces to reward and punish the independent actions of consumers, producers, and investors. It is recognized, however, that some of those actors will try to take advantage of the system, engaging in unfair competition and otherwise intentionally distorting market forces for their benefit. The Antitrust Division of the Department of Justice, in cooperation with the Federal Trade Commission, seeks to identify and stop such practices.

In the late nineteenth century "trust-busting," as it was known, became a primary responsibility of the attorney general's office. Possible domination of the economy by monopolies was a major concern during the country's late industrial revolution. After Attorney General Richard Olney in the 1890's successfully sued the "sugar trust" under the Sherman Act, the way was paved for an increasing number of antitrust suits. With such a large workload of antitrust cases, a separate Antitrust Division of the Justice Department was established in 1933.

The Antitrust Division was charged with promoting and maintaining competitive domestic markets through the enforcement of federal antitrust laws. The most important antitrust acts historically have been the Sherman Act of 1890, the Clayton Anti-Trust Act of 1914, and the Federal Trade Commission Act of 1914. Collectively, these and other laws prohibited the creation of unfair monopolies through mergers, price fixing, predatory practices, and other activities which threaten healthy competition. The antitrust laws pervaded all aspects of business, including distribution, marketing, and manufacturing, and they apply to virtually all industries.

As the twentieth century wore on, antitrust activities became less of a priority for the government and became overshadowed by competing demands on the department's resources. Much of the division's antitrust work increasingly has been in the area of international agreements. Yet the Justice Department still periodically brings high-profile domestic antitrust suits. One such suit against the American Telephone and Telegraph Company (AT&T) from the mid-1970's through the early 1980's, for example, had a tremendous impact on the telecommunications industry. The AT&T case suggested that the Justice Department was reconsidering some of the "natural monopoly" arguments that had exempted certain industries from antitrust suits. Other industries undergoing vast changes in terms of competition at the end of the twentieth century include health care and defense.

Civil Rights

In the mid-twentieth century, the enforcement of civil rights became a paramount justice issue. Particularly, although not exclusively, in the South, various local and state governments were not adequately protecting the most basic of civil rights. Indeed, in many cases it was these governments themselves which were violating civil rights, particularly those of blacks. Although the federal government would continue to pass various laws for the protection of civil rights, it would devolve on the Department of Justice to ensure their enforcement.

The Civil Rights Division of the Department of Justice was created in 1957. It is the governmental body charged with enforcing federal laws against discrimination based on race, sex, and other criteria. The Civil Rights Division grew rapidly after its inception and has come to occupy a high-profile place in the Justice Department. Many of its duties stem from the 1964 Civil Rights Act, the 1965 Voting Rights Act, the Fair Housing Act of 1968, and the Americans with Disabilities Act of 1990. The Civil Rights Division maintains separate sections which address these and other specific issues.

The Civil Rights Division encountered a dramatic challenge to its authority when the 1954 *Brown v. Board of Education* Supreme Court decision led to the court-ordered admission of black students to a Little Rock, Arkansas, high school in 1957. Governor Orval Faubus of Arkansas ordered state officers physically to prevent black students from entering the school. In response, U.S. marshals and federal troops were deployed to escort the black students to their classes. The Department of Justice further was able to secure an injunction against the governor's interference with the federal court's order. A similar victory was scored by the

Justice Department against Governor George Wallace of Alabama. Although the Civil Rights Division, and the Department of Justice generally, have by no means always been successful in enforcing civil rights laws, the early civil rights victories provided the Civil Rights Division with a momentum that propelled it for a number of years.

Environment and Natural Resources

American justice issues have increasingly expanded from the various rights of individuals to the protection of the environment and natural resources. The Environment and Natural Resources Division of the Department of Justice enforces such laws as the protection of endangered species and the monitoring of hazardous waste disposal.

The work of the Environment and Natural Resources Division largely centers on three areas: environmental crimes, environmental defense, and environmental enforcement. The Environmental Crimes Section prosecutes persons and firms that violate the nation's environmental protection laws, such as the Clean Water Act, the Clean Air Act, and the Endangered Species Act. The Environmental Defense Section defends the U.S. government against legal challenges concerning federal enforcement of environmental laws (for example, challenges that federal enforcement is too strict or too lax). This section also defends the U.S. government against charges that it is itself in violation of environmental laws. The Environmental Enforcement Section litigates most of the civil suits brought by other federal agencies, including the Environmental Protection Agency, the U.S. Coast Guard, and the Departments of Interior, Commerce, and Agriculture.

Environmental law and policy are relatively new fields, and thus much of the Justice Department's work in the area is precedent-setting. In *United States v. Robert Brittingham and John LoMonaco* (1993), for example, the Environment and Natural Resources Division obtained a $6 million criminal judgment against the chairman of the board and the president of Dal Tile Corporation. They were the highest-ranking corporate officials ever convicted of environmental offenses. The case establishes a strong precedent about personal liability for corporate violations of environmental statutes. If this and other legal trends continue, the potential influence of the Environmental and Natural Resources Division could be enormous.

Taxes

Another increasingly salient set of justice issues involves taxation. Although most of the issues are debated, decided, and administered by other agencies (such as the Congress and the Internal Revenue Service, or IRS), the preparation and conducting of the inevitable criminal and civil tax cases is done elsewhere. For many years these cases were conducted by the Treasury Department, but President Franklin Roosevelt's governmental reorganization shifted that responsibility. The Tax Division of the Department of Justice was created by executive order in 1933 to represent the United States in all criminal and civil suits connected with the internal revenue laws. The division's primary client is the IRS. Besides representing the government in tax suits, the division, in cooperation with U.S. attorneys' offices, also collects judgments.

Civil Claims

The department's Civil Division defends the various agencies, departments, and personnel of the United States government in noncriminal legal suits. The Civil Division is, in essence, the federal government's attorney. Its earlier name, the Claims Division, is perhaps more descriptive, highlighting the fact that the division defends the government against numerous claims stemming in one way or another from governmental operations: military tests, land sales, water diversion projects, and any number of other activities and mishaps. The sheer size of federal governmental operations virtually guarantees the likelihood of numerous civil suits. These suits turn on a wide array of justice issues.

Much of the work of the Civil Division is conducted by the Court of Claims Section. Congress established the Court of Claims in 1855 in response to a burgeoning number of claims against the U.S. government. The Civil Division's Court of Claims Section takes responsibility for all cases against the government with the exception of land, tax, admiralty, and American Indian claims.

Bureaus

In addition to the five divisions outlined above, the Department of Justice includes several more specialized bureaus. The Federal Bureau of Investigation (FBI) is the Justice Department's primary investigative arm. The Bureau of Prisons oversees the federal prison system. The U.S. Marshals Service provides security for the federal courts, executes court orders and arrest warrants, transports federal prisoners, and otherwise serves as a link between the executive and judicial branches of the federal government. The Immigration and Naturalization Service (INS) provides for the entry and resettlement of persons into the United States, prevents illegal entry, and administers employment and citizenship laws. The Drug Enforcement Administration (DEA) enforces laws regulating narcotics and other controlled substances. The U.S. National Central Bureau represents the United States in the International Criminal Police Organization (Interpol), an association of police agencies from 169 countries.

In addition, the Office of Justice Programs (OJP) was established in 1984 to improve the overall efficiency and effectiveness of the country's justice system. The OJP primarily collects and disseminates data and analysis on various criminal justice issues and programs.

Context and Public Perceptions

The underlying principles and rationale of the Justice Department, whatever their value, seem to elude the general public's understanding of the agency. Indeed, the ethos of the department as a whole is limited by public (and in some cases intragovernmental) perceptions of the department's component parts. The public is generally cognizant of the FBI's investigative functions, the role of the Marshals Service in apprehending federal fugitives, and the DEA's seizure of assets derived from illicit drug trafficking, for example. The work of the litigation divisions, however, only infrequently commands public attention. In general, the litigation emphasis behind the Justice Department's slogans "the world's largest law firm" and "the nation's attorney" (which appear in department publications) is limited to only a small number of high-profile cases.

One example was the federal trial in 1993 of the four Los Angeles police officers who earlier had been acquitted by a state court on charges of assault against Rodney King. Much controversy surrounded the Justice Department's efforts to secure a conviction of the officers, whose previous acquittal had sparked racial riots in Los Angeles. Although the second trial (which resulted in the conviction of two of the officers) focused on civil rights violations rather than assault charges, some observers believed that it amounted to unconstitutional "double jeopardy." In any event, the case heightened public awareness of the Justice Department's litigation role, especially as distinguished from the state of California's role in the first trial.

In the mid-1990's, the Justice Department again began to garner considerable public attention, this time in the context of investigations of and litigation against high-level government officials. The Justice Department and independent counsels appointed by the attorney general investigated agency heads, White House officials, and even cabinet secretaries. In 1994 even the assistant attorney general himself was forced to resign as criminal allegations about previous activities headed toward an eventual guilty plea. The fact that the Justice Department was investigating various other parts of the executive branch lent some credibility to its role as the chief enforcer of laws, irrespective of the positions of those it investigates and prosecutes. To that can be added the "Saturday night massacre" of 1973, when the attorney general and deputy attorney general resigned rather than carry out President Richard Nixon's order to fire Watergate Special Prosecutor Archibald Cox.

The celebrity of these few events only emphasizes that the scope of the Justice Department's activities and the importance of its role are seldom recognized. The U.S. Department of Justice has become a large, diverse, and active agency with a tremendous impact upon American justice.

—*Steve D. Boilard*

Suggested Readings

The U.S. government makes available many publications explaining the operation of the Department of Justice and of its various divisions and bureaus. The *Annual Report of the Attorney General of the United States* is published by the Department of Justice (available through the U.S. Government Printing Office) and provides a current accounting of the department's operations and goals. The Department of Justice's *Legal Activities* describes the organization, activities, and recent cases handled by attorneys with the various divisions of the department. An annual publication, *Legal Activities* is aimed primarily at potential employees. The *U.S. Government Manual* covers the entire federal government, but its section on the Department of Justice provides a thorough accounting of the institutional structure, as well as addresses and phone numbers for more specific information. A history of the department, the full text of the act which established it, and a comprehensive analysis of its operation (as of the mid-1960's) is provided in Luther A. Huston, *The Department of Justice* (New York: Praeger, 1967). Finally, there are a number of books which focus on the Justice Department's policies under particular administrations. Two examples are Victor S. Navasky, *Kennedy Justice* (New York: Atheneum, 1971), which covers Justice Department activities under Attorney General Robert F. Kennedy, and Richard Harris, *Justice: The Crisis of Law, Order, and Freedom in America* (New York: E. P. Dutton, 1970), which provides a critical account of the Justice Department in the early Nixon years, under Attorney General John Mitchell.

See also Attorney general of the United States; Attorneys, United States; Bankruptcy; Civil rights and liberties; Criminal justice system; Federal Bureau of Investigation; Federal judicial system; Law enforcement; Marshals Service, U.S.

JUVENILE CRIMINAL PROCEEDINGS

Special courts and procedures provided by each to deal with juvenile offenders; these courts differ in terminology and goals from those in the adult criminal system

In addition to the normal criminal justice system for adults, each state has a separate system for juvenile lawbreakers. The juvenile justice system differs in philosophy and goals from the adult system in that its primary purpose is to rehabilitate rather than to punish. Juveniles are accorded only some of the rights accorded to adult criminal defendants, and the terminology used in juvenile cases differs from that used in adult cases.

History and Philosophy
When the United States was first founded, there was no separate justice system for children. Instead, the common-law rule from England was adopted: Children under the age of seven

could not be tried at all for criminal acts, children between seven and fourteen years of age could be tried if the prosecutor showed that they were mentally mature enough to be held responsible for their acts, and children fourteen years of age and older were treated as adults. Children who were tried would receive adult punishments, including the death penalty.

By the beginning of the twentieth century, however, legal scholars, children's advocates, and others were convinced that delinquent children should be treated differently from criminal adults. The first juvenile court was created in Illinois in 1899, and most jurisdictions soon followed.

From their beginnings, juvenile courts were meant to operate under the doctrine of *parens patriae*. Literally meaning "parent of the country," *parens patriae* signifies in practice that the court acts as a guardian of wayward and needy children and in such children's

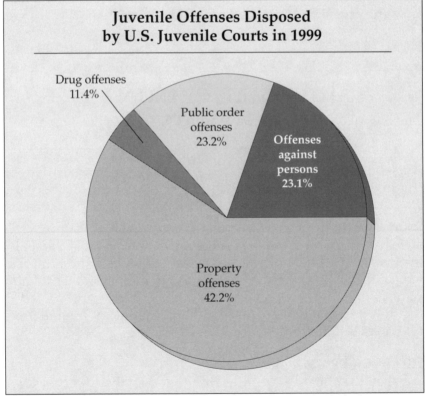

Juvenile Offenses Disposed by U.S. Juvenile Courts in 1999

Drug offenses 11.4%

Public order offenses 23.2%

Offenses against persons 23.1%

Property offenses 42.2%

Source: U.S. Department of Justice, Bureau of Justice Statistics, *Sourcebook of Criminal Justice Statistics—2001.* Washington, D.C.: U.S. Government Printing Office, 2002.

best interests. In fact, many juvenile courts have jurisdiction not only over delinquency cases but also over cases involving neglected, abused, and abandoned children and over child-custody cases. Under the doctrine of *parens patriae* a juvenile court's primary mission is to protect and rehabilitate delinquent children. Juvenile courts should provide individualized attention to each child and seek outcomes that are closely tailored to each child's needs.

Juvenile Court Jurisdiction

Juvenile courts are courts of limited jurisdiction—that is, they can hear only certain types of cases. States differ in how they define juvenile court jurisdiction. All states specify a maximum age at which a person may be tried as a juvenile for any crime. The most common maximum age is seventeen. Most states also permit some juveniles to be tried as adults under certain circumstances. This usually takes place when older juveniles commit serious or violent crimes. Depending on the jurisdiction, a statute may require that juveniles be tried in adult criminal court in certain cases. Prosecutors may have the prerogative to decide whether to try cases in juvenile or adult court. Most commonly, however, this decision is left to judges (usually juvenile court judges). Proceedings known as waiver hearings are held, in which judges determine, generally according to statutory guidelines, whether it is appropriate to try persons as juveniles or adults.

By the end of the twentieth century, a strong movement was in place in many jurisdictions to be more punitive toward juveniles. This movement was a result of the perceived increase in dangerous juvenile crime and a reaction to the perceived inadequacies of the juvenile justice system. Many states lowered the age at which persons could be tried as adults while increasing the range of offenses. Minors tried as adults are subject to the same procedures as adult defendants and may also receive the same sentences, including incarceration in prison. In some cases, minors found guilty in adult trials are kept in juvenile facilities until they reach the age of majority, at which time they are transferred to adult facilities.

Juvenile Procedures and Terminology

The precise procedures in juvenile cases differ among jurisdictions. However, most states use the same general terminology and procedures. In most juvenile cases, the first step is arrest. The

> ## Rights to Which Juveniles Are Entitled in Criminal Proceedings
>
> - A hearing before an impartial judge
> - Notice of charges against them
> - Counsel
> - The right to confront and cross-examine witnesses
> - The right against self-incrimination
> - Proof beyond a reasonable doubt
> - A written statement of the reasons for the court's decision
> - An appeal

arresting officers frequently choose to release juveniles to the custody of their parents. When a serious crime has occurred or when the officers believe that placement with the parents is unsuitable, the juveniles are taken into custody. In most instances, especially in more populous areas, this means that the juveniles will be taken to a temporary juvenile detention facility, usually called juvenile hall. However, as juvenile facilities are not always available, thousands of children each year spend some time in adult jails.

At juvenile hall an intake officer (who is usually a juvenile probation officer) determines whether to file a petition against the juveniles. A petition is a statement of formal charges against the minors and serves much the same purpose as a criminal complaint. The intake officer also determines whether to keep the juveniles in state custody for the time being. This determination may be based on factors such as the likelihood that the juveniles will commit more crimes if they are released and the potential danger to them from their parents or others. Unlike adults, juveniles do not have the right to be released on bail; instead, they may be released to the custody of their parents or other responsible adults.

The actual "trials" in juvenile cases are known as delinquency hearings. Children in delinquency hearings enjoy some, but not all, of the rights enjoyed by adults in criminal cases. Juveniles are "adjudicated delinquent" rather than found guilty, as are persons in adult trials. The idea behind this differing terminology is that being adjudicated delinquent carries less of a stigma than being found guilty, therefore helping juveniles to rehabilitate themselves and lead productive lives. For the same reason, juvenile proceedings are usually not open to the public, offenders' names are frequently not made available to the press, and delinquency records are often sealed or expunged after affected persons become adults.

Juveniles are given dispositions rather than sentences. Thus, after children are adjudicated delinquent, disposition hearings are held. The judge usually receives a report from a juvenile probation officer, which describes a juvenile's background and recommends a disposition. Most youths are placed on probation. If probation is deemed unsuitable, youths remain in state custody. Because dispositions are supposed to treat juveniles' individual problems, most states have a variety of dispositions at their disposal, including foster homes, group homes, treatment centers, wilderness programs, boot camps, and secure facilities.

Because the primary purpose of the juvenile system is rehabilitation, rather than punishment, juveniles are often given indeterminate sentences. That is, they remain in custody until they are determined to have been reformed or until they are too old to be held in the juvenile system's jurisdiction. As a result, juveniles may sometimes spend more time in custody than would adults for the same crimes. The maximum age at which persons may remain in custody pursuant to a delinquency adjudication differs from state to state. In some states it may be well past the age of majority. For example, in California the juvenile system may retain custody of persons until they reach the age of twenty-five.

Due Process in Juvenile Justice

When juvenile courts were originally created, judges were supposed to pay careful attention to each child's needs and the courts were supposed to safeguard children's best interests. For this reason, juveniles were not accorded the same protections as adult defendants under the due process clauses of the Fifth and Fourteenth Amendments to the U.S. Constitution. In practice, juvenile court dockets quickly became overloaded, and juvenile court judges were unable to pay close attention to each child. As a result, some cases became travesties of justice in which neither the best interests nor the constitutional rights of juveniles were protected.

By the mid-1960's the U.S. Supreme Court recognized that the juvenile justice system frequently did not live up to its ideals. In a series of cases, the Court ruled that juveniles must receive many of the same protections to which adult defendants are entitled. These protections were necessary, the Court believed, to prevent the juvenile justice system from becoming a kangaroo court. However, the Court refused to accord to juveniles all the rights enjoyed by adults. To do so would prevent juvenile courts from fulfilling their duties according to the doctrine of *parens patriae* and would effectively erase the differences between juvenile and adult courts. The Supreme Court was unwilling to go so far as to completely abandon the juvenile justice system. The most obvious right to which juveniles are not entitled is a jury trial.

Problems of Juvenile Justice

By the 1990's the juvenile justice system in the United States faced a number of serious problems. Primary among them was overcrowding: Juvenile court dockets and juvenile facilities were so full that offenders, especially those who had committed less serious crimes, could receive little attention. Treatment programs were inadequate and institutions were often so full that juveniles were in physical danger. Juvenile probationers could receive very little close supervision because of probation officers' large caseloads.

These problems contributed to another difficulty: The public viewed the juvenile justice system as inadequate. In many cases, this led to a push for more punitive measures, such as longer periods of incarceration, more restrictive dispositions, and more trials of juveniles as adults. These measures required the construction of more secure facilities that often resulted in the decreased availability of funds for prevention and treatment programs. At the urging of many experts, some states reacted by completely reshaping their juvenile justice systems, often with encouraging results. However, this radical reshaping required a change in philosophy for which it was difficult to gain public and political support. By the end of the twentieth century, therefore, the future of the juvenile justice system remained in doubt.

—Phyllis B. Gerstenfeld

Suggested Readings

Good starting points include *The Encyclopedia of Juvenile Justice*, edited by Marilyn D. McShane and Frank P. Williams (Thousand Oaks, Calif.: Sage, 2003), R. Barri Flowers's *Kids Who Commit*

Adult Crimes: Serious Criminality by Juvenile Offenders. (Haworth, 2002), and *Handbook of Youth and Justice,* edited by Susan O. White (New York: Kluwer Academic/Plenum Publishers, 2001). Among the many books offering general overviews of the juvenile justice system are Thomas Grisso and Robert G. Schwartz, editors. *Youth on Trial: A Developmental Perspective on Juvenile Justice.* Chicago: University of Chicago Press, 2000); *The Changing Borders of Juvenile Justice: Transfer of Adolescents to the Criminal Court,* edited by Jeffrey Fagan and Franklin E. Zimring (Chicago: University of Chicago Press, 2000); and *Will the Juvenile Court System Survive?,* edited by Alan W. Heston and Neil A. Weiner (Thousand Oaks, Calif.: Sage Periodicals Press, 1999); and John T. Whitehead and Steven P. Lab's *Juvenile Justice: An Introduction* (2d ed. Cincinnati: Anderson, 1996). Three texts that summarize important juvenile criminal proceedings are Roland V. del Carmen, Mary Parker, and Frances P. Reddington's *Briefs of Leading Cases in Juvenile Law* (Cincinnati: Anderson, 1998), Joseph J. Senna and Larry J. Siegel's *Juvenile Law: Cases and Comments* (2d ed. St. Paul, Minn.: West Publishing, 1992), and Samuel M. Davis, Elizabeth S. Scott, Walter Wadlington, and Charles H. Whitebread's *Children in the Legal System: Cases and Materials* (2d ed. Westbury, N.Y.: Foundation Press, 1997). Barry Krisberg and James F. Austin present a critical view of the contemporary juvenile justice system in *Reinventing Juvenile Justice* (Newbury Park: Sage, 1993). A fascinating narrative account of the daily workings of the Los Angeles juvenile courts is presented in Edward Humes's *No Matter How Loud I Shout: A Year in the Life of the Juvenile Court* (New York: Simon & Schuster, 1996). Studies of problem juveniles include Barry C. Feld, *Bad Kids: Race and the Transformation of the Juvenile Court* (New York: Oxford University Press, 1999), and *Securing Our Children's Future: New Approaches to Juvenile Justice and Youth Violence,* edited by Gary S. Katzmann (Washington, D.C.: Brookings Institution Press, 2002).

See also Age of majority; Arrest; Court types; Criminal justice system; Criminal procedure; Criminal records; Family law practice; Legal guardians; Probation, juvenile.

Law enforcement

Multilayered network of local state and federal law-enforcement bodies that helps to ensure compliance with governmental directives and laws throughout the United States

Laws in the United States are developed by representative legislative bodies such as the U.S. Congress, state assemblies, and city councils. Since these legislative bodies are assumed to operate with the consent of the people they govern, their laws are considered to be legitimate. In principle this legitimacy ensures that the citizens voluntarily comply with the laws. However, for a variety of reasons certain individuals at particular times might be motivated to ignore or deliberately violate laws. For this reason, law-enforcement bodies have been established by various jurisdictions of government to ensure compliance with applicable laws.

Police Power

Unlike many countries, which utilize national police forces, most law-enforcement activities in the United States are carried out by local and state police organizations. This decentralized approach to law enforcement reflects Americans' deep-rooted suspicion of centralized authority. It also has a constitutional basis: The Tenth Amendment to the U.S. Constitution states that powers not delegated to the federal government by the Constitution nor explicitly denied to the states by the Constitution are reserved by the states. Police powers—that is, authority for protecting the safety, welfare, morals, and health of the citizenry—have therefore been construed to belong to the states (and, by extension, their municipalities).

State laws and local ordinances account for most of the government regulations a person encounters on a daily basis. It therefore makes sense that state and local authorities should enforce those regulations. However, law-enforcement jurisdictions are neither clear-cut nor fixed. Instead, there is a range of overlapping municipal, state, and federal agencies that conduct a wide variety of law-enforcement functions. Most of these agencies have established their own primary areas of functional and territorial authority. Frequently, different law-enforcement agencies establish cooperative relationships over shared jurisdictions; at times they come into conflict.

Aspects of Law Enforcement

Law-enforcement functions often are divided into four categories: crime deterrence, criminal arrest, crime detection, and the maintainance of public order. The first of these is potentially the most efficient and critical of law enforcement's obligations to society. It would be virtually impossible for authorities to rely entirely on force to coercively stop all crimes that might be perpetrated in a free society. By instead working to deter the contemplation of crimes in the first place (by creating a societal expectation that the commission of a crime will result in certain arrest and unacceptably high penalties), a criminal justice system can avoid the need for excessive arrests, prosecution, and incarceration.

As some criminals will not be deterred, arrest becomes a necessary task of law enforcement. Arrest serves two main functions: First, it can halt the completion of a criminal act and thus place suspects in the hands of the criminal justice system for further action. Second, arrest can serve, by force of example, as a deterrent to other would-be criminals. The first two categories of law enforcement thus reinforce each other. Deterrence reduces the need for arrests and arrests increase the strength of deterrence.

The third category of law enforcement—crime detection—includes the detection of crimes, the identificiation of their perpetrators, and the discovery of other facts. Detection can lead to ex post facto arrest and can thus bolster deterrence. Detection is usually carried out by a distinct group of specialists within law-enforcement agencies, such as police detectives.

The fourth category of law enforcement, the maintainance of public order, does not concern criminal activity per se. Rather, it seeks to maintain orderly conditions within society. Activities in this category include enforcing crowd control, directing traffic, supervising licensed activities, and effecting rescues. Although maintaining public order, by its very nature, is not a dramatic or high-profile activity, municipal police departments devote a significant share of their resources to this task.

Overall, law enforcement is one of the main bulwarks of a democratic society. Its necessity derives from the recognition that even the citizens of a free and democratic society are subject to base motivations and temptations. Law enforcement makes effective government and civil society possible. In many ways the successful exercise of other police powers presumes effective law enforcement.

Local Police

Local police forces are the most common type of law-enforcement bodies. They maintain a highly visible presence in the community, with uniformed police officers performing such duties as walking beats, patrolling city streets, questioning persons engaged in suspicious activities, and providing directions to motorists. Municipal police departments are the modern incarnation of earlier constabularies. They are thus firmly grounded in American and English tradition and enjoy widespread public acceptance. Police departments are the most accessible and prominent form of governmental power encountered by U.S. citizens.

Police departments represent a blend of military and bureaucratic elements. They demonstrate solidarity and discipline in carrying out their work and frequently employ sophisticated communications equipment and overwhelming firepower. Police departments are usually organized with clear, hierarchical chains of command. Larger police forces are often divided into a number of precincts, with groups of officers and detectives under the control of their own precinct captains. Larger police departments also employ specialists who address certain types of crimes, such as vice and homicide. Nevertheless, most police work is carried out by patrol officers. Most police departments are overseen by a police chief, who is appointed by a city commission, mayor, or other governmental entity. Owing to the enormous power placed in the hands of the police, some jurisdictions have found it necessary to create citizen review boards to serve a watchdog function over police departments.

Municipal police departments are responsible for enforcing most of the laws that govern public activity in their communities, from parking and smoking ordinances to felonious criminal behavior. Local police perform such disparate functions as patrolling neighborhoods, maintaining the peace at community parades and demonstrations, enforcing curfews, and providing assistance in emergencies. Because police officers generally have broad discretion in assessing and responding to specific incidents, considerable emphasis is placed on the need for honesty, integrity, judgment, and accountability in law enforcement.

Urban areas also may employ a variety of specialized law-enforcement bodies to protect certain public facilities. For example, some metropolitan areas use transit police for patrolling bus and subway lines. Often these authorities transcend city boundaries and require coordination between different jurisdictions. Other institutions, such as city housing authorities, use law-enforcement powers for ensuring compliance with local ordinances.

Not all communities have formal police departments. In many areas county sheriff's departments perform most of the functions of city police departments. Their primary jurisdictions usually include only unincorporated areas. County sheriff's departments therefore tend to be active in less urbanized communities and rural regions. The emphasis of their work is tailored accordingly. Thus, they are more likely to protect public lands than to stem gang activity. In highly developed counties (with little or no unincorporated land), county sheriff's departments may be responsible for little more than transporting prisoners between jail and court.

State Law-Enforcement Agencies

State law-enforcement agencies are much more specialized than local police departments, which tend to have broad and only vaguely circumscribed authority. Even though some state law-enforcement agencies are called state "police," they do not usually make use of the range of discretionary powers assumed by local police. Instead, state police (state troopers or state highway patrols) tend to exercise most of their powers on the state's highways, freeways, interstates, and other limited venues.

Although the U.S. Constitution is interpreted as assigning police powers to the states, America's traditional suspicion of centralized authority has caused the majority of states to delegate most law-enforcement functions to their local governments. It was long feared that state police forces would represent a large step toward the creation of a national police force. With the introduction of the automobile and the construction of paved highways in the early twentieth century, however, new problems arose that could not easily be addressed by local jurisdictions. Travel across jurisdictions became easier and more common, thus allowing some criminal activity to become multijurisdictional and facilitating the easier flight of criminals from the jurisdictions in which they committed crimes. Furthermore, the mounting number of traffic accidents and moving violations created the need for a multijurisdictional force to enforce laws on the highways. By World War II all states had established their own state police forces.

Although the bulk of state police work is focused on the highways, state police organizations have carried out important work in conjunction with local authorities, particularly when extra manpower or special facilities are required. State police forces are especially necessary for bolstering authority in rural areas, since county sheriff's offices are frequently spread thin across large areas. For the most part, however, state police forces are not heavily involved in enforcing criminal law.

Other specialized state law-enforcement agencies enforce hunting and fishing laws, fire and housing codes, and other regulations. State employees whose duties bring them into relatively remote areas, such as state park rangers, often are granted considerable discretionary law-enforcement powers.

Federal Law-Enforcement Bodies

The federal government is much less involved in general and criminal law enforcement than the states and their municipalities. This is partly because only a relatively small number of the country's criminal statutes are included in federal law. The U.S. Constitution specifically assigns to the federal government jurisdiction over only a small number of crimes, such as counterfeiting and treason. However, the Constitution also grants to the Congress the power to make laws that are "necessary and proper" for implementing the federal government's enumerated powers. Over time the necessary-and-proper clause has been used to expand considerably the federal government's involvement in enforcing criminal laws. For example, in the mid-nineteenth century the U.S. Congress passed legislation defining crimes relating to the use of the U.S. mails, such as mail fraud and transmitting obscene materials. The U.S. Post Office Department (later the Postal Service) was soon involved in enforcing these laws. Other federal agencies, such as the Interstate Commerce Commission (ICC), were established in part to enforce laws and regulations affecting the movement of goods between states.

Federal narcotics agents with more than four hundred pounds of seized marijuana. (Library of Congress)

The first federal law-enforcement body to be established was the office of the attorney general. As the chief law-enforcement officer of the federal government, the attorney general advises the president and other executive officials on legal affairs and represents the United States in legal matters generally. As head of the Justice Department, which was created in the mid-nineteenth century, the attorney general oversees what amounts to an enormous law office, the sole client of which is the U.S. government. In general, the Justice Department is responsible for prosecuting violations of federal law.

The Justice Department has several bureaus and agencies with more specific law-enforcement duties. The Federal Bureau of Investigation (FBI) is the Justice Department's primary investigative arm. The U.S. Marshals Service provides security for the federal courts, executes court orders and arrest warrants, transports federal prisoners, and otherwise serves as a link between the executive and judicial branches of the federal government. The Immigration and Naturalization Service (INS) provides for the entry and resettlement of noncitizens into the United States, prevents illegal entry, and administers employment and citizenship laws. The Drug Enforcement Administration (DEA) enforces laws regulating drugs and other controlled substances. The National Central Bureau represents the United States in the International Criminal Police Organization (Interpol), an association of police agencies from 169 countries.

Further, the Treasury Department has a number of specialized law-enforcement agencies, including the U.S. Customs Service, the Internal Revenue Service (IRS), and the Bureau of Alcohol, Tobacco, and Firearms (ATF). Other federal agencies carry out specialized law-enforcement duties as part of their more general responsibilities.

Most of these federal agencies and bureaus were established in the twentieth century, as a growing population, increased mobility, and advancing technology raised certain law-enforcement issues to national prominence. Organized crime has been one area of law enforcement for which federal action is considered especially appropriate. Large crime syndicates can be national or even international in scope and are thus difficult to deal with at the local level. The federal government has therefore established a growing, although still relatively modest, matrix of law-enforcement structures for contending with organized crime.

The largest single expansion of federal law-enforcement activity took place in the 1920's and 1930's. Most of this new activity was directed at illegal alcohol sales and the criminal organizations that thrived on them. National crime again became a major public issue in the 1960's and early 1970's. In 1970 Congress passed the Racketeer Influenced and Corrupt Organization (RICO) statute, which included a range of provisions aimed at attacking organized crime with federal power. In general, the act strengthened the ability of law-enforcement authorities to gather evidence against organized crime, provided for the protection of government witnesses, revised explosives regulations, and increased penalties for "dangerous special offenders." Title IX of the act addressed "racketeer influenced and corrupt organizations," identifying illegal activities and specifying penalties. The RICO statute considerably expanded federal law-enforcement powers by making the investment of certain illegal funds in interstate businesses a federal offense.

Federal-State Cooperation

Federal law-enforcement activities presumably aim to protect federal property and other national interests of immediate relevance to the U.S. government. However, federal law-enforcement activity has also been directed at interstate crime and corrupt law-enforcement agencies at the local level. Although it is unlikely that the federal government will ever adopt full-fledged police powers, it has shown a willingness to take on law-enforcement duties when local governments appear to be poorly suited for particular tasks.

The federal government created a Law Enforcement Assistance Administration (LEAA) in 1969 to help channel federal assistance to state and local law-enforcement agencies. Although the LEAA was dismantled a decade later, its general mission and purpose has been continued through other agencies and departments. For example, the federal government helps provide technical assistance and training to law-enforcement personnel and departments through the Federal Law Enforcement Training Center. In the 1990's the presidential administration of Bill Clinton made a particularly high-profile effort to bolster local law enforcement by augmenting the number of local police officers nationwide. Clinton promised to put 100,000 new police officers on the streets within several years. Although this effort achieved mixed results, it does illustrate the preference for local control of law enforcement, albeit with the financial and moral support of the federal government.

—Steve D. Boilard

Suggested Readings

A good general reference on the subject is Mitchel P. Roth's *Historical Dictionary of Law Enforcement* (Westport, Conn.: Greenwood Press, 2001). On the general concept of law enforcement see William G. Doerner's *Introduction to Law Enforcement: An Insider's View* (Boston: Butterworth-Heinemann, 1998). Legal issues surrounding the practice and structure of law enforcement are examined in Rolando V. Del Carmen's *Briefs of Leading Cases in Law Enforcement* (Cincinnati: Anderson, 1997). A collection of articles on various law-enforcement topics is presented in *Law Enforcement Operations and Management* (New York: Garland, 1997), edited by Marilyn McShane and Frank P. Williams. A more focused treatise is offered by Jim McGee and Brian Duffy in *Main Justice: The Men and Women Who Enforce the Nation's Criminal Laws and Guard Its Liberties* (New York: Simon and Schuster, 1996). A national citizens' commission headed by Steven Donziger has issued a detailed critique of America's law-enforcement and criminal justice efforts and policy recommendations in a published report edited by Donziger called *The Real War on Crime: The Report of the National Criminal Justice Commission* (New York: HarperPerennial, 1996). Chapter 7, "Toward a New Model of Policing," is especially relevant. Charles Phillips and Alan Axelrod have compiled an encyclopedic dictionary of over six hundred important persons who have significantly affected the history of law enforcement: *Cops, Crooks, and Criminologists: An International Biographical Dictionary of Law Enforcement* (New York: Facts on File, 1996). Works focused on policing include *Policing Urban America*, by Geoffrey P. Alperts (Prospect Heights, Ill.: Waveland Press, 1997), *Critical Issues in Policing: Contemporary Readings*, edited by Roger G. Dunham and Geoffrey P. Alperts (3d ed. Prospect Heights, Ill.: Waveland Press, 1997), and *Policing*, by Michael Palmiotto (Durham, N.C.: Carolina Academic Press, 1997). Pamela H. Bucy has written an article examining the privatization issue entitled "Privatizing Law Enforcement," *Annals of the American Academy of Political and Social Science* 543 (January, 1996). For an international perspective, see *Government Ethics and Law Enforcement Toward Global Guidelines*, edited by Yassin El-Ayouty, Kevin J. Ford, and Mark Davies (Westport, Conn.: Praeger, 2000). Other specialized studies include *Challenges and Choices for Crime-Fighting Technology: Federal Support of State and Local Law Enforcement*, by William Schwabe and others (Santa Monica, Calif.: Rand, 2001); *Crime Mapping: New Tools for Law Enforcement*, by Irvin B. Vann and G. David Garson (New York: Peter Lang, 2003); *Policing Hatred: Law Enforcement, Civil Rights, and Hate Crime*, by Jeannine Bell (New York: New York University Press, 2002).

See also Arrest; Attorney general of the United States; Attorneys general, state; Citizen's arrest; Constitution, U.S.; Criminal justice system; Criminal procedure; Detectives, police; Federal Bureau of Investigation; Informants; Marshals Service, U.S.; Multiple jurisdiction offenses; Police; Prosecutors; Search warrant requirement; Sheriffs; State police.

LAW FIRM PARTNERS AND ASSOCIATES

Lawyers and the professional colleagues with whom they work in private law firms

Although many lawyers are in individual practice, most form partnerships. Law firms consist of name partners, on which the firm's name is based; equity partners, who invest in the firm; associates; and support staff, such as legal secretaries, paralegals, and clerks. Partners may be selected because of the amount of business they bring to a firm.

Legal firms specialize in many different fields of the law: municipal finances, revenue, bond financing, corporate securities, government, real estate, estate planning, the environment, international law, and litigation and general practice. Initially a law firm may depend on the character and leadership of one person. However, if the firm grows, the structure may become more corporate, moving from one-person control to corporate-style management by committee, with boards of directors and titles, such as chief executive officer and chairperson.

Businesses rely on big law firms in New York, Washington, and other centers that are aggressive in extending their practices to other states and regions. The ambitious law firm engages in strategic planning, develops mastery over specialized areas, surveys the market to consider what areas to strengthen or reduce, opens branch offices, and considers restructuring. The development of a small law firm into a full-service firm may take place through mergers. A merger rarely provides economies of scale, but it strengthens specialties and enables the firm to expand into new markets. Dealing with a different organizational culture and philosophy can lead to conflicts with partners and clients, prompting some partners to open their own practices.

People are the key to growth and development. Finding the right mix requires careful recruiting, which considers lawyers' scholastic achievements, special training, and experience. Legal secretaries are vital to the team and should be selected as carefully as attorneys. Staff development programs may include time management, total quality management, and professional development.

Young lawyers no longer expect to stay with one firm their entire careers. Moreover, aggressive cost cutting may result in layoffs of support staff and associates. Some firms use contract attorneys instead of their own associates. Associates who do not become partners must decide whether to remain at the firm, transfer to another firm, go into independent practice, or seek a government or corporate position. Women face overt and subtle discrimination in opportunities and salaries. Some lawyers become judges or receive appointments to government agencies and other prestigious positions, enhancing the law firm's reputation.

Clients want to buy solutions to legal problems, but law firms sell lawyer time. Computerization has enabled billing by the hour and even by the minute. Some firms cut costs by assigning hourly paid associates to do the work that could be done by lower-ranked employees, dealing with dissatisfaction by paying bonuses and granting salary increases.

—William L. Reinshagen

See also Attorney-client relationship; Attorney salaries; Attorney types; Attorneys; Billable hours; Law firms; Paralegals; Pro bono legal work; Public interest law.

LAW FIRMS

Private companies in which attorneys join together to share resources and assist one another in their legal practices

The concept of the national law firm is a surprisingly recent one. Historically, the best law firms in large cities, such as Cravath Swain & Moore in New York or Covington & Burling in Washington, attracted the best and brightest law graduates and exercised important influence on national legal developments. These firms, however, remained concentrated in one city while maintaining small branch offices to service clients with out-of-town needs. Few employed more than two hundred or even one hundred lawyers.

Since the 1980's the economics of law practice have conspired to create the truly national or global law firm, with offices in several cities and no single home office to which all the others report. These firms increasingly operate like national or multinational corporations, with professional management, an emphasis on bottom-line productivity, and relatively little day-to-day contact between lawyers in their various offices. Like corporations, these firms have grown both internally, by increasing the numbers of lawyers in their existing offices, and externally, by acquiring or merging with law firms in other cities and foreign countries. The practices of such firms tend to be highly specialized, emphasizing complex areas of law such as international law, sophisticated commercial transactions, and commercial litigation, in which their larger size provides an advantage over smaller competitors.

By 1997 the Chicago-based firm of Baker & McKenzie, the nation's largest law firm, had grown to 1,970 lawyers with offices in the United States and abroad. In 1996-1997 the 112 lawyers Baker & McKenzie added was greater than the size of all but a few law firms a generation earlier. Baker & McKenzie was not alone. The Cleveland-based firm of Jones, Day, Reavis, and Pogue and the New York-based firm of Skadden, Arps, Slate, Meagher, and Flom each employed more than 1,000 lawyers, and numerous other firms had joined the 400-plus "megafirm" tier.

Since large law firms resemble large corporations, it is inevitable that they would be subject to the same criticisms. In his 1993 book *The Lost Lawyer* Anthony Kronman criticizes national law firms for promoting a culture of commercialism in place of the values of prudence and practical reason that characterized the old-fashioned lawyer. The specialization of these firms exacerbates this problem, because it makes lawyers see themselves as narrow technicians rather than as pragmatic, real-world problem solvers. While Kronman's criticisms have some force, it is also true that national and multinational law firms have increased the efficiency of legal services, providing an exciting and lucrative opportunity for the most intelligent and ambitious law school graduates. The challenge for the profession may therefore consist less in preventing bigness than in trying to retain at least some of the traditional values of the profession in a large, corporate-style setting.

—*Michael A. Livingston*

See also Attorney-client relationship; Attorney fees; Attorney salaries; Attorney trust accounts; Attorney types; Law firm partners and associates; Law schools; Legal clinics; Model Rules of Professional Conduct; Paralegals; Pro bono legal work; Public interest law.

LAW SCHOOLS

Institutions that prepare students to pass bar examinations so that they can practice law; graduation from a law school is the first step to becoming a lawyer in the United States

In the colonial and immediate postrevolutionary period, as was the case in most professions or trades, a person aspiring to be a lawyer apprenticed himself for an agreed-upon period of time to someone with knowledge of the field, who, in return for supervised work, would teach the nuances of the profession and would pay a subsistence wage, often including room and board. Although Litchfield Law School was founded in 1784, and several other institutions, including Harvard, shortly thereafter began to teach the subject of law, this was not the beginning of law schools as they are now known.

The egalitarian impulses of the Jacksonian era were antithetical to all forms of professional training; as a consequence, all but Harvard's programs were shuttered. It was not until the 1850's, with the founding of schools at Columbia, New York University, and the University of Pennsylvania, that the institution of law schools truly began to flourish. By the time of the Civil War, there were at least twenty-one schools operating throughout the country.

Law Schools in the Nineteenth Century

The quality of education varied widely, but almost uniformly the standards for admission were low compared with other divisions of the same university. Furthermore, nonuniversity-based schools offering inferior training proliferated. For this reason, there grew a movement to extend the examination given to those who had completed their apprenticeship to all those seeking to practice. By 1890, successful passage of a bar examination was the

Reading room of the library of Harvard University's law school in the early twentieth century. (Courtesy of Art & Visual Materials, Special Collections, Harvard Law School Library)

normal prerequisite for practice, whether the candidate was a graduate from a law school or not. Shortly thereafter, one could not simply sit for the bar examination; in 1896, the American Bar Association (ABA), the professional association of all lawyers, promulgated more rigorous standards: a high school diploma and at least two years of law school or the practical equivalent thereof. In 1900, as part of the continuing effort to maintain and improve standards, the Association of American Law Schools (AALS) was founded.

Even with these improvements, the course and quality of study varied widely: Schools that were part of a university were often more theoretical, while proprietary schools were more practical, stressing specific facts and procedures appropriate to their local area. In 1870, Dean Christopher Langdell of Harvard Law School introduced the "case method," in which the process and evolution of law is stressed. Very quickly most schools adopted this form of pedagogy, as it appeared to be effective and allowed for large classes, meaning that the schools could generate significant profit. As a result, admissions standards fell in many schools as administrators opted for a more Darwinian solution: Those who could survive the rigors of the course could progress to the next hurdle, the bar examination. In 1926, 250 of Harvard's entering class of 700 failed. To inject some equity into the process, in 1928, Columbia included an aptitude test in the admissions process. From this would evolve the Law School Admission Test (LSAT).

Law Schools of Today

Modern law school standards are rigorous. To qualify to sit for the bar examination, a student must have completed twelve hundred class hours in three years (if a part-time student, within four years) at an accredited law school and must have studied professional skills, torts, contracts, property, and procedure. These courses are usually taken in the first year of a three-year program. The range of additional courses is broad, covering interdisciplinary topics, social justice, and a wide variety of clinical exercises. Rarely do students specialize in narrowly defined areas of the law before entering the profession; rather, they are trained to "think like a lawyer." Essentially, this entails distilling arguments, iden-

UNDERGRADUATE PREPARATION FOR LAW SCHOOL

More than 84,000 undergraduates who applied to law schools in 1994-1995 had undergraduate majors in these fields:

Social sciences:	47.6 percent
Arts and humanities:	19.7 percent
Business and management:	16.4 percent
Natural sciences:	4.6 percent
Engineering:	3.2 percent
Health professions:	1.1 percent
Computer sciences:	0.6 percent

Specific majors were:

Political science:	18.7 percent
English:	7.1 percent
Psychology:	4.8 percent
Criminal justice:	4.1 percent
Economics:	3.5 percent

tifying and ranking issues, and finding parallels with earlier cases. Accreditation standards therefore demand that the school have an adequate library, a student/faculty ratio that is low enough for easy interaction between student and faculty, and an admissions policy that is strict enough to ensure that those admitted will have a good chance of successfully completing the course of study. Only in the state of Wisconsin does graduation from an accredited law school guarantee admission to practice; elsewhere, all must pass a bar examination.

ABA and AALS efforts to raise and enforce standards put extraordinary pressures on the proprietary schools; to survive, many merged with universities or existing ABA-approved institutions. By 1958, there were only thirty unapproved institutions, most of which could be found in a smattering of states, notably California. By making its bar examination very rigorous, the state ensured the quality of those entering the practice without taking the potentially unpopular step of eliminating institutions which, for the most part, served those who could not gain admission to the more selective schools.

As of early 2003, there were 178 ABA-approved law schools throughout the nation plus five schools with provisional approval. Most required that for admission applicants take the LSAT, designed to predict how well the applicant will do in the first year of law school. Unlike the almost uniform requirements for admission to medical school, there is no specialized preparatory course of study prescribed for admission; any study that develops reasoning skills is seen as adequate training.

Both the ABA and the AALS have stressed the need for affirmative action in law school admissions, along with support systems to help ensure that those admitted will be able to complete the program. Since the early 1970's, the makeup of the typical law school class has changed dramatically. Whereas it used to be almost entirely composed of white males who were recent college graduates, by the mid-1990's roughly 50 percent of law students were female, and often more than a quarter were members of minorities.

—Theodore P. Kovaleff

Suggested Readings

Books that provide interesting views on law schools include Philip C. Kissam, *The Discipline of Law Schools: The Making of Mod-*

ern Lawyers (Durham, N.C.: Carolina Academic Press, 2003); William C. Chase, *The American Law School and the Rise of Administrative Government* (Madison: University of Wisconsin Press, 1982); Randall R. Kelso and Charles D. Kelso, *Studying Law: An Introduction* (St. Paul, Minn.: West Publishing, 1984); and Robert Bocking Stevens, *Law School: Legal Education in America from the 1850's to the 1980's* (Chapel Hill: University of North Carolina Press, 1983). Each year the Law School Admission Services, with the Association of American Law Schools, publishes the *Prelaw Handbook: An Official Guide to ABA-Approved Law Schools*. They also publish materials designed to help students prepare for the Law School Admission Test, which are carried in many college book stores. Other published guides to law schools include Gary A. Munneke, *Barron's Guide to Law Schools* (New York: Barron's Educational Series, 2000), and *The Penguin Guide to American Law Schools*, by Harold R. Doughty (New York: Penguin Books, 1999). Practical handbooks for prospective law students include William G. Weaver, *Peterson's Game Plan for Getting into Law School* (Princeton, N.J.: Peterson's, 2000); Robert H. Miller, *Law School Confidential: The Complete Law School Survival Guide: By Students, for Students* (New York: St. Martin's Griffin, 2000); and *A Woman's Guide to Law School*, by Linda Hirshman (New York: Penguin Books, 1999).

See also American Bar Association; Attorney types; Bar examinations and licensing of lawyers; Judicial clerks; Law firms; Pro bono legal work; Public interest law; Unauthorized practice of law.

LAWSUITS

Processes through which disputes are resolved in court systems

Through lawsuits, society makes binding as to specific persons and entities its norms and preferences. Lawsuits are also frequently a means by which social norms and preferences are articulated, reinforced, and made binding on all at large. Lawsuits may be brought by society itself acting through agencies of the government "in the name of the people" or they may be brought by private individuals. In either case, society, acting through its agents—the judge or jury—listens to the positions of the disputants, decides who is right and who is wrong, and grants appropriate relief to the parties. Lawsuits differ from other mechanisms for dispute resolution because they have the full backing of the authority of the state and thus may be enforced directly by the state's police powers.

The Nature of Lawsuits

A lawsuit begins with a formal complaint by a plaintiff or prosecutor that a defendant has acted (or is acting) in ways that are inconsistent with the laws of the community. Ordinarily, the plaintiff claims that such wrongful conduct has resulted in injury and that the plaintiff is thus entitled to some relief from the defendant. Lawsuits are thus categorized according to the nature of the complaint, the sort of injury complained of, and the relief sought.

Lawsuits are most commonly classified as criminal and civil. A criminal lawsuit is brought to punish a wrongdoer for conduct that society has criminalized as antithetical to the welfare of the general community. Typically, imprisonment and/or monetary fines are used to enforce compliance with such laws. The choice between imprisonment and fines depends on an evaluation of the purpose of punishment. Numerous (and in many ways conflicting) objectives are said to be served by punishing wrongdoers, and the selection of imprisonment and/or monetary fines reflects the social weight given to these objectives, which include deterring similar conduct in the future (either by the particular person or by others in the defendant's situation), rehabilitating wrongdoers to enable them to conform to the acceptable norms and practices of society, communicating the community's sense of indignation or righteous anger, and expressing to the victim the community's felt sense of atonement for the delinquency of one of its members.

Given that the potential for successful prosecution under a criminal statute will result in imprisonment, the bringing and prosecution of criminal lawsuits are very heavily regulated. Only the state, acting through a specifically authorized agent who is directly accountable either to the people through democratic elections or to the chief executive at the state or federal level may initiate a criminal prosecution. A somewhat unusual exception to this rule is the use in the federal government of the independent counsel, who investigates and prosecutes high-level officials when there is doubt as to the ability of the U.S. attorney general and the Justice Department to effectively investigate and prosecute them. Even in such cases, the principle of direct accountability to the community may be carried further by the requirement that the defendant be indicted by a grand jury composed of a cross section of the community. Thereupon, the defendant must be tried by a jury composed of the citizens of the community when the charge is a felony and unless the defendant knowingly and voluntarily gives up the right to a jury trial. The defendant may be convicted of the charged offense only if the state proves all the elements of the offense to the jury "beyond a reasonable doubt."

Civil lawsuits may be brought by the state or by private individuals. In civil lawsuits, plaintiffs are required to allege and show that a societally recognized interest has been interfered with by defendants. They must prove their cases only by a preponderance of the evidence or, in a limited number of exceptional cases (usually those involving a claim that the wrongdoer possessed an evil mind-set) by "clear and convincing" evidence. With the peculiar exception of "civil contempt," (available in the very limited circumstance in which a party defiantly refuses to comply with an order of the court necessary to the lawsuit), the deprivation of liberty by imprisonment is not an available remedy in civil suits. Rather, because the primary goal of a civil action is to compensate the injured party (and only indirectly to deter such conduct by making an example of the wrongdoer), the typical remedy available in a civil lawsuit is compensation for harm already done or an injunction to forestall imminent, threatened, or continuing harm. In exceptional circumstances, however, such as in bad faith, breach of contract, or when wrongful conduct is particularly atrocious or engaged in with an egregious mind-set, punitive or exemplary damages may be awarded against the wrongdoer as a penalty.

Boundaries of Lawsuits

One of the most difficult aspects of lawsuits is their scope. For example, if a medical doctor is struck by an automobile while crossing the street, the ultimate issue will revolve around who had the right of way at the time the accident occurred. Before it is over, however, the lawsuit may have to determine whether only the medical doctor can sue or whether others related to the doctor, such as a spouse, dependents, or patients, may also sue. Similarly, a suit may have to clarify whether only the driver of the car may be sued or whether others, such as the car owner, the seller of the car, or its manufacturer, may be sued as well. There are no fixed or preordained answers to these questions. Rather, the answers that society gives to them reflect choices and balances to encourage or discourage certain kinds of behavior and the cost to the general dispute-solving system of seeking to do justice in the particular case. To answer these questions, it is necessary to consider the substantive rights of the parties and the available procedures for enforcing those rights. Indeed, answers to these questions may vary from one jurisdiction to another and may even vary within the same jurisdiction over time. Typically, the boundaries of a lawsuit are defined by the nature of the right at stake, the magnitude of the injury claimed, the development of the administrative system for handling the claim, and the capacity and resources available to the system for enforcing its rulings.

Rights flow from legislation and from custom. For example, the legislature may have passed a law stating that an automobile driver must come to a stop when he or she sees a pedestrian crossing a street. The doctor hit by an automobile might invoke this law as the basis for his lawsuit, and it will be up to the court to decide what is meant by the broad and general language of the legislation. The court must determine if drivers must stop regardless of whether the light is red or green or only if they actually see a pedestrian crossing the street.

Many lawsuits are filed for the purpose of establishing the existence of a right or for its extension. Such lawsuits are concerned less with providing relief to particular plaintiffs (not an insubstantial goal) than with social reform. This is especially the case with regard to fundamental and constitutional rights, which are stated in very broad terms and ultimately depend for their effectiveness on the specific interpretations given to them by the courts.

Since the 1970's there has been a significant and perhaps fundamental broadening of the boundaries of lawsuits, which has affected both the nature of claims asserted and the availability of remedies. The lawsuit has become a primary vehicle for social reform and a significant factor in the economic restructuring of American society. Thus, through lawsuits American courts have played pivotal roles in determining the extent to which members of different ethnic groups attend the same schools, share public

THE U.S. LEGAL SYSTEM

facilities, and are employed on the same terms. Similarly, the degree to which women, persons with disabilities, and homosexuals receive the same treatment as other members of society has been determined as much through lawsuits as through legislative enactments. Moreover, the lawsuit has been engaged substantially in a far-reaching economic restructuring of American society through the class-action device, in which one person or a small number of persons seek to represent the claims and legal interests of a large group of persons; through the vigorous use by consumer groups and business competitors of laws regulating trusts, bankruptcies, the environment, trade practices, personal injuries, or securities; and through the increasingly flexible availability of injunctive relief. Such lawsuits influence the conduct not only of those before the court but, more important, of sellers, buyers, employers, and governmental agencies, who, although not before the court, are nonetheless directly controlled by the judicial decisions emanating from the courts.

Procedural Rules

Conscious of their quasilegislative role in the creation and shaping of substantive rights through lawsuits, courts strive to retain the judicial character of their pronouncements through a series of procedural rules. One set of those rules—referred to as "justiciability"—insists that plaintiffs must have a concrete and particularized interest in the outcome of the lawsuit. These rules are enforced through the doctrines of standing, ripeness, and mootness.

Under the doctrine of standing, a court insists that plaintiffs asserting a claim must show that a right which is properly theirs has actually been interfered with and that they have sustained the sort of injury that is amenable to redress by the judicial process. Thus, it is not sufficient that plaintiffs assert the existence of a right in the abstract or simply that their right has been interfered with. They must show both the existence of a right and actual legal injury as a result of interference with the right so as to ensure that they will prosecute their claims with the vigor and adverseness of a truly (as opposed to a hypothetically) interested party. The same concerns undergird the requirements of ripeness and mootness. Ripeness demands that plaintiffs' claims have matured, not merely that they are feasible. Mootness asserts that the injury is current, at least as of the time of the lawsuit. Thus, courts see lawsuits as vehicles not simply for righting general wrongs but for providing relief to particular plaintiffs.

Because the consequence of a lawsuit cannot be limited entirely to the plaintiff and defendant but may necessarily implicate the interests of other persons and society at large, other procedural rules expand rather than constrain the reach of the lawsuit. When this consideration is combined with a desire for the efficient use of judicial resources, the result is a tendency in judicial administration that is at odds with the concrete demands of lawsuits. Thus, plaintiffs need not only represent their own interests, but through joinder and "class action" devices they may litigate on behalf of others who possess similar rights and have been similarly injured.

As long as plaintiffs can establish requisite standing, ripeness, and lack of mootness, they may be able to advocate not only their own concrete interests but the somewhat more removed and potentially hypothetical interests of others. Nine-year-old Sarah Brown in the U.S. Supreme Court case of *Brown v. Board of Education* (1954) came to represent not only her own right to attend a racially integrated elementary school but the right of all children in the United States to attend integrated primary schools. Ultimately she represented the right of all African Americans not to be confined to separate public facilities, whether in education, hospitals, or public restrooms. Many other lawsuits and legislative interventions were necessary to flesh out the *Brown* precedent, but the concept of equal protection under the law, much like most rights in American society, depended for their elaboration and force on ordinary lawsuits commenced and prosecuted by quite ordinary plaintiffs.

Sometimes a court may insist that all potential claimants or defendants be joined in their lawsuits while at other times a court may be willing to adjudicate even far-reaching societal interests solely on the basis of the claims, interests, and defenses of a small subsection of those who will be affected by the judicial decision. Establishing the appropriate balance between the view of judicial function as simply to resolve the problem of specific litigants and the reality that the effects of a judicial decision cannot, and perhaps should not, be confined to the immediate litigants poses one of the most difficult issues in the understanding and use of lawsuits.

Other Dispute Resolution Mechanisms

In the late twentieth century the lawsuit as a dispute resolution mechanism came under significant attack. Critics contended that it is too costly, making it beyond the reach of all but the wealthy; that it is too stylized and formal, making it an inadequate tool for resolving the day-to-day informal conflicts that arise among ordinary persons; and that it tends to breed adverseness and elitism. They have proposed supposedly less costly and more informal dispute resolution mechanisms that address the specific quarrels of the parties and that do not seek to resolve broader social conflicts. Three such mechanisms are usually alluded to: negotiation, arbitration, and mediation and conciliation.

Negotiation involves direct efforts by parties or their agents to resolve their disputes without recourse to an intermediary. Arbitration is much like lawsuits in the sense that the parties leave the ultimate and conclusive resolution of their dispute to a third party, or umpire. It differs from lawsuits in that the umpire is a private person the scope of whose authority is subject entirely to the control of the disputants. Increasingly, the relatively informal structure of arbitration has been superseded by a more formal structure in which arbitration is organized by formal institutions such as the American Arbitration Association and a host of industry-specific bodies such as the New York Stock Exchange or the American Institute of Architects. Mediation and conciliation is also a privately ordered dispute resolution arrangement. However, unlike arbitration it does not seek to bind the parties to the decision of an umpire but uses a third party as a facilitator who encourages the litigants to explore the range of solutions available to them and to arrive at an optimal solution.

Alternative dispute resolution mechanisms have not proved to be a panacea. Arbitration, in certain circumstances, can be just as expensive, time-consuming, and formal as litigation. The success or failure of negotiation, arbitration, and mediation and conciliation often depends on the same sort of imbalance of power and resources that many critics of lawsuits criticize. Moreover, these alternative mechanisms lack the certainty of state-sanctioned enforcement of binding decisions inherent in lawsuits. The result is that innovative uses of alternative dispute resolution have increasingly been experimented with by litigators involved in lawsuits. Increasingly, the initiation of lawsuits has become the first step in a choreographed dispute resolution process that might employ nonbinding arbitration, mediation, and negotiation to determine if the parties can arrive at a resolution without a binding decree by a court. While some of these steps are formalized, most of them simply proceed as ad hoc steps in the litigation process. As a result, fewer than 5 percent of all lawsuits conclude with a final judgment issued by a court. Most criminal cases are resolved through plea bargaining, and the vast majority of civil cases are settled by the parties prior to trial and even sometimes after a judgment has been rendered.

—*Maxwell O. Chibundu*

Suggested Readings

Two lively studies of lawsuits are Thomas F. Burke. *Lawyers, Lawsuits, and Legal Rights: The Battle over Litigation in American Society* (Berkeley: University of California Press, 2002), and Carl T. Bogus. *Why Lawsuits are Good for America: Disciplined Democracy, Big Business, and the Common Law* (New York: New York University Press, 2001). A comparatively easy way to learn about the intricacies of lawsuits is to follow an account of a single lawsuit from beginning to end. An excellent presentation of a civil lawsuit is *A Civil Action*, by Jonathan Harr (New York: Random House, 1995), and a presentation of a criminal lawsuit is *A Crime of Self-Defense: Bernhard Goetz and the Law on Trial*, by George P. Fletcher (New York: Free Press, 1988). Judges and juries are also significant actors in lawsuits, and discussions of their roles may be found in Jeffrey Abramson's *We, the Jury: The Jury System and the Ideal of Democracy* (New York: Basic Books, 1994) and in Marianne Constable's *The Law of the Other: The Mixed Jury and Changing Perceptions of Citizenship, Law, and Knowledge* (Chicago: University of Chicago Press, 1994). Finally, the most comprehensive development of the issues presented by lawsuits may be found in books on civil procedure written for lawyers. A good one-volume treatise on the subject is Jack H. Friedenthal, Mary K. Kane, and Arthur R. Miller's *Civil Procedure* (2d ed. St. Paul, Minn.: West Publishing, 1993). For a specialized treatment of lawsuits in federal courts, see Ann E. Woodley, *Litigating in Federal Court: A Guide to the Rules.* Durham, N.C.: Carolina Academic Press, 1999. For a lightheart look at the subject, see *Whiplash!: America's Most Frivolous Lawsuits*, by James L. Percelay (Kansas City, Mo.: Andrews McMeel, 2000).

See also Adversary system; Appeal; Arbitration; Attorneys; Breach of contract; Cause of action; Civil actions; Civil law; Class action; Contracts; Defendants; Frivolous lawsuits; Harmless errors; Injunctions; Jurisdiction; Litigation; Mediation; Restraining orders, temporary; Shareholder suits; Summary judgments; Trials; Verdicts.

LEGAL CLINICS

Nonprofit community organizations established to provide legal services to people unable to afford customary attorney fees

The poor, homeless, and others of low income can obtain legal counseling at no cost or, in some cases, for a nominal fee through the services of legal clinics. These clinics are staffed by legal professionals who often donate their services at no charge. At the clinics are attorneys, paralegals, law students, and support staff. Clinics can be independent facilities or associated with a law firm, a bar association, or a law college. The facilities are overseen by a director or board of directors appointed by the local bar association or the various groups affiliated with the clinics. Funding for the clinics comes from federal, state, or local grants; from donations; and from support groups. The clinics generally serve local areas, cities, counties, or regions and are thus familiar with local problems and services.

Clinic services vary from general coverage in a variety of fields to specialized clinics that emphasize specific types of services for specific groups. The poor and homeless, for example, are generally concerned with housing, the possibility of eviction, failure to pay rent, and tenant-landlord disputes. Other concerns are food stamps, welfare insurance, employment, income tax preparation and filing, health insurance, health care, and disability insurance. Women in particular often have special problems pertaining to child custody, child care, children's rights, divorce settlements, and spousal abuse. Persons with disabilities may require assistance with job discrimination, medical insurance, housing, and transportation.

Some clinics specialize in cases involving the courts. Depending on the extent to which clinics offer such assistance, help might include client counseling, the investigation of complaints, legal research, court preparation, witness instruction, and actual representation in court. For those convicted of crimes, assistance with new trial motions, parole, and postconviction concerns can be handled by legal clinics. This form of assistance may also include the analysis of police records, the development of supporting affidavits, the study of autopsy reports, research into prior litigation, work with the courts, and discussions with prosecutors and judges.

Another area of concern for those seeking help from legal clinics is the problem of consumer credit and debt. Other clinics concentrate on aid to immigrants, noncitizens, and their dependents. These people are often victims in dealing with housing and in obtaining work permits and other legal documents, such as driver's licenses. They often need assistance in obtaining proper forms to secure permanent residence status or citizenship. Persons with the human immunodeficiency virus (HIV) and acquired immunodeficiency syndrome (AIDS) are often discriminated against in the workplace and by society in general. These people are often the least prepared to defend themselves from such abuses. Clinics specializing in their needs are available. A similar argument can be made for gay and lesbian persons. They too, if unable to afford conventional legal help, can turn to legal clinics specializing in their needs. In addition to helping individuals, nonprofit organizations unable to afford attorney fees can seek help from legal clinics that concentrate on their problems. These problems might include tax issues, the drafting of organizational bylaws, and the establishment of rules of conduct.

—Gordon A. Parker

See also Attorney fees; Attorneys, court-appointed; Bar associations; Civil rights and liberties; Contingency fees; Indigent criminal defendants; Law firms; Legal services plans; Pro bono legal work; Public defenders.

LEGAL GUARDIANS

Persons appointed by wills or courts to assume responsibility for minors or adults who are not considered competent to undertake legal obligations on their own

Parents may specify in a will whom they want to assume legal responsibility for their underage surviving children. Persons so designated become the legal guardians of such children if they are willing to assume this responsibility and if the courts agree. If minors survive parents who do not leave a will, the court appoints persons as legal guardians to assume responsibility for the children. In addition to appointing legal guardians for minor children who have been orphaned, courts may appoint guardians for other reasons. Legal guardians may be appointed to take responsibility for children who have been removed from their parents' residence or for children who have been abandoned by their parents. Legal guardians may also be appointed for children from families in which the parents' parental rights have been terminated or for children whose parents are incarcerated. In addition to appointing guardians for minors, courts may also appoint guardians for adults who for some reason, such as developmental delay or mental illness, may not be able to make decisions for themselves.

In appointing guardians for minors and for adults who are not competent, the court selects persons who will act in the best interests of the minor or incompetent person. A guardian often is a close relative of the person for whom the guardianship is being provided, but this must not be and is not always the case. When appropriate, the court may seek input about a preference for a guardian from the person for whom the guardianship is being provided.

The guardian may or may not have custody of the person for whom the guardianship is provided, but the guardian is responsible for the welfare of that person and for the protection of that person's property. A guardian is responsible for ensuring that a school-age child is enrolled in school and attends regularly. The guardian must also grant permission for the minor to be adopted. If the minor is under thirteen years of age, the guardian can apply for the minor's passport. If people under guardianship want to marry or join the armed forces, they must receive permission from their guardians to do so. Guardians must give permission for medical, surgical, and psychiatric services. They have a legal obligation to carry out the responsibilities of guardianship and can be charged for failing to do so. People who act as guardians can be deprived of their guardianship status if it is proven that they have failed to act in the best interests of the person for whom they have responsibility. In acting to deprive a person of guardianship, the court follows due process and investigates complaints about the guardian, seeking information from appropriate sources that usually include the person for whom the guardianship is provided. As guardianship is a legal responsibility, it can be terminated only through a court order.

—Annita Marie Ward

See also Age of majority; Competency; Family law practice; Indigent criminal defendants; Juvenile criminal proceedings; Probate; Probation, juvenile.

LEGAL IMMUNITY

Freedom from liability or prosecution under criminal or civil law

The privileges and immunities of U.S. citizens are included in the U.S. Constitution in Article IV, in the Fifth Amendment, and in the Fourteenth Amendment. The Fifth Amendment guarantees that no person "shall be compelled in any criminal case to be a witness against himself," while the Fourteenth Amendment provides that the states cannot pass laws that take away the privileges or immunities promised to all U.S. citizens by the Constitution. Article IV protects all the privileges and immunities of U.S. citizens by guaranteeing that each state must treat citizens of other states as it treats its own citizens. Thus, the provision for defendants and witnesses to refuse to furnish evidence that might tend to incriminate themselves is applicable on the federal and state levels to persons charged with crimes or to witnesses in any proceeding.

In the United States a frequent use of immunity occurs in criminal law when witnesses who are suspected of criminal activity are granted immunity from prosecution for their aid in testifying against other suspected criminals. Such immunity permits obtaining testimony that would otherwise be banned by exercise of witnesses' privilege against self-incrimination. In many cases, immunity deals are worked out between the defendant and the prosecution in order to obtain the defendant's testimony. Two types of criminal immunity exist in the United States: transactional immunity and use immunity. When transactional immunity is granted, the recipient cannot be prosecuted for any aspect of the criminal act in which he or she was involved. If use immunity is granted, the recipient's testimony given in return for immunity may not be used against that person or coconspirators for any criminal act unknown to the prosecutor prior to the granting of immunity.

Immunity may also be based on the official status of the people involved. For example, a presiding judge rendering a decision cannot be charged with civil or criminal libel. Likewise, U.S. senators and representatives enjoy a limited privilege of immunity while in attendance at legislative sessions. In the United States and several other countries, legislators are immune from civil liability for statements made in the course of their duties during legislative speeches and debate. They are also immune from criminal arrest, although they are subject to legal action for crimes.

Under international law diplomatic representatives of foreign governments are granted immunity from local jurisdiction, both civil and criminal, in the countries in which they serve. This diplomatic immunity extends to diplomats' offices and residences. The practice of diplomatic immunity is a matter of mutual courtesy between nations.

A sovereign governmental body is immune from civil action by private citizens unless the governmental body consents to such action. The charters or legislation of governmental corporations and authorities usually waive immunity from private actions. In the United States, the federal and state governments have established statutory procedures to allow the prosecution of claims against them.

—*Alvin K. Benson*

See also Amnesty; Bail bond agents; Civil rights and liberties; Constitution, U.S.; Diplomatic immunity; Fifth Amendment; Immunity from prosecution; Informants.

LEGAL SERVICES PLANS

System through which individual persons may obtain the legal services they need in return for fix payments made in advance

Prepaid legal services plans are formed by employers, unions, or associations. There are legal services plans in which members of credit unions make monthly payments. Many plans have panels of lawyers who agree to render legal services to credit union members. A growing number of labor unions have legal services plans. Labor union plans are typically negotiated between labor and management. When a union has a legal services plan, all dues-paying union members are entitled to services. Legal plans are typically administered by third-party law firms. Legal plans may be purchased for a business or as a benefit for employees. For example, members of the Boston Teachers Union subscribe to a legal services plan. A number of firms have employee-paid plans. Legal services plans are funded by employees through payroll deductions. A number of law firms offer legal services to small businesses. Plans vary in terms of their services and subscription rates. Many prepaid legal fees charge less than $20 per month per subscriber. Legal fees are typically paid by the plan, the sponsor, or the participant.

Panels of attorneys perform legal services for subscribers. Hyatt Legal Plans, LawPhone, and Pre-Paid Legal Services are examples of national firms marketing prepaid legal services. Each plan outlines the terms of its legal services and what services are offered. Signature's legal plan offers subscribers unlimited telephone consultation, the drafting of simple wills, unlimited legal letters, the legal review of documents, and assistance with warranty protection and small-claims cases.

Subscribers may receive legal advice by telephone, document review, and other services. Most prepaid plans charge fees for additional services. The National Resource Center for Consumers of Legal Services estimates that over 100 million Americans belong to legal services plans. The American Bar Association (ABA) generally approves of lawyers participating in such plans. However, attorneys must be permitted to exercise independent professional judgment on behalf of clients, to maintain client confidence, to avoid conflict of interest, and to practice competently.

Attorneys providing services through a plan must follow all the ethical and disciplinary rules expected of any licensed attorney. A growing number of states require that group legal services plans obtain prior approval by the state bar. New York, for example, permits that state's Superintendent of Insurance to approve prepaid legal services plans.

—*Michael L. Rustad*

See also Attorney-client relationship; Attorney fees; Attorney types; Attorneys; Billing rates; Legal clinics; Pro bono legal work; Solicitation of legal clients; Unethical conduct of attorneys.

LEGISLATIVE COUNSEL

Lawyers employed by legislative or administrative bodies with responsibility for drafting and reviewing proposed legislation and anticipating its real-world effects

Legislative counsel are lawyers who have legislatures or administrative agencies instead of private businesses or individuals as clients. For example, a member of Congress who wants to introduce a bill to clean up toxic waste sites probably does not have detailed knowledge of environmental law or the technical skill to draft appropriate language. Instead, the member of Congress (or, more likely, a trusted staffer) explains the outlines of the proposal to the legislative counsel's office, which drafts language consistent with the member's original purpose. The legislative counsel may also point out weaknesses in the proposal, suggest ways to modify the proposal without compromising its principal objectives, and address technical questions such as effective dates and transition rules. A similar function is performed by legislative counsel offices in the various state legislatures, although these are usually smaller and less specialized than at the federal level.

Although legislators are the most obvious clients, the term legislative counsel is also applied to lawyers for executive or administrative agencies who review proposed legislation and, when called upon, draft their own proposals for introduction in the appropriate legislatures. For example, the first draft of major tax reform proposals is frequently written by the Treasury Department's Office of Tax Legislative Counsel and subsequently modified by the relevant congressional staffs. Like their congressional counterparts, the holders of administrative positions usually combine a general law degree with at least some experience in private legal practice, to which some (but not all) of them return after a few years in public service.

Historically, most legislatures had only a small number of legislative counsel, each of whom wrote legislation in many fields. This remains the case in state governments, in which staffs are small and controlled by party leaders or committee chairpersons rather than by individual legislators. By contrast, the U.S. Congress saw an explosion in the size of its staffs in the late twentieth century, from fewer than three thousand in the late 1940's to more than twenty thousand in the 1990's. Although the formal House and Senate Offices of Legislative Counsel remain small, the increase in staff size means that many of the traditional roles of these offices, especially less technical functions such as evaluating proposed legislation and suggesting substantive improvements, are performed by specialized committee staffs or by the offices of individual members of Congress. The effects of this change are hotly debated. Some believe that the quality of legislation has declined with the proliferation of specialized staffs, which tend to be more politicized and perhaps less professional than those from legislative counsel offices, even when called by similar-sounding names such as "legislation counsel" or "legislative director." Others believe that the increase in staff size reduces the role of lobbyists and increases the independence and effectiveness of individual members of Congress.

—Michael A. Livingston

See also Administrative law; Attorney types; Attorneys, United States; Attorneys general, state; District attorneys; Statutes.

LESSER INCLUDED OFFENSE

Crime that contains substantially the same behavior or elements as the main offense but carries a lesser punishment than the main offense

Nearly all criminal codes are subdivided into sections of related offenses. The similarities among individual statutes within sections are often easier to see than the differences. The differences are often found in subtle variations in the *actus reus* (criminal behavior) described within the statute.

It is generally illegal to attempt to commit a crime. If persons attempt to steal a car and are caught as they try to drive away, they can be charged with either theft or attempted theft. The attempt behavior is almost the same as the stealing behavior. There are also other crimes included in the main offense. It is illegal to break into a car regardless of whether the intent is to steal something from the car or the car itself. Both the attempt offense and the breaking in offense are lesser included offenses to auto theft. There are also offenses that are physically impossible to commit without committing another offense. For example, in order to break into a house or business it is necessary to trespass. Trespassing is a lesser included offense to burglary.

Because of the double jeopardy provisions of the Fifth Amendment to the U.S. Constitution, the U.S. Supreme Court has ruled that one cannot be convicted of, or plead guilty to, both the main offense and the lesser included offense.

—*Michael L. Barrett*

See also Annotated codes; Arraignment; Confessions; Convictions; Criminal justice system; Double jeopardy.

LIABILITY, CIVIL AND CRIMINAL

Traditional distinction in the law between criminal, or public law, and private law

The division between criminal law and civil law is sometimes referred to as the public/private law distinction. Criminal law is prosecuted by public officers on behalf of society at large, whereas civil law actions are brought by private individuals. Criminal law and tort law have been traditionally regarded as separate subjects with clear lines of demarcation. Civil law subjects include the substantive fields of contract law and the law of torts. Torts are civil wrongs done by one party against another, excluding breaches of contract. The law of contracts is a branch of civil law dealing with enforceable agreements. Article 2 of the Uniform Commercial Code (UCC) governs the sale of goods. Article 3 of the Uniform Commercial Code applies to contracts governing negotiable instruments. The common law of services is a growing field of civil liability. The law of torts can be subdivided into medical malpractice, product liability, and constitutional torts. Civil liability also includes laws affecting regulated industries, environmental law, securities regulation, occupational safety and health regulations, and many other fields.

Punitive damages are a civil sanction that punish and deter conduct inimical to the public welfare. The power of punitive damages may be employed to punish individuals who are beyond the reach of criminal law. For example, a California jury awarded $25 million in punitive damages to the family of Nicole Simpson and Ron Goldman in the infamous O. J. Simpson case. The growing overlap between criminal and civil law is reflected in the expanded use of punitive damages to punish misconduct by corporations. Many legal scholars view the explosion of cases involving punitive damages as part of a collapsing boundary between criminal and civil liability.

—*Michael L. Rustad*

See also Arraignment; Case law; Civil law; Commercial litigation; Contracts; Indemnity; Joint and several liability; Negligence; Strict liability; Torts.

LITIGATION

Process of bringing a legal action, including all relevant proceedings; the primary means of seeking enforcement of rights and redress for grievances in judicial settings

When two or more individuals or entities have a disagreement ostensibly based on a violation of law, often they find themselves embroiled in litigation. In a simple lawsuit, the plaintiff, the party who voices the initial complaint, files suit with a court against the defendant, the party who has allegedly wronged the plaintiff. The rules for filing and prosecuting a lawsuit are highly formalized and vary according to jurisdiction. As a case proceeds through a given court system, it can be rejected at a number of points, often for procedural violations. If a case actually goes to trial, it can be adjudicated by a judge or a panel of judges, or by a judge and jury. If the trial results in a judgment or verdict, that determination can often be appealed to a higher court by either party—again, often on procedural grounds. Appeals often result in further appeals, some of them taken all the way to the U.S. Supreme Court.

See also Adversary system; Advisory opinions; Attorneys; Burden of proof; Commercial litigation; Contracts; Lawsuits; Litigation expenses; Paralegals; Personal injury attorneys; Public interest law; Test cases; Trials.

LITIGATION EXPENSES

Various expenses of lawsuits that include attorney fees, court filing fees, court reporting fees for depositions, and expert witness fees

A famous judge, Learned Hand, once observed about lawsuits, "I must say that, as a litigant, I should dread a lawsuit beyond almost anything else short of sickness and of death." Judge Hand no doubt had many aspects of litigation in mind when he pronounced this dire verdict on the subject, but the cost of litigation

One of the most distinguished American jurists who never sat on the U.S. Supreme Court, Learned Hand served more than thirty years on federal appeals courts and wrote more than three thousand opinions. (Library of Congress)

must be listed among its chief vexations, then and now. Litigation is an extraordinarily expensive affair. Litigants must ordinarily foot the bill for everything from relatively nominal court filing fees to extravagantly expensive attorney fees. Even minor trials can cost several thousands of dollars, and expenses in major litigation can literally amount to millions of dollars.

Generally, attorney fees are the most expensive part of litigation bills. Attorneys often charge an hourly rate, which may range from as little as $100 per hour to more than $400, depending on the experience and expertise of the lawyer and the geographic location. Some clients can avoid the enormous fees that such hourly rates may generate by finding a lawyer who will handle a matter on a contingency fee basis. Under a contingency fee arrangement, a lawyer obtains a fee only if he or she is successful in obtaining some recovery for the client, and the fee is normally paid out of this recovery. In many cases, lawyers either are not allowed or are unwilling to charge a contingency fee. In such cases, parties must generally bear the substantial costs of attorney fees, even if they are successful in their litigation claims.

Two other significant legal expenses in most cases are those relating to depositions and expert witnesses. In civil cases, pretrial discovery rules allow parties to uncover a variety of information prior to trial and thus to avoid "trial by ambush." One means of acquiring such information is to take the depositions of witnesses. In depositions, witnesses are questioned under oath about facts relevant to a case, and both questions and answers are recorded by a court reporter. Thus, depositions, which are a crucial part of most civil cases, involve the expense both of lawyers, who generally ask the questions of witnesses, and the court reporter, who transcribes the testimony. Moreover, in many cases expert witnesses are needed to testify about particular matters. Expert witnesses often charge hourly rates for their testimony equal to or greater than the hourly rates charged by the lawyers in the case. States vary considerably as to whether they allow the prevailing party in a case to recover these kinds of litigation expenses from the losing party.

—Timothy L. Hall

See also Attorney fees; Attorney trust accounts; Billing rates; Contingency fees; Court-awarded fees; Court costs; Legal clinics; Litigation; Personal injury attorneys; Private investigators; Retainers; Small-claims courts; Solicitation of legal clients.

LONG-ARM STATUTES

Any laws that allow states to make judgments that are legally binding on corporations or individuals who do not reside in the same states

Long-arm statutes are necessary because courts have interpreted the doctrine of due process guaranteed by the U.S. Constitution to include the requirement that a state have some form of minimal contact with defendants before it can issue judgments against them.

The exact form of contact required between a state and a defendant before a judgment can be made varies from state to state. In general, it is sufficient that a defendant has entered a state, either directly or through a representative, or that a defendant has dealt with a state resident for a specific purpose.

The usual forms of minimal contact specified in state long-arm statutes fall into four categories. Defendants are subject to judgment if they do business within state boundaries; if they own, use, or possess real property, such as land or buildings, within the state; if they commit a civil wrong against a person or property, known as a tort, within the state; or if they commit a tort that causes injury within the state.

—*Rose Secrest*

See also Bankruptcy; Due process of law; Jurisdiction; Multiple jurisdiction offenses; Torts.

LOUISIANA LAW

Legal system that is unique among the American states in consisting of a compilation of short, logically interrelated articles designed to regulate civil society by means of general propositions

The Louisiana Civil Code and civil law system are unique in the United States, as they are rooted in French, Spanish, and Roman traditions rather than English common law. Louisiana is the only state in the United States that has a civil law system and has enacted a civil code. While some common-law states have enacted codes addressing certain specific areas of law (such as commercial law), such codes typically attempt to reflect the law existing at the time of the codification without substantially altering or organizing it. In contrast, the Louisiana Civil Code provides logical organizations of general principles of law to be applied by deduction and extended to new circumstances by analogy. As law professor Ferdinand Stone has explained, this type of system requires attorneys to evaluate legal issues in different ways than their common-law counterparts do. The civil-law lawyer, Stone notes, has a written "blueprint plan of the universe" in his pocket; by consulting the plan, he can use "simple logic [to] deduce the appropriate answer." The common-law lawyer has no general rule but meets problems as they come, "bringing to bear upon them [his] experience and common sense."

Because the Louisiana Civil Code's vocabulary employs terminology and concepts of French, Spanish, and Roman law, attorneys from the other forty-nine states cannot readily understand it. For example, standard common-law concepts of property law such as "life estate" and "remainder" do not exist by that nomenclature. Their rough equivalents bear names derived from Latin and French, such as "usufruct" and "naked ownership."

The Structure of the Civil Code

The Louisiana Civil Code reflects a distinctively French perspective on law and society. The primary goal of early nineteenth century French civil codification was to render the law accessible by making it clear. To accomplish this goal, a civil code had to be complete in its field and had to lay down general rules in logical sequence.

In this spirit, the framers of the Louisiana Civil Code established three books that consist of a series of concisely written articles. Book 1, "Of Persons," encompasses legal personality, domicile, marriage, separation, divorce, legitimate and illegitimate children, adoption, parental authority, tutorship, and emancipation. This book regulates matters of personal status. Book 2, "Of Things and the Different Modifications of Ownership," covers the general law of movable and immovable property, personal and praedial servitudes, building restrictions, boundaries, and usufruct. Book 3, "Of the Different Modes of Acquiring the Ownership of Things," is the most comprehensive and lengthy of the three. It regulates the ways that citizens acquire and lose property, including successions, testaments, donations, delicts, community property, and many types of contracts—sale, lease, partnership, loan, deposit, mandate, surety, compromise, and pledge. In 1991, a fourth book, "Conflict of Laws," was added to the code.

Legal History of Louisiana

The legal history of Louisiana began in 1712, the year France granted Antoine Crozat a monopoly on commerce throughout the Louisiana Territory. The United States subsequently purchased Louisiana from France in 1803. The Louisiana Territory was then divided into territories, one of which, the Territory of Orleans, later became the state of Louisiana. At that time, United States officials, who were trained in the Anglo-American legal tradition, came to Louisiana and urged the adoption of a common-law system. In 1806, however, the first legislature of the Territory of Orleans passed a resolution to keep its civil law system intact insofar as it did not conflict with the U.S. Constitution. In 1808 the legislature enacted *A Digest of the Civil Laws Now in Force in the Territory*

of Orleans with Alterations and Amendments Adapted to Its Present
Form of Government, known as the Civil Code of 1808. The 1808
code was revised in 1825 and again in 1870; it remains the basis for
the current civil code.

—David R. Sobel

Suggested Readings
   Among the good sources on Louisiana civil law are Shael
Herman, *The Louisiana Civil Code: A European Legacy for the United
States* (New Orleans: Louisiana Bar Foundation, 1993); Tulane
Law School's *The Louisiana Civil Code: A Humanistic Appraisal*
(New Orleans: Author, 1981); and A. N. Yiannopoulos, *Louisiana
Civil Law System* (Baton Rouge, La.: Claitor's, 1971). More recent
studies include *A Law unto Itself?: Essays in the New Louisiana Legal
History*, edited by Warren M. Billings and Mark F. Fernandez (Ba-
ton Rouge: Louisiana State University Press, 2001), and *Louisiana:
Microcosm of a Mixed Jurisdiction*, edited by Vernon Valentine
Palmer (Durham, N.C.: Carolina Academic Press, 1999).

See also Annotated codes; Civil law; Common law; State courts;
Statutes; Uniform laws.

Marshals Service, U.S.

*Law-enforcement agency within the Justice Department that pro-
tects and supports the federal courts*

The U.S. Congress established the U.S. Marshals Service in the Judiciary Act of 1789. Appointed by the president for four-year
terms, the marshals chose their own deputies. Compensated only
for services rendered, they served warrants and other legal papers of the federal courts, protected federal property, transferred
prisoners, and pursued fugitives from federal justice. Marshals
occasionally did controversial work, such as enforcing the Fugitive Slave Act of 1850 and strikebreaking. They were subject to political patronage and poorly funded. Their authority was limited
to their judicial districts. There was little coordination between
the districts or in the sharing of resources.

In December, 1956, an Executive Office for U.S. Marshals was created to aid the exchange of ideas and information, monitor performance, and provide supervision and direction. Major reform took place between 1969 and 1974. The Executive Office became the U.S. Marshals Service. It controlled the budgets of district marshals and hired deputies. Professional standards were codified and applied to recruitment and training. New programs were established and old ones expanded. These reforms transformed the Marshals Service into a modern professional law enforcement agency. The president of the United States appoints the director of the Marshals Service, who controls operations from headquarters in Arlington, Virginia. The president also appoints a marshal to each of the ninety-five district offices. In 1977 the service had about four thousand deputies and career employees. Deputies must have a college education or equivalent experience. Women number about seven percent of the personnel and work in all branches.

Recruits spend eight weeks at the Federal Law Enforcement Training Center in Glynco, Georgia, studying general law enforcement, criminal investigation, and forensics. They also attend the U.S. Marshals Service Training Academy for six weeks of more specific training.

The Special Operations Group (SOG), created in 1971, responds to dangerous emergencies involving federal property or law, such as terrorist incidents or riots. The Missile Escort Program provides security to the U.S. Air Force and the Defense Department during the movement of missiles between military bases. The Air Operations Branch moves prisoners, transports SOG personnel, carries out international prisoner movements, and conducts prisoner exchanges between the United States and other countries. The Witness Security Program (1971) protects witnesses not only in federal courtrooms but also outside when they are judged to be threatened. Designed to facilitate the prosecution of organized crime, the program creates new identities for witnesses and their dependents.

Marshals pursue federal criminals who jump bail, violate parole, or escape from prison. Deputy marshals arrest more fugitives under warrant each year than all other federal law-enforcement agencies combined. The service's Fugitive Investigative Strike Team has organized highly successful sting operations. The service manages billions of dollars worth of property forfeited or seized by Justice Department agencies from persons convicted of drug trafficking and organized crime. Income from such property is used to benefit law enforcement.

—*Charles H. O'Brien*

See also Federal Bureau of Investigation; Federal judicial system; Justice Department, U.S.; Law enforcement; Officers of the court; Police.

MARTIAL LAW

Temporary use of military personnel to enforce laws and judicial decisions domestically, typically during public emergencies

In the United States the the concept of martial law usually refers to its imposition under orders of the president of the United States, who may employ the federal armed forces, or by state governors, who may mobilize National Guard units of their states. Martial law is a special condition during a state of emergency, not a body of laws and regulations as in civil law and military law, and the military's authority under martial law is never absolute.

Whereas the constitutions of most states authorize the governors or legislatures to proclaim martial law and dispatch the National Guard to control insurrections, the U.S. Constitution is not so straightforward about the president's powers. Article IV, section 4, enables the federal government to help a state suppress domestic violence upon the request of the legislature or governor. Article I, section 8, empowers the U.S. Congress "To provide for calling forth the Militia to execute the Laws of the Union, suppress Insurrections and repel Invasions." Since the Constitution requires that the president ensure the faithful execution of the nation's laws (Article II, section 3) and makes him commander-in-chief of federal forces, he is considered to have the power to declare martial law, although Congress must approve the suspension of writs of *habeas corpus* (applications to a court to consider whether a person in custody is being held lawfully). Precedent suggests that only war or national emergency justifies the use of martial law, but neither the U.S. Constitution nor statutory law specifies such limits.

Two presidents have declared martial law. During the Civil War (1861-1865) President Abraham Lincoln did so for Washington, D.C., and for areas of the Confederacy as they were occupied by federal troops. He also suspended the privilege of writs of *habeas corpus*. Governor Joseph Poindexter instituted martial law for

---

DOMESTIC USES OF THE MILITARY IN U.S. HISTORY

1794	President George Washington sends militia troops to Pennsylvania to suppress the Whiskey Rebellion without explicitly declaring martial law.
1814	General Andrew Jackson proclaims martial law for New Orleans.
1842	The Rhode Island legislature declares martial law to suppress Dorr's Rebellion.
1863-1865	President Abraham Lincoln declares martial law for Washington, D.C., and occupied Confederate territory and suspends the right to *habeas corpus* during the Civil War.
1895	President Grover Cleveland uses federal troops to keep the mails moving during a Pullman and railroad strike in Illinois, despite Governor John Altgeld's objection.
1919	General Leonard Wood declares "qualified martial law" to stop race riots in Omaha, Nebraska, and to police a steel strike in Gary, Indiana.
1932	General Douglas MacArthur uses Army troops to disperse the "bonus army" of veterans encamped in Washington, D.C., without a declaration of martial law.
1941-1944	Federal martial law is declared in Hawaii under the Hawaiian Organic Act.
1954	Federal troops maintain order during a mining strike in Colorado after the governor declares martial law for the mining area.
1957	President Dwight D. Eisenhower orders federal troops to enforce a federal court order admitting African American children to an all-white high school in Little Rock, Arkansas, despite Governor Orval Faubus's objection.
1992	President George Bush orders one thousand troops to quell riots in Los Angeles, California, supplementing National Guard units mobilized by Governor Pete Wilson.

Manzanar, California—one of the internment camps in which people of Japanese descent were forced to live under martial law during World War II; most were American citizens. (National Archives)

Hawaii on December 7, 1941, a move subsequently seconded by President Franklin D. Roosevelt. Roosevelt also authorized military commanders to exert direct authority over some areas of the United States; designated portions of the Western states were used to incarcerate Americans of Japanese descent.

Other federal officials have occasionally declared limited martial law to quell or prevent riots. In some instances a president, without formally declaring martial law to enforce federal laws, has sent troops to a state, even over a governor's objection.

U.S. Supreme Court decisions have limited the power of the military during martial law. During the Civil War the Court ruled that trials of civilians by federal military tribunals were invalid when civilian courts were open. Only when civil administration completely breaks down may military tribunals try civilians (*Ex parte Milligan*, 1866). In 1946 the Supreme Court decided that the military did not have jurisdiction over civilian employees of a military installation (*Duncan v. Kahanamoku*). However, the Court earlier appeared to approve some trials of civilians in state military courts by rejecting a suit for wrongful imprisonment resulting from one such trial (*Moyer v. Peabody*, 1909). The Court has also reserved the power to decide whether a governor's use of military forces is justified (*Sterling v. Constantin*, 1932).

—Roger Smith

See also Courts-martial; *Habeas corpus*; Military justice; Military police; Military tribunals.

MEDIATION

Process by which a neutral third party acts as a facilitator to assist other parties in resolving disputes

Part of the alternative dispute resolution process in the U.S. legal landscape, mediation is less formal than arbitration. Unlike arbitration, a mediator does not have the authority to render a binding decision. A mediator cannot compel parties to do anything. The role of the mediator is to assist parties in settling a dispute. Unlike arbitration, mediation involves neither hearings nor the presentation of evidence. The mediator conducts informal meetings with the parties to thoroughly understand the issues. Meetings may involve either one or both parties. On occasion it is necessary to conduct separate sessions with each party in order to acquire knowledge of the facts of the case.

All statements and information provided to the mediator is confidential and can only be disclosed with the permission of the party. The mediator's goal is to assist the parties by conducting candid discussions of the issues and the parties' priorities. The information gained from these discussions may be used by the mediator to reduce tensions between the parties, induce the engagement of meaningful dialogue, open discussions into areas not previously considered, uncover additional facts or motivations, assist in fostering mutual understanding, and communicate proposals in more palatable terms. In order to effectively perform the role of mediator, credibility and trust are essential. Credibility and trust are usually established at the beginning of mediation, when the mediator explains his role and allows the parties to explain the dispute.

Mediation is a voluntary process in which parties agree in writing that their dispute will be submitted to mediation. A number of profit and nonprofit organizations provide mediation services. The American Arbitration Association is an example of a private nonprofit organization that has been a central force in the area of alternate dispute resolution. There are two ways to start the mediation process: to agree to mediation prospectively in the terms of an existing contract or to submit an existing dispute to mediation by simply filing a form. The parties select a mediator from a list containing biographical information on qualified mediators.

Preparation for a mediation conference should include defining the issues involved, understanding the parameters of the situation, identifying needs and interests, assessing trade-offs, making reasonable proposals, comprehending the strengths and weaknesses of the case, preparing facts and documents to support positions, and listening carefully to the other side. An agreement should be made in writing, and, if the case is in litigation, motions to dismiss should be filed. If the mediation conference fails to arrive at a settlement, arbitration may become an option. Frequently, however, even if a mediation conference is initially unsuccessful, cases are settled subsequent to mediation.

Mediation saves time and money and is a very flexible process. It keeps decision-making authority in the hands of the parties and is generally available on short notice. Mediation is not an adversarial process, and it protects the future relations between parties.

—Robert N. Davis

See also Arbitration; Attorney types; Lawsuits; Legal services plans; Trials.

MEDICAL EXAMINERS

Physicians certified to conduct autopsies, the process through which causes of death can be determined

A medical examiner is an employee of a municipality. Unlike a coroner, who is usually elected to the position, a medical examiner is appointed either by the chief official of a municipality or by a commission.

To be certified as a medical examiner, a person must be a graduate of an accredited four-year college, attend an accredited medical school, receive the degree of Doctor of Medicine, and spend five years as a resident in general pathology and forensic pathology. At the end of this residency, the doctor must pass a national examination and be recognized as a diplomate by the American Board of Pathology. The doctor also may be certified by the American Board of Pathology in general pathology. In addition, the medical examiner may be trained in the law, particularly as it affects forensic medicine; however, legal training is not a requirement.

The functions of medical examiner and coroner may overlap. In some municipalities, both offices are held by one person, although they may also be separate and distinct duties. When the duties are separate, the coroner has the power to order an autopsy but not necessarily the qualifications to perform one. A medical examiner cannot order an autopsy but has the expertise to conduct one.

A medical examiner may be characterized as a detective who, using evidence gathered from internal and external examination of a body, plus evidence gathered where the body was found, tries to determine how and approximately when death occurred. The evidence gathered at the scene of the death can aid the medical examiner in determining whether death actually occurred where the body was found. This evidence is presented to the coroner and the coroner's jury, who render a formal verdict.

Information gathered by medical examiners over the course of many years has been collated to show how general facial and body characteristics correspond with age, sex, and nationality. A medical artist can use such information to draw a likeness of the person based upon these general characteristics and any specific facts provided by the medical examiner. These renderings have proved to be extremely accurate.

The first medical examiner may have been the physician Antisius, who determined that, of the twenty-three dagger wounds inflicted upon Julius Caesar, the fatal thrust was one that perforated his thorax.

See also Detectives, police; Evidence, rules of; Witnesses, expert.

MILITARY ATTORNEYS

Attorneys who perform legal services for the branches of the armed forces in which they serve

Military attorneys serve in the judge advocate general departments within all the branches of the armed forces. They practice in offices throughout the United States and several foreign countries. The military has its own laws and court system. Attorneys administer activities within the military judicial system. They do legal research, defend and prosecute court cases, and preside over military courts. In addition, they provide legal advice to military staff members and represent the services in international and civil legal matters.

Lawyers in the military give legal advice about government real estate, commercial contracts, patents, and trademarks. They also preside over court cases and make judgments based on the Uniform Code of Military Justice. The Uniform Code of Military Justice, first enacted in 1950, is the principal body of laws that applies to members of the armed forces. The military justice system is the primary legal enforcement tool of the armed forces. Military attorney tribunals interpret and enforce the Uniform Code. The code is similar to, yet separate from, the civilian criminal justice system. Several different rationales exist for a separate military justice system. The system's procedures allow for efficiency and ensure quick punishment, which are critical to military discipline. Civilian criminal justice, by comparison, is often slow, troublesome, and may yield inconsistent results. The maintenance of order and uniformity is expected from speedy military trials, for

NUMBER OF ATTORNEYS IN THE MILITARY

The military had approximately 4,000 active duty attorneys, divided as follows in the branches of the service, during the 1990's:
- The Army had 1,500
- The Air Force had 1,300
- The Navy, Marines, and Coast Guard together had 900 judge advocate general (JAG) officers

Military lawyers must have graduated from law schools accredited by the American Bar Association.

this contributes to national security. The court-martial method fulfills expectations of efficient and well-disciplined armed forces.

One of the primary clients of attorneys at military installations is the base commander, whose job is similar to that of a mayor of a city. The variety of legal problems that arise on military bases is limitless. Thus, military judge advocates are involved in numerous law disciplines, including the Uniform Code of Military Justice. They may also handle international law, which is concerned with armed conflicts regulated by treaties and the Geneva Convention of 1949; labor law, including civilian employment within the federal government and employment discrimination laws that are governed by the Civil Service Reform Act of 1978; environmental and real property law, which is concerned with reviewing the National Environmental Policy Act (NEPA) of 1969; and claims and tort litigation, by which military lawyers work closely with federal agencies, members of the local civilian bar, and U.S. attorney's offices in processing claims under numerous federal statutes, including the Federal Tort Claims Act of 1946.

Civilian attorneys work for the government, corporations, law firms, and in private practice. They perform duties that are similar to those performed by military attorneys, although they usually specialize in a particular field. However, military attorneys do not practice several types of civilian law—for example, divorce, trade, and antitrust law.

—Earl R. Andresen

See also Attorney types; Courts-martial; Military justice; Military tribunals.

MILITARY JUSTICE

System of apprehension, judgment, and punishment designed to maintain order, efficiency, security, and discipline within the military

A military justice system is usually administered by a particular arm or department of the military branch it serves. It is commanded by officers of rank comparable to those heading other departments to avoid situations in which judicial matters might be influenced—or appear to be influenced—by a higher authority in another branch.

A military justice system isolates its members from civilian control of legal issues for which the civilian judicial system is deemed inadequate or inappropriate; it also provides for the handling of crimes which are exclusively military matters

As in any other system of justice, military systems have provisions for investigation, gathering of evidence, arrest and detainment of alleged wrongdoers, trial, review, sentencing, punishment, and record keeping. Legal counsel must be provided for the accused and for those bringing charges. Sites are reserved for detainment of the accused, processing and studying evidence, trial, review, sentencing, and punishment. The severity of the charges determines to what extent isolation from the civilian population is necessary. In cases where civilian political activism is likely because of the severity or notoriety of the alleged crime or cases in which legal action against an accused is unpopular among the civilian population, the entire proceedings may be removed from civilian surroundings and made off-limits to the public and the press.

For minor lapses of discipline the accused may elect to face his accuser before only his or her immediate unit commander. While this removes safeguards involved with a formal trial by disinterested strangers, it has the benefit to the accused of being swift and private. For more serious offenses, there is a system of courts-martial.

Despite extremely detailed instructions and regulations in official military documents, there are also provisions for crimes that are not predictable or are difficult to define. These are covered in what are usually called "general articles" and relate to offenses not familiar to civilians. The very lack of specificity of these articles has placed them under attack by civil liberties advocacy groups.

In the United States, constitutional safeguards such as the Bill of Rights extend to military personnel except when the freedoms guaranteed by these rights are limited by "military necessity." The personal property of a military person, for example, is open to examination by superiors. In the closeness of military living conditions and because of the hazard that contraband poses to discipline, inspections may be conducted without prior announcement or a warrant. These examinations include the sort known familiarly as "shakedowns," in which a detailed search of living quarters is conducted if a crime is suspected. This is a violation of U.S. constitutional provisions but is generally assumed to be necessary.

Another constitutional guarantee withheld from military personnel is freedom of speech. Criticism and calumny against the president, vice president, members of Congress, secretaries, governors, and state legislators is forbidden. Activism against war or any usages of the military is also considered sowing dissension and may be acted upon.

In the military, the accused is denied access to a random selection of court, to trial by peers, to access to counsel in the lowest level of court, and to a verbatim record of the trial—all of which are guaranteed to civilians. The functions of the court, normally divided in the civilian milieu into "prosecution" and "defense," are combined in a single group, usually a judge advocate's staff appointed by the unit commander. This is justified by the cardinal military precept of "singleness of command," intended to avoid the inefficiencies of multiple command paths.

These exceptions to civilian practice have varied widely according to public reaction to the activities of the armed forces at any given time. In time of war some exceptions to the rights of military personnel are made in the name of secrecy and security. Yet military assignments which are thought "inhumane" may be refused with impunity if public opinion brings enough political pressure on the military. Cases of nonperformance of duty on the grounds of the enemy's human rights, for example, produced considerable legal wrangling during the Vietnam War.

An individual may not be tried by both military and civilian courts for any federal offense, including military offenses. Individuals tried for offenses under the laws of the states or of foreign countries, however, may be tried by the military as well.

Structure of the System

For the following discussion of a military justice system, the terms used will be those of the U.S. Army. (Parallel titles, structures, and procedures apply generally to many other modern systems.) All military justice activity except that of the informal procedure mentioned above is conducted by the organization directed by the judge advocate general. The document of law and procedure for military justice in the United States is the Uniform Code of Military Justice (UCMJ), which was adopted in 1951 to replace the antiquated Articles of War in use since revolutionary times. An auxiliary work, the Manual of Courts Martial (MCM) provides procedural rules for the conduct of courts-martial.

In addition to specific offenses, the UCMJ provides two non-specific articles: one for officers, making it an offense to indulge in "conduct unbecoming an officer and a gentleman," the other for enlisted men, forbidding "disorders and neglects to the prejudice of good order and discipline in the armed forces, all conduct of a nature to bring discredit upon the armed forces." In the MCM these are divided into more specific, but still subjective, offenses such as "being grossly drunk and conspicuously disorderly in a public place." While these "general articles" have been criticized as vague and allowing selective persecution, they have parallels in civilian law. Additionally, although the UCMJ and MCM are specific to the American armed forces, they have parallels in other modern military entities, reflecting the legal and social cultures of the various nations.

In U.S. territory, the military justice system has no responsibility for crimes not involving military property or personnel, leaving these to the civilian judicial systems. For nonmilitary offenses in foreign countries, however, the military justice system assumes responsibility. This protects the accused from possible draconian civilian jurisprudence, and it protects the civilian populace of the country from abusive behavior by military personnel.

Procedures and Provisions

Military justice differs from civilian justice in ways that reflect the danger to a nation's military mission posed by offenses which in civilian life present a much lesser danger. Except for a person

committing multiple capital crimes, a criminal in civilian life seldom imperils those much removed from his own sphere of action,
whereas in the military similar actions may have national consequences. In the United States armed forces, for example, quick
and consistent response is expected to every order, however minor. Since the courts are formed of command personnel taken
from their other duties (except for civilian counsel), there must be
a system that provides for hearing minor accusations in a simplified way so that the entire command organization is not bur-
dened.

At the least serious end of the range of offenses, an individual
may be tried in an informal session, called an Article 15 in the military because it is defined by the article so numbered in the UCMJ.
In this action the accused person's immediate unit commander
convenes, hears, judges, and sentences the accused without outside assistance, although the accused may have recourse to counsel if requested. Often in these minor actions the punishment is
assignment of short periods of onerous but necessary chores
within the unit, such as food preparation, maintenance, refuse removal, or sentry duty. There are limits to the allowed punishment
consistent with the minor nature of the offenses. If the accused
wants, he or she may request trial by a court-martial.

In the U.S. military, there are several levels of courts, with each
higher level giving the accused as well as the prosecutor greater
freedom. The highest of these courts are usually convened only
for serious crimes involving what would, in civilian life, be criminal cases. Typically, these offenses involve major bodily harm to
others, large-scale theft, or insubordination of a nature that may
threaten the outcome of a major military operation. While any
planned rebellion against orders is mutinous in the sense of refusing to follow orders, the charge of mutiny is usually reserved for
action against authority in the face of enemy activity.

Individuals have the right to claim redress for unfair or unusually harsh treatment by superiors. Like the courts-martial that
hear accusations against individuals, a court may be requested to
hear and adjudicate an individual's complaints. It is incumbent
upon the person bringing the complaint, however, to perform
whatever action he or she is assigned by competent orders. Only
then, the mission satisfied, may the individual bring complaint.
This policy is necessary to avoid having a mission jeopardized by
an individual who wishes to take the time to protest an order.

Police

The military branches provide their own police forces. These are specially trained personnel who serve many of the same functions as civilian police. On each military base there is one organization under the command of a provost marshal and the provost marshal's staff. Not under the command of any other entity on that base, the provost marshal has responsibility for order, traffic control, and property security on the base. In off-base situations, military police have the additional responsibility of protecting civilians from risks such as intoxicated and belligerent personnel on leave.

Military police carry out surveillance, arrest of wrongdoers, accumulation of evidence, and presentation of evidence in court. They are supported by the same sort of scientific facilities and communications systems as, for example, the state police of a populous state. In addition, they have the responsibility for apprehending and transporting accused personnel. They have access to federal criminal records for issues of national security. Confinement of prisoners on military bases and escort of prisoners during trials is also provided by the military police organization. In addition, it is responsible for apprehending and returning illegally absent personnel to their base for trial.

Courts-Martial

In the U.S. Army there are three levels of court-martial. In the first, or "summary" court, the convening officer serves simultaneously as judge, jury, prosecutor, defense counsel, and court reporter. If requested, a military lawyer is provided for the accused. The safeguards of individual rights found in a civilian court are not required to be observed, but the summary court is restricted in the severity of its sentences—typically they involve a short (not exceeding forty-five days) confinement, reduction of pay, or demotion of one grade level.

The next higher, or "special" court-martial, provides competent, trained counsel and three experienced officers as judges. While the special court involves greater safeguards of the accused person's rights, it also carries with it the potential of severe sentences, including "bad conduct" discharges or prolonged imprisonment.

A general court-martial is heard by at least five officers of senior rank, when available, and is preceded by an investigation to determine whether assurance of guilt is sufficient to warrant pressing the charge. If convicted of a serious offense in the general court-martial, an individual may face a "dishonorable" discharge, prolonged imprisonment, or, in cases involving default in the face of enemy action, the death penalty. In the two higher courts, the accused may request the replacement of up to one-third of the officers hearing the case by enlisted (non-officer rank) personnel. This is intended to lower the cultural and social bar between the accused and his judges. Should the accused desire, the trial may be conducted by a single officer rather than a board.

The protections against self-incrimination and double jeopardy are identical to those guaranteed for civilians by the Bill of Rights and are specifically described in the UCMJ. Because of the intimidation implicitly present in a situation involving personnel interrogated by those of substantially superior rank (and therefore, power) the UCMJ requires that the accused be informed of their rights and the nature of the accusation. This is a parallel to the "Miranda" procedure in civilian police procedure, in which a person is warned that testimony, freely given, may be used against the person in court.

Review and Appeal

Upon conviction, the prisoner is allowed an "administrative review," an interview with the presiding (trying) officer at which the prisoner and counsel may make arguments for mitigation or suspension of the sentence. It is common for the commander bringing the charges to ask for the maximum sentence provided by the UCMJ so that he can mitigate it if indicated.

After the administrative review, judgments may be reviewed by a civilian court of military appeals (COMA). The COMA is a board appointed by the president, each member serving fifteen years. In major issues, such as cases involving top-grade officers or in offenses providing for the death penalty, review by the COMA is automatic.

For offenses such as those providing for the dismissal of an officer, for a bad-conduct discharge from service, or for more than one year's incarceration, the accused may request review by a court of military review (COMR). In addition to these avenues of review, cases which may have involved the alleged denial of the prisoner's constitutional rights may be heard by the U.S. Supreme Court.

If no relief is allowed by these reviews and an individual believes that he has been wrongly treated, he may request a formal legal procedure in which the judge advocate general's staff serves in the role of judge and arranges for counsel for the plaintiff if necessary. The accused may request counsel from others in the military, such as a doctor or chaplain.

Military justice procedures contain additional safeguards for the accused person awaiting trial. While in confinement the accused is exempt from any work not involved in the cleanliness of his own living quarters and person. He is not usually required to live in close proximity with convicted prisoners. He is protected from hazing or unusually severe discipline. Mail pertaining to his case is exempt from invasion. Any physical force applied to his person and the conditions of his confinement are limited in severity to those needed to ensure his presence at the trial. Unlike civilian practice, however, there is no provision for release on parole or bail.

Punishment

Convicted offenders may be reduced in rank, fined, or imprisoned. Incarceration of convicted military personnel for limited periods (less than a year) may be in a facility (stockade) on the military installation to which the accused is assigned unless the antisocial nature of his offense makes a change of station advisable. For longer terms of confinement, federal prisons are employed.

There are several offenses for which the death penalty may be invoked. Mutiny, deserting in the face of enemy action, and murder are the most likely. In most countries having a military force, the crime of desertion in war is a capital crime, but the death penalty for military crimes in the U.S. has generally become obsolete in the light of the extensive appeals available to condemned criminals.

There have been executions since World War II, including one of a deserting soldier in the period immediately following the Vietnam War, but these occurred during the period of conscription. Pressure from antiwar activists led to the cessation of the draft in 1972. With one of the few all-volunteer military establishments in the world, the U.S. is unlikely to suffer further desertions of any consequence.

—*Loring D. Emery*

Suggested Readings

Two surveys of the history of military justice are Jonathan Lurie's *Military Justice in America: The U.S. Court of Appeals for the Armed Forces, 1775-1980* (Lawrence: University Press of Kansas, 2001) and *Evolving Military Justice*, edited by Eugene R. Fidell and Dwight H. Sullivan (Annapolis, Md.: Naval Institute Press, 2002). A useful work on procedures and principles is Michael J. Davidson, *A Guide to Military Criminal Law* (Annapolis, Md: Naval Institute Press, 1999). A historical perspective of the military is found in Samuel Huntington's *The Soldier and the State* (Cambridge, Mass.: Belknap Press of Harvard University Press, 1967), which treats the evolution of military leadership and documents the struggle between American political culture and the military. The social and political development of the military is treated by Peter Karsten in *The Military in America* (New York: Free Press, 1986), which discusses the development of civilian control of the military and the emergence of human rights movements in the military. In *The Military Establishment* (New York: Harper & Row, 1971) by Adam Yarmolinsky, one finds a carefully annotated attack on every phase of the United States military, from the military-industrial "conspiracy" to the arbitrary nature of military justice. The rights of personnel in the military justice system are described by Robert Rivkin in his *The Rights of Servicemen* (New York: Avon, 1972), a handbook prepared by the American Civil Liberties Union for dealing with military justice and securing individual rights in the system. *History of the United States Army* by Russell Weigley (Bloomington: Indiana University Press, 1984), is a comprehensive work on the history of the American military establishment from colonial times to 1983.

See also Courts-martial; Criminal justice system; Martial law; Military attorneys; Military police; Military tribunals.

MILITARY POLICE

Military personnel assigned to guard battle areas in combat zones, protect military installations in peacetime, and maintain discipline in the armed forces by enforcing laws and regulations

Law-enforcement specialists have different names in the various armed forces of the United States: In the Army and Marine Corps they are called military police (MPs), in the Navy and Coast Guard, shore patrol, and in the Air Force, security police. They share a common mission: to guard military property, protect personnel, and maintain discipline. The Marines, Army, and Air Force have permanently organized units composed of officers, warrant officers, and enlisted women and men; the Navy and Coast Guard draw from ship personnel to provide shore patrols when ships are in port. In the Navy the Naval Investigation Service conducts criminal investigations. The Army's counterpart is the Criminal Investigation Division.

An outgrowth of the wartime provost marshal system, the first permanent military police unit was formed in 1941 in the Army. Since then the responsibilities of military police have steadily expanded as military doctrine has changed and interaction with civilians has increased. Traditionally, the primary mission of military police has been to fight crime, enforce regulations, and assure troop discipline, whether in camps, aboard ships, or on the battlefield. However, the military police also control traffic, recover stolen or lost property, guard prisoners of war, provide such passive antiaircraft defense as enforcing blackouts, take measures against gas warfare, and conduct security investigations. Since the Korean War (1950-1953) MP units have sought to control black markets near U.S. bases overseas, provide convoy security, guard highways and bridges, destroy tunnels, and direct the movement of refugees. For the highly fluid battlefields foreseen in the Air-Land Battle doctrine of the 1990's, military police personnel were given more firepower and mobility in order to protect against attacks from the rear. Additionally, MPs are expected to join regular combat units when needed at the front lines.

Because they control refugees, investigate black markets, and oversee sailors and other personnel in foreign cities, the military police have extensive dealings with foreign civilians. In the United States they coordinate with local civilian police forces near

MILITARY POLICE

Each military branch provides its own force of specially trained police who serve many of the same functions as their civilian counterparts. Every military base has a military police organization under the command of a provost marshal. Provost marshals are responsible for order, traffic control, and property security on their bases. Off the bases, military police have the additional responsibility of protecting civilians from risks such as intoxicated and belligerent personnel on leave.

Military police carry out surveillance, arrest of wrongdoers, accumulation of evidence, and presentation of evidence in court. They are supported by the same types of scientific facilities and communications systems as state police. In addition, they are responsible for apprehending and transporting accused personnel. They have access to federal criminal records for issues of national security. Confinement of prisoners on military bases and escort of prisoners during trials is also provided by the military police organization. In addition, it is responsible for apprehending and returning illegally absent personnel to their base for trial.

military bases to apprehend criminals and deserters. Military personnel who commit crimes off base usually fall under the jurisdiction of civilian police. Inside military facilities the military police have jurisdiction, although they may turn over suspects to civilian authorities for some felonies committed during peacetime. Additionally, military police patrol civilian communities near military facilities to ensure that troops conduct themselves properly. In large cities where two or more branches of the armed services have installations, the Armed Forces Police, a detachment of law-enforcement personnel from each branch present, work closely with local police departments. The military police of each service have all-service authority.

The Posse Comitatus Act of 1878 prohibits the use of the military and military police to enforce civilian laws among the general population unless the president of the United States declares martial law or the U.S. Congress suspends the act.

—*Roger Smith*

See also Courts-martial; Marshals Service, U.S.; Martial law; Military attorneys; Military justice; Military tribunals; Police.

MILITARY TRIBUNALS

Courts that administer military justice according to established codes and procedures

In the United States, the codes and procedures regulating military tribunals are outlined in the Uniform Code of Military Justice, passed by Congress in 1950 and implemented a year later. This code is applied to all branches of the service and is designed to prohibit abuses of military justice and to ensure the fair administration of military justice in the armed forces of a democratic state.

Historically, the use of military tribunals to pass judgment on military offenses has been a mainstay of U.S. military justice. Traditionally, tribunals usually consisted of three officers and a prosecuting officer. Defendants were not guaranteed legal representation. Juries, or judges as they are called in military terms, were rarely used. This was affirmed in the *Ex parte Milligan* decision (1866). Since World War II, with the passage of the Uniform Code of Military Justice, military courts have taken on a regularized form. Tribunals, which use more than one judge on a panel, are convened only in the appeals process.

Lambdin P. Milligan was a civilian who was tried by a military commission on charges of conspiring to seize Union munitions during the Civil War. When he appealed his conviction, his case rose to the U.S. Supreme Court. The Court's Ex parte Milligan decision rejected the government's argument that the Bill of Rights could be suspended during time of war. (Indiana Historical Society)

The nature of an offense and the type of sentence determine which type of court sits in judgment. Jurisdiction is now divided into three levels of courts: general, special, and summary. A general court is

used for capital offenses and other more serious crimes. A mili-·
tary judge oversees the proceedings and issues instructions to a
jury, which usually consists of seven officers. Only a general court
can impose the death penalty, for which a unanimous vote is required. All death penalty convictions are automatically appealed.
Special courts deal with lesser, noncapital offenses and are restricted in the range of punishments they may impose. Special
courts cannot sentence convicted persons to imprisonment for
more than six months, for example. Summary courts are often
convened to deal with minor infractions of the Uniform Code and
punishments are likewise restricted. Summary courts do not require trained military judges, but defendants still have the right
to legal counsel. In summary courts, judges are usually brigade-
level commanders.

In each type of court defendants are offered legal representation and protected against self-incrimination and double jeopardy. With the adoption of the Uniform Code of Military Justice,
much effort has been made to ensure fairness, especially at the
general and special court levels, which require that sitting judges
be officers from outside defendants' immediate command structures. Appeals go first to the service-level appellate courts and
then, if necessary, to the U.S. Court of Military Appeals.

Two months after the September 11, 2001, attacks on the Penta-
gon and New York City's World Trade Center, President George
W. Bush sign an executive order that authorized military tribunals to try noncitizens charged with acts of terrorism against the
United States. The president insisted that the use of such tribunals
for this purpose had been approved by the Supreme Court in *Ex
parte Quirin* in 1942. In that decision, the Court upheld the convictions of eight German saboteurs who had been captured in the
United States and tried by military tribunal order by President
Franklin D. Roosevelt. The American Bar Association subsequently supported the use of military tribunals to try al-Qaeda
terrorists who were believed to be responsible for the September
attacks, for war crimes.

—*William Allison*

See also Capital punishment; Court types; Courts-martial; Martial law; Military attorneys; Military justice.

MIRANDA RIGHTS

Requirement that arresting officers inform suspects of their right against self-incrimination and their right to counsel during custodial interrogation

Miranda rights were created by the Supreme Court's 5-4 decision in *Miranda v. Arizona* (1966). Miranda, a suspect in a kidnaping and rape case, confessed after being interrogated for two hours. The confession was admitted in trial, and Miranda was convicted. The Court overturned his conviction, ruling that the confession was inadmissible because the police failed to inform Miranda of his constitutional right to avoid self-incrimination and to obtain counsel before questioning him during a custodial investigation. The Court established guidelines, known as the Miranda rights, for informing suspects of their Fifth Amendment rights.

The *Miranda* ruling has been continually reexamined since its inclusion in the U.S. justice system. It left a number of unanswered questions, including how to determine whether the accused was in fact in custody (and therefore needed to be read his or her rights), whether the suspect's statements were spontaneous or the product of an investigation (and needed to be preceded by the reading of rights), and whether the individual effectively waived his or her rights. Subsequent cases helped answer these questions and define when the practice of reading suspects their rights can be suspended, which is usually if the questioning is being conducted in certain contexts and if larger issues—notably public safety—are concerned. Although the *Miranda* decision has been frequently criticized as an exercise in judicial activism, the Supreme Court reaffirmed the decision in *Dickerson v. United States* in 2000.

A Question of Time and Place

In *Orozco v. Texas* (1969), the Court upheld a lower court's ruling that four police officers should have read the Miranda rights to a suspect before questioning began in the suspect's bedroom at four o'clock in the morning. However, in *Beckwith v. United States* (1976), the Court held that statements received by Internal Revenue Service agents during a noncoercive and noncustodial interview of a taxpayer under a criminal tax investigation conducted in a private residence did not require a reading of the Miranda rights, provided that the taxpayer was informed that he was free to leave the interview at any time.

In its 1966 ruling, the Court stated that the reading of the rights is necessary only if the suspect is in custody or deprived of freedom in a significant way. In the case of *Oregon v. Mathiason* (1977), the suspect entered the police station after an officer told him that he would "like to discuss something with him." It was made clear to the suspect that he was not under arrest. During his visit to the police station, the suspect confessed, and his confession was ruled admissible, despite the suspect not having been read his Miranda rights. The Court, in *North Carolina v. Butler* (1979), stated that "the trial court must look at all the circumstances to determine if a valid waiver has been made. Although an express waiver is easier to establish, it is not a requirement."

Still many questions remained unanswered, and further interpretations of *Miranda* followed. In *Smith v. Illinois* (1984), the Court declared that suspects taken into custody could invoke their Miranda rights very early in the process, even during the interrogator's reading of their rights, effectively ending their ques-

---

The Miranda Warning

The implications of *Miranda v. Arizona* are far-reaching, even into the world of films and television. The basic Miranda warnings that must be given to a suspect prior to a custodial interrogation are familiar to many viewers of police and detective stories:

> You have the right to remain silent. Anything you say can be used against you in court. You have the right to an attorney. If you cannot afford an attorney, one will be appointed to you prior to questioning.

Some law enforcement jurisdictions have added warnings beyond the basic Miranda:

> Have any promises been made to you? Have you been threatened in any way? If you decide to answer questions now, you still have the right to stop answering the questions at any time you wish.

tioning before it starts. In *Berkemer v. McCarty* (1984), the Court determined that the Miranda rights must be read any time "in-custody" interrogation regarding a felony, misdemeanor, or minor offense takes place. However, it stated that routine questioning during traffic stops did not place enough pressure on detained people to necessitate officers' warning them of their constitutional rights.

Some Exceptions

In *New York v. Quarles* (1984), the Court ruled six to three that there is a "public safety" exception to the requirement that Miranda rights be read. In *Quarles*, police officers arrested a man they believed had just committed a rape. They asked the man where he had discarded a gun. The arrest took place in a super-market, and the suspect was thought to have concealed the gun somewhere inside the supermarket. The gun was found and used as evidence. In such circumstances, the Court declared, "The need for answers to questions in a situation posing a threat to the public safety outweighs the need for the prophylactic rule protecting the Fifth Amendment's privilege against self-incrimination." *Quarles* was a significant ruling, eroding *Miranda*'s influence.

Subsequent cases challenged the Court's interpretation of *Miranda*. In *Oregon v. Elstead* (1985), police officers received a voluntary admission of guilt from a suspect who had not yet been informed of his constitutional rights. The suspect made a second confession after he had been read his Miranda rights and had signed a waiver. Regarding the second confession, the Court ruled that "the self-incrimination clause of the Fifth Amendment does not require it to be suppressed solely because of the earlier voluntary but unwarned admission." Furthermore, in *Pennsylvania v. Muniz* (1990), the Court decided that the routine questioning and video-taping of drivers suspected of driving under the influence was permissible even if the Miranda rights had not been recited.

In addition, the Court held that reciting the Miranda rights is not required when the suspect gives a voluntary statement and is unaware that he or she is speaking to a law enforcement officer. In *Illinois v. Perkins* (1990), an undercover government agent was placed in a cell with Perkins, who was incarcerated on charges unrelated to the subject of the agent's investigation. Perkins made statements that implicated him in the crime that the agent sought to solve, but he later claimed that the statements should have

(continued on page 484)

SUPREME COURT DECISIONS ERODING MIRANDA RIGHTS

Year	Case	Ruling permits use in trials of:
1970	*Parker v. North Carolina*	Defendant's admission of guilt made during allegedly coercive police interrogation conducted a month after his arrest.
1971	*Harris v. New York*	Damaging statements made by a defendant who is not read his Miranda rights to impeach his testimony at trial.
1972	*Milton v. Wainwright*	Confession made by an indicted defendant to an undercover police officer whom he thought was a fellow prisoner.
1975	*Oregon v. Haas*	Damaging statements made by a defendant while riding to jail in a police car. After receiving Miranda warning and asking for legal counsel, defendant was told he could not call a lawyer until he was driven to a police station.
1975	*Michigan v. Mosley*	Damaging statements made by a defendant without the presence of an attorney two hours after he said that he wanted to remain silent when he was read his Miranda warning.
1976	*Beckwith v. United States*	Incriminating statements made to an Internal Revenue Service agent in noncustodial interview without Miranda warning.
1977	*Oregon v. Mathiason*	Incriminating statements made by a parolee during a voluntary interview at a police station, who was arrested afterward on basis of incriminating statements.
1979	*North Carolina v. Butler*	Testimony of a defendant who did not expressly waive his rights during police interrogation.
1981	*California v. Prysock*	Testimony made when police read a defendant his rights in language not precisely that of the Miranda warning.

Year	Case	Ruling permits use in trials of:
1983	*Oregon v. Bradshaw*	Testimony of a defendant who voluntarily initiated conversation with police.
1983	*California v. Beheler*	Testimony of a defendant who visited police station voluntarily for questioning without issuing a Miranda warning, since he was allowed to exit the station before being arrested.
1984	*Minnesota v. Murphy*	Testimony collected by a probation officer who did not give a defendant a Miranda warning.
1985	*Oregon v. Elstead*	Damaging statement made to police by a defendant not given a Miranda warning because statement was given in defendant's home.
1986	*Moran v. Burbine*	Testimony collected by police from a defendant whom they failed to tell that his sister had hired a lawyer, who was trying to reach him.
1987	*Arizona v. Mauro*	Statement made by a defendant in a phone call to his wife after he was informed of his rights and requested an attorney.
1988	*Pennsylvania v. Burder*	Testimony of defendants arrested in ordinary traffic stops who are not read their Miranda rights.
1989	*Duckworth v. Eagan*	Testimony collected by arresting police officers who deviate from exact wording of Miranda rights.
1990	*Michigan v. Harvey*	Damaging statements made by defendants after they request an attorney in a conversation started by police.
1990	*New York v. Harris*	Damaging statements made in a nonconsensual, warrantless search of defendant's home.
1990	*Illinois v. Perkins*	Testimony collected by undercover police informer who failed to inform defendant of his Miranda rights when latter was jailed but not yet arraigned.

(continued)

Year	Case	Ruling permits use in trials of:
	SUPREME COURT DECISIONS ERODING MIRANDA RIGHTS (CONTINUED)	
1991	*McNeill v. Wisconsin*	Testimony collected by police who fail to inform a defendant of his Miranda rights, even when he has an attorney, provided they question him about a different crime.
1993	*Brecht v. Abrahamson*	Harmless errors; federal courts may set aside convictions challenged for errors only if the errors have had a "substantial and injurious effect" that produces an "actual prejudice."
1994	*Davis v. United States*	Damaging statements made by defendant whose request to consult with an attorney is not sufficiently strong and insistent.
2003	*Chavez v. Martinez*	Arresting officers and government agents cannot be sued for violating a defendant's Miranda rights if testimony obtained through the violation is not later used in court.

been inadmissable because he was not read his Miranda rights. However, even though Perkins was unaware that his cell mate was a government agent, his statements—which led to his arrest—were deemed admissible.

—Dean Van Bibber

Suggested Readings

Bergman, Paul, Sara J. Berman-Barrett. *The Criminal Law Handbook: Know Your Rights, Survive the System.* 5th ed. Berkeley, Calif.: Nolo Press, 2003).

Carmen, Rolando Videl. *Criminal Procedure.* West Publishing, 1998.

Schmalleger, Frank. *Miranda Revisited: The Case of Dickerson v. U.S. and Suspect Rights Advisements in the United States.* Englewood Cliffs, N.J.: Prentice Hall, 2001.

See also Arrest; Confessions; Fifth Amendment; Police; Presumption of innocence; Reversals of Supreme Court decisions by Congress; Self-incrimination, privilege against; Suspects.

MISDEMEANORS

Criminal offenses viewed as less serious than felonies; examples include prostitution, disorderly conduct, and many traffic offenses

Federal and state definitions of felony and misdemeanor vary somewhat, but in all states the distinction is important. Felony and misdemeanor are large categories that indicate the seriousness of various types of crime. Misdemeanors are less serious offenses, such as disorderly conduct, many traffic offenses, and many "vice" offenses such as prostitution and some gambling activities. Felonies are more serious crimes, such as murder, rape, and armed robbery. Federal guidelines define a felony as any crime "punishable by death or by imprisonment for a term exceeding one year."

Most states maintain similar definitions, although some states classify crimes according to the place of incarceration for offenders. If incarceration is to be in a state prison, the offense is a felony; if it is punishable by a term in a local jail, it is considered a misdemeanor. In some jurisdictions an offense may be considered either a felony or a misdemeanor depending on a number of factors. Larceny (theft), for example, may be classified as a felony (grand larceny) if the value of the item or items stolen is sufficiently high or a misdemeanor (petty larceny) if their value is relatively small. Occasionally the first conviction for an offense is a misdemeanor, with subsequent convictions being defined as felonies; an example is driving under the influence (DUI).

In most states there are separate court systems for felonies and misdemeanors. Felonies are tried in county courts, or courts of general jurisdiction. Misdemeanors are handled by local courts with limited jurisdiction. These local courts (also called minor or inferior courts) are not "courts of record"; that is, transcripts of the proceedings are not kept. By far, most criminal cases are handled by local courts, partly because so many charges are only misdemeanors and partly because felony charges are sometimes reduced to misdemeanor charges before a trial begins. Misdemeanor cases proceed through the courts very quickly (the process has been called "factory-like" and has been the subject of considerable criticism), and many of the safeguards of defendants' rights that apply in felony cases are not required. In contrast to felony cases, misdemeanor cases are usually decided at one time, with hearing, arraignment, and sentencing all combined in one short hearing. Many local courts must process a tremendous volume of misdemeanor cases every day. The handling of felony cases, on the other hand, is complex, and cases may take more than a year.

The term "misdemeanor" derives from a combination of the French words *mes* and *demener*, and therefore means "to conduct oneself ill." The felony and misdemeanor categories come from English common law; in England, misdemeanor originally meant a "trespass against the peace." Eventually the term broadened to incorporate any criminal act that was not considered a felony or treason. The misdemeanor/felony distinction was discontinued in England in 1967, but in the United States most jurisdictions maintain the classifications.

Another classification of lesser criminal acts is infractions, or violations. Many traffic offenses are infractions, as are such things as peddling without a license. Infractions are punishable only by fines, not by incarceration.

See also Criminal justice system; Criminal records; Felonies; Principals (criminal); Torts.

MISTRIALS

Trials that are aborted or ruled invalid because of either fundamental errors or hung jurys; because mistrials are equivalent to no trials, retrials become necessary if defendants are to be convicted of crimes

The most common reason for a mistrial is the inability of the jury to agree on a verdict. A judge may also declare a mistrial when a violation of evidentiary or procedural rules is so prejudicial that a fair trial becomes impossible. A "harmless error" provides no basis for a mistrial, because it does not affect substantive rights.

In order to protect a defendant's Fifth Amendment right against double jeopardy, the Supreme Court in *Oregon v. Kennedy*

(1982) divided mistrials into two categories. First, when a mistrial is declared over the defendant's objection, a retrial is not permitted except when the judge acts from "manifest necessity." Second, when the mistrial occurs with the consent of the defendant, a retrial is permitted unless the prosecution intentionally commits an error designed to obtain a second trial.

See also Double jeopardy; Harmless errors; Judicial review; Jury nullification; Lawsuits; Trials; Verdicts.

MODEL PENAL CODE

Proposed criminal code drafted by the American Law Institute in 1962 that has strongly influenced a number of states in the drafting of their criminal law statutes

Before the American Law Institute sponsored and published the Model Penal Code in 1962, the criminal codes of the fifty states were far from uniform. In criminal law matters, states were guided by the decisions of the common law, often replete with inconsistencies and contradictions. The Model Penal Code was drafted by judges, lawyers, and law teachers with the goal of eliminating the inconsistencies found in the common law and providing a uniform set of criminal codes. It was designed as a model for state legislatures to follow in drafting their own criminal codes, and as such it has influenced the drafting of criminal codes in approximately forty states.

See also Annotated codes; *Black's Law Dictionary*; Common law; Criminal justice system; Judicial conduct code; Louisiana law; Model Rules of Professional Conduct; Sentencing; United States Code.

MODEL RULES OF PROFESSIONAL CONDUCT

Uniform framework of ethical standards that regulate the practice of law

The Model Rules of Professional Conduct were adopted by the House of Delegates of the American Bar Association (ABA) in 1983 to replace the Model Code of Professional Responsibility. Their principal objective, as set forth in the preamble, is to guide lawyers in avoiding the "difficult ethical problems [that] arise from conflict between a lawyer's responsibilities to clients, to the legal system and to the lawyer's own interest in remaining an upright person while earning a satisfactory living."

The Model Rules have since been adopted by almost all the state supreme courts, which have the ultimate authority to regulate the admission to the bar and the practice of law in each state. The rules are divided into several articles, which pertain to all aspects of an attorney's duties: the client-lawyer relationship, the lawyer's role as an advocate and counselor, transactions with persons other than clients, law firms and associations, public service, information about legal services, and professional integrity. Each article contains rules followed by comments to be used as guidelines to interpret them. While some of the rules are very specific, others lay out general standards that give lawyers broad discretion as to how to act ethically.

—*Kurt M. Saunders*

See also American Bar Association; Attorney confidentiality; Attorney trust accounts; Attorneys as fiduciaries; Bar associations; Effective counsel; Grievance committees for attorney discipline; Solicitation of legal clients; Unethical conduct of attorneys.

MULTIPLE JURISDICTION OFFENSES

Offenses that involve more than one jurisdiction

Law enforcement was originally a local activity. Increasingly, criminal activity crosses state lines. A growing number of federal statutes take into account multiple jurisdiction offenses. The National Computer Crime Squad of the Federal Bureau of Investigation (FBI), for example, investigates violations of the Federal Computer Fraud and Abuse Act of 1986. Computer crimes are classic examples of offenses that frequently take place across state and national boundaries. The multiple jurisdiction offense permits a computer crime to be prosecuted in a number of states.

Gambling, drug trafficking, and other multijurisdictional criminal activities frequently involve individuals and conduct that cut across national and international boundaries. Drug activity, for example, may involve a regional or national illegal distribution network. Congress has enacted a number of statutes against multiple jurisdiction offenses to prosecute illicit activities that occur across state lines. Prior to multiple jurisdiction offenses, criminal justice officials were unable to prosecute activities involving more than one state.

Many drug statutes provide for the prosecution of offenses in multiple jurisdictions. An example of a state dealing with a multiple jurisdiction offense is the federal statute against the distribution of controlled substances. When a drug offense or any element of a drug offense is committed in an aircraft, vehicle, train, or other mode of transportation, criminal activity may occur in several jurisdictions. The federal criminal code permits the offense to be tried in any jurisdiction through which the defendant or the illicit drugs passed. Statutes against multiple jurisdiction offenses are useful in prosecuting defendants who transport stolen property across state lines. When the offense involves the unlawful taking or receiving of property, the offender may be tried in any jurisdiction in which the property was taken or received. Similarly, when the offense is a conspiracy, the offender may be tried in any jurisdiction in which the conspiracy or any of its elements occurred.

During the late twentieth century, the U.S. Congress began passing many statutes that provide for continuing jurisdiction without regard to state boundaries. For example, the U.S. Code defines criminal offenses involving the use of the mails as a continuing offense. A federal crime involving the use of the mails may be prosecuted in any district from which mail was transported or imported. Many states set out rules granting multiple jurisdiction in cases involving marriage and family relationships. An example of a multiple jurisdiction offense is the abandonment or nonsupport of children.

—*Michael L. Rustad*

See also Criminal justice system; Jurisdiction; Law enforcement; Long-arm statutes.

NEGLIGENCE

Theory of liability that allows an injured party (plaintiff) to recover compensation for damages caused by a defendant's careless conduct; the term is also used to describe the particular conduct of the defendant

American law presupposes that people have a duty to act with reasonable care; many civil suits involve charges of negligence, or acting carelessly or recklessly. When a person suffers an injury caused by someone else's conduct, the injured person may have the right to "recover," or collect an award to compensate for damages, for the injury. The injured party (the plaintiff) could bring a cause of action against the defendant under one of several theories of liability, depending on the facts of the case.

The law imposes on everyone a duty to act carefully. This means that people should not act in a way that creates unreasonable risks of harm to others. This duty is usually referred to as the duty of the "reasonable person under the circumstances." A person is negligent when his or her conduct is below this standard of care. The test for negligence is thus objective in that it does not matter whether the person intended or knew the consequences of the act. The conduct is compared with, and judged against, that of the hypothetical reasonably prudent person under the same circumstances. If the person's conduct is an act that the reasonable person would not have done under the circumstances, or if it is failure to act under circumstances where the reasonable person would have acted, he or she is considered "negligent" and may be found liable for the damages others suffer because of the risk created.

The word "negligence" is also used to describe that legal right, or cause of action, that the plaintiff has against the defendant to recover damages for the injury. In addition to showing the damages suffered, in order to have a cause of action the plaintiff will have to show that the defendant had a specific duty toward him or her, that the defendant breached that duty, and that the defendant's conduct that constituted the breach caused the injury.

There may be instances where the law has designed a different standard of conduct for particular circumstances. For example, the standard of conduct for children is that of similar children of the same age, experience, and intelligence under the circumstances. The standard for physicians is that of the medical profession's recognized practice in the particular field.

See also Breach of contract; Cause of action; Joint and several liability; Liability, civil and criminal; Punitive damages; Restitution; Strict liability.

NIGHT COURTS

Court proceedings conducted at times other than those considered normal working hours—a system that became increasingly common in the late twentieth century

Almost entirely criminal courts, night courts have become a necessity as a result of several federal court rulings. Due process requirements, mandated by state and federal courts, and state statutes, require that individuals arrested or detained by the police must be brought before a magistrate and given formal notice of charges against them within twenty-four to forty-eight hours in an effort to minimize the time a presumably innocent individual spends in jail.

Jurisdictions unable to handle staggering case loads during regular working hours have been forced to operate courts twenty-four hours a day, seven days a week as a result. The Criminal Court of New York City, for example, the largest and busiest court in the United States, handled approximately 40 percent of its 1997 arraignments during the night and early morning hours. Many other court systems, especially those in densely populated areas, have been forced to establish similar courts or risk being forced to release criminals who might be denied their due process rights.

—*Donald C. Simmons, Jr.*

See also Attorneys; Court types; Small-claims courts.

Nolo contendere PLEAS

Pleas of criminal defendants that neither admit nor deny guilt of the crimes with which the defendants are charged

The Latin phrase *nolo contendere*, meaning "I will not contest it," is a plea in a criminal case by which defendants answer the charges made in an indictment by declining to dispute or admit the fact of their guilt, while accepting a fine or sentence pursuant to it. Defendants who plead *nolo contendere* submit to judgments fixing a fine or sentence that are the same as if they had pleaded guilty. The essential difference between a plea of guilty and a plea of *nolo contendere* is that a guilty plea may be used against the defendant in a civil action based on the same acts and may later be used to prove wrongdoing in a civil suit for monetary damages, whereas a plea of *nolo contendere* may not be so used. *Nolo contendere* is especially popular in antitrust actions, such as price-fixing cases, in which it is likely that civil actions for treble damages will be initiated after the defendant has been successfully prosecuted.

A defendant may make a plea of *nolo contendere* only with the permission of the court. Such a plea shall be accepted by the court only after due consideration of the views of the parties and the interest of the public in the effective administration of justice.

—*John Alan Ross*

See also Arraignment; Civil actions; Defendants; Defendant self-representation; Effective counsel; Pleas; Plea bargaining.

NOTARY PUBLICS

Person certified by a state government to witness legal transactions, administer oaths, and authenticate signatures

The office of a notary public is an ancient one that was recognized as far back as ancient Rome. The primary function of a notary is to certify that legal transactions of various sorts have taken place. In cases of international law, federal certification of the notary public is necessary, but in most cases he or she is certified by a state government and practices in a particular geographical area.

A notary public is not necessarily a member of the legal profession. Although requirements vary somewhat among the states, as a general rule the only necessity is that the notary be an adult of good moral character, a rather vague term that is rarely challenged. It is not even necessary for a notary to be a U.S. citizen; statutes barring aliens have been struck down by the courts on the grounds that citizenship is not relevant to an individual's ability to attest to the authenticity of a legal transaction. To become a notary an individual files an application with a government office, pays a small fee, and is usually required to pass an examination. He or she then swears to an oath of office and is issued an official notary stamp.

Although notaries have had many broad functions throughout history, including such important duties as administering oaths of office, in modern times their primary activity is to attest the authenticity of signatures on legal documents. A very important case in which notarization is required is in the transfer of property. In order for a title of ownership to be registered with the land records office or other relevant state agency, the transfer of ownership must be notarized.

Although it is not always legally required, notarization is advisable in any case in which the authenticity of a signature or the understanding of the parties involved may be called into question. In the case of a last will and testament, for example, notarization of the document is likely to allow the survivors to avoid time-consuming and expensive litigation if any aspect of the will is called into question. When a power of attorney is granted, it is crucial that the party granting such power swear before a notary that he or she understands and consents to the consequences of this action.

The services of a notary public are particularly crucial in the matter of contracts and other legal agreements and in statements that might be used as legal evidence in court proceedings. In such cases, the only requirement, apart from certification, is that the notary have no interest in the matter at hand. The parties involved swear before the notary that their testimony is true, and the notary may require proof of identity. If any aspect of the agreement is later called into question, the notary's seal is considered as direct evidence that the parties have knowingly entered into such agreements.

—*Marc Goldstein*

See also Affidavits; Contracts; Evidence, rules of; Probate.

OBJECTION

Recorded statement of protest against an action during the course of a trial that may become critical when a case comes up for appeal

An objection is a formal statement of disapproval concerning a specific activity or procedure that occurs during the course of a trial. In general, an objection is made when one side in a trial makes a protest to the judge that an action taken by the opposing side is unfair or illegal. The judge then makes a ruling on the objection, either sustaining it by agreeing with it and forcing the opposing side to withdraw the action or overruling it by disagreeing with it and allowing the action to continue. If either side disagrees with the decision, it makes an objection to the ruling, known as an exception.

The recording of objections during a trial is important because it allows a higher court to make judgments on any possible errors made by a lower court if a case comes up for appeal. Under unusual circumstances, a higher court may reverse a lower court's decision without a record of objection if an obvious error has been made. Under normal conditions, however, the higher court only makes rulings on procedures or decisions that were objected to during the trial.

In some courts, a bill of exceptions must be submitted before an appeal can be heard. This document consists of the objections made to the decisions of the lower court.

—Rose Secrest

See also Appeal; Defendants; Discovery; Evidence, rules of; Privileged communications; Reversible errors; Trials; Witnesses; Witnesses, confrontation of.

OBSTRUCTION OF JUSTICE

Interference with the operation of a court or its officials in a way that may deny a party the right to due process or justice

Obstruction of justice is an attempt to impede justice by any means. Obstruction includes physical disruption of a trial court in session, an attempt to interfere with a judge or court officials, including jurors, or an attempt to bribe or create doubt regarding the integrity of those involved in a court proceeding. Concealing or falsifying evidence obstructs justice, as does resisting a court-appointed process server.

Because police are officers of the court, intentional interference with their duties may be considered an obstruction of justice. In federal practice, obstruction extends to agencies, departments, and committees conducting their work. A witness concealing evidence from an investigation by a congressional committee is as guilty of obstruction as a person concealing evidence in a trial court.

See also Contempt of court; Criminal procedure; Gag orders; Subpoena power; Trials; Witnesses.

OFFICERS OF THE COURT

Concept that lawyers—despite the fact that they are expected to be vigorous advocates of their clients' interests—also have a responsibility to help uphold the judicial system

Lord Henry Peter Brougham, the lawyer for Queen Caroline of England during her famous early nineteenth century trial for adultery, is remembered among lawyers for his defense of the queen. In possession of evidence that might have embarrassed the king, Brougham explained to the court why he was bound to use this evidence if it served the interests of his client. An advocate, he declared, "in the discharge of his duty, knows but one person in all the world, and that person is his client." This bold statement of the advocate's duty toward the client captures an important aspect of legal practice. Nevertheless, it does not portray a complete picture of that practice. Coupled with zealous service on behalf of clients is a longstanding recognition among lawyers that they are "officers of the court."

Lord Henry Peter Brougham. (Library of Congress)

The declaration that lawyers are officers of the court serves to limit the zeal with which they may represent clients. It presupposes that lawyers must conduct themselves with a certain measure of dignity and respect toward the court. More controversially, the notion that lawyers owe significant obligations to the judicial system underlies one much debated provision of most legal ethics rules. The Model Rules of Professional Conduct, in force in most states, requires that lawyers in some circumstances inform the court if they know that a client or witness has lied in the proceedings. This obligation, clearly at odds with normal duties of confidentiality and loyalty owed to clients, has its roots in the principle that lawyers must serve the interests of the justice system as well as those of their clients.

—*Timothy L. Hall*

See also Adversary system; Bailiffs; Clerks of the court; Court types; Marshals Service, U.S.; Prosecutors; Trials.

OPINIONS

Written explanations by court of the reasons for their decisions in cases

The American judicial system generally expects that judges who decide cases will explain the bases for their decisions in written opinions. Opinions written by relatively important courts—state appellate courts and federal courts—are then collected and preserved and form the basis for subsequent judicial decisions. Later courts strive to adhere to the results of previously published opinions in keeping with the judicial principle of *stare decisis*, which means, "Let the decision stand." To facilitate his reliance on previous opinions to guide subsequent ones, legal publishers have traditionally collected judicial opinions into bound volumes referred to generically as "reporters." Reporters may collect all the opinions of a specific court, such as the *United States Reports*, which includes the opinions of the U.S. Supreme Court. Other reporters contain the opinions of courts in a particular geographic region, such as the *Pacific Reporter*, which includes opinions from

TYPES OF JUDICIAL OPINIONS

Majority opinion: Issued by the controlling majority of justices to explain a decision

Concurring opinion: Issued by one or more judges who agree with the result of a case but wish to provide a separate discussion of their reasons for joining in this result

Dissenting opinion: Issued by justices who disagree with the majority's result in a case

Per curium: Issued by the entire court rather than one written by a particular judge

the courts of California and other western states. Computerized databases and Internet sites make most, if not all, reported opinions available to those without access to bound volumes of reporters.

In the U.S. system appellate judges write most opinions. Appellate courts generally have three or more members, a majority of whom determine the outcome in particular cases. One member of this majority then typically writes the opinion explaining the result, or holding, of the case. This opinion is called the majority opinion. Sometimes a judge who agrees with the majority's result in a case may nevertheless not agree with the reasoning offered by the majority opinion or may wish to explain the decision in some fashion other than that adopted by the majority. This judge may write what is referred to as a concurring opinion. A judge who disagrees not only with the reasoning of a case but with the result reached by the majority might write a dissenting opinion to express this disagreement. Finally, in a few cases judges may agree about a decision and publish a *per curiam* opinion, which bears the name of no particular author. Courts publish *per curiam* opinions most frequently to express decisions in minor or noncontroversial cases.

—*Timothy L. Hall*

See also Advisory opinions; Appeal; Appellate practice; Case law; Courts of appeals; Judicial clerks; Judicial review; Precedent; Reporters, Supreme Court; Supreme Court, U.S.

PARALEGALS

Persons with limited legal training who perform certain legal functions under the supervision of accredited attorneys

Paralegals are not authorized to practice law, but they assist lawyers and clients in law-related matters. The paralegal profession was developed in order to increase access to legal services at a reduced cost. Paralegals work among attorneys in private law firms, corporations, government offices and agencies, banks, and insurance and real estate organizations. Paralegals may not give legal advice requiring the exercise of independent legal judgment, represent clients in litigation, or fail to disclose that they are not attorneys. Some of their general duties include the compilation of legal documentation and pretrial materials, the search for court dockets and files, and the preparation of law memorandums, leases, mortgages, deeds, citations, summons, depositions, and subpoenas. They also assist attorneys in areas of litigation, divorce law, domestic relations, probate and estate law, and corporate law.

Paralegals in private law firms conduct research, interview clients, gather information, and prepare agendas for meetings and complex transactions. In the public sector, paralegals assist clients in filling out forms, negotiate with agencies, represent clients before certain administrative authorities, and disseminate materials on legal concerns affecting the local community. Paralegals are in particular demand by the federal government for handling many of the functions traditionally provided by more highly paid lawyers. For example, agencies involved in Social Security administration have programs that employ paralegals to conduct some prehearing conferences, research issues, and write decisions.

Formal training in paralegal services started in the late 1960's. In the United States paralegal programs exist at many colleges, universities, and law schools, as well as at private training institutions, government agencies, and bar associations. In 1995 there were 500 paralegal programs in the United States, but only 185 were approved by the American Bar Association (ABA). Paralegal students do not need prior legal experience, and most have never been inside a law office. Prospective paralegal students should ask prior to selecting a program whether a program in which they are interested is a two- or four-year program, what the program's educational objectives are, whether the program is ABA approved, what the reputation of the institution and program is, what the quality of the faculty is, and whether the program provides assistance with career development. Some of the courses a paralegal student might take include legal research, legal writing, legal ethics, interviewing, litigation, estates and trusts, real estate law, business law, criminal law, family law, and computer skills.

About 188,000 paralegals were employed by law firms and agencies in the United States in 2000, and the paralegal field was the eighth fastest growing profession in the United States. In some states, after paralegals have successfully completed their academic work and their on-the-job training, they are allowed to take bar examinations to become accredited attorneys.

—Alvin K. Benson

See also Administrative law; Attorney types; Attorneys; Law firm partners and associates; Law firms.

PARDONING POWER

Power granted to the president of the United States and state governors to forgive offenses or crimes, thereby removing any punishments or penalties attached to the charged offenses and legally restoring the pardoned persons to a state of innocence regarding the crime

A pardon is an "act of grace" to mitigate the punishment the law demands for a crime and to restore the rights and privileges forfeited because of the offense. The executive authority can either commute or pardon the convicted criminal. To commute is to reduce the penalty, such as the length of time in prison. To pardon is to excuse the person from any penalty under the law. In *Ex parte Garland* (1867), the Supreme Court stated, "When the pardon is full, it releases the punishment and blots out of existence the guilt, so that in the eyes of the law the offender is as innocent as if he had never committed the offense."

In September, 1974—less than a month after succeeding Richard Nixon as president—Gerald Ford stunned the nation by announcing that he had pardoned Nixon for any and all crimes that he may have committed during his presidency. (Library of Congress)

An amnesty is a group pardon of several or many people. "Pardon" applies to one individual. A pardon totally restores the individual, whereas a "parole" simply releases the person early, subject to the supervision of the public authority. A person violating the conditions of parole may be returned to imprisonment. This is usually not the case with a pardon, but there can be a "conditional pardon" that requires the pardoned person to meet some condition such as leaving the state or refraining from certain actions. A violation of the condition could lead to the revocation of the pardon.

There can also be a partial pardon, which remits only a part of the punishment or only the part for a specific portion of the legal consequences of a crime. Most pardons, though, are absolute or unconditional. No further legal actions can be taken against a recipient of a complete pardon. This legally applies to collateral as well as direct consequences of an incident. Governors and the president have a systematic procedure to consider applications for pardons. The official in the Department of Justice who considers these applications and makes recommendations to the president is known as the pardon attorney.

The most famous, and probably most controversial, pardon in American history was granted to former President Richard Nixon by President Gerald Ford in 1974. Before Nixon could be impeached by Congress for his role in the Watergate cover-up, Ford granted him a "full, free, and absolute pardon."

See also Amnesty; Parole; Probation, adult; Probation, juvenile.

PAROLE

Release of prisoners before the end of their sentences on the promise that they will not break the law again or violate certain specified conditions

The word "parole" comes from the French word *parol*, which means "word of honor." Originally, it referred to the practice of releasing prisoners of war who promised not to resume fighting. Modern parole is the conditional release of prisoners by a parole board before the expiration of their sentences. Parole does not mean that a felony offender is free from the legal custody and supervision of the state. Parole is a privilege granted by the state, which could just as easily keep the prisoner in jail.

Purpose of Parole

The mission of parole is to prepare, select, and assist offenders who, after a reasonable period of incarceration, could benefit from early release. At the same time, the state protects the public through the conditions of release and supervision. The state and the prisoner sign a contract under which the prisoner promises to abide by certain conditions in exchange for conditional freedom. The state justifies parole on the grounds that prisoners need supervision and help if they are to readjust to freedom successfully. Most parole failures occur relatively soon after release. In fact, approximately one-quarter of parole failures occur within the first six months.

Incarceration ensures the protection of society, acts as a deterrent to criminal activity, and functions as punishment for criminal acts. However, it is limited in its ability to prepare offenders for return to the free world. Parole is based on the belief that the majority of offenders can benefit from a period of transition back into the community. Conditional release affords a continuing measure of protection to the public while supporting parolees in their effort to become productive, law-abiding citizen. If parolees violate the conditions of their parole or commit crimes, parole can be revoked and the offenders returned to jail.

Not all offenders have the same potential and motivation to earn or to benefit from conditional release. Offenders must be judged on their own merits and in light of their offenses, sentence lengths, and personal backgrounds. Parole authorities use risk assessment tools to evaluate the potential success of offenders if paroled. These studies help determine whether prisoners should be released and the conditions of parole.

Society benefits from a successful parole program. Most incarcerated offenders eventually complete their sentences and return to the community. Parole is viewed as a positive means of promoting successful reintegration. It also helps reduce unnecessary expenses at correctional institutions while, at the same time, maintaining an appropriate degree of supervision and control to ensure the protection of society. Parole also mitigates the harshness of criminal law, equalizes disparities in sentencing, and helps prison authorities maintain order and reduce crowding.

The purpose of parole is to improve public safety by reducing the incidence and impact of crime committed by parolees. Parole is not leniency or clemency but a logical extension of the sentence to provide the opportunity to return offenders to society after a reasonable period of incarceration and when they are assessed to have the capability and desire to succeed and live up to the responsibilities of their release.

Offenders who comply with the conditions of their parole and do not violate the law receive an absolute discharge at the end of their sentences. The parolee may be required to abstain from alcohol, keep away from undesirable associates, maintain good work habits, and not leave the community without permission. The revocation of parole occurs when the parolee commits a new crime or violates the conditions of parole. Half of all convicted felons are released on parole. Parole boards release approximately 99 percent of prisoners from prison to serve the remainder of their sentences outside prison walls. An estimated 35 to 40 percent of all parolees have their paroles revoked and are sent back to prison.

Legal Issues

The U.S. Constitution does not require states to maintain a parole system. There is no constitutionally protected right to parole or to due process in release hearings unless state statutes or regulations create a liberty interest in parole release. The parole board can do just about anything it pleases with respect to a prisoner's parole release. Whatever the board decides and does prevails, because it enjoys immense discretion in the parole decision process. While parole boards are not constitutionally required to provide reasons for denying release, the use of state-mandated parole guidelines provides prisoners with such information.

Prisoners' federal constitutional rights with respect to parole are limited. For example, the U.S. Constitution places few limits on parole boards. Boards may rely on allegations of conduct of which the prisoner was found innocent or may even consider information from charges of which the prisoner was not convicted. The board can deny parole because of the severity of a prisoner's crime. The parole board may not consider race or inaccurate information to make its decision. To obtain judicial relief, prisoners must show that their files contain errors and that the board relied on false information in denying or revoking parole or time off for good behavior. Prisoners must also show that they requested prison authorities to correct their files but that the latter refused to do so. Often state law and regulations provide prisoners with greater rights. Even when an offender has a federal constitutional claim, a prisoner must exhaust remedies available in state courts before a federal court will intervene.

History of Parole

The American parole system originated in the late 1870's. Well-behaved prisoners in the reformatory in Elmira, New York, had their prison sentences shortened. This system was based on programs developed in England and Ireland. The concept of parole was created by Alexander Maconochie (1787-1860), who was superintendent of the British penal colony on Norfolk Island, off the coast of Sydney, Australia. Sir Walter Crofton (1815-1897) was influenced by Maconochie's work. Crofton was director of the Irish prison system. A modified version of the Irish system, under which a prisoner could earn early release from prison, was adopted in England and then at Elmira. Other American prisons copied the Elmira system.

A feature of the Elmira system was the indeterminate sentence. Under this system a judge imposed a prison sentence with a minimum and a maximum length. The parole board determined the prisoner's release date. In most states inmates who followed prison rules were entitled to good time off—time deducted from a prisoner's maximum sentence. A prisoner could shorten his sentence by one-third under the good-time-off system. A side effect of indeterminate sentencing was that different persons convicted of the same crime could receive different sentences.

Under determinate sentencing systems, a judge imposes a sentence of a specific length. This sentencing system provides for early release because of good behavior—often one day off a sentence for every day served. In theory, this system promotes prison discipline. Violation of prison rules could result in jail time being added to the sentence.

The idea of parole release spread slowly throughout the United States until the Great Depression of the 1930's. Pressing economic conditions—notably the cost of incarceration, not the press of prison reform—led to the rapid spread of parole release systems. Conditional release is the term used to describe prisoners released on good time.

Many efforts to abolish or change the parole system have been tried. For example, the Sentencing Reform Act of 1984 abolished parole eligibility for federal offenders who committed offenses after November 1, 1987. It also provided for the abolition of the U.S. Parole Commission on November 1, 1992. However, the Judicial Improvements Act of 1990 and the Parole Commission Phaseout Act of 1996 extended the commission in five-year increments through November 1, 2002.

The history of prisons and parole in the United States shows that parole release has been used, and possibly misused, to maintain prison discipline and to reduce prison overcrowding. Parole boards evolved out of the power of governors to issue pardons to selected prisoners. Before the creation of parole boards, governors often used their pardoning powers to relieve overcrowding in state prisons. For example, in the mid-nineteenth century, pardons accounted for over 40 percent of prisoner releases.

The Parole Decision

The goal of all parole decisions is the protection of society. In the short term, the parole board examines whether there is a high degree of risk to society if it releases the prisoner. To meet the longer-term goal, the board considers whether parole would help the offender return to the community.

Parole may be discretionary or mandatory. Discretionary parole occurs when the parole board voluntarily grants parole before the offender completes a sentence. Mandatory parole is the automatic release of an offender upon completion of the sentence (less any good time credit). Under many state parole systems, the department of corrections determines when an offender is eligible for parole. The corrections department uses a formula that includes, but is not limited to, length of sentence, institutional adjustment, treatment or educational program involvement, and prior prison experience.

To guide its decision, the board conducts a risk assessment. The assessment has two parts—a preliminary risk assessment and a special factor evaluation. The first part includes gathering information about the offender. The information includes details of the offense, criminal history, social problems such as alcohol or drug use and family violence, mental status (especially if it affects the likelihood of future crime), performance on earlier releases, information about family relationships, and employment prospects. The board then consults statistical guidelines that assess the probability that the offender will commit another crime. The guidelines indicate how often a group of offenders with characteristics and histories similar to those of the prisoner under review commits new offenses. The second step focuses on a review of reports from psychologists, police, victims, and prison authorities.

After considering the evidence and holding a hearing with the prisoner, the board decides whether to grant parole. If denied, another parole review date may be set. The offender usually has the option to appeal the board's decision when errors in fact, unknowingly considered during the review process, are identified later. The board reconsiders cases when significant new information is presented that was unavailable when the case was originally examined. If parole is granted, the board determines the conditions of release. A parole board may be independent of the prison system or a division of the organization that administers correctional institutions. In most states, parole board members are appointed by the governor.

The core services of parole boards are to help offenders develop release plans and to supervise persons released on parole. Parole authorities may also provide employment and life skills counseling, halfway house accommodations, counseling, community work programs, and family services. Parole board members usually hold release hearings in the state prison. Prisoners usually do not have legal representation at such hearings.

In the 1990's many states permitted victims or their next of kin to appear before the parole board. Some states permitted victims to introduce written statements at parole hearings. Such statements could include information concerning the crime, the extent and severity of the personal or family injury and economic loss, and the victim's attitude toward the offender's potential parole release. All parole boards consider opposition to an inmate's parole from the police and news media. The parole board determines the actual amount of time to be served based on the prisoner's institutional adjustments as measured by the prisoner's accomplishments, vocational education, academic achievement, work assignments, therapy, and interpersonal relationships with other inmates and prison authorities. Other factors include the prisoner's prospects for outside employment, education, training, eligibility for community services such as halfway house placements and help with personal problems.

Underfinanced and overcrowded prisons pressure parole boards into accelerating the release of inmates. Unfortunately, there are too few parole officers to cope adequately with all the parolees.

During most of the twentieth century, parole boards decided when most prisoners would be released. With the advent of determinate sentencing and parole guidelines, releasing power has essentially been taken away from the parole boards in many states.

Parole Violations

If after a reasonable length of time parolees continue to show that they can obey all the rules of parole, they may be discharged from parole supervision. At that time, they receive a certificate stating that the current sentence and parole obligations have been met and discharged.

Every paroled prisoner signs an agreement to abide by certain regulations, including obeying the law and not possessing or using narcotics or carrying weapons. Parole violations are either technical violations or new offense violations. Technical violations occur when the conditions of parole are violated. New offense violations involve an arrest and criminal prosecution and conviction. Parolees alleged to have committed a violation are given a preliminary hearing to determine whether there is probable cause to believe the conditions of parole were violated. If probable cause is determined, the offender is held in custody pending a hearing to determine whether parole should be revoked. The purpose of the revocation hearing is to determine whether the violation is serious enough to revoke parole and return the parolee to prison. If probable cause is not determined, the prisoner is released. Prisoners are entitled to due process at parole revocation hearings.

Reinventing Parole

Parole boards are often criticized when a parolee commits a high-profile crime. Studies of intensive-supervision programs for high-risk parolees have found that the programs cut neither recidivism nor costs. Critics have favored some types of "three strikes and you're out" laws or a no-parole policy after three convictions for some categories of violent and repeat felons. In an effort to reinvent the parole system, some experts have advocated use of a voucher system. For a specific period, parolees can use the voucher to seek an education, job training, drug treatment, or other services from state-selected providers. If parolees want to help themselves, they can. If not, they are on their own. Parolees who commit new crimes are sent back to prison to do their time and are given additional time for the new violation.

Some experts have advocated privatizing the parole system. Providers of bail bonds would manage the parole system. With their own money at risk, bondsmen would supervise their parolees closely. Privatizing the parole system would save taxpayers money. Prisoners eligible for parole would be required to post a financial bond against specified violations such as reporting regularly to their bail bond agents or submitting to drug testing. Persons violating parole would forfeit their bond, generating revenue for the state and victim compensation. Bond would be set by the courts or parole boards based on the criminal's history and prospects for a productive, law-abiding life.

—*Fred Buchstein*

Suggested Readings

To understand how parole fits in the correctional system, see *Probation, Parole, and Community Corrections,* by Dean J. Champion (Upper Saddle River, N.J.: Prentice Hall, 2002); *American Corrections* by Todd R. Clear and George F. Cole (Belmont, Calif.: Wadsworth, 1997); and *When Prisoners Come Home: Parole and Prisoner Reentry,* by Joan Petersilia (New York: Oxford University Press, 2003). For an examination of parole from the perspective of a former parole officer and deputy sheriff who became a professor of criminal justice see *Probation and Parole: Theory and Practice* (Englewood Cliffs, N.J.: Prentice-Hall, 1994). Other treatments of parole include *Paroling Authorities: Recent History and Current Practice* by Edward E. Rhine, William R. Smith, and Ronald W. Jackson (Laurel, Md.: American Correctional Association, 1991) and *Prisoners Among Us* (Washington, D.C.: Brookings Institution, 1976). A self-help guide for prisoners seeking parole is found in *Prisoners Self-Help Litigation Manual* by John Boston and Daniel E. Manville (Dobbs Ferry, N.Y.: Oceana, 1995). *The Criminal Law Handbook: Know Your Rights, Survive the System,* by Paul Bergman, Sara J. Berman-Barrett (5th ed. Berkeley, Calif.: Nolo Press, 2003), covers all aspects of criminal cases, through parole, in a question-and-answer format.

See also Bail system; Bonds; Community service as punishment for crime; Due process of law; Good time; House arrest; Pardoning power; Personal recognizance; Probation, adult; Probation, juvenile; Three-strikes laws.

PERJURY

Crime in which a person deliberately lies or bears false witness while under oath, either in court or in such extrajudicial testimony as sworn affidavits and depositions

Because it can confound justice, perjury is considered an extremely serious crime; undetected, it can result in the conviction of the innocent or the acquittal of the guilty. Although the Ninth Commandment, in the Old Testament book of Exodus, proscribed bearing false witness, laws against perjury are of relatively recent derivation. In England until the fourteenth century, coerced confessions or trials by ordeal or combat, rather than eyewitness testimony, were normally used to determine guilt. Even as English common law and the jury system developed, witnesses were first limited to a suspect's accusers. They were not even required to appear at trials; if they did appear, they were treated as jurors. Verdicts, but not testimony, could be found false through "the writ of attaint," under which juries could be punished and their verdicts nullified.

In England, testimony of Crown witnesses given under oath was first allowed in the sixteenth century, but it was not until 1702 that sworn testimony of witnesses for the defense was permitted. By that time, juries no longer had a testimonial function. Witnesses had become the only means of bringing evidence before criminal courts, and perjury was a punishable offense under common law. One important concept that shaped early laws against perjury involved the "material" nature of sworn testimony. That is, for a person to be convicted of perjury, his or her perjured testimony had to be significant enough to influence the outcome of the trial. Most modern state statutes defining perjury retain the "material" qualifier, though a few state laws no longer make it a mandatory requirement. Even in those states where materiality is required, it has served not so much as an impediment to conviction as a factor in determining the severity or grade of the crime.

While convictions for perjury have at times hinged on some subtle distinctions, the basis of perjury remains the same: A witness must deliberately lie while presenting testimony under oath. In many states, perjury is not limited to lying while under oath in court. It has been extended to include lying or "false swearing" before governmental agencies empowered to subpoena witnesses and take sworn testimony. Further, a witness may commit perjury even giving true testimony if the witness believes that the testimony is actually false. Perjury thus depends not only on the truth or falsity of a sworn statement but also on the intent to deceive. Inconsistent or contradictory testimony does not constitute perjury if no such intent is involved.

Perjury, a felony, carries major penalties, including both heavy fines and imprisonment. It is, however, difficult to prove. In most cases, perjury convictions must meet the "two-witness rule" requiring some corroboration of testimony that contradicts the allegedly perjured testimony. For this reason the charge of perjury is more often threatened than invoked.

See also Affidavits; Attorney confidentiality; Community service as punishment for crime; Confessions; Jury nullification; Testimony; Witnesses; Witnesses, confrontation of.

PERSONAL INJURY ATTORNEYS

Lawyers who specialize in representing persons who have been injured against those responsible for the injuries

Among the less flattering images of unscrupulous lawyers is that of the ambulance chaser, the lawyer who arrives shortly after an accident to find among the injured and bleeding a new client. In fact, ambulance chasers are outlaws among attorneys, subject to disbarment for their unethical solicitation of clients. However, people who have been injured in some way nevertheless frequently need legal representation, and personal injury attorneys specialize in such cases. Personal injury lawyers may handle cases as varied as those involving relatively minor traffic accidents and those involving the injuries and deaths produced by the crash of an airliner.

Personal injury lawyers usually rely on a particular kind of fee arrangement, called a contingency fee agreement. This agreement

FACTORS TO CONSIDER IN PERSONAL INJURY CASES

- Types of injuries
- Frequency, duration, and severity of pain
- Nature of any permanent damage
- Length and nature of treatment
- Cost of medical care
- Extent of lost earnings as a result of injuries
- Jurisdiction in which the case is brought (some juries are more liberal in their awards, others are more conservative)

ACCIDENT STATISTICS

- Accidental injuries kill more Americans between the ages of one and thirty-four than all diseases put together. These fatalities drain the economy of more years of people's working lives than cancer and heart disease combined.
- Among the ten leading causes of death in the American population, nonvehicular accidents rank fourth. Car accidents rank sixth.
- For every fatal accident there are approximately ten nonfatal accidental injuries.
- In 1988 thirty-five deaths and more than eighteen thousand injuries requiring hospital treatment occurred as a result of power lawn-mower accidents.
- Each year an estimated 350 children under the age of five drown in residential swimming pools and spas.
- Each year approximately 4,600 children under the age of five are treated in hospital emergency rooms following water accidents.
- An average of 90,000 children under the age of fifteen annually received hospital emergency room treatment as a result of injuries from toys.
- One out of twenty-five Americans is likely to be an accident victim.

provides that the personal injury attorney will not recover a fee in a case unless the attorney obtains some recovery for the client. In addition, personal injury attorneys generally pay the expenses needed to prepare a case for trial and deduct these from any ultimate recovery. These expenses, which include the fees of expert witnesses and the cost of pretrial discovery of facts about the case, can be very substantial and would be beyond the means of most individuals. However, by setting aside money from prior successful cases, personal injury attorneys are able to keep a reserve of cash for use on the expenses of subsequent cases. Consequently, by using the contingency fee agreement and by paying litigation expenses up front, personal injury attorneys are able to provide representation to individuals regardless of their financial standing.

But these financial aspects of personal injury practice are also controversial. The first and perhaps most important element of a successful personal injury practice is obtaining cases involving personal injury plaintiffs. This need to find clients causes some personal injury lawyers to engage in television or radio advertising, which is viewed as demeaning to the profession by more conservative lawyers. Furthermore, the need to find clients also tempts some personal injury lawyers to violate established rules against soliciting clients: in short, to engage in ambulance chasing.

Even after personal injury attorneys find their clients, they may be tempted to provide funds to these clients to cover medical and living expenses prior to trial or settlement. Personal injury clients are sometimes lured into accepting artificially low settlements of their injuries because they lack the financial resources to survive the lengthy period of time it normally takes to win a verdict at trial and sustain it on appeal. However, the law has long disfavored allowing persons to encourage litigation by offering support or other encouragements to litigating parties. The legal doctrines of champerty and maintenance, for example, make it a crime in many jurisdictions for persons to offer such support. Furthermore, rules of legal ethics prohibit attorneys from providing medical or living expenses to their clients.

—*Timothy L. Hall*

See also Attorney fees; Attorney types; Contingency fees; Damages; Litigation expenses; Negligence; Solicitation of legal clients; Torts.

PERSONAL RECOGNIZANCE

Means by which criminal defendants who are considered good risks are released from prison before their trials without having to post surety bonds

The traditional means of ensuring that criminal defendants will appear at their trials if they are released from prison is to require that they post a surety bond, backed by cash or property, either personally or through the services of a bail bondsman. This approach has permitted many individuals to enjoy pretrial freedom while penalizing them by the loss of their deposit should they attempt to flee the court's jurisdiction. Its main drawback is that individuals who cannot afford to post bail are forced to remain in jail until their trials, even if they are innocent.

In 1961 the Vera Foundation in New York City established a trial Bail Project to encourage the release of defendants on their own recognizance. Operating on the assumption that defendants with strong ties to the community would be unlikely to flee, the project evaluated applicants on such factors as their length of time in the area, employment, and family ties. Foundation representatives kept in touch with those released to remind them of their court appearances. Although judges always had the power to release defendants on personal recognizance, the program encouraged the release of far more defendants than ever before. Moreover, the Bail Project had a much lower rate of flight than did bail bondsmen. Similar projects have worked in other jurisdictions, and programs to release people on personal recognizance are common.

—Arthur D. Hlavaty

See also Bail bond agents; Bail system; Bonds; House arrest; Parole.

PLEA BARGAINING

Negotiation process in which defendants agree to plead guilty in exchange for the expectation of fewer or lesser charges or more lenient punishments

In the American justice system, more than 90 percent of all criminal convictions are obtained through guilty pleas produced after negotiations between the prosecution and the defense. Nevertheless, in the minds of the public, decisions about the guilt or innocence of criminal defendants are supposed to be made after lawyers battle one another in the courtroom under the watchful eyes of a judge and jury. The central role of trials in the American justice process is emphasized in a variety of information sources, ranging from textbooks to television dramas. In reality, however, more than 90 percent of all criminal convictions are obtained through negotiations between the prosecution and the defense. The negotiation process through which the prosecution attempts to reach an agreement with the defendant is called "plea bargaining." The defendant voluntarily admits responsibility for the crime by entering a guilty plea, and, in turn, the prosecution agrees to reduce the number or severity of criminal charges pursued against the defendant or, alternatively, recommends that the judge impose a less-than-maximum sentence. Although the American public had little recognition of the existence of plea bargaining prior to the 1960's, historical studies show that such activities have taken place in American courts since the nineteenth century.

Plea Bargaining and the Law

Although the Sixth Amendment to the U.S. Constitution guarantees that people charged with serious crimes have a "right to a speedy and public trial by an impartial jury," there is no requirement that cases actually go to trial. The U.S. Supreme Court permits people to waive their constitutional rights as long as such waivers are undertaken knowingly and voluntarily. When criminal defendants enter guilty pleas, they are, in effect, waiving their right to a jury trial.

In several judicial decisions, the Supreme Court has endorsed and provided rules for plea bargaining. In particular, the Court has insisted that guilty pleas be entered voluntarily and that both prosecutors and defendants fulfill promises made during the bargaining process. Defendants, for example, will often gain a lighter sentence by pleading guilty and promising to testify against other individuals. If they do not testify, their plea agreement can be nullified. Prosecutors often promise to recommend a specific sentence, and they must keep their promises if those promises were a primary inducement to gain the guilty plea. The Supreme Court also permits prosecutors to pressure defendants during the plea negotiations by threatening severe charges or punishments if a guilty plea is not forthcoming.

Plea-Bargaining Process

Plea bargaining may begin at any time after a defendant is arrested and may continue throughout the justice process. In fact, some plea agreements are even reached after the prosecution and defense have begun to present evidence in front of a jury. Some plea bargains involve actual negotiated exchanges between the prosecution and defense. For example, the prosecutor may agree to drop serious charges if the defendant will agree to plead guilty to one lesser charge. Alternatively, some plea bargaining involves the prosecutor and defense attorney in merely settling the facts of the case. Both lawyers may know, for example, that a certain judge always imposes specific sentences for first-degree burglary and "breaking and entering." Thus the plea-bargaining discussions involve reaching agreement on the provable facts in the case, to determine which crime the prosecutor is likely to be able to prove. The defendant will then plead guilty to whatever crime both sides agree can be proved. In this way the defendant gains certain knowledge about what the sentence will be and avoids uncertainty about which punishment is likely to be imposed after a trial.

Plea bargaining exists because it serves the interests of all parties involved in criminal cases. Prosecutors gain certain convictions without expending the resources required for trials. Defendants gain fewer charges as well as punishments that are less than the maximum possible. Defense attorneys have cases resolved so that they can move ahead to work on other cases. Judges gain efficiency in the quick processing of criminal cases that might otherwise absorb weeks of court time in trials.

Critics of plea bargaining claim that it is an illegitimate process that permits criminals to escape the harsh punishments that they deserve. Defenders of plea bargaining assert that such negotiations tend to give offenders precisely what they deserve by focusing on a determination of provable facts and also save significant time and money by keeping cases from going to trial. Some prosecutors and legislatures have attempted to abolish plea bargaining for specific charges, but most studies indicate that plea bargaining never disappears. Because the process serves the interests of all involved, it will continue to occur informally whenever prosecutors and defense attorneys talk to one another at various stages of the justice process. Although many members of the public believe that the prevalence of plea bargaining is one of the worst flaws in the American justice system, most professionals who work in the courts view plea bargaining as a desirable and necessary process that permits the courts to conclude cases quickly and impose punishment efficiently.

—Christopher E. Smith

Suggested Readings

Two up-to-date studies of the subject are Hedieh Naheri, *Betrayal of Due Process: A Comparative Assessment of Plea Bargaining in the United States and Canada* (Lanham, Md.: University Press of America, 1998), and *Plea Bargaining's Triumph: A History of Plea Bargaining in America*, by George Fisher (Stanford, Calif.: Stanford University Press, 2003). The ways in which lawyers and judges learn about plea bargaining are discussed in Milton Heumann, *Plea Bargaining* (Chicago: University of Chicago Press, 1978). Plea-bargaining strategies are examined in Douglas Maynard, *Inside Plea Bargaining* (New York: Plenum Press, 1984), and Lynn Mather, *Plea Bargaining or Trial?* (Lexington, Mass.: Lexington Books, 1979). Studies of plea bargaining in specific court contexts can be found in Peter F. Nardulli, James Eisenstein, and Roy B. Flemming, *The Tenor of Justice: Criminal Courts and the Guilty Plea Process* (Urbana: University of Illinois Press, 1988). Efforts to reform plea bargaining are discussed in Candace McCoy, *Politics and Plea Bargaining* (Philadelphia: University of Pennsylvania Press, 1993).

See also Attorneys, court-appointed; Confessions; Criminal justice system; Defendants; Defense attorneys; Lesser included offense; *Nolo contendere* pleas; Pleas; Prosecutors; Public defenders; Trials.

PLEAS

Formal responses of criminal defendants to the indictments brought against them

The plea is a significant component in the arraignment phase of the criminal process. During the arraignment the judge presents the criminal charges, advises defendants of the right to court-appointed counsel, schedules hearings, determines the trial date, and resolves issues with regard to bail. At the arraignment defendants respond with a plea of not guilty, guilty, or *nolo contendere*. The defendants' choice of pleas is critical, as the disposition of the case rests on the plea.

Not Guilty and Guilty Pleas

The first option, and the one most often selected, is not guilty. The not guilty plea allows defendants time to consider the strength of their cases and to determine the chances of a favorable outcome in court. Therefore, the plea does not necessarily mean that defendants are innocent; it means that they wish to have their cases heard in court and want a judge or jury to determine whether there is enough evidence to return a guilty verdict. If defendants do not enter a plea, the court automatically enters a not guilty plea based on the precept that one is innocent until proven guilty. Persons who plead not guilty have a right to have a judge or jury trial. At trial the decision makers listen to the evidence. In order for a judge or jury to return a guilty verdict in a criminal proceeding, the prosecutor must demonstrate guilt beyond a reasonable doubt.

Defendants may also choose to plead guilty. The implications of this decision are serious. Defendants waive their right to a trial and to prepare a defense, the right against self-incrimination, the right to confront witnesses, and the right to appeal the decision. Thus, when defendants relinquish such fundamental rights, the judge must question them to determine whether they understand the implications of the guilty plea. The judge must determine whether the plea is voluntarily made or whether threats or promises were made to force a guilty plea. The judge also must ensure that defendants understand the charges against them and the corresponding sentences or fines.

Last, the judge must ascertain the factual basis of the plea to make sure that there is proof that defendants have actually engaged in the conduct with which they are charged. If defendants choose this plea and the judge has determined that they understand the ramifications of pleading guilty, the court may immediately convict as if a judge or jury returned a guilty verdict in a trial. Defendants may be sentenced at the arraignment or the judge may order a presentencing report and schedule a sentencing hearing.

Nolo Contendere

The last plea option allows defendants to plead *nolo contendere*, which means no contest, or "I do not wish to contend." Typically, defendants use this plea in order to avoid an admission of wrongdoing in the event of a subsequent civil suit regarding the same matter. If defendants are sued for monetary damages, a guilty

---

Reasons to Plead Not Guilty, Guilty, or
Nolo Contendere

A defendant should plead *not guilty* if he or she
- is innocent
- has a believable defense
- wants to claim the right to a trial
- has a broader issue at stake that he or she wishes to defend
- wishes to avoid a criminal record
- is factually guilty, but could still be found legally not guilty

A defendant should plead *guilty* if he or she
- is guilty
- is not able to challenge strong opposing evidence (beginning with first contact with police)
- desires to get the court process over with quickly
- equates a written confession to the police as a guilty plea
- is encouraged by his or her lawyer to plead guilty
- chooses a plea agreement that reduces the sentence or fine
- wants to create a positive impression by not wasting court time
- wishes to protect other persons by "taking the rap"
- is arrested far from home and does not want to return to the jurisdiction for court appearances
- cannot afford to take time off work to fight the case
- fears that delay might give a prosecutor more time to bring additional and perhaps more harmful evidence to light
- cannot afford an attorney, does not qualify for a court-appointed attorney, and does not desire self-representation

A defendant should plead *nolo contendere* if he or she
- wants to avoid the stigma of a guilty plea
- wants to avoid proof of committing a crime in case of subsequent civil action
- wants to avoid the psychological trauma of admitting guilt

---

verdict would provide evidence of wrongdoing, whereas a plea of *nolo contendere* would not. When defendants plead *nolo contendere*, a conviction is handed down, just as a guilty plea is adjudicated. The defendants relinquish their rights just as persons who plead guilty and are subject to the same sentences or fines as persons who plead guilty and are convicted. The judge must take the same precautions to ensure that defendants are aware of the relinquishment of rights involved in the plea of *nolo contendere* and that the decision is voluntary.

—Ann Burnett

Suggested Readings

A good, reader-friendly and basic overview of the criminal process is *The Criminal Law Handbook: Know Your Rights, Survive the System*, by Paul Bergman and Sara J. Berman-Barrett (5th ed. Berkeley, Calif.: Nolo Press, 2003). Also useful is Jay M. Feinman's *Law 101: Everything You Need to Know About the American Legal System* (New York: Oxford University Press, 2000). Briefer, but general overviews also include *The Ordering of Justice: A Study of Accused Persons as Dependents in the Criminal Process*, by Richard V. Ericson and Patricia M. Baranek (Toronto: University of Toronto Press, 1982), *An Introduction to the Legal System of the United States*, by E. Allan Farnsworth (3d ed. New York: Oceana, 1996), and *Introduction to Law and the Legal System*, by Harold J. Grilliot and Frank A. Schubert (4th ed. Boston: Houghton Mifflin, 1989). For more complex discussions see *Trial Manual for the Defense of Criminal Cases*, by Anthony G. Amsterdam (Philadelphia: American Law Institute, 1974), and *The Law of Criminal Procedure: An Analysis and Critique*, by David A. Jones (Boston: Little, Brown, 1981).

See also Arraignment; Criminal justice system; Defendants; Defendant self-representation; Defense attorneys; Fifth Amendment; *Nolo contendere* pleas; Plea bargaining; Presumption of innocence; Reasonable doubt; Trials.

POLICE

Modern law enforcement agencies that are generally the principal law enforcement bodies in cities and towns

The word "police" has its origin in the ancient Greek word *polis*, which the Greeks used for their form of city-state government. *Polis*, broadly associated with government, has a distinctly urban connotation; other words derived from the same root are "polity," "politics," and "policy." The concept of the police force has evolved substantially through the years but is still associated with the law enforcement agency that governs concentrations of people in villages, towns, and—particularly—large metropolitan areas. Nearly every municipality refers to its law enforcement agency as the police, whereas many counties refer to their law enforcement agency as the sheriff or sheriff's department.

The first law enforcement in the United States was provided by the "night watch" system, prevalent in the East until the early nineteenth century. The night watch usually was overseen by local businessmen, who took turns maintaining nightly guard duty at their stores. These "solid citizen" law enforcement figures gave a parochial cast to law enforcement that has survived until the present day. As villages grew into towns, the night watch was supplemented with a day patrol. Constables were added in some areas. In the South and West, the local law enforcement officer was usually the sheriff. Eventually, however, the need for round-the-clock law enforcement agencies became clear.

Modern police departments originated in Europe in the nineteenth century as people moved to the cities during the Industrial Revolution. Using the London police department as its model, New York City established a police department with eight hundred officers in 1844. It in turn became a model for other large American departments. Local police forces had become fairly common by the late nineteenth century; they were locally funded. Local tax revenues are still the biggest single source of support for municipal police departments. By the early twentieth century, police departments were an accepted part of most communities. Slowly the problems of the early years, such as corruption, incompetence, and lack of training, were being recognized and addressed. Municipal police maintain a broad role in the enforcement of federal, state, and local laws and the apprehension of all types of criminals.

In the years immediately after World War II, police training and roles expanded noticeably. In the 1950's, police became increasingly involved in enforcing traffic laws. Also, as cities and their suburbs expanded, foot patrolmen were replaced by police officers in patrol cars. Police could thus patrol larger areas, but the fact that they were in automobiles isolated them from the people they were protecting. This trend began to be reexamined in the 1980's, and many communities attempted to return to what has become known as "community-oriented policing," emphasizing foot and bicycle patrols.

Functions of Police Departments

The traditional jobs that Americans want their police departments to perform include preventing crime, preserving order or peace, protecting people and property, and protecting personal liberties. Patrolling designated areas (whether on foot or in automobiles), educating the public through crime-prevention programs, and working with others in the criminal justice system (such as the district attorney) have been the main approaches to achieving the first goal. Preserving public order involves activities ranging from crowd control to traffic control to responding to domestic violence complaints. Both the general public and most police officials view the police's most important task as protecting the well-being and property of law-abiding citizens. In order to accomplish this goal, the police enforce laws, apprehend violators, recover stolen property, investigate suspected criminal activities, and assist in the prosecution and conviction of violators.

A newer and in some ways simpler model has also been proposed for police departments. The new model holds that police should fill three basic roles: responding to citizens' complaints, providing services to the community, and arresting suspected criminals. Proponents of this model note that a significant number of calls to police involve not crimes per se but immediate needs for help in a wide variety of areas, as when a person's automobile is disabled or when parents discover drugs in the possession of their children.

Organization

The typical large American municipal police organization is quasi-military in nature. Officers are promoted to ranks such as sergeant, lieutenant, and captain; a rigid hierarchy is involved. On the plus side, this allows a tight organization and a clearly delineated chain of command; on the minus side, it does not allow much adaptability or flexibility. The chief of police is at the top of the chain of command, and below him are one or more deputy chiefs. Below them are commanders and precinct captains; below them are lieutenants, sergeants, and patrol officers. Each person in this structure should have no more than one supervisor. This policy is complicated by the fact that police departments operate twenty-four hours a day, so personnel frequently have different supervisors on different days and at different times. Organizational charts, rules, and manuals define the divisions of authority within the department.

The patrol officer, although low in the hierarchy, is in many ways the central figure in the police department's law enforcement efforts. Investigations are most often initiated by patrol officers. The duties of patrol officers comprise a wide range of activities, including patrolling assigned areas, responding to emergencies, investigating suspicious situations, issuing traffic citations, administering first aid to injured people, searching for stolen or lost property and missing persons, providing public information, and maintaining effective relationships with other law enforcement agencies and personnel.

Large police departments also have specialized officers to handle such matters as juvenile delinquency, vice and narcotics, traffic control, and plainclothes (detective) investigations. There are also support personnel who maintain records (which are crucial when criminal cases go to court) and maintain the department's communication system as well as its communications with other parts of the criminal justice system.

The Evolution of Modern Police Techniques

Before the development of identification techniques such as fingerprinting, police had to rely on eyewitness testimony or the help of informants. One method was to arrest petty criminals and give them partial immunity for their crimes if they would help law enforcement officials to locate other wrongdoers. These informants would provide information that would lead to the arrest of more serious criminals. The use of informants continues to this day. The identification of criminals took a great stride with the invention of fingerprinting, using a system developed by Francis Gaulton in Great Britain. Fingerprinting, now one of the most widespread methods of identifying criminals, has been supplemented by the analysis and classification of footprints, tire marks, bloodstains and other body tissues and fluids, and by the use of deoxyribonucleic acid (DNA) tests to identify the perpetrator of a crime.

Modern communication via radio, television, computer networks, and a whole range of satellite facilities has materially increased the ability of police agencies to communicate with one another and to receive reports of crime. For the apprehension of criminals and recovery of stolen property, modern techniques include the use of computers to track license plates, vehicle identification numbers (VINs), and serial numbers on stolen property, particularly firearms. The comparatively recent development of the 911 emergency calling system, which provides quick access to firefighting and emergency medical services, is said to be a deterrent to crime.

Training of Police

As the number and range of crimes grew along with U.S. cities, specialized training for police officers became increasingly imperative. Any large city today maintains its own academy for the training of police officers. The Federal Bureau of Investigation (FBI) also plays an important support role for state and local police by providing national crime laboratories, extensive legal services, and specialized training. No longer can police forces maintain a simple "watchman" function or limit themselves to the apprehension of criminals. The role of the police in mediating domestic disputes, for example, has grown dramatically in the late twentieth century. Thus, police find themselves extending their training beyond mere law enforcement into the family-service area. The complexity of the legal and cultural environment in which police officers operate, and the resultant need for psychological and sociological training, has made sophisticated training of police mandatory.

Police Brutality and Corruption

Despite the growth of professionalism and the increased availability of training, major concerns remain about two related issues that erode professionalism: police brutality and corruption. Both these problems are related to the parochial origin of police in the United States. Police forces are generally funded by local taxpayers, who use the purse strings to maintain local control over the police. Local police, in turn, nearly always favor residents over outsiders, majority ethnic groups members over minorities, and the well-to-do over the poor. Outsiders, minorities, and poor people are the most likely targets for police brutality. Police corruption nearly always involves the differential application of law enforcement. Again, local well-to-do citizens are most likely to benefit from corruption by obtaining favorable treatment from the police. Local control of both city and county law enforcement continues to make these problems endemic. Attempts to combat corruption and brutality nearly always require the intervention of state or federal agencies.

Suggested Readings

Robert M. Fogelson, *Big City Police* (Cambridge, Mass.: Harvard University Press, 1977), is a history of police reform in the United States. David R. Johnson, *American Law Enforcement: A History* (St. Louis: Forum Press, 1981), is an overview that includes discussion of the federal government's role in fighting crime. Roger G. Dunham and Geoffrey P. Alpert, eds., *Critical Issues in Policing: Contemporary Readings* (Prospect Heights, N.J.: Waveland, 1992), is a comprehensive collection of essays by a variety of specialists. A solid account of basic organization among various law enforcement agencies can be found in Robert H. Langworthy, *The Structure of Police Organizations* (New York: Praeger, 1986). The link between police behavior and public policy is made by Stuart A. Scheingold in *The Politics of Law and Order: Street Crime and Public Policy* (New York: Longman, 1984). A classic book on police behavior is James Q. Wilson's *Varieties of Police Behavior* (Cambridge, Mass.: Harvard University Press, 1968). Important recent critical studies of police include *Militarizing the American Criminal Justice System: The Changing Roles of the Armed Forces and the Police*, edited by Peter B. Kraska (Boston: Northeastern University Press, 2001); *The System in Black and White: Exploring the Connections Between Race, Crime, and Justice*, edited by Michael W. Markowitz and Delores D. Jones-Brown (Westport, Conn.: Praeger, 2000); *Policing and Violence*, by Ronald G. Burns and Charles E. Crawford (Upper Saddle River, N.J.: Prentice Hall, 2002); *Patterns of Provocation: Police and Public Disorder*, edited by Richard Bessel and Clive Emsley (New York: Berghahn Books, 2000); *Civilian Oversight of Policing: Governance, Democracy, and Human Rights*, edited by Andrew J. Goldsmith and Colleen Lewis (Portland, Oreg.: Hart, 2000); and *Police Liability: Lawsuits Against the Police*, by Dennis M. Payne (Durham, N.C.: Carolina Academic Press, 2002).
—*Richard L. Wilson*

See also Arrest; Chain of custody; Detectives, police; Federal Bureau of Investigation; Informants; Law enforcement; Marshals Service, U.S.; Military police; Miranda rights; Sheriffs; State police; Suspects.

PRECEDENT

Prior court decision that guides a later interpretation of the law

When judges see factual similarities between a current case and an earlier one, they look for the rule of law on which the earlier case was based and apply it to the present case. The earlier case is called a precedent.

Much law is written in terms that do not lend themselves to a single, unequivocal interpretation. For example, the First Amendment to the U.S. Constitution states that "Congress shall make no law . . . abridging the freedom of speech." However, because the authors of the Bill of Rights did not anticipate the invention of radio and television, contemporary judges must decide whether electronic communications broadcasts over the airwaves are a form of "speech."

When judges confront such ambiguous situations for the first time, they apply the written Constitution according to what they consider just principles. In doing so they effectively fill in the blank spaces in the document. In that sense they are actually making constitutional law. Since judges are bound to follow established law when they make decisions, all judges in similar cases in the future must follow the precedent established in the earlier case.

Law made by legislatures—called "statutory law"—is often characterized by the same ambiguity. When the U.S. Congress passed the Sherman Anti-Trust Act of 1890, the Supreme Court had to decide whether the law's prohibition of "every contract, combination . . . or conspiracy in restraint of trade or commerce" made union organized strikes illegal. In *Loewe v. Lawlor* (1908) the Court said that a union strike was such an illegal restraint of trade. This decision prompted Congress to amend the antitrust law six years later to exempt union activity from its coverage.

U.S. legislators do not write laws to cover every conceivable circumstance. If judges find that there simply is no applicable statute, they must make a decision in the case on the basis of their understanding of justice. Such judge-made law is called common law and is found in judges' written decisions. Once a judge has made a common-law decision, the decision carries the force of law, and other judges must apply the principle in deciding future cases.

A precedent is binding only in the jurisdiction in which it has been decided. Thus, if a Maine court decides that an optometrist's failure to test for glaucoma constitutes negligence, that decision does not bind a Mississippi judge. When it comes to federal constitutional and statutory law, the U.S. Supreme Court's interpretations govern the entire country.

It is possible to overturn a precedent. Common law can be overruled by a statute. A court's interpretation

Chief Justice Harlan Fiske Stone, chief justice of the United States from 1941 to 1946. (Collection of the Supreme Court of the United States)

of a statute may be overruled by a subsequent statute. A court may overrule itself but rarely does so. A precedent may or may not be a good law, but as former U.S. Supreme Court Justice Harlan Fiske Stone said, "It is often more important that a rule of law be settled than that it be settled right."

—*William H. Coogan*

See also Annotated codes; Case law; Common law; Constitution, U.S.; Jurisdiction; Opinions; Trials; Uniform laws; United States Code.

PRELIMINARY HEARINGS

Early-stage pretrial procedures that are used to determine whether
sufficient evidence exists to try persons charged with crimes

Preliminary hearings occur early in the legal process when persons are charged with serious criminal offenses, typically felonies. The purpose of such hearings is to allow an independent judicial officer to determine whether probable cause exists to transfer cases to the main trial court of the jurisdiction. These hearings are most frequently considered screening devices to eliminate cases that involve excessive charges, questionable grounds, or insufficient evidence. Such cases are costly both to the defense and the state and serve no purpose in the eyes of justice.

Many jurisdictions do not provide for preliminary hearings, and the U.S. Supreme Court has never stated that they are constitutionally required. Those jurisdictions that provide for them also allow prosecutors and defense attorneys to avoid them. Defendants waive preliminary hearings in about half of all cases. Judges dismiss cases in about 5 to 10 percent of all preliminary hearings.

Most often, the defense benefits from preliminary hearings. Testimony heard in such hearings is admissible when cases go to trial. For example, defense attorneys gain access to testimony in preliminary hearings that can be used to impeach witnesses at trial if they change their statements. These hearings also provide the defense with early discovery opportunities—that is, opportunities to discover relevant information prior to trial. Prosecutors may also benefit from preliminary hearings, as statements by witnesses are admissible at trial even if such witnesses are not available when cases go to court.

—*Michael L. Barrett*

See also Criminal procedure; Discovery; Grand juries; Hearings; Judicial review; Probable cause; Testimony.

PRESUMPTION OF INNOCENCE

Notion that persons accused of crimes need not prove their innocence; instead, the prosecution must prove them guilty

The presumption that an accused person is innocent until proven guilty is an essential element of the American criminal justice system. The idea traces its roots to Roman law. Its role in the early common law of England is obscure, but it was clearly established by 1802. In England and the United States it is viewed as the source of the "proof beyond a reasonable doubt" requirement in criminal trials.

The presumption of innocence is not explicitly provided for in the Constitution. It is inferred from the due process clauses of the Fifth and Fourteenth Amendments (as held in the Supreme Court cases *Coffin v. United States*, 1895, and *Taylor v. Kentucky*, 1978, respectively). The presumption of innocence describes the right of a defendant to offer no proof of innocence in a criminal case. It also describes the duty of the prosecution to offer evidence that the defendant committed the crime charged and to convince the jury beyond a reasonable doubt that, in the light of the offered evidence, the defendant is guilty of the crime charged. The fact that a jury is instructed to presume that a defendant is innocent until proven guilty assists the jury in understanding the limited circumstances under which it should vote to convict a defendant. It also cautions a jury to not convict based on the fact the defendant was arrested and is being tried or on mere suspicion that the defendant committed the crime charged. In this sense the presumption of innocence aids the jury in understanding the requirement that the prosecution prove its case beyond a reasonable doubt, a concept which can be difficult for a jury to understand.

A defendant charged with a federal crime is entitled to receive a presumption of innocence jury instruction if he or she requests it, as established in *Coffin v. United States*. This is not the rule in state crime trials. Despite the long history of its importance and function, the Supreme Court has held that a presumption of innocence instruction need not be given to every jury in state criminal trials. The Supreme Court has interpreted the due process clause of the Fourteenth Amendment as requiring it only when the failure to give such an instruction in the case would deprive a defendant of a fair trial in the light of the totality of the circumstances. Many states, however, have held that the presumption of innocence charge to a jury is required by their state constitutions or statutes.

If a defendant is presumed innocent, then what is the justification for holding a criminal defendant in jail pending trial? Holding the defendant in jail prior to trial certainly seems to be imposing punishment before the defendant has been found guilty, which would appear to be logically inconsistent with the ideal of the presumption of innocence. In *Bell v. Wolfish* (1979), the Supreme Court explained why the presumption of innocence does not apply to pretrial proceedings. The Court held that the role of the presumption of innocence is limited to the guilt-determining process at the defendant's trial. Before trial, the defendant's right to freedom is defined by the Fourth, Fifth, and Eighth Amendments. The government may need to hold a defendant in jail prior to trial to ensure that he or she appears for the trial or to protect the community from possible criminal conduct by the defendant prior to trial. In many, but not all, circumstances, the Eighth Amendment provides that a defendant has a right to bail before trial.

See also Arrest; Bill of Rights, U.S.; Counsel, right to; Defendants; Grand juries; *Habeas corpus*; Miranda rights; Pleas; Probable cause; Public defenders; Search warrant requirement; Self-incrimination, privilege against.

PRINCIPALS (CRIMINAL)

Primary perpetrators of crimes; however, the practical distinction between principals and accessories to crimes has minimal significance in the modern U.S. justice system

Under the common law, people who acted together to commit a crime were distinguished as either principals or accessories. Principals were the main actors who participated in an actual offense while accessories were people who aided the principal either before or after the commission of the offense. An example of this would be a principal who plans to rob a bank but who needs a vehicle and firearms to effectuate the robbery. A person who supplies the principal with the firearms and the vehicle, knowing of and agreeing to the criminal purpose, would be an accessory before the fact under the common law. A person who met up with the principal after the robbery in order to assist in the concealment of money and evidence would be an accessory after the fact. The principal is the person who actually commits the robbery or anyone who is actually or constructively present who aids in the commission of the robbery.

These distinctions have for the most part been rendered moot by modern statutes which generally provide that all persons who participate in a criminal venture may be prosecuted as principals. Thus, a person who advises or encourages another in the commission of an offense may be found guilty as a principal even if that person is too far away from the actual scene of the crime to aid in its actual commission. An example of this would be a person who sets up a sale of narcotics by introducing a seller and a buyer by way of a telephone call. Even if not present at the actual exchange, that person could be prosecuted as a principal under a statue prohibiting the distribution of narcotics. In some states, these secondary actors are prosecuted and punished as principals under conspiracy statutes.

Most modern statutes that abolish the practical distinctions between principals and accessories do so by stating that people are guilty of criminal offenses that they commit themselves or that are committed by the conduct of other persons for which they are legally accountable. Such statutes define accomplices as a class of persons who are legally accountable for the conduct of others—that is, principals. Under such statutes, accomplices may be held liable as principals even if the primary actor has not been prosecuted or convicted. An accomplice may be charged as a principal if there is proof that the crime was committed and that the accomplice acted in furtherance of the crime. This is true even if the person who is claimed to have actually committed the offense is acquitted. Similarly, accomplices may be prosecuted as principals even if they would ordinarily be considered legally incapable of committing the offense.

—*Michele Leavitt*

See also Acquittal; Common law; Criminal justice system; Defendants; Felonies; Misdemeanors; Statutes.

PRIVATE INVESTIGATORS

Individual persons, partnerships, or corporations—which are generally licensed by the states—who offer investigative services for hire to attorneys, insurance companies, government entities, and private individuals

The services provided by private investigators are similar to those provided by police officers and detectives in that they all investigate the circumstances surrounding certain events. However, private investigators have no police powers. Often private investigators are retired law-enforcement officers, but that is not a requirement for licensure. It is estimated that five thousand private investigations agencies employ 200,000 persons.

Private investigators are often referred to as "private I's" or "private eyes." The origins of this slang term can most likely be traced to the 1850's with the Pinkerton agency, which is still one of the largest private investigations firms in the United States. The Pinkerton agency was the first to use the slogan "We never sleep" and an open eye for its logo.

Private investigators supplement police forces by charging fees for investigative work for defense attorneys (who do not have the resources of the state to conduct investigations for them), insurance companies (when there are suspicions that certain claims may be false), and private individuals (whose concerns may not warrant police intervention, such as marriage or custody disputes). Some private investigations firms provide personal and contract security services, background checks for employment and insurance applications, investigations into workers' compensation claims, and surveillance services to investigate shoplifters, pilferers, and even in-home child-care workers.

Private investigators are licensed in most states, and those states require a criminal background check as well as either experience or training in the specific field of investigations. For example, the state of Florida licenses its private investigators through the State Department and requires either prior police and investigative experience or the service of a two-year term of internship under a currently licensed private investigator.

Even though many private investigators are former law-enforcement officers, their powers are much more limited than those of police officers. Private investigators have no more power than an average citizen to make arrests. They generally limit their activities to gathering information for courts or to reporting to parties requesting their services. Proprietary officers (those working directly for malls, factories, department stores, or government facilities) are often called upon to challenge employees who work in such environments. These officers actually have somewhat more latitude to make searches than police officers, as they are not confined by the search and seizure constraints defined by the U.S. Constitution. Therefore, with proper notification, proprietary officers and investigators may search employees' personal automobiles, purses, and effects.

The numbers of persons involved in private investigations and private security operations have increased at the significant rate of 8 percent per year, as compared to 4 percent for public police officers. This can be attributed to the fact that police resources are limited by local tax bases and that there are more lawsuits filed than ever before. Private suits promising large settlements require investigative services to provide background information and factual data. Also, with the increase in sophisticated surveillance techniques and the perceived need for scrutiny in daily affairs, the demand for the services of private investigators is on the rise.

—*C. Randall Eastep*

See also Defense attorneys; Detectives, police; Evidence, rules of; Federal Bureau of Investigation; Law enforcement; Litigation expenses; Police.

Privileged communications

Statements made by individuals within protected relationships— such as those between attorney and client, husband and wife, physician and patient, cleric and penitent, and journalist and news source—that the laws of some states protect from compelled disclosure at trials or depositions

Privileged communication laws encourage full and free disclosure between certain classes of individuals when the speaker needs to be able to make confidential statements, including statements about the person's own misdeeds, with the assurance that the recipient of this information cannot be compelled to reveal it at a later date

Legal scholars, such as John Wigmore, have observed that there are four fundamental conditions necessary to the establishment of a privilege against the disclosure of communications. First, the communications must originate in a confidence that they will not be disclosed. Second, the element of confidentiality must be essential to the maintenance of the relation between the parties. Third, the relationship must be one which, in the opinion of the community, ought to be diligently fostered. Finally, any injury which would occur to the relationship by disclosure of the communication must be greater than the benefit which would be gained by requiring it to be revealed.

The concept of privileged communications goes against the fundamental judicial principal that the courts have a right to require anyone who may have relevant information to testify. Therefore, the courts strictly construe such privileges and accept them "only to the very limited extent that permitting a refusal to testify or excluding relevant evidence has a public good transcending the normally predominant principal of utilizing all rational means for ascertaining the truth" (*Elkins v. United States*, 1960).

Attorney and Client

Clients have a privilege to refuse to disclose, and to prevent their attorneys from disclosing, confidential communications made for the purpose of facilitating the rendition of professional legal services to them. The attorney-client privilege has been justified by the theory that disputes which could result in litigation can be handled most expeditiously by attorneys who have been candidly and completely informed of the facts by their clients. Such full disclosure will best be promoted if clients know that their disclosures cannot, over their objections, be repeated by their attorneys in court. In the criminal context, the attorney-client privilege is necessary to protect the accused's Fifth and Sixth Amendment rights to the effective assistance of counsel.

Privileged attorney-client communications can be waived only by the client. Further, if the client is called to testify during trial, the client can assert the privilege when asked by the opposing counsel what he told his own attorney. In most states, the death of the client will not relieve the attorney from the privilege that existed while the client was alive.

The privilege is not recognized if the client's purpose is the furtherance of an intended future crime or fraud. The privileged communications may be a shield of defense as to crimes already committed, but it cannot be used as a sword or weapon of offense to enable persons to carry out contemplated crimes against society (*Gebhart v. United Railways Co.*, 1920).

Husband and Wife

This privilege is considered necessary for the encouragement of marital confidences, which promote harmony between husband and wife. It is most commonly asserted in criminal proceedings, in which accused persons can prevent their spouses from testifying against them. Either spouse may assent the privilege.

In some states, the privilege extends past the death of one of the spouses. Communications between the husband and wife before marriage or after divorce are not privileged, however, and the privilege does not extend to proceedings in which one spouse is charged with a crime against the person or property of the other or against a child of either.

Physician and Patient

The American physician-patient privilege originated in a New York testimonial provision of 1828 which reads:

> No person authorized to practice physic or surgery shall be allowed to disclose any information which he may have acquired in attending any patient, in any professional character, and which information was necessary to enable him to prescribe for such patient as a physician, or to do any act for him as a surgeon.

This statute set forth the general scope and purpose of the privilege. In some states it has been extended to communications between a patient and nurse, psychologist, psychotherapist, or social worker. The policy behind the privilege is that the physician must know all that a patient can articulate in order to identify and treat disease; barriers to full disclosure would impair diagnosis and treatment.

For the privilege to apply, the patient must have consulted the physician for treatment or diagnosis. Only that information which is necessary to enable the doctor to prescribe or act for the patient is privileged. The privilege is not recognized where the patient sees the physician at the request of another, such as a public officer. It does not apply in an examination by a court-appointed doctor or prosecutor or in an examination requested by the patient's own attorney for personal injury litigation purposes. The privilege is not recognized if the patient has an unlawful purpose in the consultation, such as to secure an illegal abortion, to obtain narcotics in violation of the law, or to have his or her appearance disguised by plastic surgery when a fugitive from justice.

In most jurisdictions, an implicit waiver of the privilege occurs when a plaintiff files a civil suit for personal injury damages. Plaintiffs are not permitted to sue for personal injuries while preventing their doctors, pursuant to the physician-client privilege, from disclosing pertinent treatment information. The privilege is also often statutorily waived in actions for workers' compensation, prosecutions for homicide, assault with a deadly weapon, commitment proceedings, and will contests.

Cleric and Penitent

The cleric-penitent privilege recognizes the need to disclose confidentially to a spiritual or religious counselor what are believed to be flawed acts or thoughts and to receive guidance in return. This privilege also recognizes that members of the clergy often assume roles as counselors, doing much work that overlaps with psychiatrists and psychologists, both of whom have the benefit of privileged physician-patient communications in most states.

—*David R. Sobel*

Suggested Readings

A number of general works include good discussions of privileged communications, among them Charles Tilford McCormick, *McCormick on Evidence* (4th ed. St. Paul, Minn.: West Publishing, 1992); *American Jurisprudence* (2d ed. Rochester, N.Y.: Lawyers' Co-operative, 1979); Eric D. Green, *Problems, Cases, and Materials on Evidence* (Boston: Little, Brown, 1993); and John Henry Wigmore, *Evidence in Trials at Common Law* (2d. ed. Boston: Little, Brown, 1961). More specific discussions include Alan B. Vickery, "Breach of Confidence: An Emerging Tort," in *Columbia Law Review* 82 (November, 1982), and "Communication to Clergyman as Privileged," in *American Law Reports* (3d ed. Rochester, N.Y.: Lawyers' Co-operative, 1975). William H. Simon, *The Practice of Justice: A Theory of Lawyers' Ethics* (Cambridge, Mass.: Harvard University Press, 1998), has chapters on confidentiality. *The Criminal Law Handbook: Know Your Rights, Survive the System*, by Paul Bergman, Sara J. Berman-Barrett (5th ed. Berkeley, Calif.: Nolo Press, 2003), covers everything that goes on in criminal cases in a question-and-answer format.

See also Attorney-client relationship; Attorney confidentiality; Attorneys, court-appointed; Trial publicity; Unethical conduct of attorneys; Witnesses.

PRO BONO LEGAL WORK

Controversial requirement that lawyers perform free legal services for the good of the public—"pro bono publico"—to maintain their licenses to practice law

Pro bono work involves the free delivery of legal services to persons of limited means or to charitable, religious, civic, community, governmental, and educational organizations in matters primarily designed to address the needs of poor persons. It also involves providing free legal assistance to individuals, groups, or organizations seeking to obtain or protect civil rights, civil liberties, or public rights. In addition, it means providing free legal services to charitable, governmental, or educational organizations in matters that further their goals and in which payment would significantly deplete their funds. There is no universally accepted definition of pro bono work. The model codes of ethics enacted by bar associations only provide general guidance.

Lawyers who volunteer their time do so for a variety of reasons. They may feel passionate about an issue or type of client. They may want to gain litigation experience or learn a new area of law. According to several studies, approximately 85 percent of the legitimate legal needs of the poor go unmet. The needs of the poor include adequate food, decent shelter, and protection from abuse. Many pro bono programs recruit volunteers to handle public benefits hearings, public housing issues, spousal abuse, and appeals pertaining to Medicaid (a federal health insurance program). Typically, a pro bono program cannot provide legal assistance to every person of limited means who desires assistance. The demand for such services outstrips the supply of lawyers capable of providing them.

Pro bono programs may be established to assist all persons of limited means in a geographical area and to serve special populations such as battered spouses or the homeless. Other programs address a wide range of issues or a particular issue, such as immigration or community economic development. Some programs provide full-case legal representation, while others provide advice only. An example of a pro bono program is that established by the Arizona Asian American Bar Association to assist Americans of Japanese ancestry who suffered a loss of their civil rights during World War II. Another example is the Massachusetts Black Lawyers Association, which created the Macon B. Allen Civil Rights Clinic in Boston. This clinic serves low-income people who wish to pursue claims of employment discrimination on the basis of race, sex, or national origin.

In addition to pro bono lawyers, the poor receive legal aid through alternative dispute resolution programs and nonlawyer legal services. Other providers include judicare programs, in which the government pays private attorneys to aid indigent clients. Governmental support of legal services for the poor is provided through the Legal Services Corporation (LSC), a federally financed nonprofit organization that provides staff attorneys in civil cases for low-income Americans.

Pro Bono Precedents

The first experience with legal aid was the Freedman's Bureau. Between 1865 and 1868 the bureau retained attorneys in the District of Columbia and some southern states to represent poor African Americans in criminal and civil cases. The first private legal aid society in the United States was the German Legal Aid Society, established in 1876 by German immigrants. The Legal Aid Society of New York was the nation's first legal aid organization to be financed by a combination of funds from bar associations, community chests, individuals, and businesses.

The legal aid movement developed slowly in the twentieth century. In 1963 the U.S. Supreme Court ruled in *Gideon v. Wainwright* that indigent defendants in state felony cases must be provided with counsel. As a result of this ruling, government-sponsored public defender offices opened nationwide to provide legal assistance to felony defendants who could not afford to hire attorneys. Federal funds for legal assistance to the poor were allocated to the Office of Economic Opportunity (OEO), which was part of President Lyndon B. Johnson's "war on Poverty." In 1966 Congress created the OEO Legal Services Program (LSP). This program used the legal system to reform laws and practices perceived as biased against the poor. The LSP's reform initiatives sparked considerable political opposition. In 1974 Congress created the Legal Services Corporation (LSC). The LSC was a quasi-governmental agency governed by a nonpartisan board of directors. It, too, came under attack. In 1987 Tulane Law School in New Orleans, Louisiana, became the first law school to require that its students provide a minimum of twenty hours of legal aid to indigent individuals.

The American Bar Association (ABA) has long recognized the responsibility of lawyers to engage in pro bono work. In 1908 the ABA Canon of Ethics recognized the inherent duty of lawyers to provide legal aid to the indigent in criminal cases. In 1969 the ABA adopted the Model Code of Professional Conduct, which states that every lawyer, regardless of prominence or workload, has the responsibility to find time to serve the disadvantaged. No time requirement was specified. In 1975 the ABA House of Delegates adopted the Montreal Resolution, which states that it is the basic professional responsibility of each lawyer to provide free, public-interest legal services, such as poverty and civil rights law. In 1983 this policy was incorporated into the Model Rules of Professional Conduct.

In December, 1987, the *ABA Journal* and the *American Medical Association Journal* jointly called on lawyers and doctors to contribute fifty hours each year to serving the poor. In 1988 the ABA's House of Delegates adopted the Toronto Resolution, which urges all lawyers to devote no less than fifty hours per year to pro bono and other public-interest services for the needy or to improve the law, the legal system, or the legal profession. The pro bono provision is the only rule in the Model Rules that is not mandatory.

Opposition to Mandatory Pro Bono Service
The proposal that lawyers be required to perform pro bono legal work first surfaced in the late 1970's when the State Bar of Cal-

ifornia and the Association of the Bar of New York City established an expectation of forty hours of pro bono service annually. The proposals sparked intense opposition and were defeated. Later mandatory pro bono proposals experienced a similar fate. State bar associations are reluctant to adopt mandatory pro bono requirements, because not all lawyers can afford to donate their time.

Lawyers generally agree that access to the courts is a basic right in American society. Courts are a forum in which people can present their grievances and in which wrongs can be corrected. Lawyers also agree that people need legal representation in order to have their disputes resolved relatively quickly, fairly, and as inexpensively as possible. The poor do not have equal access to the law because they have little money. Lack of legal assistance for the poor undermines their right to equal justice under the law and access to the legal system.

Opponents resist mandatory pro bono activities on the basis that it is an unwarranted encroachment on their personal freedom. They generally agree that equal access to the legal system is a serious problem. However, they believe that imposing pro bono work on lawyers is a form of involuntary servitude and an ineffective method for solving the legal problems of the poor. Opponents contend that the courts cannot, and should not, mandate acts of charity. They argue that the shortage of legal services for the poor is a broad social problem. It is undemocratic to require that lawyers be the only professionals to have to solve a problem that must be solved by society as a whole. Opponents are also concerned about the difficulty of documenting and enforcing a mandatory pro bono obligation.

Proponents argue that because pro bono representation is a bedrock professional duty, lawyers simply must do it. By the late twentieth century an overwhelming majority of states had pro bono provisions in their legal ethics codes. These provisions hold that mandatory pro bono is necessary because legal service programs and calls for voluntary help have been insufficient to meet the needs of the poor.

Rules of Conduct
American Bar Association's Model Rule 6.1 (adopted in 1993) sets forth that lawyers should perform fifty hours of pro bono service per year. If lawyers cannot provide pro bono services, they

should donate the monetary equivalent of fifty hours of service to organizations providing free legal services. This section of the organization's Model Rules of Professional Conduct indicates that a "substantial majority" of this commitment should be spent on behalf of people of limited means or for organizations primarily concerned with the needs of persons of limited means. The law firm Pro Bono Project recommends that lawyers in large law firms perform between fifty and eighty hours of pro bono service per year. The committee that wrote the rule in 1993 said that the private bar alone cannot be expected to fill the gap for service for the poor. It argued that the federal government, by adequately funding the LSC, should bear the responsibility for fixing the problem of unmet legal needs. The government exacerbated the situation by failing adequately to fund the LSC.

A variety of solutions has been offered to resolve the debate over the obligation to provide free legal representation to the poor. For example, mediators have focused on passive enforcement, which is instituted only when practitioners commit ethical violations. This approach is similar to that of mandatory seat belt laws. Under such laws police officers cannot issue citations for violations unless drivers have been stopped for other offenses. Another approach holds that lawyers must pay a user fee or tax in exchange for a license to practice law. Because the license entitles lawyers to use the public asset of client confidentiality or secrecy, they must donate time to pro bono work.

Since the 1970's the organized bar has pressed lawyers to expand their pro bono efforts. At the same time, bar associations have avoided mandating that they do so. Pro bono work is a goal to which lawyers should aspire. Lawyers' responsibility to provide representation to those who cannot afford to pay for it is likely to remain a controversial issue.

—*Fred Buchstein*

Suggested Readings

For an overview of the pro bono debate see *The Law Firm and the Public Good* (Washington, D.C.: Brookings Institution/Governance Institute, 1995), edited by Robert A. Katzmann. Jeremy Miller and Vallori Hard trace the history of pro bono service in "Pro Bono: Historical Analysis and a Case Study" in *Western State University Law Review* 21 (Spring, 1994). Consumer activists Ralph Nader and Wesley J. Smith discuss the pro bono activities of large law firms in *No Contest: Corporate Lawyers and the Perversion of Justice in America* (New York: Random House, 1996). Other works on the legal profession may be found in Sol Linowitz's *The Betrayed Profession* (New York: Charles Scribner's Sons, 1994) and Mary Ann Glendon's *A Nation Under Lawyers* (New York: Farrar, Straus & Giroux, 1994). The ABA's Center for Pro Bono is a clearinghouse for information on the private bar associations' involvement in legal services for the poor. The ABA's Center for Professional Responsibility is a source for national and state codes of conduct. Broader studies of ethical issues include *Ethical Standards in the Public Sector: A Guide for Government Lawyers, Clients, and Public Officials*, edited by Patricia E. Salkin (Chicago: Section of State and Local Government Law, American Bar Association, 1999) and *Ethics in Practice: Lawyers' Roles, Responsibilities, and Regulation*, edited by Deborah L. Rhode (New York: Oxford University Press, 2000). Both books have chapters on pro bono work.

See also American Bar Association; Attorney fees; Bar associations; Billable hours; Law firm partners and associates; Law firms; Legal clinics; Model Rules of Professional Conduct; Public defenders.

PROBABLE CAUSE

Standard of proof necessary for representatives of the government to make an arrest or to search and seize a person's belongings

The Fourth Amendment to the U.S. Constitution states, "The right of the people to be secure in their persons, houses, papers, and effects, against unreasonable searches and seizures, shall not be violated, and no Warrants shall issue, but upon probable cause, supported by Oath or affirmation, and particularly describing the place to be searched, and the persons or things to be seized." The authors of the Constitution were very concerned about government intrusion into the lives of citizens, and through the Fourth Amendment they sought to ensure that individual privacy would be respected.

The question as to what constitutes probable cause has been considered a number of times by the U.S. Supreme Court. In 1949, in deciding the case of *Brinegar v. United States*, the Court stated, "probable cause is the facts and circumstances within the officers' knowledge and of which they had reasonably trustworthy information and are sufficient in themselves to warrant a man of reasonable caution in the belief that an offense has been or is being committed." This requires that the officer or agent of the government be fairly certain (to have some tangible proof, even if it is not admissible in court) before making an arrest or search or before making application for a warrant.

Probable cause, as a standard of proof, may best be considered as lying on a continuum with mere suspicion at one end and absolute certainty at the other end. Courts have held that reasonable suspicion, a level of proof somewhat lower than probable cause, is needed to stop and frisk suspects. On the scale somewhat higher than probable cause is preponderance of evidence, which is the standard of proof necessary to determine liability in civil cases.

Observational and Informational Probable Cause

There are two basic ways probable cause can be developed: through observation and information. Observational probable cause is formulated by police officers by using their five senses. If they can see, hear, smell, taste, or touch evidence that a crime has been or is being committed, an arrest or a search may be made. When determining the sufficiency of observational probable cause, courts take into consideration police officers' training and experience. Thus, a police officer trained to detect the scent of marijuana is recognized as being able to distinguish that odor to develop probable cause, even if an ordinary citizen may not make that distinction. With observational probable cause the "totality of circumstances" standard is often used by the courts. With this standard, surveillance and other observations over time are compounded to determine whether probable cause exists. Informational probable cause is usually developed through investigations that yield certain facts about suspects. Included here are statements given by witnesses to crimes, victims' statements, and statements given by other police officers and informants. Although probable cause is always required to arrest or search, warrants are not always necessary.

Warrantless Searches

It is clear from the language of the Fourth Amendment that the Founders intended for agents of the state to produce warrants prior to searching or arresting citizens. However, the courts have recognized the impracticality of that requirement in modern society. As early as 1925 a challenge to the need for officers to actually produce a physical document (warrant) was made by a man named Carroll whose car was searched during Prohibition. After government agents seized illegal liquor from his vehicle, Carroll appealed his conviction, alleging that the search was unconstitutional because the agents had no warrant. The U.S. Supreme Court, in deciding for the government in *Carroll v. United States*, reasoned that automobiles can be moved before a warrant can be obtained and that the police need flexibility when probable cause exists.

A lesser standard of proof, reasonable suspicion, is needed by police officers before officers may stop a car. Once the car is stopped, probable cause for a full search may be developed by the circumstances. For example, a police officer may stop a car because it is weaving and, while talking to the driver, may smell marijuana. Although the weaving was not probable cause to search the car (it was reasonable suspicion to stop the car), the smell of marijuana provides the officer with probable cause to search. The U.S. Supreme Court has ruled in *Ross v. United States* (1982) that once probable cause to search a vehicle has been established, the police have the right to search the entire vehicle, including all containers therein. The probable cause requirement for police to conduct a valid search can be waived if the party consents to the search. The consent must be voluntary and intelligently given. Evidence seized without consent or probable cause is subject to exclusion from criminal proceedings pursuant to the exclusionary rule.

Reasonable Expectation of Privacy

Although the Fourth Amendment protects people and not places, not every location is protected by the language of the Fourth Amendment. The U.S. Supreme Court has determined that the requirement for probable cause is restricted to areas in which there is a reasonable expectation of privacy. Evidence or contraband which is in plain view of a police officer is subject to seizure without probable cause. Likewise, if marijuana is grown in an open field behind one's home, no reasonable expectation of privacy exists. The courts have held that persons have a reasonable expectation of privacy in a closed public phone booth but that they do not have a reasonable expectation of privacy while being detained in the rear seat of a police car. Issues related to the expectation of privacy have often generated controversy as increasingly sophisticated surveillance techniques have been developed.

Although police officers are the most likely criminal justice practitioners to develop probable cause, an independent tribunal (a judge or magistrate) must verify probable cause prior to the issuance of a search or arrest warrant. The police officer applying for a search or arrest warrant must outline the probable cause in an affidavit and the judge or magistrate must decide if the evidence is sufficient to support the warrant. As a systemic check, a probable cause hearing is held during the pretrial stage after an arrest so that a judge can ensure that probable cause exists. If it does not exist, the defendant must be released.

—*C. Randall Eastep*

Suggested Readings

Thoughts on probable cause are best expressed through legal texts and texts dealing with criminal procedures. Gilbert B. Stuckey's *Procedures in the Justice System* (4th ed. New York: Macmillan, 1991), Harvey Wallace and Cliff Robertson's *Principles of Criminal Law* (White Plains, N.Y.: Longman, 1996), and Neil C. Chamelin and Kenneth R. Evans's *Criminal Law for Police Officers* (4th ed. Englewood Cliffs, N.J.: Prentice-Hall, 1987) are good basic guides. John M. Scheb and John M. Scheb II's *Criminal Law and Procedure* (St. Paul, Minn.: West Publishing, 1994) and Daniel Hall's *Survey of Criminal Law* (2d ed. Albany, N.Y.: Delmar, 1997) are also excellent sources. For an extended discussion on application see Rolando V. del Carmen's *Criminal Procedure: Law and Practice* (3d ed. Belmont, Calif.: Wadsworth, 1995).

See also Arrest; Attorney fees; Bench warrants; Preliminary hearings; Presumption of innocence; Reasonable doubt; Search warrant requirement; Suspects.

PROBATE

Legal process that occurs after a person dies to ensure that the person's property is distributed according to the person's wishes, as stated in a last will and testament or in the absence of such a document according to the laws of the state in which probate occurs

Probate law, like all constitutional and common law in the United States, was adopted from English law, being derived from the king's courts, also called common-law courts, in which the procedures were complex and protracted. England replaced the king's courts with ecclesiastical courts charged with handling estate matters in a less complex and faster way. Equity courts were later established in England to transfer the ownership of titled property, such as land, stocks, and bank accounts, with considerably less delay and confusion than was the case in the king's courts. From its beginnings, the United States modeled its probate system on England's complex king's courts.

The Probate Process

The term "probate court" is used in the United States to identify courts that deal with estate matters. In some states such designations as "orphans' courts," "surrogate courts," and "chancery courts" are used to identify courts that attend to probate matters.

If decedents leave a last will and testament, it is the duty of the executor appointed in this document to present the will to the probate court to verify that it meets the legal requirements of the state and that it has been duly dated, signed, and witnessed. When decedents do not leave a will, the court appoints an administrator, whose duties are essentially those of an executor. Usually the family of the deceased has little voice in determining who that administrator shall be.

In most states, two or three people witness the signatures of testators. These witnesses may be called into the probate court to verify their signatures and to affirm that they were present when the will was signed. They may also be asked to attest to the testator's mental state to assure that the testator was capable of understanding its provisions. In most states, if the signed and witnessed will is notarized, the witnesses do not have to appear in court unless the document is being contested. Most states consider handwritten, or holographic, wills valid as long as they have been dated, signed, and witnessed. The form of the will is not specifically set, but it must clearly state the desired distribution of the testator's property.

A decedent's survivors may avoid probate until such time as they wish to transfer the title of property to their names. If a spouse dies leaving a house or an automobile, the surviving spouse may continue to live in the house or drive the automobile for an indefinite period. However, when the survivor wishes to take title of the house or the automobile, he or she must do so through the probate process.

The probate court is sometimes asked to act prior to the death of persons deemed incapable of handling their own financial affairs because of illness or senility. In such cases, the probate court may appoint a conservator to act on behalf of the disabled person. The court may also appoint guardians to act for minors who own property but have not yet reached legal age.

A decedent's place of residence determines where the estate will be probated, although when people own property and reside for part of the year in more than one state, each state may claim the estate and file a motion to have the will probated in a state other than the one in which the person drew up the will and in which the person died.

FUNCTIONS OF PROBATE COURTS

- They verify the validity of a last will and testament or, in the absence of a will, appoint an administrator to oversee the probate process and the distribution of the estate
- They ensure that public notice of a decedent's death is printed in newspapers so that creditors and potential heirs can file claims before the estate is distributed
- They receive an inventory of a decedent's estate
- They require the executor or administrator to have the estate appraised
- They ensure that all just claims against the estate are paid
- They verify that all income and inheritance taxes are paid
- They supervise the distribution of the residual estate according to the directions of the will or, lacking a will, in accordance with the laws of the state

The Cost of Probate

Probate is time-consuming and costly. Although an estate's executor may serve in that capacity without meeting any specific requirements, a probate attorney is usually required to attend to matters that must come before the probate court. Besides paying the probate attorney, the estate must pay probate fees and fees for such other matters as the appraisal of the estate.

The executor or administrator may be paid according to a formula, which, in most states, permits payment of two or three percent of the estate's total value. Although probate attorneys in many states can charge whatever they wish, executors usually determine in advance what the attorney's fees will be. They should not exceed the fees that executors are permitted by law.

Most attorneys, if asked about their fees in advance, work within these parameters, although the amount charged for legal help in settling an estate of $10,000 may run as high as 10 percent, whereas the fee for dealing with an estate valued in the millions might be one or two percent. Individual cases vary considerably, but fees negotiated before an attorney is authorized to act for an estate are generally lower than those that are set during the probate process or at its conclusion. The probate court also levies charges against the gross estates with which it deals. These charges vary, but they can run as high as seven percent in some cases or even more if an estate is particularly complicated.

In most cases, it takes between one and two years to settle an estate, although the process may drag on for four or five years, particularly when bequests are made to citizens of foreign countries or when some of the decedent's assets are not liquid. Not all assets are subject to probate. Assets contained in a living trust are available immediately to those named in the trust, although they must pay the appropriate inheritance taxes on them.

Other Probate Issues

In twenty-eight states and the District of Columbia all estates, regardless of size, are subject to probate. In twenty-two states, however, small estates may escape probate. The cut-off point in Minnesota, South Dakota, and Wisconsin, for example, is $5,000, whereas in California no estate with a value under $60,000 need be probated.

Some people mistakenly think that because the federal government exempts the first $625,000 of one's assets from federal inher-

> ## ASSETS EXEMPTED FROM PROBATE
>
> - Assets held in living trusts
> - Proceeds from life insurance policies and certain annuities if left to specific beneficiaries rather than to the estate of the deceased
> - Mutual funds, individual retirement accounts (IRAs), and other securities that include a transfer-on-death provision
> - Property, including real estate and bank accounts, held in joint tenancy or in tenancy by the entirety
> - A surviving spouse's half of community property held in community property states

itance tax (which is in the process of being gradually raised to $1 million), estates under that amount are not subject to probate. This misconception can be costly to those who do not understand that nearly all estates over $10,000 are subject to probate in most states.

Once an estate is probated, all the documents relating to it, including copies of the last will and testament and of the appraisal of the estate, are available to anyone who requests them. This freedom of information robs families of privacy in estate matters and, in many cases, subjects them to harassment from unscrupulous sales people trying to entice them into schemes that will, in the end, cost them dearly.

The only way to protect the privacy of the deceased and his or her family is through a living trust, which does not become part of any public record. People who draw up living trusts must remember to transfer their assets into the trust. In most cases, they should also have a will to assure the distribution of any property not included in the trust and to specify final arrangements. Because such wills are considerably less complex than those that distribute all of one's assets, the probate process should be faster and less costly than it would be if all bequests were made through the will. Also, if the bulk of one's estate is contained in a living trust, the remainder may be so small as to escape probate in some of the twenty-two states that exempt small estates from probate.

Living trusts serve another purpose. As real estate prices have increased significantly throughout the United States, the majority of people who die leave estates large enough to require probate.

THE U.S. LEGAL SYSTEM

In order to avoid probate, many people establish revocable living trusts that hold their assets for their own use during their lifetimes and are distributed as specified upon their deaths.

The Future of Probate

The probate process has been soundly criticized for many years as unnecessarily expensive, unwieldy, and unfair, particularly as it relates to relatively small estates. The system, however, continues, and it is unlikely to be drastically changed because change must be legislated and many legislators are attorneys who benefit from the process.

In the 1930's New York City reform mayor Fiorello La Guardia declared the probate court to be the most expensive undertaking in the world, yet he was unable to effect any change in it. Lawyers who draw up wills and are generally appointed as the probate attorneys look upon the fees they receive for their services as sinecures that will assure them of a substantial income far into the future.

Because of abuses in the probate process that came to light during the late twentieth century years and that have been widely publicized, many people, even those of modest means, have resorted to living trusts as a means of avoiding or minimizing probate.

During the late 1990's, the state legislature of California passed a law that permits the trustee of a living trust simply to file an affidavit with the probate court and to publicize a decedent's death in the newspaper so that creditors can file their claims, after which an estate is settled without probate. The state of Washington has approved similar legislation.

It is anticipated that several other states will soon pass legislation to permit estates to be settled without undergoing probate. In all such instances, however, testators must establish living trusts to qualify for exemption from probate.

—*R. Baird Shuman*

Suggested Readings

Authoritative recent studies of probate include *American Probate: Protecting the Public, Improving the Process*, by Paula A. Monopoli (Boston: Northeastern University Press, 2003) and *The Living Trust: The Failproof Way to Pass Along Your Estate to Your Heirs Without Lawyers, Courts, or the Probate System*, by Henry W. Abts III

(Chicago: Contemporary Books, 2003). Similar in nature is Norman F. Dacey's *How to Avoid Probate!* (New York: Macmillan, 1990). Charles A. DeGrandpre and Kathleen M. Robinson's *Probate Law and Procedure* (Salem, N.H.: Butterworth, 1990) is useful and practical, as is Kay Osberg's slender volume, *Probate: How to Settle an Estate* (New York: McKay, 1990), which is written for the nonprofessional. Jens C. Appel and F. Bruce Gentry's *The Complete Probate Kit* (New York: Wiley, 1991) is directed at the nonprofessional as well. A practical guide to lay people is Theodore E. Hughes and David Klein's *A Family Guide to Wills, Funerals, and Probate: How to Protect Yourself and Your Survivors* (New York: Facts on File/Checkmark Books, 2001).

See also Court types; Executors; Family law practice; Legal guardians; Uniform laws.

PROBATION, ADULT

Sentencing procedure by which adults convicted of crimes are released by courts and do not go to prison, so long as they adhere to certain conditions set by judges

In the 1990's probation was the most commonly used punishment in the U.S. criminal justice system. There were about 3,600,000 people on probation in the United States, compared with approximately 1,500,000 persons in prisons and jails. The number of people on probation amounts to one out of every thirty-eight adults and one out of every twenty-one males. Most people on probation have committed relatively minor crimes, such as driving with a suspended license, committing petty theft or larceny, or possessing small amounts of drugs or other controlled substances. The offenders have typically been released to the community under the supervision of a probation officer and are usually required to meet briefly with the officer once a week or perhaps only once a month for counseling.

Probationers must usually meet a series of requirements. Sometimes probationers must stay away from certain persons, such as wives or children they may have harassed or threatened, or from particular places, such as street corners at which drugs are sold. Judges may also order that probationers stay free of drugs or alcohol or that they find and hold a job. Employers generally do not need to be told that a job applicant is on probation. Breaking any of these conditions can lead to imprisonment for violating probation procedures.

The average cost of probation nationwide is about $850 a year per offender, which compares favorably with the average $22,000 a year it costs to keep someone in prison. In many states some of the costs of probation are recovered by requiring probationers to pay part of the cost of their supervision. This cost-effectiveness is one reason that the number of persons on probation began increasing dramatically during the late twentieth century.

History and Goals of Probation

Probation comes from the Latin *probatus*, which means "tested" or "proved." In the early United States, persons convicted of crimes were eligible for a suspended sentence if they promised to behave well and offered proof that they could observe the laws. The modern system began in Boston in 1841, when John Augustus, a businessman and advocate of rehabilitation, began bailing out convicted offenders, found them jobs, and gave the court monthly reports on their progress toward a better life. Augustus gained the release of more than two thousand prisoners using this method, most of whom were effectively rehabilitated. In 1878 Massachusetts became the first state to allow judges to choose probation as an alternative to a prison sentence. By 1940 all states allowed probation for juvenile offenders and all but six permitted adult probation. Not until the 1980's, however, did all states and the federal government provide for adult probation. The first statistics on probation were collected in 1976, when it was reported that nearly 1,000,000 adults were found to be on probation and 457,528 persons were in prison in the United States.

Probation began as an alternative to imprisonment and was justified as a method of rehabilitation that would save many people, especially nonviolent criminals, from the horrors and potential violence of prison life. Since prisons did not seem to do a very good job of reforming convicts and always seemed to be terribly overcrowded, judges would have an alternative to sending people to the penitentiary. The goal was to reduce crime by allowing offenders an opportunity to prove their fitness for society. The principal goal was rehabilitation, reforming the guilty party, rather than simply punishment, retribution, or revenge.

Central to probation is the notion that persons found to be "good risks" can be placed on probation and that they will not commit more crimes if they are given supervision and counseling. The philosophy of probation is that convicted persons can become law-abiding again. All they need is to be provided with treatment programs, employment, and other services. The focus is not on the harm done by the criminal but on the future reduction of criminal behavior, which can be achieved through proper treatment and supervision.

Violations of probation can be controlled by the ever-present threat that violators will be sent to prison if they break the rules. The idea of probation challenges the "just deserts" school of criminal justice, which proclaims that the purpose of the system is to make those convicted of crimes pay for the damage they have done by undergoing imprisonment. The goal of this method of criminal justice is to punish offenders, not to rehabilitate them.

Probation Decisions

The decision to place a convicted person on probation is one alternative available at a sentencing hearing. The judge is usually informed of the details of the offense in each case and makes the decision to place a person on probation after considering a variety of factors. These include the defendant's prior criminal record, social history, and family and employment record. This information is usually provided by a probation officer assigned to investigate the case. Normally, probation is given only in felony cases, not in misdemeanor cases.

Probation is granted by the judge in most cases if the probation officer recommends it. Two key factors are involved in this decision: the seriousness of the crime and the report on the person's prior criminal record. In most cases the seriousness of the crime is the single most important factor. Generally, persons convicted of having committed nonviolent crimes are much more likely to receive probation than those who have committed violent or drug-related criminal acts. The judge's decision is also influenced by the likelihood of rehabilitation. Persons considered "good risks" are very likely to receive probation, especially if their crimes did not involve violence.

Only a few studies have been done on the revocation of parole. Decisions to end probation and send people to prison follow no particular pattern or set of rules. There seems to be no consistent standard in revocation hearings. Judges are often inconsistent in arriving at these decisions. Generally, however, revocation depends on the nature of the probation violation. Failure to appear at meetings with parole officers is considered particularly grave. Revocation also depends on the probationer's age, prior record, and employment history. For example, the failure to find or retain a job can lead to revocation. However, any decision to revoke probation must be made by a judge, not simply by a probation officer.

Intensive Probation

One alternative to sending a violator to prison for violating probation is to order more intensive probation. This method can also be applied in cases in which a convicted person has committed a serious or violent crime. Intensive probation provides much closer supervision of offenders and is over three times more expensive than regular probation. Offenders in intensive programs are required to contact parole officers very frequently, sometimes as often as once a day or at least once a week.

Georgia, a state with a large investment in intensive probation, requires that serious nonviolent offenders have five face-to-face contact with probation officers every week. The failure rate in this program is about 16 percent, or about one-half the failure rate for regular probationers. Prisoners on either type of probation are extremely unlikely to commit violent crimes, since most have never been convicted of violent crimes. Less than 1 percent of violent crimes in the United States (0.8 percent to be exact) are committed by probationers.

Probation Officers

The major problem with the probation system is the huge caseloads carried by most probation officers. Experts consider thirty cases per officer the best possible situation. However, the average officer in the United States has at least two hundred cases each month. Such huge caseloads prevent many officers from getting actively involved with their clients. Instead, all probationers receive the same treatment, regardless of whether they have been convicted of income tax evasion or armed robbery. Few probationers can get the individual attention they need to remain successfully employed and motivated. The problem seems not to be the idea of probation but the way the system works. There is too little money and too few probation officers to do an effective job.

Another problem since the 1980's has been the fundamental belief on the part of many criminal justice practitioners, from police officers to judges, that probation does not reduce crime. A majority of the U.S. public seems to accept this view. This has led to a major shift in how judges determine sentences. In the 1960's and 1970's probation officers and judges believed that their mission was to reform and rehabilitate persons under their supervision and authority. Probation was supposed to help people convicted of crimes work their way back into society through employment opportunities and counseling. Probation officers saw their job as helping their clients overcome drug or alcohol dependency while meeting their family obligations.

In the 1980's, however, a much harsher form of criminal justice was instituted, with "just deserts" being the most prominent philosophy. In this view, punishment rather than rehabilitation was the goal, and parole officers responded by focusing their attention on catching probation violators and reporting them to the courts for confinement. New technologies and monitoring devices have made this practice more common. Electronic monitoring devices attached to probationers' legs or ankles enable officers to know where a subject is every minute of the day. House arrest is much more possible with such new devices, many of which have been available only since the mid-1990's. Nevertheless, probation is primarily reserved for people convicted of nonviolent crimes.

The costs of normal, nonintensive probation are still about one-twentieth the cost of imprisonment, and a majority of probationers do not commit additional crimes. Probation is a system that works well to reduce future criminal activity by providing rehabilitation for offenders. It has been shown to be the best sentencing alternative to imprisonment.

—*Leslie V. Tischauser*

Suggested Readings

Discussions of the procedures and guidelines used in considering probation can be found in *Probation, Parole, and Community Corrections,* by Dean J. Champion (Upper Saddle River, N.J.: Prentice Hall, 2002); Lynn S. Branham's *The Law of Sentencing, Corrections, and Prisoners' Rights in a Nutshell* (St. Paul, Minn.: West Publishing, 2002); and *Probation, Parole, and Community Corrections* (New York: John Wiley & Sons, 1976), edited by Robert M. Carter and Leslie T. Wilkins, and in Frederick A. Hussey and David E. Duffee's *Probation, Parole, and Community Field Services: Policy, Structure, and Process* (New York: Harper & Row, 1980.) An evaluation of the effectiveness of probation versus incarceration is found in Douglas Lipton, Robert Martinson, and Judith Wilks's *The Effectiveness of Correctional Treatment: A Survey of Treatment Evaluation Studies* (New York: Praeger, 1975). A state-by-state description of probation systems is presented in the U.S. Bureau of the Census's *State and Local Probation and Parole Systems* (Washington, D.C.: U.S. Department of Justice, Law Enforcement Assistance Administration, National Criminal Justice Information and Statistics Service, 1978). For an interesting discussion of alternatives to imprisonment see Norval Morris's *The Future of Imprisonment.* (Chicago: University of Chicago Press, 1974). *Plea Bargaining's Triumph: A History of Plea Bargaining in America*, by George Fisher (Stanford, Calif.: Stanford University Press, 2003), examines the relationship between plea bargaining and probation.

See also Criminal justice system; Criminal records; Good time; House arrest; Pardoning power; Parole; Probation, juvenile; Sentencing.

PROBATION, JUVENILE

Sentencing procedure by which juveniles convicted of crimes are released by courts and do not go to prison, so long as they adhere to certain conditions set by judges

Probation is a general term for alternative sentencing, allowing convicted criminals to live outside prison, either in the community or in supervised residential programs. The emphasis is on rehabilitation. By the use of education, training, and counseling, it is hoped that the convict will be able to lead a useful life and not continue criminal activities. Because youthful offenders are often perceived as more likely than older ones to change their outlooks and because prison is often viewed as a "school for criminal activities," juveniles are very often sentenced to probation.

Probation has its roots in the harsh laws of the Middle Ages in Europe, where corporal or even capital punishment was imposed for crimes that would be considered minor by modern standards. Judges sometimes suspended sentences or imposed lesser punishments than those ordinarily called for, especially when children were involved.

The modern American system of probation began in the nineteenth century. The first paid probation officer was hired in Boston in 1878. In the latter half of the twentieth century, as Americans became more interested in social problems and the welfare of underprivileged citizens, probation, especially of inner city youth, became widespread.

The Rationale Behind Probation

There have long been a variety of responses to antisocial activities in society. The biblical method of "an eye for an eye," combined with Christian concepts of good and evil, led to a general attitude that those who harm others must suffer pain in retribution. By the nineteenth century and the onset of the Industrial Revolution, this attitude began to change, at least in part thanks to the writings of reformers, notably Charles Dickens, whose novels emphasized the difficult conditions among which members of the working class were forced to live.

In the wake of the Industrial Revolution and the sudden increase of immigration to the United States by people who had few skills, little education, and little knowledge of the English language, an underclass developed, and crime became the only solution for many persons. The problem became more intense in the twentieth century, as American cities became increasingly populated by minority groups, often living in desperate conditions. Reformers became interested in improving the conditions under which such people lived rather than sending them to prison. By the late twentieth century, there was increasing concern that U.S. prisons are overcrowded and that people convicted of relatively minor offenses should be given alternative sentences.

The result of these changes in attitude was a system of alternatives to actual jail sentences, especially for young offenders. Particularly in the latter part of the twentieth century, young criminals began to be viewed as victims of society as much as villains, and new methods were proposed.

The Mechanics and Types of Probation

In modern times the process of sentencing begins with an arraignment, at which time accused persons are brought before a judge and their alleged crimes are stated. At this stage, a probation officer may file a petition with the court if it is felt that an alternative to incarceration is advisable. The decision is based on the seriousness of the crimes, the likelihood of reform, and the environment to which the accused will be returning.

If probation is imposed, it is always conditional. Criminals are assigned probation officers, who monitor their activities. Conditions are generally imposed; persons on probation must refrain from criminal activities, attend school or training programs, and often confine themselves to a particular geographical area. Probationers are kept under regular surveillance, sometimes by electronic means. If they violate the conditions of probation, they may be resentenced to prison. After the probational period has expired, they may be released into society as free citizens.

Juvenile probation is an attempt to give youthful offenders a second chance at leading useful lives in society. There are a great many opinions as to what sort of environment is most likely to allow and encourage youth to take such a course. The first consideration is the environment in which they lived before being arrested. If they came from reasonably sound homes, they would probably be returned to the custody of their parents and be supervised by a probation officer. They would be required to attend school on a regular basis and might also be assigned to community projects. This method was common in the 1960's but was perceived as less desirable in later decades.

Intensive supervised probation, begun in the 1960's for adults and expanded to include juveniles in the 1980's, is a more structured version of community probation. Probationers are often monitored electronically and may be required to pay restitution to their victims. Intensive counseling is also involved.

At the end of the twentieth century, residential programs for juvenile probationers became far more common. Such programs had their origins in the reform schools of the nineteenth and early twentieth centuries, but many varieties were developed. At one extreme is the boot camp system, modeled on military training methods. Probationers are given intensive physical and educational training and their lives are very highly structured. It is hoped that such harsh discipline will be effective in teaching the youths to abide by the rules of society.

Somewhat less restrictive are group homes, in which the juveniles live together in the community, under the supervision of adults, who either live on the premises or work in shifts. The probationers may be entirely restricted to the home, may be taken on supervised outings, or even given limited privileges in the outside environment, depending on their behavior. The rationale behind this system is to allow offenders to gradually work their way back into the community.

Another system, which became increasingly popular in the 1980's, was to involve youths with the natural environment. This might involve something very much like a year-round summer camp, involving sports, swimming, hiking, arts and crafts, and educational programs. It may be an intensive wilderness survival program. In either case, useful work for the Forestry Service or other government agencies may be involved, including the improvement of trails and the cleanup of wilderness areas. The wilderness approach is often considered especially appropriate for juveniles from inner city areas. It is suggested that an extreme change of environment may change youths' outlook and priorities.

If the court has determined that probationers have broken the law primarily because of an unfortunate home environment, the probationers may be placed in foster care. It is hoped that given a more supportive environment, they will change their ways. Parental visitation may or may not be granted. Along with these methods, a tactic called "shock probation" was introduced late in the twentieth century. Youths are taken to prisons, where they are shown the conditions in the hope that they will change their behavior in order to avoid going to prison themselves.

The Effectiveness of Probation

There is a great deal of controversy surrounding the effectiveness of assorted types of juvenile probation and the effectiveness of actual time in prison. Many statistical and individual studies have been conducted, but they have produced mixed results.

It is necessary to balance the welfare of juvenile offenders with the safety of the communities in which they live. At one extreme are those who believe that prisons are a bad influence in themselves. Young people who may be arrested for relatively minor offenses, such as vandalism or petty theft, will associate with hardened criminals and learn to adopt their lifestyle. Also to be considered is that there is a great deal of violence within the prisons, including sexual abuse of young inmates, both male and female.

On the other hand, there are those who cite an apparent increase in crime among youths and stress that lawful members of the community must be protected. These people often point out that a disproportionate number of juvenile offenders come from inner-city environments, in which crime and drug use is rampant, and that if they return to these communities, they are likely to return to crime.

The increasing use of alcohol and illegal drugs among youths confuses the situation further. The use of alcohol by someone under the legal age or the use of relatively benign drugs such as marijuana is a highly significant factor in the statistics involving youthful crime. As opinions on the law involving such offenses vary widely, the statistics are very often biased according to the viewpoints of those doing the studies.

Generally, it has been found that residential programs involving community involvement and useful training has at least some effect, although accurate figures are difficult to come by. Releasing offenders into the community is generally ineffective, especially if the community involved is an area in which both adult and juvenile crime is common.

Conclusions

The prevalence of criminal activities among young people in modern times has led to various attempts to control this problem. Beginning in the late twentieth century there was an increasing call for youths who commit serious crimes, especially violent crimes, to be tried and punished as if they were adults, even including subjecting them to capital punishment. At the same time, there were many attempts to consider alternative punishments in order to prevent young offenders from becoming lifetime criminals.

The problem is not easy to solve. On one hand, there is a natural tendency to want to treat children as gently as possible in the hope that they can overcome unfortunate environmental conditions and become useful members of society. On the other hand, the increasing presence of street gangs and juvenile criminal activity causes great fear among the adult population.

—*Marc Goldstein*

Suggested Readings

Elliott Currie's *Crime and Punishment in America* (New York: Metropolitan Books, 1998) is a general discussion of sentencing alternatives, including probation, based on the premise that traditional prisons are not effective. A general discussion of juvenile crime, with the emphasis on alternatives to actual imprisonment, can be found in Alan R. Coffey's *Juvenile Corrections: Treatment and Rehabilitation* (Englewood Cliffs, N.J.: Prentice-Hall, 1975). Dean L. Champion's *Criminal Justice in the United States* (2d ed. Chicago: Nelson Hall, 1997) is a general summary of the modern legal system of the United States, with an extensive treatment of juvenile crime and alternatives to incarceration. A statistical analysis of assorted probation methods can be found in *Probation, Parole, and Community Corrections* by Robert M. Carter, Daniel Gluer, and Leslie T. Wilkins (3d ed. New York: John Wiley and Sons, 1984). A study of assorted methods of dealing with juvenile crimes is *Beyond Probation* by Charles A. Murray and Louis A. Cox, Jr. (Beverly Hills: Sage, 1979). In *Juvenile Delinquency and Juvenile Justice* (New York: John Wiley and Sons, 1987) Joseph W. Rogers and Larry Mays provide a general discussion on juvenile crime and assorted attempted solutions. Both *Adolescent Gangs: Old Issues, New Approaches*, edited by Curtis W. Branch (Philadelphia: Brunner/Mazel, 1999), and *Securing Our Children's Future: New Approaches to Juvenile Justice and Youth Violence*, edited by Gary S. Katzmann (Washington, D.C.: Brookings Institution Press, 2002), consider the issue of juvenile probation.

See also Age of majority; Criminal records; Family law practice; Juvenile criminal proceedings; Legal guardians; Parole; Probation, adult; Sentencing.

PROSECUTORS

Government attorneys responsible for investigating and pursuing
charges against defendants accused of violating criminal laws

The prosecutor is a central figure in the criminal justice system. By making discretionary decisions about which cases to pursue and which charges to bring, prosecutors play a significant role in determining the fate of people suspected of committing crimes. Prosecutors must work closely with the police in determining how to investigate crimes and which defendants to pursue. After the police make an arrest, the prosecutor takes charge of the case and sees it through to its conclusion, whether charges are dropped or the defendant is convicted and sentenced to prison. Because most American prosecutors are elected officials, they are responsive to the values of their local communities in deciding which charges to apply against criminal defendants.

The Organization of Prosecution

Prosecution in the United States is organized in conjunction with the different levels of government. In particular, the prosecution of federal criminal cases is handled separately from the prosecution of cases alleging violations of state laws and local ordinances.

The attorney general of the United States, an appointed member of the president's cabinet and the head of the U.S. Justice Department, bears overall responsibility for the prosecution of federal crimes. Federal crimes are those acts made punishable by statutes enacted by the U.S. Congress. Examples of federal crimes include smuggling, bank fraud, counterfeiting, drug trafficking, and bank robbery. Many people convicted of federal crimes engaged either in white-collar crimes, such as bank fraud, or in drug trafficking. The prosecution of each federal criminal case occurs in the U.S. district court whose jurisdiction encompasses the city or town where the crime occurred. The federal prosecutor who actually presents the case against the defendant is called a U.S. attorney, and there is one such attorney in each of the ninety-four districts throughout the United States. U.S. attorneys are appointed by the president of the United States and supervised by the U.S. attorney general.

Most crimes, such as burglary, murder, sexual battery, and larceny, are violations of state law. Local prosecutors in each city or county bear primary responsibility for prosecuting state crimes. Depending on the state, these prosecutors are called county prosecutors, district attorneys, or state's attorneys. In most states, local prosecutors are elected officials who must please the public with their performance in order to stay in office. Elected local prosecutors do not answer to any authority other than the voters. There is typically no judge or higher prosecutor who can tell them to pursue or drop particular cases. In only a few states are attorneys general, the chief legal officers of their states, responsible for overseeing the decisions and actions of local prosecutors. State attorneys general, who are usually selected by voters in statewide elections, typically have authority to prosecute only specific categories of cases, such as consumer fraud that occurs statewide. State attorneys general work closely with local prosecutors and share information, but local prosecutors make their own decisions about which defendants to pursue and which charges to file.

The Prosecutor's Duties

The prosecutor's success depends on the police doing a good job in gathering evidence. If the police make mistakes during an investigation, the prosecutor may be deprived of key evidence, either because the police overlooked the evidence or because a judge ruled the evidence inadmissible after it was obtained improperly. Thus, the prosecutor works closely with the police to identify and investigate criminal suspects and thereby helps to

---

TYPES OF PROSECUTORS

U.S. Attorney: Prosecutor for the United States government in each of the ninety-four federal judicial districts nationwide, who is responsible for prosecuting defendants accused of federal crimes

State Attorney General: Chief legal officer in state government, typically elected by the voters, who represents the state in legal matters and prosecutes defendants accused of violating specific state criminal laws

District Attorney or County Prosecutor: Local official, elected by the voters in most cities and counties, who is responsible for prosecuting the majority of criminal defendants accused of violating state criminal laws

ensure that proper evidence is obtained. In many cities the police
seek the prosecutor's approval before asking a judge to issue an
arrest or search warrant.

After an arrest is made, the prosecutor may make arguments to
the court about whether bail should be set and the amount of bail
money that suspects must present in order to gain pretrial release.
The prosecutor must also present evidence at preliminary hearings in order to persuade a judge that enough evidence exists
against a suspect to justify moving the case forward. In order to
obtain evidence, the prosecutor interviews witnesses and victims
while relying on evidence gathered by the police. Most important,
the prosecutor decides which charges to file against the defendant. In a homicide case, for example, the prosecutor must evaluate the suspect's motives and actions in order to decide which
charges to pursue. If there is evidence that a killing was premeditated, the charge may be first-degree or aggravated murder. If the
killing was intentional but not premeditated or was the result of
negligence, the prosecutor may pursue charges of second-degree
murder or manslaughter. In some cases the prosecutor decides to
drop the charges when there is insufficient evidence, when there
are serious doubts about the suspect's guilt, or when the offense is
too minor to be worth absorbing the time of staff members in the
prosecutor's office.

As cases proceed through various preliminary hearings toward trial, prosecutors decide whether to discuss a plea agreement with the criminal defense attorney representing the defendant. In order to obtain a sure conviction and avoid the time and
expense of trial, prosecutors engage in plea bargaining in most
cases. In exchange for the defendant's agreement to plead guilty,
the prosecutor may offer to reduce charges or to recommend a
specific sentence to the judge.

Prosecutors sometimes intentionally overcharge defendants
by filing multiple charges, including some for which there is little
evidence. By overcharging, prosecutors have more bargaining
chips to give away in the plea bargaining process without risking
that the defendant will receive a lesser sentence than one that
would likely be imposed after conviction at trial. If no plea agreement develops, the prosecutor takes the case to trial.

In addition to their formal duties, local prosecutors often maintain active communications with the news media to keep the public informed of current developments. They also maintain contact

with political party leaders in order to enhance their own prospects for reelection. In large cities and counties the prosecutor may not handle any cases directly. Instead, a large staff of assistant prosecutors handles the actual plea bargaining and trials while the prosecutor supervises the assistants, oversees the annual budget, and maintains relations with the news media and governmental offices. Thus, a prosecutor may act as a political figure and government administrator rather than as an actual courtroom attorney. The office of prosecutor is the traditional stepping stone to higher political office, and many judges, legislators, and governors first began their careers as local prosecutors.

The Prosecutor and the Criminal Trial

The prosecutor represents the state in the courtroom by presenting evidence of the defendant's guilt and attempting to persuade the judge or jury to render a guilty verdict.

During jury selection the prosecutor must question prospective jurors in order to exclude those who might be biased. The trial begins when the prosecutor makes an opening statement describing the charges and the evidence that will be presented to prove the defendant's guilt. The prosecutor then bears the burden of presenting sufficient evidence to prove the case, presenting and questioning witnesses, submitting documents and objects into evidence (such as physical evidence), and making arguments about how the evidence demonstrates the defendant's guilt. When the defense presents witnesses and counterarguments, the prosecutor can ask additional questions about testimony and evidence. The prosecutor can also respond to the arguments made by the defense. The trial concludes when the jury or judge renders a verdict. There can be a guilty verdict only when the prosecutor presents evidence and arguments to persuade the jury or judge that the defendant is guilty beyond a reasonable doubt.

As an officer of the court, the prosecutor is obligated to ensure that the defendant's rights are protected and that a fair trial takes place. However, because local prosecutors are elected officials, critics fear that they feel pressured to please the public by ensuring that someone is convicted for every crime that occurs. Thus, they may become too zealous about their role in stopping criminals and thereby lose sight of their duties to protect defendants' rights and to ensure that the available evidence clearly establishes a defendant's guilt.

When a defendant pleads guilty or is convicted at trial, the prosecutor may recommend a sentence to the judge. In jurisdictions in which judges have discretion to determine sentences, they often place great weight on prosecutors' recommendations. In other jurisdictions, the sentences for specific crimes are mandated by the legislature through sentencing guidelines. Thus, the prosecutor's influence over the ultimate sentence stems from the choice of charges originally pursued rather than from a sentence recommendation after conviction.

Decision Making by Prosecutors

Prosecutors may use different approaches to determine which cases to pursue and how to pursue them. Some prosecutors feel obligated to proceed with any case in which there is evidence that a suspect may be guilty of a crime. In some cases, the prosecutor may be unsure about the defendant's guilt and simply leave it to the jury or judge to decide. In such situations, the prosecutor recognizes that some defendants will ultimately be acquitted at trial because a jury or judge did not believe that the evidence proved guilt beyond a reasonable doubt. Other prosecutors pursue cases only when they themselves are convinced of the defendant's guilt and believe that enough evidence clearly exists to convict them at trial. Such prosecutors are likely to dismiss charges against defendants when the evidence against them is uncertain or weak.

In other jurisdictions prosecutors' decisions about which cases to pursue may be influenced by the available resources in the criminal justice system. If the assistant prosecutors are busy with cases involving serious crimes, defendants charged with minor offenses may have the charges dropped and be set free. Similarly, if the county jail is nearly full, prosecutors may need to take account of available cell space in making bail recommendations or deciding which cases to pursue.

Because local prosecutors are elected officials who frequently want public attention in order to seek higher office, there are risks that prosecutors use political considerations in deciding which cases to prosecute. In some situations, prosecutors have launched investigations against political opponents while ignoring misdeeds committed by political supporters. Other prosecutors have engaged in discriminatory actions against minority religious or racial groups.

—Christopher E. Smith

Suggested Readings

A discussion of federal prosecutors is presented in James Eisenstein's *Counsel for the United States: U.S. Attorneys in the Political and Legal System* (Baltimore: Johns Hopkins University Press, 1978). The duties and roles of local prosecutors are examined in Lief Carter's *The Limits of Order* (Lexington, Mass.: D.C. Heath, 1974) and David Neubauer's *Criminal Justice in Middle America* (Morristown, N.J.: General Learning Press, 1974). Discussions of decision-making prosecutors are presented in Joan Jacoby's *The American Prosecutor: A Search for Identity* (Lexington, Mass.: D.C. Heath, 1980) and William McDonald's *The Prosecutor* (Beverly Hills, Calif.: Sage, 1979). For an inside look at prosecution from a prosecutor's perspective see David Heilbroner's *Rough Justice: Days and Nights of a Young D.A.* (New York: Pantheon, 1990) and Judith Rowland's *The Ultimate Violation* (New York: Doubleday, 1985). *The Prosecutors: A Year in the Life of a District Attorney's Office*, by Gary Delsohn (New York: E. P. Dutton, 2003), is a journalistic account of the work of assistant district attorneys in Sacramento, California.

See also Attorney types; Attorneys general, state; Criminal justice system; District attorneys; Law enforcement; Officers of the court; Public defenders; Suspects; Trials.

PUBLIC DEFENDERS

Attorneys compensated by the government for providing legal representation to criminal defendants who are too poor to hire their own lawyers

The public defender is a key actor in the American adversarial system of criminal justice because this attorney is responsible for ensuring that each defendant's rights are protected and each defendant's case is presented in a forceful, professional manner. Public defenders represent criminal defendants who cannot afford to hire their own attorneys. Although public defenders are paid by the government, they bear the professional responsibility of vigorously defending accused persons, even those against whom there is clear-cut evidence of guilt.

Public defenders must make sure that each indigent defendant's constitutional rights are protected and that the prosecution proves its case before any poor person is convicted of a crime and receives a sentence of incarceration or death. Public defenders must play this role through the processing of criminal cases, from the initial police interrogations of suspects through jury trials and initial appeals. American history has demonstrated that when there are no lawyers assigned to represent poor defendants, there are grave risks that innocent people will be convicted of crimes or that police officers and prosecutors will violate constitutional rights in the course of seeking criminal convictions.

The Constitution and Adversarial Justice

The colonists who established the United States and wrote the U.S. Constitution brought with them from England a profound distrust of governmental power. From English legal traditions they borrowed institutions and practices that they hoped would diminish the risk that police and prosecutors could arrest, convict, and imprison people unfairly. In the Bill of Rights, they established people's rights to fair trials, trial by jury, freedom from compelled self-incrimination, and other mechanisms designed to reduce the risk that prosecutors would wield excessive power. In drawing from these English traditions, the American founders established an adversarial system of justice in which the defendant would have the right to present arguments and evidence in opposition to the prosecution before a decision was rendered by a neutral group of citizens making up the jury. A key element of this adversarial system established by the Sixth Amendment was Americans' right to counsel during criminal proceedings.

During the nineteenth century, the Sixth Amendment right to counsel was interpreted in a limited fashion. The provision was considered to apply only in federal cases, and it was regarded as barring any governmental effort to prevent defendants from hiring their own attorneys. As a result, poor defendants' access to adversarial justice was limited to whatever ability they possessed to represent themselves in making arguments and presenting evidence. Illiterate, uneducated, and inarticulate defendants were inevitably overwhelmed by the prosecution, regardless of their actual guilt or innocence. Eventually, the Supreme Court inter-

---

PUBLIC DEFENDERS AND THE SIXTH AMENDMENT

The office of government public defenders owes its existence to the final phrase of the Sixth Amendment:

In all criminal prosecutions, the accused shall enjoy the right to a speedy and public trial, by an impartial jury of the State and district wherein the crime shall have been committed; which district shall have been previously ascertained by law, and to be informed of the nature and cause of the accusation; to be confronted with the witnesses against him; to have compulsory process for obtaining witnesses in his favor, and to have the assistance of counsel for his defence.

---

preted the Sixth Amendment to require that the government supply attorneys to represent poor defendants in federal cases, so that all defendants would have genuine access to the adversarial process (*Johnson v. Zerbst*, 1938).

During the twentieth century, many states acted on their own to supply attorneys for indigent criminal defendants in state court cases. By the early 1960's, fewer than a dozen states still refused to supply attorneys for poor defendants. The Supreme Court remedied this problem by reinterpreting the Sixth Amendment to require that attorneys be provided free of charge to represent indigent defendants facing felony charges in state courts (*Gideon v. Wainwright*, 1963). This interpretation was expanded to require representation in initial appeals after conviction (*Douglas v. California*, 1963) and, subsequently, in any case in which a defendant faced the possibility of incarceration (*Argersinger v. Hamlin*, 1972). As a result of these judicial decisions, state and county governments were required to develop methods for hiring, compensating, and assigning attorneys to represent indigent criminal defendants.

Methods of Providing Representation

Three primary means have developed for providing attorneys for indigent criminal defendants. In most urban areas, states and counties have established public defender offices, employing salaried attorneys full time to provide representation for indigent defendants. These attorneys become specialists in criminal law and frequently bring great zeal to their representation of defendants, having made a conscious career choice to become public defenders. Although these attorneys benefit from specialized training and expertise, they are often hampered by relatively low salaries and high caseloads. If there is a surge in criminal cases, each attorney in the office will have to assume a greater burden, because limited government budgets frequently preclude the possibility of hiring additional attorneys. Many attorneys suffer from "burnout," and the high turnover rate in the office means that many public defenders are young, inexperienced attorneys who may not stay with their initial career choice long enough to develop the expertise necessary for skilled advocacy. In addition, these attorneys often find that their clients are uncooperative. Because the defendants know that their attorneys are on the government's payroll, they sometimes erroneously believe that the public defenders are actually working for the prosecution. When the defendants do not cooperate in supplying information necessary for mounting a vigorous defense, public defenders' jobs are made much more difficult.

Many states and counties, especially those outside urban areas, provide representation through an appointed counsel system. Attorneys in private practice ask to be placed on the local court's list of lawyers willing to accept appointments to represent indigent defendants. As the need arises, an individual lawyer will be asked to represent a specific poor defendant. The government pays the lawyer a modest hourly rate for handling each case. In some counties, the court clerk simply assigns the next available attorney from the list when a defendant cannot afford to hire a lawyer. In other places, judges choose attorneys for each assignment. When the list is not followed in order, there are risks that judges will steer cases to their political supporters and allies.

Attorneys who participate as appointed counsel do not always possess interest or expertise in criminal law. Frequently, inexperienced attorneys fresh out of law school take criminal case appointments as a means to pay their bills while they work toward establishing a law practice for tax cases, corporate matters, or other legal issues that interest them. As a result, there may be questions about the enthusiasm and skill employed by these attorneys on behalf of indigent defendants. Many defendants believe that their appointed attorneys were too quick to engage in plea bargaining simply because they were not interested in mounting a vigorous defense. Moreover, the relatively low hourly pay scale can encourage appointed attorneys to seek quick plea bargains rather than risk assuming uncompensated costs in preparing for expensive, time-consuming trials. Some private attorneys earn all of their income from handling a high volume of quick plea bargains in order to accumulate fee payments for many cases. As a result, there are serious questions about the quality of representation provided for indigent defendants by appointed counsel.

The third method of providing representation is used in only 10 percent of counties nationwide. In the contract counsel system, each year attorneys bid for the opportunity to represent all the indigent defendants in a county. One attorney or law firm will be awarded the contract to handle all cases for a specified hourly rate or predetermined annual fee. The quality of representation will vary according to the skill and dedication of the attorney or attorneys who win the annual contract.

The American mechanisms for providing public defenders do not exhaust all possible solutions. Denmark seeks to ensure that defendants receive skilled representation by limiting appointments to experienced attorneys who are certified to represent criminal defendants. In Ontario, Canada, defendants are given vouchers that they can use to select their own attorneys, who will be compensated by the government by taking the case. In a few countries, and occasionally in American counties that exhaust their annual budget for public defense before the end of the year, judges require attorneys to represent indigent defendants without any compensation. In such situations, however, the attorneys have little incentive to prepare and present an extensive defense on behalf of the defendant.

Process of Indigent Representation

The U.S. Supreme Court issued several decisions identifying which stages in the justice process require the opportunity to be represented by counsel. Fairness in an adversarial system of justice requires professional representation early in the criminal process in order to monitor and counteract the actions taken by the prosecution and police in gathering evidence. Yet public defenders often have fewer resources than prosecutors. While the police serve as investigators who gather evidence for the prosecution, public defenders are often completely on their own in gathering evidence and preparing a case.

Indigent people arrested for crimes are entitled to be represented by a public defender during any questioning by police or prosecutors. The public defender is responsible for ensuring that the suspect's constitutional right against compelled self-incrimination is not violated through improper or coercive questioning techniques. The presence of the defense lawyer also guards against the risk that the police or prosecutor may testify untruthfully about what the suspect said during questioning. Although defendants have a right to have a public defender present, many poor defendants waive their right to have a lawyer present during questioning, either because they do not understand the importance of professional representation or because they believe that they gain leniency by immediately cooperating with the police.

Poor defendants also have a right to a public defender during other preliminary stages. Bail hearings are a particular important stage for these defendants because they are unlikely to be able to secure release if a judge requires them to post cash in order to be released from jail pending trial. The public defender must attempt to persuade the judge that the indigent defendant can be released on his or her own recognizance without posing a risk of flight or danger to the community.

In most cases, public defenders seek favorable plea bargains in which the indigent defendant will enter a guilty plea to a reduced charge. Such plea bargains terminate more than 90 percent of cases that are not dismissed for lack of evidence early in the proceedings. Plea agreements may be discussed with the prosecution during each stage of the criminal process until an agreement is reached. Many indigent defendants do not realize that all defense attorneys, including those representing affluent clients, discuss possible plea bargains with the prosecution. Poor defendants may automatically assume that their public defender is "selling them out" because they are too poor to hire their own attorney. There may be some truth to this assumption if the public defender is not aggressively advancing the client's interests during the negotiations. Such perceptions can contribute to friction and a lack of cooperation between indigent defendants and public defenders.

Public defenders play an important role in the adversarial justice process. Yet because they are frequently hampered by low pay, limited resources, high caseloads, and uncooperative clients, there are continuing questions about whether poor criminal defendants receive adequate representation and protection of their constitutional rights.

—*Christopher E. Smith*

Suggested Readings
   Studies of public defenders in trial courts are presented in Lisa McIntyre, *The Public Defender: The Practice of Law in the Shadows of Repute* (Chicago: University of Chicago Press, 1987); Lynn Mather, *Plea Bargaining or Trial? The Process of Criminal-Case Disposition* (Lexington, Mass.: Lexington Books, 1979); and Robert Hermann, Eric Single, and John Boston, *Counsel for the Poor: Criminal Defense in Urban America* (Lexington, Mass.: Lexington Books, 1977). One study of public defenders' appellate work is David T. Wasserman, *A Sword for the Convicted* (New York: Greenwood Press, 1990). One of the most famous articles discussing public defenders is Jonathan Casper's "Did You Have a Lawyer When You Went to Court? No, I Had a Public Defender," *Yale Review of Law and Social Change* 1 (Spring, 1971).

See also Attorney types; Criminal procedure; Defendants; Defense attorneys; Indigent criminal defendants; Presumption of innocence; Prosecutors; Suspects.

PUBLIC INTEREST LAW

Law practice that involves group legal activity, particularly litigation that goes beyond the interests of individual clients and strives for legal reform that benefits the larger public

Public interest law came into being because reformers considered the American legal system to be flawed. The legal system in the United States is described as an adversary system in which the parties to a conflict do battle, through their lawyers, in the arena of a courtroom. It was long assumed that this was the best way to arrive at truth, and from truth justice would emerge. In the 1960's and 1970's, however, critics of the adversary system came to believe that it works well only when the two sides have substantially equal resources, such as information and wealth. Often they do not.

Redressing Inequity

Reformers recognize that some groups and interests are unrepresented or underrepresented because they lack economic and political power. Reformers seek to correct this inequity not by radically changing the system but by creating public interest law firms to defend the interests of those who have been harmed by economic or political forces that they, on their own, cannot match. Such law firms seek to promote the public interest by making the legal system, as well as American society, more closely approximate democratic ideals. While private law firms seek to make profits, public interest law firms do not. They promote a cause. Their cause may include environmental protection; consumer protection; the protection of children; equitable treatment of minorities, women, or the disabled; or protection against government restrictions on the use of private property.

Consumer advocate Ralph Nader rose to fame during the early 1960's, when he challenged the safety of American automobiles.

To better promote a cause, public interest lawyers and law firms try to attract favorable publicity. Publicity is a means for furthering their cause when it results in increased contributions to the organization. Such contributions increase the firm's ability to promote its vision of the public interest—whatever that may be. Publicity can be beneficial to a cause even when a test case in the courts does not secure the plaintiff's goal, as when Ralph Nader, perhaps the nation's best known public interest lawyer, was unable to end the airline practice of overselling flights and bumping ticket holders after all seats were filled. The publicity from Nader's case led the Civil Aeronautics Board to regulate the awarding of compensation in the interest of bumped passengers, which it might not have done otherwise.

Public Interest Lawyers

Lawyers who practice public interest law earn less money than attorneys of comparable age and experience who work with private law firms. According to the *National Law Journal*, the median starting salary in small, private law firms (two to ten lawyers) in 1997 was $35,000 per year. The starting salaries for lawyers with public interest law firms varied, but it rarely exceeded $35,000 per year, and most such lawyers earned less than that. Associates hired by top private firms specializing in such fields as intellectual property or securities law receive much higher starting salaries. Because there are large profits to be earned in these fields, private firms can afford to offer high starting salaries to attract some of the most talented recent law-school graduates. Public interest law firms, however, are nonprofit organizations which, therefore, cannot offer competitive salaries.

The low salaries paid by public interest law firms do not, however, result in their being staffed by lawyers of little talent. The characteristics of public interest lawyers are more like those of lawyers in top private law firms than of those hired into small law firms with starting salaries of $35,000. Public interest lawyers are more likely to have graduated from prestigious law schools, to have been in the top 25 percent of their class, and to have been on the law review. Public interest lawyers are more likely to have clerked for a judge, a mark of prestige, than lawyers in small private firms. But if these highly competent people spend their whole careers in public interest law, they will earn far less than partners in major private law firms.

Public interest lawyers are attracted to the practice of public interest law by something other than money. They appear to be motivated by a desire to do good, to make U.S. society better. When asked whether it is worth the loss of income, they say that it is. In addition to the satisfaction derived from the feeling that they are doing good, there are other benefits that may attract them. They sometimes have the opportunity to associate with powerful government officials and other high-profile people. They also have opportunities to handle important cases that sometimes attract much media attention considerably earlier in their careers than they would as young associates in a private, for-profit law firm.

Funding

Since public interest law firms do not receive fees from their clients, they must raise funds from other sources to meet their expenses. In the 1960's and well into the 1970's philanthropic foundations were a major source of such funding. By the mid-1970's, even though these foundations contributed at substantially the same rate, the number of public interest law firms increased. Thus, the proportion of their funding that came from foundations declined. The late 1970's saw individual foundations, such as the Ford Foundation, actually decreasing their contributions to public interest law firms. The situation was made worse by a weak economy. The decade of the 1980's was a time when those who ran philanthropic foundations were pessimistic about the ability to solve social problems, and they looked with disfavor on litigation, which is the primary tactic of public interest law firms. While foundations in the 1990's were less generous to public interest law firms than they were in the 1960's, they remained a significant source of funding.

With the decline in foundation funding and cuts in federal spending on social programs and environmental protection during the presidency of conservative Republican Ronald Reagan in the 1980's, liberal public interest firms utilized direct mail techniques to raise money and build a base of political support for their efforts. They added many individuals to their membership lists and added corporate donors as well. Besides contributing money, corporate donors sometimes provided access to photocopiers and computers.

Another source of support on which public interest law firms have relied is court-awarded attorney fees. There are several federal statutes that permit the awarding of such fees to successful plaintiffs in matters considered to be in the public interest. In this way, government has itself encouraged public interest litigation. When public interest lawyers are successful and a court awards them fees, the awards are generally at the going rate for private, profit-making lawyers. Since the salaries of public interest lawyers are low, their firms are able to use court-awarded fees to finance other cases.

EXAMPLES OF PUBLIC INTEREST LAW FIRMS AND THEIR OBJECTIVES

- **Earthjustice Legal Defense Fund (1997), formerly Sierra Club Legal Defense Fund (1971):** Protects the environment from pollutants and works toward the preservation of species and habitats
- **Center for Democracy and Technology (1994):** Promotes public policies that advance civil liberties and democratic values in new computer and communications technology
- **Landmark Legal Foundation (1976):** Promotes individual rights, government accountability, and conservative values
- **National Right to Work Legal Foundation (1968):** Opposes compulsory union membership as a condition of employment
- **NAACP Legal Defense and Education Fund (1940):** Defends African Americans against all forms of racial discrimination and supports affirmative action

---

Public interest law firms have found still other ways to raise funds. Some have participated in workplace fund-raising drives, in which employees may choose to contribute to them. Some have raised funds by publishing attractive magazines, which they send to their dues-paying members. Such magazines can lure sympathetic members of the public into joining the organization. Environmental organizations have successfully used this technique. The National Wildlife Federation produces Ranger Rick, a publication for children.

Some law schools and their alumni organizations have formed public interest law foundations. These foundations offer fellowships to students planning to practice public interest law. They also finance internships at public interest law firms and loan-forgiveness programs for graduates who go into public interest law. In 1993 Ralph Nader's Harvard Law School class of 1958 went beyond this and established the Appleseed Foundation, the aim of which was to establish Appleseed Centers for Law and Justice in communities. The purpose of these Appleseed Centers is to engage in community organizing as well as litigation. A major criticism of liberal public interest law firms has been that they have overemphasized litigation and neglected community organizing.

Ideological Clash

The Appleseed Centers for Law and Justice reflect the goals and values of the left, or liberal, side of the political spectrum. Indeed, most early public interest law firms established in the 1960's and early 1970's reflected the goals and values of political liberals, and Ralph Nader and his supporters were active in the establishment of several of them. By the early 1970's, however, conservatives saw a need to present their own interpretations of the public interest to the courts. They feared that liberal public interest groups had achieved a near monopoly on the legal interpretations being placed before the judiciary and hoped to rectify that situation.

The first conservative public interest law firm, the Pacific Legal Foundation, was established in 1973 in Sacramento, California. In its early years, it had difficulty raising funds, but it presented its conservative view of the public interest through the submission of *amici curiae* (friend of the court) legal briefs in cases in which it took an interest but did not directly represent either party. This is a tactic used by both liberal and conservative public interest groups. It is less costly than actually litigating a case. However, the Pacific Legal Foundation sponsored some cases itself, and, as it began to win and generate some favorable publicity, additional contributions began to flow to the firm, allowing it to grow in size and activity. The Pacific Legal Foundation has been less likely than liberal public interest firms to bring test cases. Instead, it has assisted government agencies being sued by liberal public interest firms. In some civil suits brought by private individuals against businesses, the Pacific Legal Foundation has assisted the businesses in appealing large judgments against them.

Other conservative public interest firms have been created across the United States. Most have remained smaller than the Pacific Legal Foundation. While some conservative organizations have generally supported private property rights and opposed government regulation of business, others have represented conservative positions on social issues. Americans United for Life, for example, has opposed abortion and euthanasia. As ideological clashes take place in other parts of government, they also take place in the courts.

—*Patricia A. Behlar*

Suggested Readings

Criticism of lawyers for allying themselves with the powerful and neglecting the weak of American society can be found in Ralph Nader and Wesley J. Smith, *No Contest: Corporate Lawyers and the Perversion of Justice in America* (New York: Random House, 1996), and Jerold S. Auerbach, *Unequal Justice: Lawyers and Social Change in Modern America* (New York: Oxford University Press, 1976). A very thorough and objective study of public interest law is Burton Weisbrod, Joel F. Handler, and Neil K. Komesar's *Public Interest Law: An Economic and Institutional Analysis* (Berkeley: University of California Press, 1978). General readers will find a wealth of information in this work. More recent and more accessible to the general reader is Nan Aron, *Liberty and Justice for All: Public Interest Law in the 1980s and Beyond* (Boulder, Colo.: Westview Press, 1989). Most of the information in this book is drawn from liberal groups. For an examination of the conservative public interest movement, see Lee Epstein, *Conservatives in Court* (Knoxville: University of Tennessee Press, 1985).

See also Adversary system; *Amicus curiae* briefs; Attorney types; Civil actions; Court-awarded fees; Law firm partners and associates; Law firms; Law schools; Test cases.

PUNITIVE DAMAGES

Damage awards over and above the amount assigned for restitution of loss that are intended to punish a defendant rather than to provide victims with compensation

Punitive damages, sometimes called exemplary damages because they seek to make an example of a wrongdoer, punish offenders for extreme wrongdoing, notably in cases involving gross negligence, fraud, violence, or malice. A system was developed in England in the thirteenth century in which monetary penalties, called amercements, were awarded by the courts in civil cases. The awards became frequent and often excessive. As a result, the Magna Carta included provisions limiting amercements and attempted to allow only amounts reasonable for the wrongdoing.

Similarly, the Eighth Amendment to the U.S. Constitution reads, "Excessive bail shall not be required, nor excessive fines imposed, nor cruel and unusual punishment inflicted." There have been several constitutional challenges to the legality of punitive damages, among them *Bankers Life & Casualty Co. v. Crenshaw* (1988) and *Pacific Mutual Life Insurance Co. v. Haslip* (1991). Nevertheless, these awards have become more frequent since the 1960's—so much so that many insurance policies now exclude payment of loss for punitive damages. There have been awards of more than one million dollars when actual damages were relatively small.

See also Breach of contract; Civil law; Commercial litigation; Compensatory damages; Damages; Indemnity; Judgment proof; Liability, civil and criminal; Restitution; Strict liability; Torts.

REASONABLE DOUBT

Standard applied in a criminal case to justify a verdict of not guilty when the case against the defendant is insufficiently conclusive

The requirement that a defendant in a criminal case should be convicted only if a jury is persuaded of the person's guilt beyond a reasonable doubt has a long history in Roman law and common law dating to the fourth century. By the eighteenth century the requirement of proof beyond a reasonable doubt was established in its current form. The requirement of proof beyond reasonable doubt in criminal cases reflects society's judgment that it is better to allow a few guilty defendants to go free than to increase the chance of an innocent defendant being convicted.

In a criminal trial, the prosecution must prove each element of a crime beyond a reasonable doubt, or the defendant is entitled to acquittal. This requirement applies to both state and federal criminal trials, and it is based on the due process clauses of the Fifth and Fourteenth Amendments. Without the benefit of a proper instruction to the jury on the concept of proof beyond a reasonable doubt, a defendant is functionally deprived of the Sixth Amendment right to a trial by jury (*Sullivan v. Louisiana*, 1993).

Some courts and commentators have stated that reasonable doubt is an undefinable term. Others have said either that it is best left undefined or that what constitutes reasonable doubt should be left to the common sense of the jury. The due process clauses of the Fifth and Fourteenth Amendments do not require a court to define reasonable doubt for a jury, but many courts do define it for juries.

What, then, is reasonable doubt? Clearly, reasonable doubt does not exist if the doubt is based only on a hunch or mere suspicion of innocence. Nor can doubts based on imaginary suppositions or fanciful scenarios, or on a wish to avoid making an unpleasant or difficult decision, be considered "reasonable." Reasonable doubt should be based on evidence or lack of evidence. It must be doubt that a reasonable person would entertain in making a serious decision. The reasonable doubt concept does not require a jury to find that the elements of a crime are proved to an absolute or mathematical certainty. Rather, it means that a defendant should be convicted if a reasonable person would find that a strong probability exists—in the light of the evidence presented in the case—that the defendant is guilty.

See also Acquittal; Appellate practice; Burden of proof; Directed verdicts; Due process of law; Pleas; Presumption of innocence; Probable cause; Trials; Verdicts.

RELEASE

Settling or giving up of a claim a cause of action or a right to be enforced

A release is an abandonment of a claim generally in the form of a written settlement agreement. A release means that a party gives up rights. In tort litigation, which involves civil wrongs done by one party against another, more than 95 percent of cases settle prior to a final verdict. The settlement agreement contains a release of a tort cause of action.

Releases of claims exist in other fields of the law as well. For example, a party may agree to release the other party from a contractual duty. A creditor may release a debtor from a debt owed. A guarantor of a promissory note may be released or discharged from the note. A promissory note may be renegotiated. In the field of real property, a quitclaim deed is regarded as a release deed. In the field of bankruptcy, property may be released from the bankruptcy estate for equitable or statutory reasons.

—*Michael L. Rustad*

See also Consent decree; Contracts; Dismissal; Torts; Trials.

REPORTERS, SUPREME COURT

Employees of the U.S. Supreme Court responsible for publishing and disseminating decisions of the justices in an accurate, timely, and uniform manner

Although unheralded and little known except to legal historians, Supreme Court reporters provide access to the judicial opinions that are the primary source of law in the U.S. system of justice. Reporters are the conduits through which the Court disseminates its opinions on the spirit and letter of the law.

On a daily basis, reporters provide draft opinions and other working documents that the justices employ in their decision-making process. Other duties include editing the Court's opinions before publication. The reporters also add the preface or headnote and record how the justices voted. They supervise printing of the opinions in *United States Reports*, the Court's official publication. Reporters also keep rough drafts of the justices' decisions secret from the public until publication. If a copy of the draft opinion leaked before finalization, the effects could harm the litigants or even society at large.

When the first U.S. Congress established the federal judiciary in 1789, neither the legislators nor the justices envisioned the need for a Court reporter. Lawyers had local court decisions in manuscript form and printed English law books, which included the decisions of the English common-law courts. As a practical matter, the Court did not have any decisions to disseminate when it began its work in New York City in 1790. It was not until 1816 that the Court appointed its first official reporter.

Publishing the Court's Decisions

A legal entrepreneur, Philadelphia lawyer Alexander J. Dallas, published the first comprehensive volume of U.S. law reports in 1790. Dallas published the first *United States Reports* for profit and without a single decision of the new nation's highest court. The book contained Pennsylvania decisions dating from 1754. Justices provided Dallas with written decisions to the extent that they existed; justices were not required to submit their decisions in writing. For oral decisions, Dallas relied on notes taken by him or others in attendance. He published the Court's opinions from 1790 until 1800. When the Court moved from Philadelphia to Washington in 1800, a District of Columbia judge, William Cranch, became the unofficial reporter. He published the Court's decisions until 1815.

Congress officially created the Court reporter's office in 1816. The Court then appointed attorney Henry Wheaton as its first official reporter in 1817. A bitterly contested lawsuit erupted between Wheaton and Richard Peters, Wheaton's successor, over Peters's reissuing the volumes of Court decisions originally published by Wheaton. Peters planned to publish Wheaton's twenty-five volumes of reports in a six-volume digest for less than a third of the price of the originals. Wheaton contended the action violated his copyright and thus threatened the market for his volumes.

In *Wheaton v. Peters* (1834), the first decision on copyright law, the Court held its opinions were in the public domain. Protection applied only to the reporter's commentaries and other notes. It was not until 1834 that the Court even required the filing of opinions. The printed record of the Court began in 1837. From 1863 to 1871, two records of opinions, a printed version and a manuscript version, coexisted.

Greater Access

The Court's decision in *Wheaton v. Peters* was a milestone in the history of legal publishing. Where case reports had once been scarce because of the high prices charged by copyright holders, publishers in various states raced to publish less expensive editions for use by lawyers, judges, and other citizens. The Court was playing an ever-greater role in shaping the laws of the growing country. Contemporaries of the early reporters sometimes criticized them for publishing the opinions too slowly and without careful editing.

Early reporters summarized case facts, prepared the preface or headnote to the opinion, transcribed the arguments of counsel, and provided useful indexes to the volumes they edited. Nineteenth century reports that cited the reporter by name gave the impression the reporter was more important than the justices. The shift to identifying reports by state name diminished visibility of the reporter. In 1874 Congress appropriated funds for publishing the Court's opinions under government auspices. The first anonymous reporter was William Tod Otto. Private printers published the reports until 1921 when the Government Printing Office took over the job.

The official Court reporter, *United States Reports*, includes a brief preface explaining the decision or points of law. Because of the slow publication schedule for this report, many lawyers rely on private companies that publish and annotate official Court decisions. Major publishers include West Publishing Company, Lawyers Cooperative Company, and the National Bureau of Affairs. The Court's opinions are immediately entered into commercial on-line databases such as WESTLAW and LEXIS. *United States Law Week* publishes the full text of Court decisions within days.

Court reporting has changed since Dallas sought his fortune as a publisher of Court decisions. The justices write their own decisions and do not rely on others to record their opinions and decide what is important. That is the job of the justices. Rather than legal entrepreneurs, the anonymous reporters are employees of the Court. New information technologies, especially the Internet and CD-ROMS, make access to the justices' opinions easier for other judges, lawyers, and citizens. In a society ruled by law, the reporter's function remains an important one.

—*Fred Buchstein*

Suggested Readings

Brenner, Susan W. *Precedent Inflation*. New Brunswick, N.J.: Transaction, 1992.

Domnarski, William. *In the Opinion of the Court*. Urbana: University of Chicago Press, 1996.

Epstein, Lee, et al. *The Supreme Court Compendium: Data, Decisions, and Developments.* Washington, D.C.: CQ Press, 2003.

Frederick, David C. *Supreme Court and Appellate Advocacy: Mastering Oral Argument.* St. Paul, Minn.: West Publishing, 2003.

Hall, Kermit L., ed. *Judicial Review and Judicial Power in the Supreme Court.* New York: Garland, 2000.

_____, ed. *The Oxford Guide to United States Supreme Court Decisions.* New York: Oxford University Press, 1999.

Surrency, Erwin C. *A History of American Law Publishing.* New York: Oceana, 1990.

Lewis, Thomas T., and Richard L. Wilson, eds. *Encyclopedia of the U.S. Supreme Court.* 3 vols. Pasadena, Calif.: Salem Press, 2000.

See also Advisory opinions; Court reporters; Opinions; Supreme Court, U.S.

RESTITUTION

Restoring or compensating a person for something that was wrongly taken away from that person—an example of one of the oldest forms of justice in the world

The concept and practice of restitution has its origins in the ancient Semitic civilizations of the fertile crescent. It was part of both the Code of Hammurabi and the Mosaic Code of the Old Testament. In the case of theft, the offender was to restore "ten-fold" what had been stolen. Other crimes involved various forms of compensation; if someone cut another person's hand off, for example, either maliciously or through negligence, compensation had to be paid to cover (to use modern terms) medical expenses, lost wages, and pain and suffering.

This principle, though common in history, generally fell into disuse in the United States. In the American legal system, offenders must go to prison or pay a fine to the state, but victims are usually uncompensated for their losses. (If a person is found guilty in a criminal court, however, the victim can then sue the person in a civil court in an effort to recover monetary damages.) This situation began to change in the 1980's, however, as more laws and courts used the principle of compensation and restitution. In a sense, restitution can be seen as combining the civil law's concern with compensating victims and criminal law's concern with punishing offenders. In one scenario, an offender may be given probation on the condition that he or she make continuing payments to compensate the victim of the crime.

See also Common law; Community service as punishment for crime; Damages; Negligence; Punitive damages; Sentencing.

RESTRAINING ORDERS, TEMPORARY

Temporary commands by courts to preserve the status quo pending trials

Often the relief sought in a judicial proceeding is monetary: One party seeks money from another for an injury. However, sometimes a party may seek from the court an order requiring another person or entity to do or not do something. One business that believes another business has stolen trade secrets might obtain an order from a court preventing the use of the trade secrets. Court orders of this kind are generally referred to as injunctions. To obtain an injunction a party must file a lawsuit. If the party prevails in the suit, it may obtain the order it seeks, which is referred to more precisely as a permanent injunction.

The law provides temporary orders of two types between the time a party files a lawsuit and the time the party finally obtains a permanent injunction. A court may hold a hearing to decide whether the party seeking an injunction seems likely to prevail in the case. If the court believes that the party is likely to prevail, it may order a preliminary injunction, which is essentially the same as a permanent injunction but merely exists until the trial is over and the court enters a final order granting the permanent injunction. However, because even hearings may take time to schedule and conduct, rules of civil procedure generally permit a party to seek an even more temporary injunction, one designed merely to last until the court has an opportunity to conduct a full hearing of the issue. This kind of temporary injunction is referred to as a temporary restraining order.

—*Timothy L. Hall*

See also Civil actions; Consent decree; Hearings; Injunctions; Lawsuits.

RETAINERS

Formal agreements between attorneys and clients through which the attorneys are hired to take the clients' cases

The deposit or advance payment made by a client to an attorney for some of the fees and costs anticipated in a legal case is termed a "retainer," as is the actual agreement between the client and attorney specifying the nature of services to be rendered, costs, and related matters. The retainer fee is held in a trust account that typically pays no interest. In effect, a retainer authorizes an attorney to begin work on a legal case and also assures the attorney that payment will be made. If an attorney were to begin work on a case before actually being hired by a client, the attorney's actions would not be considered legally binding.

There are various types of retainers. When an attorney takes on a specific case, the agreement is called a special retainer. If an attorney agrees to act for a client when needed, it is termed a general retainer. A full payment retainer is payment in full in advance. This is common practice when the client is a credit risk, such as a person involved in a criminal case. This retainer is also used for flat fee matters that can be completed in less than thirty days, such as incorporation or simple wills. With a partial payment retainer an attorney asks for part of the fee in advance (typically half) and the balance on completion of the case. This is appropriate for more expensive flat fee work that will turn around in less than sixty days, such as an estate plan or an immigration hearing. A replenishing retainer is typically used for hourly work. The retainer fee is placed in escrow, and at the end of each month the client is billed to replenish the retainer to its original amount.

An attorney generally asks for a retainer fee in order to have an available fund from which to draw a salary and for any out-of-pocket expenses pertaining to the case. The retainer covers an attorney's knowledge and experience, the time spent working for the client, and any office expenses associated with the client's case. Costs not covered by a retainer but payable by a client are costs for filing a case in court; for copies of official documents; for telephone calls, photocopying, and express mail; and for court reporters who take testimony from witnesses who cannot appear in court and from expert witnesses, such as doctors or scientists. A retained attorney takes money from the retainer fund only as costs or fees are incurred on the client's behalf. If a client changes attorneys or if the attorney concludes the case and has not utilized all of the retainer, the client is refunded the difference.

—*Alvin K. Benson*

See also Attorney-client relationship; Attorney fees; Attorney salaries; Attorney trust accounts; Court costs; Litigation expenses.

REVERSALS OF SUPREME COURT DECISIONS BY AMENDMENT

Overturning of Supreme Court rulings interpreting provisions of the Constitution by constitutional amendments

According to Article V of the U.S. Constitution, two-thirds majorities of both houses of Congress or a convention called by Congress at the request of two-thirds of state legislatures can propose an amendment to the Constitution. The amendment must be ratified by three-quarters of the states through their legislatures or special conventions. These amendments enable Congress to overturn a Supreme Court ruling involving a constitutional issue. In contrast, if Congress wishes to overturn a Court ruling interpreting a federal statute, it can do so simply by passing another law. Among the amendments successfully proposed by Congress, five—the Eleventh, Thirteenth, Fourteenth, Sixteenth, and Twenty-sixth—can be interpreted as overturning Court rulings.

The Eleventh Amendment, ratified in 1795, overturned *Chisholm v. Georgia* (1793) by limiting the federal courts' right to hear suits brought against states by citizens of other states. In *Chisholm*, the Court had allowed a citizen of South Carolina to sue the state of Georgia. Because a number of state governments were in default on their debts at the time, the states feared that the *Chisholm* case would make them vulnerable to a flood of lawsuits.

In *Scott v. Sandford* (1857), the Court denied Congress the power to outlaw slavery in any of the territories under federal jurisdiction and declared that no African American, free or slave, could ever be a citizen of the United States. This ruling was overturned by the Thirteenth Amendment (1865), which eliminated slavery, and the Fourteenth Amendment (1868), which conferred citizenship on every person born or naturalized in the United States.

The Sixteenth Amendment (1913) gave Congress the power to levy an income tax, overturning *Pollock v. Farmers' Loan and Trust Co.* (1895), in which the Court had ruled such a tax unconstitutional. The Twenty-sixth Amendment (1971), by granting eighteen-year-olds the right to vote in elections at all levels, overturned the Court's ruling in *Oregon v. Mitchell* (1970) that Congress could set age qualifications only for federal elections—not for state and local elections.

—*William H. Coogan*

Suggested Readings

Biskupic, Joan, and Elder Witt.*The Supreme Court and Individual Rights*. Washington, D.C.: Congressional Quarterly, 1997.

Epstein, Lee, et al. *The Supreme Court Compendium: Data, Decisions, and Developments*. Washington, D.C.: CQ Press, 2003.

Frederick, David C. *Supreme Court and Appellate Advocacy: Mastering Oral Argument*. St. Paul, Minn.: West Publishing, 2003.

Friendly, Fred, and Martha Elliott. *The Constitution, That Delicate Balance*. New York: McGraw-Hill, 1984.

Hall, Kermit L., ed. *Judicial Review and Judicial Power in the Supreme Court*. New York: Garland, 2000.

_____, ed. *The Oxford Guide to United States Supreme Court Decisions*. New York: Oxford University Press, 1999.

Hall, Kermit, William Wiecek, and Paul Finkelman. *American Legal History: Cases and Materials*. 2d ed. New York: Oxford University Press, 1996.

Lewis, Thomas T., and Richard L. Wilson, eds. *Encyclopedia of the U.S. Supreme Court*. 3 vols. Pasadena, Calif.: Salem Press, 2000.

Seidman, Louis Michael. *Our Unsettled Constitution: A New Defense of Constitutionalism and Judicial Review*. New Haven, Conn.: Yale University Press, 2001.

See also Constitution, U.S.; Reversals of Supreme Court decisions by Congress; Supreme Court, U.S.

REVERSALS OF SUPREME COURT DECISIONS BY CONGRESS

Overturning of Court decisions through the power of congressional legislation to rewrite the law

Beginning with its earliest decisions, the Supreme Court created controversy and occasionally prompted Congress to overturn its decisions. Under the Constitution, Congress can override federal court decisions through constitutional amendment or by rewriting a piece of legislation. Because the amendment process requires supermajorities of both houses of Congress and the state legislatures, most overturning of Court decisions involves ordinary legislation.

Many of the Court's decisions involve the interpretation of federal law and its application to legal disputes. These interpretative powers provide the Court with some ability to legislate by defining the meaning of words in a piece of legislation, producing conflict with Congress. Over two hundred years of Court history, such conflict has led to approximately two hundred laws being passed in order to overturn a Court decision.

The Congress Reaction

During the first fifty years of the Court's existence, the justices engaged in little interpretation of federal law. It was not until the

Capitol building in which the House of Representatives and Senate hold their sessions. (Digital Stock)

1850's that Congress became involved in attempting to reverse a Court decision. Congress's action came in *Pennsylvania v. Wheeling and Belmont Bridge Co.* (1852). The case centered on whether the Wheeling Bridge constituted an obstruction to interstate commerce. In its decision, the Court ruled the bridge was an obstruction and ordered that the owner either raise or remove it.

After losing before the Court, the bridge owners appealed to Congress. In response, legislation was passed declaring that the bridge was a legal structure and necessary for the transportation of the mails. This law was challenged before the Court. In *Pennsylvania v. Wheeling and Belmont Bridge Co.* (1856), the Court upheld the law as a constitutional congressional reversal of a Court decision.

However, overturning a Court decision does not always require that Congress pass legislation. Because the Court depends on Congress for funding and political support of its decisions, the threat of legislation to overturn a Court ruling can cause the justices to change their minds. In *Watkins v. United States* (1957), the Court limited Congress's investigatory powers. The justices' main target was the House Un-American Activities Committee. According to the Court, the committee's investigation of communists in labor unions exceeded the scope of its charter.

The congressional response to *Watkins* came in the form of the Jenner bill. Senator William F. Jenner's proposed legislation allowed committee chairpersons to determine the scope of a congressional investigation. The wording implicitly overruled *Watkins*. Though the Jenner bill did not pass the Senate, the Court received Congress's political message. In *Barenblatt v. United States* (1959), the Court reversed itself on *Watkins*, allowing Congress greater power in defining its own investigations.

Constitutional Conflicts

After the 1950's, Congress and the Court became more involved in conflict over constitutional interpretation and the meaning of federal legislation. With the Court creating new constitutional interpretations, Congress found itself in conflict with the justices. The ruling in *Miranda v. Arizona* (1966) required police officers to read suspects their rights in order to prevent coerced confessions. Congress reacted with the 1968 Omnibus Crime Control and Safe Streets Act in which federal courts were allowed to ignore Miranda warnings and create their own standards for coerced confessions. The Fourth Circuit Court of Appeals in *United States v. Dickerson* (1999) ruled that the congressional act overruled *Miranda* and that federal law enforcement officials were not required to read suspects their rights.

Many of the liberal civil rights provisions passed during the 1960's were scrutinized by the conservative Supreme Court appointees of Richard M. Nixon and Ronald Reagan. Their conservative interpretations of the law prompted Congress to legislate in order to overturn those decisions. One such ruling was *General Electric v. Gilbert* (1976), in which the Court ruled that the 1964 Civil Rights Act's prohibition against gender discrimination in employment did not forbid discrimination against pregnant workers. Congress responded with the 1978 Pregnancy Discrimination Act, specifically overruling the *Gilbert* decision by making pregnancy protected under the civil rights law.

The Court under Chief Justice William H. Rehnquist reinterpreted the Constitution and federal law, prompting a flurry of legislation to overturn Court decisions. Three decisions, *Patterson v.*

MacLean Credit Union (1988), *Wards Cove Packing Co. v. Atonio* (1989), and *Martin v. Wilks* (1989) made it more difficult for claimants in racial discrimination cases to prove their case. In response, Congress passed the 1991 Civil Rights Act, which made it easier to prove race discrimination at the workplace.

The Court's decision in *Employment Division, Department of Human Resources v. Smith* (1990), produced more congressional legislation. In *Smith*, the Court ruled that the free exercise clause did not apply to general applicable laws that only incidentally restricted religious freedoms. In 1993 Congress passed the Religious Freedom Restoration Act, which required government to show a compelling interest for restricting any religious belief or practice. This overruled the Court's standard in *Smith*. The Religious Freedom Restoration Act was itself challenged in Court in the case of *Boerne v. Flores* (1997). In *Boerne*, the Court struck down the act as an unconstitutional use of congressional power to overturn a judicial decision. According to the Court, in overturning its decision in *Smith*, Congress had changed the meaning of the free exercise clause, a power reserved for the courts.

Throughout the Court's history, congressional disagreement with the justices' decisions has prompted legislative action. As the Court interprets the law, Congress is likely to find it necessary at times to overrule those interpretations.

—Douglas Clouatre

Suggested Readings

Abraham, Henry. *The Judicial Process*. Cambridge, England: Oxford University Press, 1993.

Biskupic, Joan, and Elder Witt.*The Supreme Court and Individual Rights*. Washington, D.C.: Congressional Quarterly, 1997.

Epstein, Lee, et al. *The Supreme Court Compendium: Data, Decisions, and Developments*. Washington, D.C.: CQ Press, 2003.

Frederick, David C. *Supreme Court and Appellate Advocacy: Mastering Oral Argument*. St. Paul, Minn.: West Publishing, 2003.

Lewis, Thomas T., and Richard L. Wilson, eds. *Encyclopedia of the U.S. Supreme Court*. 3 vols. Pasadena, Calif.: Salem Press, 2000.

Murphy, Walter. *Congress and the Court*. Chicago: University of Chicago Press, 1962.

Seidman, Louis Michael. *Our Unsettled Constitution: A New Defense of Constitutionalism and Judicial Review*. New Haven, Conn.: Yale University Press, 2001.

Sunstein, Cass R. *One Case at a Time: Judicial Minimalism on the Supreme Court.* Cambridge, Mass.: Harvard University Press, 1999.

Swisher, Carl. *The Taney Period.* New York: Macmillan, 1974.

Warren, Charles. *Congress, the Constitution and the Supreme Court.* 1925. Holmes Beach, Fla.: Gaunt, 2001.

See also Constitution, U.S.; Reversals of Supreme Court decisions by amendment; Supreme Court, U.S.

REVERSIBLE ERRORS

Errors affecting the rights of parties to actions that may lead to miscarriages of justice

The finding of reversible error is limited to appellate review of a lower court's decision, at which time the error becomes apparent. A reversible error justifies reversing a judgment, even if there was no objection to the matter that caused the error in the lower court. The error must be something that would reasonably be expected to prejudice the rights of the party complaining or against whom the error was committed.

Reversible errors also includes judicial errors, actions committed by the court themselves that affect parties' rights to fair trials. Reversible errors include allowing hearsay evidence, allowing unduly damaging evidence that was presented and not objected to during the course of the proceeding, or the failure of a judge to instruct the jury as to the proper limitation of consideration of such testimony, when such instruction was normal and necessary.

See also Appeal; Bill of Rights, U.S.; Court types; Harmless errors; Objection; Verdicts.

SEARCH WARRANT REQUIREMENT

Necessity of obtaining warrants from judges, based on meeting certain criteria, before law enforcement personnel can conduct searches

While under British rule, the thirteen North American colonies were subject to a system of law, one aspect of which was the writ of assistance, which allowed government officials to conduct general searches. The writ of assistance empowered local authories to search anywhere for contraband. British judges did not need to hear any facts regarding illegal activity before a writ was issued and a search conducted. A search could be conducted on mere suspicion and at any location. After the American Revolution, the citizens of the new country were interested in limiting government searches. The Bill of Rights, ratified in 1791, contained the Fourth Amendment, which protected people from unreasonable searches. The Fourth Amendment set out the requirements the government must meet before a search warrant can be issued. The amendment states a warrant cannot be issued "but upon probable cause, supported by Oath or affirmation, and particularly describing the place to be searched, and the persons or things to be seized."

Requirements of a Search Warrant

Through numerous cases, the Supreme Court has defined the exact requirement of the warrant clause. The Court has repeatedly defined the "probable cause" needed for a search warrant to be issued. To obtain a search warrant, law enforcement officers must show they have reliable and sufficient facts that would cause a reasonable person to believe a criminal act has been committed and that items or a person subject to seizure are at the location to be searched. Probable cause for the warrant cannot be based on what the subsequent search uncovers, only on the facts known when the warrant was issued. The Court also ruled that the probable cause must have been obtained legally. If law enforcement obtains information through an illegal search, it cannot remove the unconstitutional taint on the evidence by later applying for a search warrant. The amount of time between the gathering of probable cause and the execution of the search warrant may make the warrant "stale." If an inordinate amount of time passes and doubt arises whether the object of the warrant is still at the location, then the warrant may become invalid because of outdated probable cause.

The warrant must particularly describe the place to be searched or the item or person to be seized. The place to be searched must be described in the warrant to the extent that it can be set apart from all other locations. The Court has ruled that if an officer can with reasonable effort ascertain and identify the place to be searched then the warrant will be valid. The warrant must also describe items to be seized well enough that an officer can exclude all other items. Failure of the description to be precise enough to exclude other locations or failure to adequately describe an item or person to be seized will make the warrant invalid and the search illegal.

Although the Fourth Amendment does not expressly state that a warrant will be issued by a neutral and detached magistrate, it is generally regarded to be inherent. One of the purposes of a warrant is to allow a neutral party to decide whether law enforcement has probable cause to conduct a search. It is an essential part of the search warrant process to have a detached party review the facts and issue a warrant only if probable cause is present. Failure to have a warrant issued by an impartial and unbiased party will invalidate the warrant and make the search illegal.

The final requirement of the search warrant clause requires the warrant to be supported by an oath or affirmation. The oath or affirmation must be administered by the party issuing the warrant before testimony about probable cause. The Court has held that if the person supplying the probable cause recklessly disregards the truth or knowingly gives false evidence, the search warrant is invalid.

Exceptions

The Supreme Court has found six instances in which a search is reasonable and valid without a warrant. When an officer arrests a suspect, the officer may conduct a search incident to an arrest. However, the Court ruled that only the person and the immediate area are subject to search in *Chimel v. California* (1969). The arrest must be lawful or the evidence may be deemed inadmissible under the exclusionary rule. Under the automobile exception established by *Carroll v. United States* (1925), if the police have probable cause to believe that an automobile contains evidence of a crime, fruit of a crime, or contraband, a search may be conducted without a warrant. If law enforcement observes evidence of a crime, and they have a legal right to be at the location, they may make a warrantless search under the plain view doctrine. The Court has recognized that a citizen may waive his or her Fourth Amendment rights by voluntarily and intelligently consenting to a search, allowing an officer to make a legal warrantless search. In *Terry v. Ohio* (1968), the Court concluded that officers may conduct a limited search of a person (by frisking him or her) for weapons if they have a reasonable suspicion that the person is armed and dangerous. The Court also held that when an officer is in hot pursuit, or where evidence may be destroyed or hidden away, or the evidence is a threat to public safety, an officer may make a warrantless search.

—*Steven J. Dunker*

Suggested Readings

Bergman, Paul, Sara J. Berman-Barrett. *The Criminal Law Handbook: Know Your Rights, Survive the System*, 5th ed. Berkeley, Calif.: Nolo Press, 2003.

Ferdico, John N. *Criminal Procedure for the Criminal Justice Professional*. 3d ed. St. Paul, Minn.: West Publishing, 1985.

Franklin, Carl J. *Constitutional Law for the Criminal Justice Professional*. Boca Raton, Fla.: CRC Press, 1999.

Klotter, John C. *Legal Guide for Police: Constitutional Issues*. 5th ed. Cincinnati: Anderson, 1999.

O'Brien, David M. *Constitutional Law and Politics: Civil Rights and Liberties*. 3d ed. 2 vols. New York: W. W. Norton, 1997.

See also Bench warrants; Bill of Rights, U.S.; Presumption of innocence; Probable cause; Suspects.

SELF-INCRIMINATION, PRIVILEGE AGAINST

Privilege found in the Fifth Amendment to the U.S. Constitution that protects persons from being compelled to be witnesses against themselves in criminal proceedings

The privilege against self-incrimination is an important procedural safeguard against the awesome power of the government in the accusatorial system of criminal justice, designed to protect the individual. It originated in England in the twelfth century, when English subjects were summoned to appear before the ecclesiastical courts, the courts of High Commission, and the infamous Star Chamber to take oaths *ex officio*. Without being informed whether they were being accused of any crime, suspects were obliged to swear that they would answer truthfully any and all questions put to them.

To object, subjects invoked the ancient maxim *nemo tenetur* ("no man is bound to accuse himself"), insisting that they could not be required to accuse themselves of crimes before formal judicial proceedings, and the courts relented. Parliament prohibited administration of oaths *ex officio* and, by the eighteenth century, English courts had extended to defendants and witnesses in criminal trials the right to refuse to testify against themselves. Because the accused was disqualified from testifying at the trial, the privilege became the chief protection against forced confessions.

Fifth Amendment

The privilege was carried over to the American colonies. The fact that twelve of the twenty-three rights in the Bill of Rights (the first ten constitutional amendments, ratified in 1791) deal with criminal procedures is some indication of the importance of balancing individual rights against the government's power to prosecute crime. The Fifth Amendment reads, in part: "No person . . . shall be compelled in any Criminal Case to be a witness against himself." The Fifth Amendment acted as a limitation only on the federal government for a time. Beginning in the 1930's, the Supreme Court relied on the Fourteenth Amendment to reverse state criminal convictions based on confessions that it determined were involuntary under a "totality of the circumstances" evaluation (*Brown v. Mississippi*, 1936). Then, in *Malloy v. Hogan* (1964), the Court decided that the right against self-incrimination itself was so fundamental that it should be applied in state criminal prosecutions, under the so-called incorporation doctrine.

The values underlying the privilege against self-incrimination form the core of the American criminal justice system, which is based on an accusatorial rather than an inquisitorial system of criminal justice. The privilege obliges the government to meet its burden of proving guilt beyond a reasonable doubt without forcing the accused to join the prosecution. The Supreme Court has recognized the premium this system places on individual dignity, even the dignity of those accused of serious crime. The privilege obliges the government to play by the rules: Police and prosecutors may not rely on physical abuse, inhumane techniques, or deceit and trickery. A criminal defendant need not testify at all. The prosecutor may not comment on the failure to testify, and the jury may not take the defendant's silence as any indication of guilt.

The privilege is not without limits. It applies in civil or administrative proceedings only if an answer might tend to be incriminating in a later criminal proceeding. It can be claimed only by individuals and not by corporations, and thus business records usually may be seized. It protects only evidence elicited from the defendant, not incriminating statements of a third party. It is limited to testimonial evidence; a defendant may be obliged to furnish real evidence such as fingerprints or a blood sample. Even a person with a valid claim of privilege may be compelled to testify if the government grants immunity and promises not to use the testimony in any later criminal prosecution.

Interrogations

The Supreme Court first took a Sixth Amendment right-to-counsel approach to custodial interrogations and held that an accused had the right to be informed by his lawyer of his privilege against self-incrimination, once an investigation had focused on him (*Escobedo v. Illinois*, 1964). Then in 1966, the Court decided the landmark case *Miranda v. Arizona*, and held that without a waiver, the assistance of counsel during interrogation is necessary to vindicate the right against self-incrimination.

The police must deliver the well-known Miranda warning to the suspect: He has a right to remain silent; anything he says may be used against him in court; he has a right to a lawyer's assistance before and during interrogation; a lawyer will be appointed if he cannot afford one. If the suspect requests a lawyer or invokes the right to remain silent, then the interrogation is supposed to stop. Unless the suspect is expressly and fully afforded this warning and knowingly and voluntarily waives these rights, any confession or statement is not admissible in evidence at trial.

This decision touched off a heated public argument over the advisability of requiring this warning, which was part of a larger debate over the appropriateness of the U.S. Supreme Court elaborating rights for those accused of crime. In numerous subsequent decisions, the Supreme Court has refined the Miranda holding and its exceptions in an apparent effort to accommodate legitimate interests in law enforcement. The central requirement of a formal warning has remained intact.

—*Thomas E. Baker*

Suggested Readings
The best history of this subject is Leonard W. Levy, *Origins of the Fifth Amendment* (New York: Oxford, University Press, 1968). An able summary of Supreme Court cases is Mark Berger, *Taking the Fifth: The Supreme Court and the Privilege Against Self-Incrimination* (Lexington, Mass.: Lexington Books, 1980). Three noteworthy books debate the constitutional values underlying the privilege: Erwin N. Griswold, *The Fifth Amendment Today* (Cambridge, Mass.: Harvard University Press, 1955); Lewis Mayers, *Shall We Amend the Fifth Amendment?* (New York: Harper & Brothers, 1959); and Milton Meltzer, *The Right to Remain Silent* (New York: Harcourt Brace Jovanovich, 1972). The subject is also considered in a broader context in *Constitutional Law: Civil Liberty and Individual Rights* by William Cohen and David J. Danelski (New York: Foundation Press, 2002). Practical advice for lay people can be found in Jay M. Feinman's *Law 101: Everything You Need to Know About the American Legal System* (New York: Oxford University Press, 2000) and *The Criminal Law Handbook: Know Your Rights, Survive the System*, by Paul Bergman and Sara J. Berman-Barrett (5th ed. Berkeley, Calif.: Nolo Press, 2003).

See also Bill of Rights, U.S.; Confessions; Fifth Amendment; Presumption of innocence; Suspects; Testimony.

Sentencing

Process through which judges impose punishment on offenders following their convictions

In some criminal trials, juries deliver the verdicts; in others—in cases in which no jury is involved—the judges do so. Judges have considerable leeway in imposing sentences, allowing them to consider mitigating and aggravating circumstances. The sentencing of a defendant who has been declared guilty, however, is up to the judge (there are situations in which a jury may make recommendations). Judges are expected to have the experience, legal knowledge, and impartiality needed to hand down fair and appropriate sentences. Although various guidelines exist, the judge has a great deal of discretion in how severe a sentence is imposed. Sentencing is arguably the least codified aspect of the criminal justice system, and it is certainly one of the most critical. In general, states have penal codes that set minimum and maximum punishments for various crimes. These punishments represent a combination of the actual damage or injury caused by the crime and society's moral feeling about the crime. Violent crimes are punished most heavily.

For relatively minor crimes, sentencing is often done promptly at the conclusion of a trial. For more serious offenses, sentencing is delayed (usually two or more weeks) and is done at a special hearing. At the hearing, the results of a pre-sentence investigation are presented, generally by a probation officer. The investigation provides information on the defendant's character, background, criminal history, and relevant details of the particular crime; the judge is expected to take the information into account when sentencing. The sentence may be lenient, as in a fine, a suspended sentence (in which no penalty is imposed so long as the offender promises to make restitution or to reform), or the imposition of a period of release into the community under supervision (probation). In other cases it may be severe, involving many years in prison or, in murder cases in some states, the death penalty. Most people tend to equate sentencing with prison sentences. Actually, however, of the 4.5 million offenders who were under some form of correctional custody in 1990, fewer then one million (approximately 25 percent) were in prisons.

There are three broad approaches to imposing sentences involving prison terms. An indeterminate sentence is one in which a judge specifies a maximum and minimum term, which may be reduced by good time (good behavior) in prison or by the granting of parole. A determinate sentence is a fixed term; it also may be reduced. A mandatory sentence, as the term implies, cannot be reduced: The specified time must be served in its entirety. Two other variations come into play if a person is convicted of more than one crime. The person may serve consecutive sentences, in which the sentences for the crimes are added together (with ten years plus five years equaling a fifteen-year sentence), or concurrent terms, in which the terms overlap (a five-year sentence could be considered to be served at the same time as the first half of the ten-year sentence).

Judicial Discretion

The sentencing procedure is purposely designed to give judges considerable discretion, because the circumstances of particular crimes and perpetrators vary widely. This discretion is controversial, however, because it frequently results in criminals convicted of similar crimes being given widely different sentences. There are a number of factors involved in sentencing discrepancies. One factor, often termed "bench bias," is simply the differences in individual judges' attitudes regarding the causes of crime (in some respects, whether the judge is a political liberal or conservative) and whether the primary purpose of punishment should be retribution or rehabilitation.

Judges who think in terms of rehabilitation tend to be more lenient. There are "hard" and "soft" judges. Other factors involved in the severity of sentencing include the nature of the particular crime, the judge's determination of the criminal's character, public attitudes about crime (or about a particular type of crime) at the time, the criminal's demeanor in court, and whether the case has generated publicity. Moreover, the element of chance comes into play—some judges have admitted that certain sentencing decisions essentially amounted to a "coin toss"—as may, unfortunately, such irrelevant factors as whether the previous case was particularly aggravating, what the judge had for breakfast, or whether the judge is having an argument with his or her spouse.

Goals of Sentencing

In imposing a sentence, judges usually have multiple goals. The most ancient goal is retribution, or "just deserts." The basic concept behind retribution is hurting offenders for the pain they have inflicted by their crimes. This motivation has been modified by the notion that punishment should be equitable and in proportion to the crime committed. A second goal is deterrence: the idea that the threat of punishment will influence individuals not to commit crimes in the future. General deterrence focuses on society and the belief that potential offenders will be deterred because of fear of being punished. Specific deterrence assumes that if the punishment imposed on a specific offender is severe enough, that offender will not commit crimes in the future.

A third goal is rehabilitation. Rehabilitation is based on the notion that offenders can be helped through such programs as psychological counseling and vocational training in such a way as to lessen the probability that they will commit crimes in the future. A final goal is to separate an offender from society by imprisonment. If an offender is imprisoned, the kind of sentence imposed can have a significant impact on other goals of punishment. For example, if the goal of punishment is rehabilitation, an indeterminate sentence will be imposed so that an offender can be paroled early if he or she responds to programming. In the 1980's and 1990's, the philosophy of "just deserts" and tailoring punishment to fit the crime generally prevailed. Under this philosophy, the indeterminate sentence was replaced by a determinate, nonparolable sentence for some crimes.

Two relatively recent developments in sentencing are intermediate punishments and sentencing guidelines. Intermediate punishments refer to community corrections with more stringent conditions than traditional probation, such as house arrest, electronic [electronic monitoring] monitoring, and demands for significant restitution. Sentencing guidelines are designed to control judicial discretion and to reduce disparities in sentencing. Generally, such guidelines require that a judge specifically consider offenders' behavior and risk factors in a consistent manner in setting a sentence. The United States Sentencing Commission, organized in 1985, for example, has developed a system involving the plotting of the specifics of a case and a criminal's background on two axes that is designed to produce consistent sentences in federal courts.

See also Community service as punishment for crime; Criminal records; Cruel and unusual punishment; Damages; Good time; House arrest; Incapacitation; Probation, adult; Probation, juvenile; Three-strikes laws; Trials.

SHAREHOLDER SUITS

Actions brought by stockholders on behalf of the corporations in which they own stock

When a corporation initiates an action to recover for some injury it has suffered, the board of directors typically sues the party who has wronged the company. In some cases, however, the directors or management of the corporation do not sue and the corporation does not recover for its injuries. In such cases the law allows a stockholder of the corporation to sue on behalf of the corporation in a shareholder suit. This is sometimes called a shareholder's derivative action, since the shareholder is not really the party who is wronged and acts to protect the corporation's interests. The cause of action derives from the corporation. The corporation is a necessary party and is thus made a defendant in the shareholder's derivative action along with the defendant wrongdoers.

Any recovery in a shareholder suit belongs to the corporation, because it is the corporation and not the individual shareholder who has been injured by the actions of wrongdoing defendants. However, a shareholder may recover the reasonable cost from the corporation of bringing the action if he or she is successful in the suit. This recovery may include attorney's fees.

Often shareholder derivative actions are brought to remedy breaches of fiduciary duties of care and loyalty owed to the corporation and its shareholders by its managers and sometimes even directors. These wrongful actions may have benefited a majority of the shareholders, who will not be willing to bring suit to remedy the wrong and thereby give up the benefit they have received. Moreover, it is difficult to get directors to sue themselves or the officers they have selected. In the late twentieth century derivative actions were controlled by statutes or court rules.

State and federal laws have restricted shareholder suits, recognizing that the corporation is governed by the board of directors who normally have the right to decide to bring or not bring lawsuits in the name of the corporation. Typically, laws require that the shareholder be an owner of stock at the time of the wrong and at the time the lawsuit is commenced; that the shareholder demand of the directors (and sometimes the other shareholders) that the corporation bring the lawsuit or give a good reason why this demand should be excused, such as when the wrongdoers are in control of corporate decision making as directors and majority shareholders; and that any settlement of the lawsuit be approved by the court.

Court approval of a shareholder suit is required in order to avoid strike suits, in which a shareholder with a small investment brings the action only for its nuisance value and the corporation pays off the shareholder to go away without any real recovery to the corporation. Otherwise the corporation must spend management time and incur legal expenses as the defendant, since the action is really brought on behalf of the corporation by the shareholder. Some statutes require that a shareholder post a bond to cover the corporation's expenses as a defendant. These are known as a security for expenses statutes and effectively discourage shareholder strike suits.

A shareholder suit is thus one way that the courts and corporation laws have developed to permit shareholder monitoring of those persons who are supposed to act in the corporation's best interests. These suits ensure that if these persons do not protect corporate interests fully, the shareholder may do so derivatively.

—*J. Kirkland Grant*

See also Breach of contract; Cause of action; Class action; Commercial litigation; Lawsuits.

SHERIFFS

Chief law-enforcement administrators in counties, who are usually elected officers

Sheriffs, as counties' chief law-enforcement administrators, are responsible for maintaining public order within their jurisdictions. The performance of various other duties may also be required, including the execution of the mandates and judgments of criminal and civil courts, the delivery of writs, the summoning of juries, and the maintenance of county jails. The responsibilities of sheriffs are often so vast that sheriffs' offices are the largest employers of law-enforcement personnel in many areas of the country. In 1987 more than one in five law-enforcement officers (22.4 percent) served in sheriffs' departments. In states that legally require sheriffs, the duties and responsibilities of the office vary widely as do the requirements for holding the office. It is not unusual in many states for individuals to be elected who possess little or no educational training in law enforcement.

The Sheriff in England

The office of sheriff originated in England prior to the Norman conquest of 1066. Each shire, or county, was administered by a representative of the king known as a reeve. The appointed reeve was usually a baron who was an ally of the king. These officials had nearly absolute power within their jurisdictions. Eventually the title "shire reeve" evolved phonetically into "sheriff." The sheriff in the English countryside collected taxes, commanded the militia, delivered writs, and served as judge and jury in all criminal and civil cases. After the reign of William the Conqueror (c. 1028-1087), the sheriff's power and status were dramatically diminished. Under Henry II (1133-1189) the position assumed a law-enforcement role. By the end of the Protestant Reformation in England, specifically during the reign of Elizabeth I (1533-1603), most of the duties and powers once reserved exclusively for the sheriff had been assumed by the newly created offices of constable and justice of the peace.

Early American History

The English settlers of colonial America referred to their first law-enforcement officials as constables, as they had responsibilities very similar to those of their English namesakes. However, the governor of colonial New York appointed sheriffs who functioned in much the same manner as they had in England, exercising considerable power in their county. The sheriff in colonial New York was also responsible for the total oversight of elections, which led to widespread claims of corruption and abuse of power. The office of sheriff was stripped of much of its power following the American Revolution (1775-1783) and sheriffs as the law-enforcement agents of frontier justice did not emerge until after the American Revolution.

American sheriffs prior to the Civil War (1861-1865), who were typically appointed to their position by state, territorial, or city governments, exercised wide-ranging powers. Their many duties included maintaining order, collecting taxes, apprehending criminals, conducting elections, and maintaining local jails. Frontier sheriffs led particularly dangerous lives. They were poorly trained and often ill-equipped to deal with the hardships required of their office. In the Western territories of California, Oregon, Utah, New Mexico, Colorado, Nevada, and Texas they were called upon to travel great distances to apprehend criminals and perform other duties. When granted the authority, sheriffs also appointed deputy sheriffs to assist them in carrying out the duties of their office, especially the apprehension of fleeing criminals. It was not uncommon for sheriffs to "deputize" dozens of volunteers when circumstances required, especially during emergency situations. As the former Western territories achieved U.S. statehood, sheriffs increasingly became elected officeholders.

The Modern Sheriff

By 1900 population shifts in many states from the countryside to the cities required the creation of new law-enforcement agencies, such as city and state police departments. These new agencies assumed much of the work and duties performed by sheriffs' offices. The complexities of organized crime and other developments, especially the automobile and the expanding highway system, necessitated the creation of highly trained and skilled state and federal police agencies capable of dealing with the challenges of modern criminal activity. Most sheriffs, generally popularly elected, did not have the training or professional qualifications to deal with the modern criminal, who could move rapidly from one jurisdiction to another.

Another often-heard complaint was that the sheriffs in many communities were nothing more than servants of the local elites. In 1940 sheriffs around the country who were concerned about the level of professionalism and expertise needed to survive in the ever-changing field of criminal justice began organizing what evolved into the National Sheriffs' Association (NSA). The NSA offers training, information, and other services to sheriffs, deputies, and other personnel throughout the United States, allowing law-enforcement professionals to network and share information about trends in law enforcement and policing. In 1972 the National Sheriff's Institute (NSI) was established by the NSA to provide sheriffs and their administrative staffs with high-quality, low-cost training and programs. Jail administration, liability issues, crime prevention, and public relations are but a few of the many concerns addressed by NSI classes. The NSA also publishes the *Sheriff* magazine, *Community Policing Exchange*, *Sheriff Times*, and several other periodicals.

There are more than 3,000 sheriffs' departments in the United States, which serve as a critical part of the law-enforcement community. Issues of concern for modern sheriffs as they enter the twenty-first century include funding, community policing, coping with law-enforcement stress, and rising medical costs. In many sparsely populated and unincorporated areas of the United States the locally elected sheriff is still the primary source of law-enforcement protection. Alaska and New Jersey are the only states that do not maintain sheriffs' offices. Sheriffs are elected in forty-six states, and most states require that all law-enforcement personnel, including sheriffs, undergo training before acting in their capacity as law-enforcement officers.

—Donald C. Simmons, Jr.

Suggested Readings

The best historical treatments of the role of the sheriff in English and early American colonial government are *The History of Local Government in England*, edited by Bryan Keith-Lucus (New York: Augustus M. Kelly, 1970), and *Town and Country: Essays on the Structure of Local Government in the American Colonies*, edited by Bruce C. Daniels (Middletown, Conn.: Wesleyan University Press, 1978). Those interested in the gunfighting sheriff may refer to Joseph G. Rosa's *The Gunfighter: Man or Myth?* (Norman: University of Oklahoma Press, 1969) and Frank R. Prassel's *The West-*

ern Peace Officer: A Legacy of Law and Order (Norman: University of Oklahoma Press, 1971). For information on the role of the modern American Sheriff, see Paul and Shari Cohn's *Careers in Law Enforcement and Security* (New York: The Rosen Publishing Group, 1990), Lane W. Lancaster's *Government in Rural America* (2d ed. New York: Van Nostrand, 1952), and Herbert Sydney Duncombe's *Modern County Government* (Washington, D.C.: National Association of Counties, 1977). *Challenges and Choices for Crime-Fighting Technology: Federal Support of State and Local Law Enforcement*, by William Schwabe and others (Santa Monica, Calif.: Rand, 2001), looks at sheriffs in the context of national law enforcement.

See also Criminal justice system; District attorneys; Execution of judgment; Law enforcement; Police; State police.

SMALL-CLAIMS COURTS

Special courts, often subdivisions of regular courts, that expeditiously, informally, and inexpensively settle small claims, generally defined as claims of less than $1,000

The informality of the small-claims system makes it possible for small disputes to be settled without attorneys and formal legal procedures; the expenses involved are quite small. Proceedings in such courts are generally informal. Plaintiffs and defendants usually represent themselves without the benefit or expense of attorneys. However, in some cases it may be wise to get the advice and suggestions of an attorney before going to a small-claims court in order to understand better one's legal situation. Reading the appropriate law books in a local library, however, may be all that is necessary. Often all the court does is to arrange for the payment of small claims and accounts. The tone is conciliatory, and the judge tries to work out a fair settlement.

Almost all of the fifty states have small-claims courts. These courts handle such cases as a person seeking restitution from a dry cleaner who has ruined a suit, a couple wanting a car dealer to repair a car he sold them, or one party trying to get another to pay back a debt that is owed. Contract law is involved if an agreement has been signed. If it has not, the law still recognizes spoken and implied contracts.

There are no juries in small-claims court, and the judge must follow the formal standard of proof as in a regular civil trial; proof must be demonstrated by a preponderance of the evidence. The judge must determine the facts in the case and then apply the law the best he or she can.

Small-claims courts are not a separate level of justice, but rather a special procedure that is part of a larger, more formal court. Judges rotate in and out of the court, typically spending only a week there at a time. Part of the purpose of the courts is to expedite the case load, so small-claims hearings customarily last only fifteen to thirty minutes. Sometimes the judge will interrupt an explanation and say that he has heard enough and has a strong enough basis for a judgment. Most small-claims courts have a $1,000 limit on claims they can hear. The plaintiffs usually win, perhaps as much as 80 percent of the time. When the plaintiff does not win, it is usually because the jurisdiction of the court does not extend as far as the plaintiff's description of the situation.

It is sound judicial administration to have small-claims courts, not only because of the speed of the process and the settlement of many disputes but also because of the effect on the parties involved. A large-scale political or judicial system often seems so complicated and slow that many citizens feel alienated from their government. Small-claims courts have an opposite psychological effect and serve a worthwhile purpose in showing that the government can be responsive to their own small problems.

Small-claims courts should not be confused with the Court of Claims, created in 1855 solely to try claims against the United States government. The United States government is not a party in a small-claims court. Small-claims disputes are between two private citizens in a civil matter.

—*William H. Burnside*

Suggested Readings

Three sources that deal exclusively with small-claims courts are Christopher J. Whelan, editor, *Small Claims Courts: A Comparative Study* (New York: Oxford University Press, 1990); Robert L. Spurrier, *Inexpensive Justice: Self-Representation in the Small Claims Court* (3d ed. Port Washington, N.Y.: Associated Faculty Press, 1983), and Steven Weller and John C. Ruhnka, *Practical Observa-*

tions on the Small Claims Court (Williamsburg, Va.: National Center for State Courts, 1979). Any standard law dictionary, such as Henry A. Black, *Black's Law Dictionary* (5th ed. St. Paul, Minn.: West Publishing, 1979), gives succinct definitions of relevant terms. Other useful works are Bernard Schwartz, *The Law in America: A History* (New York: McGraw-Hill, 1974), and Alexander H. Pekelis, *Law and Social Action*, edited by Milton R. Konvitz (New York: Da Capo Press, 1970).

See also Court types; Litigation expenses; Night courts; Trials.

SOLICITATION OF LEGAL CLIENTS

Practices by which lawyers try to find legal clients, notably through the mails but not through direct telephone soliciting or personal contacts

Among the most noxious images of lawyers is that of the "ambulance chaser," the lawyer who races to the scene of an accident in the hope of finding a client among twisted metal and bloody pavement. In fact, legal ethics rules almost invariably prohibit lawyers from approaching potential clients in person for the purpose of obtaining legal fees. Generally, potential clients are viewed as all too susceptible to the beguiling wiles of lawyers and too likely to be unduly influenced when encountering them directly over the telephone or in person.

The prohibition against ambulance chasing does not apply to all forms of solicitation. The speech of lawyers seeking clients receives some protection from the U.S. Constitution's First Amendment guarantee of free speech. As a consequence, the U.S. Supreme Court has held that legal ethics rules cannot categorically ban all forms of solicitation, especially those that do not involve in-person or live telephone contact between lawyers and potential clients. Thus, lawyers may, with limited exceptions, solicit clients through the mails either by sending anonymous announcements or by targeting individuals whom they believe might have need of particular legal services. For example, a lawyer might find from the local courthouse a list of those persons against whom real estate foreclosure proceedings have been inaugurated and send a letter to those persons offering to provide legal assistance. Furthermore, the Supreme Court has held that even the rules against in-person solicitation do not apply to lawyers who do not solicit clients for the purpose of earning fees. Thus, public interest lawyers may generally solicit clients—even in person—when they do not plan to charge the clients a fee.

Just because lawyers use the mails to solicit clients does not mean that legal and ethical scrutiny of solicitation ends. First, some states have imposed waiting periods before lawyers may attempt to contact accident victims, even through the mails. The Supreme Court has upheld this kind of restriction. Moreover, even when a form of solicitation is permissible in principle, lawyers may not make misrepresentations to potential clients or exert undue influence or badger them after having been told to stop soliciting.

Persons who believe themselves to have been improperly solicited by lawyers may register complaints with the state or local bar association. A lawyer who engages in an improper solicitation may be found guilty of an ethical violation. In such a case, the bar may sanction the guilty lawyer in a variety of ways, including through reprimanding, suspending, or disbarring the lawyer.

—Timothy L. Hall

See also Attorney-client relationship; Attorney fees; Contingency fees; Legal services plans; Litigation expenses; Model Rules of Professional Conduct; Personal injury attorneys; Unauthorized practice of law.

SPEEDY TRIAL REQUIREMENT

Presentation of an accused person for trial within a reasonable amount of time to expedite justice and to prevent defendants from languishing in jail indefinitely

The guarantee of a speedy trial for persons accused of criminal wrongdoing is a concept rooted in English common law. Although the Sixth Amendment to the U.S. Constitution guarantees the right to a speedy trial, it does not specify what length of time is appropriate. The Supreme Court has refrained from clearly separating permissible trial delays from unconstitutional delays, preferring instead to evaluate delays on a case-by-case basis according to a balancing approach. Under this approach, developed in *Barker v. Wingo* (1972), the Court considers the length and reason for the delay as well as whether the delay was to the defendant's advantage or disadvantage. The Court left the task of setting more definite time limits to state and federal legislatures. In 1974 Congress passed the Speedy Trial Act, which set a normal deadline of one hundred days between arrest and trial in federal courts; many states later passed similar laws.

Although the guarantee of speedy trial is derived from the Constitution, Court decisions interpreting the due process and equal protection clauses of the Fourteenth Amendment have provided for speedy trials in state criminal proceedings; for example, in *Klopfer v. North Carolina* (1967), the Court ruled unconstitutional a North Carolina law allowing the indefinite postponement of a trial. It also ruled in *Strunk v. United States* (1973) that dismissal of charges was the only acceptable remedy for violation of a defendant's right to speedy trial.

—*Michael H. Burchett*

See also Bill of Rights, U.S.; Change of venue; Due process of law; Gag orders; Statutes of limitations; Trials.

STANDARDS OF PROOF

Rules that determine how much and what sort of evidence is enough to win in a court of law in order to ensure that all defendants and involved parties receive fair trials

There are three separate standards of proof, two for "civil" (noncriminal) cases and another for criminal cases. In most civil cases, the standard is generally said to require proving a case "by a preponderance of the evidence." This means convincing the court that one side's position is more likely true than the other side's position. In these cases, the same standard applies to both sides.

In some civil cases, such as those involving fraud, the party bringing the lawsuit is required to prove a case by providing "clear and convincing evidence." Under this standard, the court must be persuaded that the accusation or claim is highly probable, not merely more likely true than not true.

These civil standards are basically "judge-made"; that is, they were developed as part of the English common law, and those traditions have been followed by American courts. The distinction between the two types of civil cases has its origin in ancient English law, where there were two court systems, one of law and one of "equity." Cases heard in law courts were decided under the "preponderance" standard, while those heard in courts of equity were decided under the "clear and convincing" standard.

Although most modern American court systems have only courts of law, the ancient distinction still remains. Sometimes the standard to be applied is included in the law the court is asked to enforce; where the statute does not say, however, the courts resort to the common-law tradition and to their understanding of the legislature's purposes in passing the law.

In a criminal case, the party bringing the case is the government, which is usually far more powerful and with much less to lose than the other side. A much higher standard of proof is applied to the government: Before it can win, it must prove its position "beyond a reasonable doubt." That means the accused person cannot be found guilty unless the court is convinced that the government has definitely proved every necessary part of its case. This standard has long been followed in both England and the United States, and it has been expressly required in American criminal cases since 1970, when the United States Supreme Court formally adopted that language in *In re Winship* (1970).

See also Burden of proof; Chain of custody; Dismissal; Evidence, rules of.

STANDING

Jurisdictional requirement in federal court that a litigant has been injured or threatened with imminent injury by the governmental action of which he or she complains; sometimes called "standing to sue"

Unlike the other federal justiciability doctrines—mootness, ripeness, political question, and the ban on advisory opinions—standing focuses primarily on the party bringing an issue before the court and only secondarily on the issues the party seeks to adjudicate. To have standing, any litigant raising an issue in federal court must meet three constitutionally mandated requirements: injury, causation, and redressability. In addition, the Supreme Court has imposed nonconstitutional, or "prudential," restrictions, prohibiting third-party claims and generalized grievances. Plaintiffs challenging agency action under a federal statute must satisfy a third prudential requirement: The rights they are attempting to vindicate must fall within the "zone of interests" protected by the statute. The so-called prudential requirements, not being constitutionally mandated, may be waived by Congress.

A variety of reasons have been articulated by the Court and by scholars for the standing requirements. By requiring that a plaintiff have a personal stake in the outcome of a case, standing was said in *Baker v. Carr* (1962) to improve judicial decision making by ensuring the "concrete adverseness which sharpens the presentation of issues upon which the court so largely depends for illumination of difficult constitutional questions"; it is also said to promote judicial efficiency by preventing a deluge of lawsuits brought by persons with nothing more than a political or ideological interest in the outcome. By ensuring that plaintiffs can litigate only their own rights, standing is said to promote fairness by excluding meddlers who may be trying to protect the interests of those who do not want or feel the need for such protection. Finally, and probably most important, standing limits the availability of judicial review of congressional and executive decisions and thus promotes the separation of powers, which the Court has called the "single basic idea" of standing in *Allen v. Wright* (1984).

As a jurisdictional requirement, standing cannot be waived by the parties; even when the defendant does not raise it, the court may do so *sua sponte,* or voluntarily, at any stage of the proceedings, even on appeal. If a decision is ultimately made against standing, the case is dismissed, even if the matter has already been decided on the merits by the trial court and has gone through one or two appeals.

Injury

The Court ruled that a plaintiff must "show he personally has suffered some actual or threatened injury" in *Valley Forge Christian College v. Americans United for Separation of Church and State* (1982). The requirement ensures the existence of an actual dispute between litigants and is at the heart of the standing doctrine. The "personal" component was emphasized in *Sierra Club v. Morton* (1972), where the Court denied standing in an environmental case to an organization that had failed to allege that any of its members had used the land threatened by the challenged governmental policies and therefore could not show any injury to the members. The "actual or threatened" component was explained in *City of Los Angeles v. Lyons* (1983). A black man who had been injured when subjected to a choke hold by police officers was permitted to sue for damages, but he was denied standing to seek an injunction against future use of the life-threatening choke hold by police officers because he could not show that he himself was likely to be subjected to it again.

No rule or defining principle exists to determine what kind of injury will satisfy standing. However, clearly injuries to common law (personal injury, contract, property), constitutional, and statutory rights are sufficient to confer standing. In addition, the court has recognized the fact or threat of criminal prosecution (*Wisconsin v. Yoder,* 1972), economic harm (*Barlow v. Collins,* 1970), and injury to aesthetic interests (*Lujan v. Defenders of Wildlife,* 1972). Injuries that the court has held insufficient to afford standing include stigmatization by a governmental policy of granting tax-exempt status to private schools that discriminate on the basis of race (*Allen v. Wright*) and a threat to marital happiness because state abortion laws force a choice between refraining from normal sexual relations and endangering the wife's health (*Roe v. Wade,* 1973).

Mere existence of an injury is not enough. A plaintiff must also show that the injury was caused by the governmental action of which he or she complained and is likely to be redressed by the requested relief. Originally treated as a single test in which one or the other must be proved in *Warth v. Seldin* (1975), causation and redressability later became two separate tests, each of which must be established, in *Allen v. Wright.* The concepts are closely enough related that ordinarily either both or neither will be met. *Simon v. Eastern Kentucky Welfare Rights Organization* (1976), for example, involved a challenge to an Internal Revenue Service (IRS) regulation reducing the amount of free medical care that tax-exempt hospitals were required to provide. Plaintiffs argued that they were injured by the denial of needed medical care. The Court nevertheless denied standing because it was "purely speculative" whether the plaintiffs' loss of medical services could be traced to the IRS ruling and because there was no substantial likelihood that victory in the case would ensure the plaintiffs received the hospital care they sought.

No Third-Party Claims

The legal rights and interests asserted must be those of the plaintiff, not those of a third person not a party to the lawsuit. In *Warth v. Seldin*, taxpayers of Rochester, New York, sought to challenge allegedly discriminatory zoning in the suburb of Penfield, alleging that they were injured by higher property-tax rates resulting from Rochester's need to provide additional low-income housing. The Court refused to allow the Rochester taxpayers to assert the constitutional rights of low-income minorities allegedly excluded from Penfield.

Four well-established exceptions exist. First, a third-party claim will be allowed when the third party is unlikely to be able to sue or have an incentive to do so. In *Griswold v. Connecticut* (1965), a physician charged with distributing contraceptives to a married couple was permitted to raise the substantive due process rights of the couple, and in *Powers v. Ohio* (1991), a black criminal defendant convicted by an all-white jury was permitted to raise the rights of black jurors excluded from the jury. Second, a third-party claim may also be allowed when there is a close relationship between the plaintiff and the third party. In *Pierce v. Society of Sisters* (1925), a religious school was permitted to raise the constitutional rights of its students and their parents when the state attempted to require that children attend public school. Third, an association will be permitted to assert the rights of its members, as in *National Association for the Advancement of Colored People v. Alabama* (1958).

A fourth exception to the third-party rule is the overbreadth doctrine. In First Amendment cases, a litigant has been permitted to make a facial challenge to a statute even though the law, if narrowly construed, could constitutionally prohibit the litigant's activity. Such a facial challenge is permitted when the law appears to be overly broad and thus possibly having a chilling effect on constitutionally protected activity. In *Schad v. Borough of Mount Ephraim* (1981), an adult bookstore was prosecuted for presenting nude dancing in an area where the zoning laws excluded all live entertainment. The Court, even while assuming that nude dancing was not protected by the First Amendment, still allowed the store owner to raise in defense the First Amendment rights of others to present constitutionally protected live entertainment.

Other Prudential Requirements

The Court will ordinarily deny standing when a plaintiff's only injury is as a taxpayer or citizen asserting an interest in having the government obey the law. In *Frothingham v. Mellon* (1923), the Court denied standing to a taxpayer who challenged the constitutionality, under the Tenth Amendment, of the Federal Maternity Act of 1921. Although the improper expenditure of taxpayers' money may arguably amount to an injury to an individual taxpayer, her interest was "comparatively minute and indeterminable." In *Schlesinger v. Reservists Committee to Stop the War* (1974), the Court held that plaintiffs in their capacity as U.S. citizens lacked the capacity to challenge, under Article I, section 6, of the Constitution, the practice of allowing members of Congress to hold commissions in the armed forces reserves. In *Flast v. Cohen* (1968), the Court created a narrow exception by allowing standing when the taxpayer alleged that Congress was violating a particular constitutional prohibition, such as the establishment clause of the First Amendment, rather than merely exceeding its delegated powers, as in *Frothingham*.

In cases where a claim is brought under a federal statute and the plaintiff is not directly subject to the contested regulatory action, the Court has established an additional requirement: that the right or interest the plaintiff is attempting to vindicate be within the zone of interests protected or regulated by the statute. The Court stated in *Clarke v. Securities Industries Association* (1987) that the zone-of-interests requirement is not meant to establish a high barrier for plaintiffs and that it is the defendant who bears the burden of proving the congressional intent to preclude judicial review in such cases. This is an example of a congressional waiver of a prudential requirement. The Court's willingness to find standing to challenge an administrative action under a statute, while it would likely deny standing to such a general claim brought under the Constitution, is a reflection of the Court's concern with judicial restraint and its proper role vis-à-vis the other branches.

A Controversial Doctrine

Standing is among the most analyzed and most criticized of judicial doctrines. The Court's treatment of it over the years has been called incoherent, erratic, and bizarre. It has even been suggested that there should be no standing doctrine at all, that the question of standing is part of the merits of the litigant's claim. Much of the problem stems from the Court's inability to develop a consistent philosophy of standing and to relate it to a view of the proper role of the judiciary in a system of checks and balances and of the proper role of a national judiciary in a federal system. Although there is much to be said for the efforts of, particularly, the Burger Court (1969-1986) to respect the separation of powers and to avoid unnecessary judicial intervention in the affairs of the other branches of government, it should be recognized that an overly narrow view of standing will deny legitimate litigants their day in court.

Suggested Readings

Fairly detailed surveys of the standing doctrine may be found in the standard general treatises on U.S. constitutional law. A particularly comprehensive and useful example is the four-volume work by Ronald D. Rotunda and John E. Novak, *Treatise on Constitutional Law: Substance and Procedure* (2d ed., Vol 1., St. Paul, Minn.: West Publishing, 1992). A briefer review is available in Rotunda and Novak's one-volume edition, *Constitutional Law* (5th ed., St. Paul, Minn.: West Publishing, 1995). Other reliable single-volume treatises include Erwin Chemerinsky's *Constitutional Law, Principles and Policies* (New York: Aspen Law & Business, 1997) and Charles Alan Wright's *The Law of Federal Courts* (St. Paul, Minn.: West Publishing, 1994). Lawrence H. Tribe's *American Constitutional Law* (3d ed., Mineola, N.Y.: Foundation Press, 2000) offers a somewhat different organizational perspective. Most of the serious analysis and criticism of the doctrine is to be found in the law reviews. Among the more interesting and influential commentaries is Antonin Scalia's defense (before he became a Supreme Court justice) of a narrow concept of standing in "The Doctrine of Standing as an Essential Element of the Separation of Powers," *Suffolk Law Review* 17 (1983), and two arguments for a broader approach, Mark Tushnet's "The New Law of Standing, a Plea for Abandonment," *Cornell Law Review* 62 (1977), and William Fletcher's "The Structure of Standing," *Yale Law Journal* 98 (1988). A well-reasoned critique of the ban on generalized grievances can be found in Donald Doernberg's "We the People: John Locke, Collective Constitutional Rights, and Standing to Challenge Government Action," *California Law Review* 73 (1985). A particularly interesting and creative proposal helped to shape the view of a generation of law students: Christopher D. Stone, "Should Trees Have Standing?—Toward Legal Rights for Natural Objects," *Southern California Law Review* 45 (1972).

—*William V. Dunlap*

See also Advisory opinions; Judicial review; Lawsuits; Litigation.

STATE COURTS

Courts that can hear cases subject to state constitutions and laws, in contrast to federal courts, established under Article III of the U.S. Constitution, which hear cases involving federal law

Much of the judicial activity that takes place in the United States falls within the jurisdiction of state courts, which range from traffic courts and police courts to state supreme courts. State courts hear cases that do not directly involve federal laws, although underlying every decision such courts reach is the mandate that there be no violation of the rights of plaintiffs as guaranteed by the U.S. Constitution, which provides for a national court system.

The Supreme Court and State Courts

The sovereignty of states is a fundamental part of the U.S. system of government. States' rights have been jealously and zealously guarded since the nation's inception. Even those who favor a strong central government are generally convinced of the necessity of permitting states to reflect the cultural and societal norms of their various populations.

Under the independent and adequate state grounds doctrine articulated in *Murdock v. Memphis* (1875), the Supreme Court must accept the interpretation by state courts of the constitutions of their particular states, although such interpretations must not violate the Constitution. In all matters where state laws conflict with federal mandates, judges are enjoined by law to uphold the federal mandates.

The Supreme Court does not review the decisions of state courts unless federal questions are introduced early in the proceedings so that such questions can be heard at every level of the state's jurisdiction. The Court also denies petitions for the appeal of cases involving federal questions if the petitioners have failed to comply with the procedures and policies of the state courts. Further, the Court has ruled that it will consider no *habeas corpus* petitions until the petitioners have exhausted all remedies available to them at the state level.

The Court has final authority in accepting or rejecting cases that petitioners wish to bring before it. It accepts fewer than 10 percent of the state court cases it is asked to review. Some of the cases that come before the Court proceed from lower federal court decisions in cases that originated in state courts and later were transferred into the federal venue because they involved federal law.

Judicial Federalism
Relations between state courts and federal courts, including the Supreme Court, are referred to as judicial federalism. This concept establishes a hierarchical structure of appeals and redress. The state courts, although they are established by the constitutions of their states and function under the legal codes of those states, are required under the law to give precedence to federal law if it conflicts with state law. The U.S. Constitution prevails in cases where a state constitution conflicts with it in some way.

Judicial federalism was established during John Marshall's term as chief justice of the Court, which ran from 1801 to 1835. Resisting strong opposition from some state courts in the early years of the fledgling republic, Marshall fought for and won the right of the Court to be the final arbiter in deciding whether state laws were consistent with the Constitution, laws, and treaties of the United States.

Although the Court has the ultimate and decisive power in adjudicating legal matters arising from state court decisions, it has generally been scrupulous in observing comity, or the courtesy that one jurisdiction accords another by upholding its laws. Comity is not legally imposed on the Court but has arisen because of its respect and historical deference to state courts. In some cases, such as *Commonwealth v. Aves* (1836), comity has been set aside. In this case, the supreme judicial court of Massachusetts, a free state, released a slave brought from Louisiana to Massachusetts by a visitor. The Court found in favor of Massachusetts, rejecting arguments that this northern state should accord comity to the slave laws of Louisiana.

Division of Labor

From the nation's beginnings until about 1920, state and federal courts existed side by side largely to distribute the judicial responsibilities and the labor involved in them in what seemed the most reasonable and manageable fashion. State courts were to enforce the laws and constitutional guarantees of the various states. Federal courts were to enforce the guarantees of the Constitution, particularly the Bill of Rights. The duties and jurisdiction of the two court systems were clearly if somewhat informally defined, and for the most part, each system enjoyed considerable autonomy.

Between 1920 and 1950, however, the Supreme Court began gradually to increase its supervision of state courts. It nullified the findings of a number of state court decisions, particularly those from southern states that reached the appellate level and were related to the Fourteenth Amendment's guarantees of due process and equal protection under the law.

The Court maneuvered around petitions from prisoners who had been convicted in state courts and sought the protection of the Fourth, Fifth, Sixth, Seventh, and Eighth Amendments that federal defendants were accorded. Rather than considering such cases in the light of the amendments cited, the Court, observing comity and acceding to the state courts' jurisdiction, usually invoked the Fourteenth Amendment's guarantees of due process and of a fair trial for defendants who did not have legal representation.

The Court did what it could to provide the state courts with the latitude they needed to operate effectively. In so doing, it articulated precepts of fundamental fairness and due process that were vague and subjective at best. The judges in many state courts made strenuous efforts to base their proceedings and decisions on legal precedents. Some judges, however, used the absence of definitive guidelines to promote their own social agendas.

Earl Warren and State Courts

Earl Warren served as chief justice of the United States from 1954 until 1969. The social upheaval that followed the assassination of President John F. Kennedy and grew out of widespread discontent over the Vietnam War raged during the later years of Warren's tenure.

Firmly committed to protecting the civil rights of Americans, Warren insisted that the Bill of Rights be applied to the nation's state courts, many of which were dealing with the thorny issues of racial segregation, draft evasion, and civil disobedience. Warren's resolve resulted in the Court's overturning many decisions rendered by state appellate and supreme courts in regard to criminal defendants, especially those arrested for participating in public demonstrations related to race relations and the Vietnam War.

The Warren Court aroused the animus of nearly every state court justice in the United States. Warren's violations of comity resulted in widespread calls for his impeachment, although what he was doing was protected by the provisions of Article III of the Constitution and provided no substantial grounds to warrant impeachment.

The Burger and Rehnquist Courts

After Warren's retirement, Warren E. Burger was appointed chief justice, serving from 1969 until 1986. Under his leadership, the Court became less activist. It substantially abridged the impact of many of the Warren Court's civil liberties decisions. Some state supreme courts, stung badly by the limitations the Warren Court had imposed on them, now sought to alter their state constitutions to provide broader protections from federal interference than had been available to them during Warren's term of office.

The Burger court encouraged the new judicial federalism that such initiatives suggested. In time, however, the Court reversed many more state court decisions in cases involving civil liberties

Under Chief Justice Warren Burger, the Supreme Court initially took a less activist role in overseeing state court decisions. Eventually, however, the Court overturned many state court decisions. (Supreme Court Historical Society)

or, if not overturning these decisions, returned them to the state courts for further consideration, clearly indicating their unacceptability.

In the Burger Court and that of William H. Rehnquist, the next chief justice, there was a curtailment of lower federal court grants or *habeas corpus* petitions in matters relating to search and seizure and to the death penalty. Because modern federal courts hear so few appeals from state prisoners, whose access to federal courts is denied much more often than it is permitted, the authority of state courts has been increased substantially.

State Court Defiance

Generally Court decisions are honored by the state courts, of which compliance is required under the law. Although compliance is the rule, exceptions occur. Often when state courts openly defy federal mandates, their defiance is overlooked. The Court sometimes makes efforts to placate state courts or to accommodate them. On rare occasions, the Court capitulates to a defiant state court. In deciding how to deal with defiance, the Court has to consider how much of its judicial energy it is willing to expend on the matter.

As early as 1821, in *Cohens v. Virginia*, the state court of Virginia challenged the appellate authority of the Supreme Court, citing section 25 of the Judiciary Act of 1789, under which the Court was granted the right to review federal questions decided on by state courts. In the Court's decision, Marshall upheld the concept of federal supremacy.

In the late twentieth century, the Court granted state courts considerable time to implement mandates in regard to race relations and to clarify ambiguous rulings. It permitted state courts, after hearings at the highest state and federal judicial levels, to prevail in capital cases that involve complicated legal procedures. The Court at times was influenced substantially by state court decisions. It was particularly receptive to the guidance of state supreme courts in matters such as reapportionment, freedom of religion, defendants' rights, and obscenity, where local considerations are of paramount importance. At times, state supreme court rulings directly affected decisions of the Supreme Court. The California high court's decision in *Purdy and Fitzpatrick v. State* (1969) ruled that according special treatment to aliens was a form of discrimination not permitted under the Fourteenth Amendment. Two years later, in a similar case, *Graham v. Richardson* (1971), the Supreme Court reached an identical conclusion.

Although the relationship between state courts and the Supreme Court has frequently varied, the general preference of the Court is to grant as much leeway to the state courts as it reasonably can within the boundaries set by the U.S. Constitution. By shifting authority from federal to state courts as much as it legally is able to do, the Court makes its own workload manageable and reduces the number of appeals with which it has to deal.

—*R. Baird Shuman*

Suggested Readings

One of the most useful essays on this topic by Justice William J. Brennan, Jr., is entitled "Some Aspects of Federalism." It appeared in the *New York University Law Review* 39 (1964): 945-961 and, despite its age, is highly relevant to the topic of state courts. Also informative is *Human Rights in the States: New Directions in Constitutional Policymaking* (Westport, Conn.: Greenwood Press, 1988), edited by Stanley H. Friedelbaum. A number of its essays provide solid insights into the creative tensions that exist between state and federal courts. Archibald Cox presents a fascinating and detailed account in *The Warren Court: Constitutional Decision as an Instrument of Reform* (Cambridge, Mass.: Harvard University Press, 1968) that sheds light on what an activist court can accomplish. G. Alan Tarr and Mary C. Porter delve into the functioning of state supreme courts and their relationship to the Supreme Court in *State Supreme Courts in State and Nation* (New Haven,

Conn.: Yale University Press, 1990). Henry Julian Abraham's *The Judicial Process: An Introductory Analysis of the Courts of the United States, England, and France* (7th ed. New York: Oxford University Press, 1998) has several chapters on state courts.

See also Advisory opinions; Appellate practice; Attorneys general, state; *Certiorari*, writ of; Change of venue; Common law; Counsel, right to; Court types; Criminal justice system; Criminal procedure; District attorneys; Diversity jurisdiction; Judicial appointments and elections; Judicial review; Jurisdiction; Jury duty; Louisiana law.

STATE POLICE

Law-enforcement organizations that operate directly under the authority of state governments, state police carry out certain specific functions—principally highway safety and criminal investigations

The U.S. Constitution assigned to the states the responsibility for maintaining law and order. Until 1900, however, the states entrusted policing mainly to local communities. In case of riots or other serious disorders, governors called out the militia. In Texas the Rangers, a mounted militia, kept the peace in isolated areas in addition to fighting Native Americans and patrolling the Mexican border. Between 1865 and 1875 Massachusetts experimented with a state constabulary. In the late nineteenth century public sentiment remained hostile toward the idea of professional state police forces.

Early State Police Forces

In the 1890's the United States underwent rapid industrialization and grew more interdependent, its parts connected by a vast network of railroads. Crime became more mobile and complex, challenging the resources of local police. At the dawn of the twentieth century there was a pressing need for more specialized, better-trained police at the state level.

The first state to meet that need was Pennsylvania. Like many other newly industrialized areas of the Northeast and Midwest since the Civil War (1861-1865), Pennsylvania suffered chronically from severe social unrest, especially among workers in its coal mines and factories. A fierce, lengthy strike in the anthracite mines in 1902 aroused public opinion to demand that other, more civilized means be found of calming industrial disputes than the indiscriminate clubbing of mine workers by private police. This outcry set in motion a reform movement led by Governor Samuel W. Pennypacker to create a state police. The governor sent John C. Groome, a former officer in the Philippine Constabulary, to Ireland, where he studied the Royal Irish Constabulary (RIC). In 1905 Groome organized the Pennsylvania State Police, recruiting 228 men with military backgrounds, some of whom had also been officers in the Philippine Constabulary. They were given rigorous training and then deployed in four units in western Pennsylvania, where they proved to be impartial and effective at quelling disorder.

Fourteen states established police forces during the next twenty years, the eastern states generally following Pennsylvania's example. Western states, such as Nevada and Colorado, created forces that were extremely brutal and partial to the interests of wealthy absentee employers, especially in the mining industry. In the 1920's modern highways spread out across the United States, creating a new task for state police: traffic control. This required a new approach to policing. Persons wealthy enough to own or drive automobiles were likely to be prosperous merchants and professionals rather than foreign-born coal miners. Police had to be recruited and trained who could deal civilly with middle-class taxpayers, offering traffic safety programs and courteously enforcing traffic regulations.

At the same time, the expense of installing the technology to fight crime led many states to establish bureaus of criminal identification. By 1940 highway patrols or state police were at work in more than 80 percent of the states. They had earned reputations as "elite lawmen." Since World War II state police have continued to be concerned mainly with traffic control, while assuming a more significant role in criminal investigation. State police agencies are characterized by their narrow, specific mandates, reflecting public distrust of centralized policing in the European tradition.

Organization of State Police

The term "state police" is broadly understood to refer to the various agencies of law enforcement that function directly under the authority of the governments of the states, in contrast to county and local police agencies and federal police agencies. This broad definition of state police includes highway patrols, state police forces, and a variety of state investigative agencies. In 1999 there were a total of 55,892 sworn state police officers, joined by 29,550 civilian employees of state police agencies. All U.S. states except Hawaii have state policing agencies. Twenty-six states have highway patrols and twenty-three have state police agencies. Thirty-five states have investigative agencies that are separate from highway patrols or state police. There are, in addition, a great number of specialized investigative bodies, such as fire marshals and fish and wildlife agents. All state law-enforcement entities derive their authority to investigate wrongdoing or enforce the law from the state legislatures, from which they receive most of their funds.

State law enforcement is organized differently from state to state. In some states several agencies are centralized in one department. The Iowa Department of Public Safety, which is headed by a commissioner who reports to the governor, oversees the divisions of state patrol, criminal investigation, fire marshal, capitol security, communications, and administrative services. In other states, law-enforcement agencies are organized in various departments. The California Highway Patrol, for example, is organized in the Business, Transportation, and Housing Agency while the state's investigative agencies are grouped together in the Division of Law Enforcement under a director appointed by the state attorney general. Some state police agencies are controlled by commissions and others by state governors.

State Police Powers

State police in the narrow sense, in contrast to highway patrols, have state-wide powers to arrest persons suspected of both criminal and traffic offenses. Most state police agencies have plainclothes and uniformed agents. They provide the auxiliary services of record-keeping, training, communications, and forensics. Pennsylvania has the largest state police agency and Idaho the smallest.

State highway patrols are usually limited to enforcing traffic regulations, but they are empowered to assist any law-enforcement officer upon request. The investigation of crime is generally left to separate state investigative agencies. California has the largest highway patrol and Wyoming the smallest.

Investigative agencies with statewide authority to arrest have primary jurisdiction in certain crimes. Criminal investigative personnel are plainclothes officers who provide a variety of auxiliary services. They are distinguished from other state investigative agents, such as fish and game inspectors, whose powers are limited to a particular area of enforcement. Florida has the largest state bureau of investigation and North Dakota and South Dakota the smallest.

Role of State Police Broadly Considered

All state law-enforcement agencies require that applicants be U.S. citizens and state residents. Most state police agencies provide a basic course of instruction and training, usually at police academies, and in-service training. The minimum educational requirement is usually a high-school diploma or equivalent. The investigative agencies of California and several other states require that applicants must have completed two or more years of college, concentrating on police sciences.

Regardless of how differently state police systems are organized, they share common functions within law enforcement. They investigate certain crimes as prescribed by state law and provide forensic and other technical services to local police. They also provide specialized investigators, such as narcotics squads, to assist investigations by local agencies. State police enforce, with the power of arrest, state traffic laws and laws pertaining to certain criminal offenses. Usually state constitutions assign to county and municipal police the general responsibility for enforcing state laws and keeping the peace. If rural or unincorporated areas are unwilling or unable to perform these functions, they may contract or arrange for service by state police, as is the case in Alaska, Rhode Island, and Connecticut.

On rare occasions state governments may call upon their police to temporarily assume law-enforcement duties in municipalities, as in New York City in 1935 and Trenton, New Jersey, in 1983. With a few exceptions, the state police's authority to carry arms and to arrest is limited to the areas within state borders. States may enter into mutual agreements with one another that allow their respective police to cross borders in pursuit of fugitives.

STATE POLICE FORCES

Highway Patrols	State Police Agencies
Alabama	Alaska
Arizona	Arkansas
California	Connecticut
Colorado	Delaware
Florida	Idaho
Georgia	Illinois
Iowa	Indiana
Kansas	Kentucky
Minnesota	Louisiana
Mississippi	Maine
Missouri	Maryland
Montana	Massachusetts
Nebraska	Michigan
Nevada	New Hampshire
North Carolina	New Jersey
North Dakota	New Mexico
Ohio	New York
Oklahoma	Oregon
South Carolina	Pennsylvania
South Dakota	Rhode Island
Tennessee	Vermont
Texas	Virginia
Utah	West Virginia
Washington	
Wisconsin	
Wyoming	

State police forces provide information to themselves, to local police within their states, and to other state and federal agencies. Every state has access to the National Crime Information Center of the Federal Bureau of Investigation (FBI). They all have computer information systems for processing criminal records. The effectiveness of communication is improved by regional cooperation, as in the New England State Police Compact, under which police forces share resources in the investigation of organized crime. In most cases state law-enforcement agencies are responsible for collecting, transmitting, and publishing states' crime statistics. State law-enforcement agencies also supply forensic services to their own personnel and to other criminal justice agencies. For the most part, the employees of states' forensic institutions are civilians.

Examples of State Police Forces

Established in May 1905, the Pennsylvania state police was the first state police force in the United States. It is also the largest. Its organization is centralized under a commissioner, who is appointed by the governor and has the rank of colonel. Reporting directly to the commissioner is the Bureau of Professional Responsibility, the Office of General Counsel, the Office of the Budget, and Public Information. A chief of staff responsible for several bureaus of technical and administrative services also reports to the commissioner. A deputy commissioner responsible for a bureau of highway patrol, a bureau of criminal investigation, and five area commands also reports to the commissioner. In addition to the main forensic laboratory in Harrisburg, there are four regional crime laboratories serving local police. The Bureau of Criminal Investigation includes divisions of general investigation, organized crime, fire marshal, and drug-law enforcement.

Recruits to the Pennsylvania state police must be U.S. citizens, state residents, and high-school graduates, and they must meet certain physical requirements. Cadets undergo a twenty-week trooper course at the training academy in Hershey followed by field training and periodic in-service instruction.

Founded in 1929, the California Highway Patrol has grown to be the largest agency of its kind in the United States that focuses on traffic control. Situated in the Business, Transportation, and Housing Agency, it is led by a commissioner, who is appointed by the governor. It is one of two primary state law-enforcement agencies, the other being the California Division of Law Enforcement, which is responsible for criminal identification and investigation and forensic and other technical investigative services. The California Highway Patrol requires its recruits to be U.S. citizens, holders of valid California driver's licenses and high-school graduates. Moreover, they must meet certain physical and legal requirements. Recruits undergo a basic training course of twenty-two weeks at the academy in Yolo County.

—*Charles H. O'Brien*

Suggested Readings

Kenneth H. Bechtel's *State Police in the United States: a Socio-Historical Analysis* (New York: Greenwood Press, 1995) is a thorough, well-balanced study that examines the evolution of state policing in the political, economic, and social context of the early twentieth century. Donald A. Torres's *Handbook of State Police, Highway Patrols, and Investigative Agencies* (New York: Greenwood Press, 1987) thoroughly treats the organization and administration of state police forces. This book is enhanced by many tables illustrating state police organization, illustrations of state uniforms and badges, and a detailed catalog of state police agencies. David R. Johnson's *American Law Enforcement: A History* (St. Louis, Mo.: Forum Press, 1981) provides a chapter on the history of the state police. Bruce Smith's *The State Police: Organization and Administration* (Montclair, N.J.: Patterson Smith, 1969) is an early, influential study favorable to the concept of a centralized, professional state police force. Individual state police forces are described in Phillip M. Conti's *The Pennsylvania State Police. A History of Service to the Commonwealth, 1905 to the Present* (Harrisburg, Pa.: Stackpole Books, 1977) and Scott M. Fisher's *Courtesy, Service, Protection: The Iowa State Patrol* (Dubuque, Iowa: Kendall-Hunt, 1993). John Stark's *Troopers: Behind the Badge* (West Trenton: New Jersey State Police Memorial Association, 1993) is a journalist's lively, anecdotal account of the men and women in one of the larger state police agencies. John P. Kenney's *The California Police* (Springfield, Ill.: Thomas, 1964) is a brief overview of the largest state law-enforcement system. Frank R. Prassel's *The Western Peace Officer: A Legacy of Law and Order* (Norman: University of Oklahoma Press, 1972) offers useful information on policing in the Western states. Two explorations of the role of state and local police within the broader context of law enforcement are *Challenges and Choices for Crime-Fighting Technology: Federal Support of State and Local Law Enforcement*, by William Schwabe and others (Santa Monica, Calif.: Rand, 2001), and *Militarizing the American Criminal Justice System: The Changing Roles of the Armed Forces and the Police*, edited by Peter B. Kraska (Boston: Northeastern University Press, 2001).

See also Criminal justice system; Federal Bureau of Investigation; Law enforcement; Police; Sheriffs.

STATUTES

Laws enacted by legislative bodies and interpreted by courts, administrative agencies, and practicing lawyers of the appropriate jurisdiction

Statutes, or laws written by legislatures, are often contrasted with common law—that is, law arising primarily from judicial decisions and only later, if ever, codified in statutory or similar form. In the United States, Great Britain, and other English-speaking countries most law was traditionally of the common-law variety, the decision of legal questions being based on results in prior cases (precedent) and judges' own sense of equity or fairness in the case at hand. In the twentieth century the vastly increased pace of regulatory legislation, including antitrust, securities, environmental, labor, and various antidiscrimination laws, together with tax and commercial law statutes, meant that statutory law had become as important or more important than common law, especially at the federal level. Indeed, courts and practicing attorneys still spend much of their time dealing with the interpretation and application of federal and state statutes. In this sense, the difference between the English-speaking countries and the so-called civil law jurisdictions, such as France and Italy, which do not have a common-law tradition and have always relied primarily on statutory law, has been reduced in recent times.

Statutes create work for lawyers at all levels of the legislation and interpretation process. Many senators, congressmen, and state legislators are themselves practicing attorneys, and legislative committees employ staff attorneys to provide technical assistance in drafting various bills. At the administrative level—for example, the Internal Revenue Service (IRS) for tax laws and the Justice Department for antitrust or antidiscrimination statutes—still more lawyers are required to write regulations and supervise enforcement efforts. Finally, many private attorneys emphasize statutory law in their day-to-day practice, especially in specialty areas that are largely statutory in nature. This type of practice is highly challenging, because it requires familiarity with legislative and administrative sources together with more widely known judicial or court decisions. Thus, a tax lawyer must remain up to date about new and proposed tax legislation, IRS regulations and rulings, and judicial decisions in tax-related cases.

A major debate has focused on the interpretation of statutes. While U.S. Supreme Court Justice Antonin Scalia and others have argued that statutes should be interpreted according to their literal language, their opponents have argued that legislative history, including committee reports and floor debates, should be accorded greater and at times decisive weight. A parallel debate has focused on the degree of deference that courts should accord to administrative agency decisions that delineate the scope or breadth of particular statutes. How these debates will turn out is uncertain, but the vehemence with which they have been conducted highlights the increasing importance of statutory law throughout the American legal system.

—Michael A. Livingston

See also Annotated codes; Capital punishment; Civil law; Common law; Contracts; Court-awarded fees; Ignorance of the law; Judges; Legislative counsel; Lesser included offense; Long-arm statutes; Multiple jurisdiction offenses; Statutes of limitations; Three-strikes laws; Uniform laws.

STATUTES OF LIMITATIONS

Periods of time during which actions may be brought to enforce legal rights; the principle reflects the notion that legal challenges should be made in a timely fashion and defendants should not be required to defend stale claims

Statutes of limitations restrict the period of time during which an action may be brought to enforce legal rights. The requirement of a statute of limitations encourages lawsuits to be brought promptly when evidence is fresh and also grants defendants the comfort that after a reasonable time they will be free from potential claims. Statutes of limitations in the civil context are often called "statutes of repose."

The statute of limitations requires that a party must file a suit in a court of competent jurisdiction before the statute expires (or "runs," in common parlance) if the court is to have jurisdiction over the matter. If a party attempts to file a suit after the expiration of the statute, the defendants will plead as an "affirmative defense" that the statute of limitations has expired. If indeed it has, the case will be dismissed.

A statute of limitations has three parts. First, it defines when the limitations period begins to run. For example, for a tort action, the statute usually begins when the injury occurs. For a contract action, the alleged breach of contract starts the statute of limitations running. Second, the statute of limitations states the period of time during which actions may be brought. Different types of actions have different limitation periods. Disfavored actions, such as defamation of character, have relatively short statutes of one year or so. Negligence actions usually have a two-year to three-year period of limitations, while contract actions and actions based on written instruments have limitation periods of five or six years. Third, a statute defines what "tolls" the limitations period—that is, stops it from running. For example, the commencement of an action by filing suit tolls the statute of limitations, and a statute is often tolled during the legal incapacity of the plaintiff (for example, during the period of time the plaintiff is a minor).

Statutes of limitations also apply in criminal law: The state must indict or otherwise bring official charges against a defendant within the specified period of time. If the statute runs without charges being filed, the defendant is forever protected from prosecution and may even confess without fear of punishment. In the criminal context, a statute of limitations is an act of grace of the state, which surrenders its right to prosecute alleged wrongdoers. Thus, the state is more likely to surrender the right to prosecute for minor crimes than for serious ones. For example, the statute of limitations for a misdemeanor assault is typically one year. By contrast, there is no statute of limitations for murder, and in difficult cases the state can (and often does) bring charges after many years.

See also Breach of contract; Contracts; Indictments; Speedy trial requirement; Statutes.

STRICT LIABILITY

Liability that is imposed on a person or entity that disregards who is at fault when a person or party is injured

Historically, legal liability was imposed only if a party causing an injury was at fault. The minimum degree of fault for imposing liability was negligence. Strict liability is considered a radical theory by many academics because it imposes legal liability without an individual or entity being at fault. The rationale for imposing liability without fault is that often traditional legal theories fail to redress injuries unless a party is at fault. The purpose of strict liability is to shift the loss from the injured party to the party who was in the best position to prevent the injury.

Strict liability has been applied in extremely hazardous and abnormally dangerous activities such as the use of explosives. Courts have recognized that even though a person may use explosives properly and with the proper degree of care, explosives are somewhat unpredictable and may injure others. In these types of circumstances, strict liability may be imposed.

Strict liability has also been applied in situations involving animals that cause injury to others. For example, strict liability has been imposed where a party keeps a wild animal outside its natural environment and the animal causes property damage or personal injury. Strict liability may also be applied to damage caused by domestic animals that have exhibited dangerous propensities, such as a vicious dog. Strict liability also has been imposed on the owners of livestock when that livestock trespasses on another's property and causes damage.

Products liability is an area where strict liability has become increasingly important. In strict product liability, a manufacturer, distributor, or vendor of a product can be held strictly liable if a product is defective and unreasonably dangerous and causes injury to the user because of the defect.

States have also enacted statutes that extend strict liability to certain situations. Workers' compensation statutes impose strict liability on employers for injuries to employees that occur in the workplace, regardless of fault. Payments are made to an injured employee from a common insurance fund created from employer-paid premiums. Statutes also impose strict liability on certain crimes.

Examples of strict liability crimes include adulterating or misbranding drugs, polluting the air and water, and statutory rape.

Still other states have enacted statutes codifying court decisions regarding strict liability. For example, several states have statutes that impose strict liability on dog owners for damages suffered by persons bitten by their dogs.

There are defenses to strict liability; they focus on the injured party's contribution of fault to the injury. For example, misuse of a product or assumption of the risk may be valid defenses to certain strict liability actions. Further, privileges may exist to defend against injuries occurring in ultrahazardous activities where there is a desirable social benefit from the activity.

See also Joint and several liability; Liability, civil and criminal; Negligence; Punitive damages; Torts.

SUBPOENA POWER

Power of the courts to require persons with knowledge of relevant events to testify at trial, to ensure that accused persons receive the most effective defense possible

Among other important rights guaranteed to accused persons by the United States Constitution, the Sixth Amendment of the Bill of Rights guarantees a person the basic right "to have compulsory process for obtaining witnesses in his favor." That process is the right to request that a subpoena be issued to compel people who have direct knowledge of one's case to appear in court to testify on one's behalf. Regardless of whether they are "too busy" or do not want to appear, the law compels them to testify.

If subpoenaed, a person is legally required to appear in court. Failure to appear can result in a fine or imprisonment for contempt of court. Sometimes testimony can be postponed or taken by deposition (sworn testimony put into writing), but a subpoenaed person is not given the option of refusing to testify.

The technical term for an ordinary subpoena ordering someone to testify in court is *subpoena ad testificandum*. There is also a type of subpoena that orders someone to turn over specific documents or papers to the court. That is called a *subpoena duces tecum*.

Occasionally a person not wanting to turn over a paper to a court may plead the right of privacy or attempt to invoke the Fourth Amendment prohibition against warrantless searches and seizures. Courts have seldom paid much attention to such protests. Even the Fifth Amendment provision against self-incrimination has seldom prevented courts from ordering documents turned over. Administrative agencies in the executive branch normally have these same powers of subpoena. The federal government has always taken a broad interpretation of its own powers. The argument for these powers is the right of the accused to build as strong a case as possible in his or her own defense.

See also Affidavits; Bench warrants; Bill of Rights, U.S.; Clerks of the court; Discovery; Grand juries; Judges; Summons; Witnesses.

SUMMARY JUDGMENTS

Judicial decisions made on lawsuits without going through the process of trials—decisions that can only be issued by courts when the facts of cases are not in question

A summary judgment is a decision made by a court at the request of a party involved in a lawsuit without the need for a trial. The decision can be made without hearing evidence only if the two sides do not dispute the facts involved in the case. The judgment is made strictly on the court's interpretation of the laws that apply to the situation.

Summary judgments can only be made in civil actions. They are not allowed in criminal cases. Either party involved in a lawsuit can make a request for a summary judgment by claiming that the facts of the case are not in doubt. If the other side disagrees, it can submit a list of specific facts in dispute.

State and federal regulations determine how a request for summary judgment can be made. For example, it may be necessary for a party involved in a lawsuit to make a request for summary judgment at least twenty days after the lawsuit was first initiated. It may also be necessary to make the request at least ten days before the date set to hear such requests. In general, one side involved in a lawsuit is allowed to make a request for summary judgment immediately after the opposing side has made its own request.

—*Rose Secrest*

See also Civil actions; Dismissal; Lawsuits; Verdicts.

SUMMONS

Legal document notifying a person to appear in court and answer a complaint or charge

When legal action is initiated against persons, those persons receive a summons stating that they are defendants and must file an answer with the court by a specified date. Attached to the summons is a complaint, typically involving a lawsuit, with details of the charges. A summons is usually prepared by an officer of the court or, in some cases, by the plaintiff's attorney. In contrast to a subpoena, a person receiving a summons does not break the law by not appearing in court, but if the defendant is absent, the plaintiff will most likely win the case.

In general, a summons must be handed directly to the defendant. However, if the defendant is a nonresident of a state, most states allow the publication of a summons as a notice in a newspaper. If a defendant is a state resident and leaves the state for the purpose of concealment, then most state statutes allow mailing a copy of the summons to the last known address, leaving the summons with a person of suitable age and discretion at the defendant's residence, or, if such a responsible person cannot be found, attaching the summons to the door of the residence. Even if the defendant never receives a copy of the official summons, a plaintiff can pursue the case as long as the summons was delivered by the specified time according to a method described in the state's laws.

—*Alvin K. Benson*

See also Civil actions; Defendants; Injunctions; Jurisdiction; Jury duty; Lawsuits; Subpoena power.

SUPREME COURT, U.S.

Highest court in the United States and the final interpreter of whether the laws and actions of the United States government, states, cities, and its citizens are permissible under the U.S. Constitution

The Supreme Court defines the authority and powers of the national government, states, and cities and the nature of individual rights. Individual rights, such as the freedom of speech and the right to privacy, protect citizens from the abuses of government authority. The present size of the Supreme Court, nine, was last set by the U.S. Congress in 1869. The most important power of the Supreme Court is its power of judicial review, through which its justices determine whether national, state, or city laws violate the Constitution. Judicial review is also its most controversial power, because in exercising it nine justices can nullify the decisions of government bodies that are democratically elected. Some of the Supreme Court's most controversial decisions have been *Roe v. Wade* (1973), which protected women's right to abortion as part of the right to privacy and thus declared state criminal abortion laws to be unconstitutional, and *Brown v. Board of Education* (1954) which outlawed racial segregation in the schools, thus overturning decades of segregation in the U.S. South. Supreme Court power is also very substantial when it interprets what a law passed by Congress means.

Appointment and Jurisdiction

Supreme Court justices are chosen by the president of the United States with the advice and consent of the U.S. Senate. It is not unusual for presidential nominees to withdraw their names from consideration when negative information about them comes to light, nor is it unusual for nominees to be turned down by the Senate for many reasons, including Senate opposition to a nominee's views on legal questions. Appointment to the Supreme Court is for life or good behavior. Only through resignation, death, or impeachment by the U.S. House of Representatives and trial by the Senate do justices leave the Supreme Court. Only one justice has been formally impeached.

Article III of the Constitution specifies that the Supreme Court has both original and appellate jurisdiction. It has original and exclusive jurisdiction—that is, it is the court of first resort—in controversies between two or more states. It has original but not exclusive jurisdiction in cases involving public ministers and consuls and in all actions by a state against citizens of another state or against aliens. However, late twentieth century practice was for the Court to take most cases on appeal from federal district and circuit courts or the highest level state appellate courts. Parties seeking Supreme Court action request the Court to reply positively to writs of *certiorari*, writs to direct lower courts to supply the Supreme Court with the records in a case. The Supreme Court has complete discretion as to whether it hears cases.

The Rule of Four

For the Court to agree to hear a case, four justices must agree to take it. This is known as the rule of four. In the 1990's most justices allowed their law clerks, individually or in pools, to review the appeals to the Court for action. Clerks make summaries of legal issues, on the basis of which the justices decide whether to hear a

CHIEF JUSTICES OF THE UNITED STATES		
Chief Justice	**Years Served**	**Appointed by**
John Jay	1789-1795	George Washington
Oliver Ellsworth	1796-1800	George Washington
John Marshall	1801-1835	John Adams
Roger B. Taney	1836-1864	Andrew Jackson
Salmon P. Chase	1864-1873	Abraham Lincoln
Morrison R. Waite	1874-1888	Ulysses S. Grant
Melville W. Fuller	1888-1910	Grover Cleveland
Edward D. White	1910-1921	William Howard Taft
William Howard Taft	1921-1930	Warren G. Harding
Charles Evans Hughes	1930-1941	Herbert Hoover
Harlan Fiske Stone	1941-1946	Franklin D. Roosevelt
Fred M. Vinson	1946-1953	Harry S. Truman
Earl Warren	1953-1969	Dwight D. Eisenhower
Warren E. Burger	1969-1986	Richard M. Nixon
William Rehnquist	1986-	Ronald Reagan

case. Losing parties in federal district and circuit courts, in specialized courts that have been set up by Congress such as the tax Court, and in state supreme courts appeal to the U.S. Supreme Court to reverse the actions of these lower courts. For a case to be taken on appeal from a state court it must present a substantial federal question—for example, a state law's violation of the U.S. Constitution. In many instances the Supreme Court takes cases when the federal circuit and district courts have conflicting interpretations of constitutional rights and federal laws, especially when the issues in conflict are important to the nation. A good example of this is the Court's 1992 decision to reaffirm the central holdings of *Roe v. Wade*. By so doing, the Supreme Court ensures that the Constitution, the laws of the United States, and its treaties continue to be the "supreme law of the land" and binding on all courts and individuals in the United States.

In the 1990's more than 4,500 cases were brought to the Supreme Court. However, in fewer than 130 of these cases did the Supreme Court hear oral arguments and write full opinions. Another 75 to 125 cases each year were reviewed by the Court through brief decisions without oral arguments.

Briefs

All cases require that there be real controversies between two parties, such as individuals, states, cities, or corporations. The opposing parties must present detailed legal briefs. These documents must marshal all possible relevant legal principles and precedents. Although the crux of each brief usually focuses on the interpretation of the specific statute or legal principle at issue in the case, some influential briefs in the Court's history have used social science data in support of their positions. For example, in *Brown v. Board of Education* the lawyers representing the children seeking to end racial segregation supplemented their legal brief with psychological studies showing the adverse effects of school segregation on the development of African American children. Whether social science data should be used in determining individual rights is controversial, because it is feared that any change in this data might undermine the individual rights defined by the Supreme Court.

At the Court's invitation or at the mutual request of both parties to a case, advocacy groups may file *amicus curiae* briefs on a party's behalf. These briefs, however, differ significantly from the primary briefs of the two parties. They are usually filed by groups that are interested in preserving or extending certain legal principles rather than in the outcomes of the specific cases they are addressing. A group such as the National Association for the Advancement of Colored People (NAACP) might file a brief in a school desegregation case in order to further its larger goal of African American equality. A group such as the American Civil Liberties Union (ACLU) might file a brief in a flag burning case because it wishes to see the First Amendment's freedom of speech and assembly preserved. In approximately half of the cases during each Court term, the Justice Department files a brief on behalf of the U.S. government.

Oral Argument and Voting

After the justices have read the briefs filed by the opposing sides in a case, they set a date to hear oral argument. In their oral arguments, the attorneys for each party present their side of the case for an allotted period of time, usually thirty minutes. The justices often interrupt the attorneys with questions and discuss legal issues among themselves. In most cases oral argument plays a minor role in the final decision. However, in some cases oral argument is crucial. For example, in landmark decisions, such as *Brown v. Board of Education*, the Supreme Court asks that important constitutional questions be reargued in a later round of oral arguments.

A few days after hearing oral argument the justices confer to discuss and vote on cases. Conferences are secret. At times the notes of justices offer a clue to conference proceedings. Chief Justice William H. Rehnquist has introduced the practice of first allowing the justices to state their views on a case before permitting debate. Workload constraints limit the time the justices spend discussing cases in conference. Only occasionally do these conferences win over an undecided justice to a particular position.

Opinion Writing

After the justices vote on a case in conference, they must decide who writes the majority opinion stating the legal findings of the Court. If the chief justice votes with the majority, he either writes the opinion himself or assigns it to another justice who has voted with the majority. If the chief justice dissents in a case, the senior justice who voted with the majority either writes the opinion or

Justices of the Supreme Court during the 1990's. From left to right, seated: Antonin Scalia, John Paul Stevens, Chief Justice William H. Rehnquist, Sandra Day O'Connor, and Anthony Kennedy; standing: Ruth Bader Ginsburg, David Souter, Clarence Thomas, and Stephen Breyer. (Collection of the Supreme Court of the United States)

assigns it. The majority opinion is the most important written opinion in each case and is always printed first. Any justice may decide to affirm the majority decision or dissent. Members of the Court who agree entirely or to some degree with the majority decision may choose to write a concurring opinion. They usually do so for a number of reasons. First, they may agree with the majority decision but disagree with the legal principles that were used to support it. A concurring opinion allows them to offer an alternative justification for a decision.

Second, justices might agree with both the majority decision and its reasoning but wish to clarify their own views on the case or respond to one or more issues raised by a dissenting opinion. Finally, in some cases justice may write both a concurring opinion and a dissenting opinion on some aspect of the majority opinion with which they disagree. Concurring opinions were rare for most of the Court's history. They became more common in the mid-twentieth century and especially prevalent in the 1960's and 1970's. In the late twentieth century each member of the Court usually wrote from four to twelve concurrent opinions each term.

Conference voting is only an initial show of justices' positions. During the drafting of written opinions justices circulate drafts of written opinions for comment. Any justice might contribute to the draft of a colleague's opinion, make suggestions for revisions, or, in rare cases, even switch sides. Compromises over the language in opinions is common. They result from justices' efforts to win support for their views. For example, a justice writing an opinion may tone down language or add or subtract a principle to win over another justice. Despite the role that such compromise can play in Supreme Court decision making, justices change their initial conference votes in less than 10 percent of the cases they hear. Furthermore, changes in voting alignment usually serve only to increase the size of the majority.

Usually, dissenting opinions are not as legally significant as the majority opinion, for they do not form a precedent that justices feel obliged to follow in later cases. However, dissenting opinions can prove to be more important than even some majority opinions. Such opinions might be unusually forceful or eloquent, as was Justice Oliver Wendell Holmes, Jr.'s dissent in *Gitlow v. New York* (1925), or might advance a novel or influential method of interpretation, as did Justice Thurgood Marshall's unique "sliding-scale" principle in *San Antonio Independent School District v. Rodriguez* (1973). A dissenting opinion might subsequently prove so influential that it informs the majority opinion in later cases, giving justices who are not in the majority a chance to have great influence on future Court decision making.

—*Ronald Kahn*

Suggested Readings

Three excellent and up-to-date reference works on the Court are *The Oxford Guide to United States Supreme Court Decisions*, edited by Kermit L. Hall (New York: Oxford University Press, 1999); *The Supreme Court Compendium: Data, Decisions, and Developments*, by Lee Epstein et al. (Washington, D.C.: CQ Press, 2003); and *Encyclopedia of the U.S. Supreme Court*, edited by Thomas T. Lewis and Richard L. Wilson (3 vols. Pasadena, Calif.: Salem Press, 2000). Two of the best treatments of the Supreme Court as a decision-making institution include David M. O'Brien's *Storm Center* (3d ed. New York: W. W. Norton, 1993) and Henry J. Abraham's *The Judicial Process* (7th ed. New York: Oxford University Press, 1998). An important book on how the Supreme Court decides what to place on its agenda is *Deciding to Decide: Agenda Setting in the United States Supreme Court* (Cambridge, Mass.: Harvard University Press, 1991) by H. W. Perry, Jr. A book that describes how

Supreme Court justices apply legal principles in writing opinions is Ronald Kahn's *The Supreme Court and Constitutional Theory, 1953-1993* (Lawrence: The University Press of Kansas, 1994). See Gerald N. Rosenberg's *The Hollow Hope: Can Courts Bring About Social Change?* (Chicago: University of Chicago Press, 1991) for the view that elected American political institutions, not the Supreme Court, are the major causes of social change. For a contrasting view see Lee Epstein and Joseph F. Kobylka's *The Supreme Court and Legal Change: Abortion and the Death Penalty* (Chapel Hill: The University of North Carolina Press, 1992), which analyzes how legal advocacy groups influence social change by bringing cases to the Supreme Court. Other recent studies of the Court include *Supreme Court and Appellate Advocacy: Mastering Oral Argument*, by David C. Frederick, with a foreward by Justice Ruth Bader Ginsburg (St. Paul, Minn.: West Publishing, 2003); *Judicial Review and Judicial Power in the Supreme Court*, edited with an introduction by Kermit L. Hall (New York: Garland, 2000); and *One Case at a Time: Judicial Minimalism on the Supreme Court*, by Cass R. Sunstein (Cambridge, Mass.: Harvard University Press, 1999).

See also *Amicus curiae* briefs; Appeal; Appellate practice; Case law; *Certiorari*, writ of; Constitution, U.S.; Court types; Courts of appeals; Criminal procedure; Cruel and unusual punishment; Federal judicial system; Judicial review; Reporters, Supreme Court; Reversals of Supreme Court decisions by amendment; Reversals of Supreme Court decisions by Congress; State courts.

SUSPECTS

Persons believed to be involved in crimes; they may be briefly questioned and quickly searched for weapons but may not be arrested or undergo full searches without probable cause

Suspects are individuals whom police officers believe may have committed a crime or are about to commit a crime. Police officers are allowed to subject suspects to a procedure known as a stop and frisk. This procedure involves briefly questioning the sus-

San Francisco police officer collecting evidence at the scene of a crime. (Robert Fried)

pects and patting the outside of their clothing to determine if they are carrying weapons. If the stop and frisk reveals no weapons and no other evidence of illegal activity, the police must release the suspects.

In order to arrest suspects or to conduct a more thorough search, police officers must have probable cause. Probable cause requires evidence that a particular crime has been committed or is about to be committed and that specific suspects are responsible.

In public places or in emergency situations, the police may arrest suspects or conduct searches without warrants. A hearing is then held to determine if the police had probable cause to make the arrests or conduct the searches. In order to arrest suspects or conduct searches in private places when no urgency exists, a hearing is first held to determine probable cause, and then an arrest warrant or a search warrant is issued.

—Rose Secrest

See also Arrest; Counsel, right to; Criminal procedure; Defendants; Detectives, police; Miranda rights; Police; Presumption of innocence; Probable cause; Prosecutors; Search warrant requirement; Self-incrimination, privilege against.

TEST CASES

Legal cases brought to courts primarily to test specific points of law

All state and federal laws must comport with the Constitution of the United States. The adversarial system of trial, which underlies the U.S. judicial system, permits judges to declare laws unconstitutional only in the context of deciding actual legal disputes. Thus, individuals and organizations opposed to a particular law who wish the courts to invalidate it must resort to litigation. The purpose of such litigation is to test in the courts the constitutionality or a particular interpretation of a law.

Test cases are a regular feature of American politics, because the stakes in many constitutional disputes are high. Groups have an incentive to initiate such cases when the rewards of success or costs of failure are substantial. Examples of famous test cases are *Scott v. Sandford* (1857), in which the Court decided that a slave could not be considered a citizen; *Tennessee v. Scopes* (1925), also known as the Scopes "monkey" trial, which dealt with the teaching of evolution in the schools; and *Griswold v. Connecticut* (1965), in which the Court recognized a constitutional right to privacy.

In the 1850's the country was divided over the question of the extension of slavery to the western territories. Abolitionists believed the Missouri Compromise of 1820 was unconstitutional because it permitted slavery in the territories southwest of Missouri. In order to force the Supreme Court to resolve this divisive issue, a group of abolitionists arranged for a slave, Dred Scott, to sue his master in a U.S. district court. The Supreme Court accepted the case on appeal and struck down the 1820 act of the U.S. Congress but for reasons favorable to the South. The law was unconstitutional, said Chief Justice Roger Taney, because it closed the territories west and north of Missouri to slaveholders. The decision helped to precipitate the Civil War.

Test cases often begin with an act of civil disobedience. Those who believed in the strict separation of church and state opposed laws supporting Christianity in public institutions and looked for an opportunity to bring the question before the courts. In 1925 John Scopes, a biology teacher in Dayton, Tennessee, was persuaded to defy a state law prohibiting the teaching of Charles Darwin's theory of evolution. The state's prosecution of the teacher provided an opportunity to test the constitutional validity of such laws.

When Chief Justice Roger B. Taney wrote his majority opinion in the Dred Scott case in 1857, he argued that slaves are not human beings with rights but mere property. His opinion is regarded as one of the most notorious in Supreme Court history. (Collection of the Supreme Court of the United States)

Liberal interest groups were appalled at a Connecticut statute proscribing the use of birth control devices and the dissemination of information on their use. Because it was a criminal statute, Planned Parenthood was unable to launch a successful test case in the absence of a prosecution. The U.S. Supreme Court dismissed cases in 1943 and 1961 on the grounds that the appellants had suffered no harm. Prosecutors finally charged Estelle Griswold, the executive director of Planned Parenthood, with a misdemeanor after she openly defied the law. On appeal, the U.S. Supreme Court found the statute in violation of the Constitution's implied right of privacy.

Organizations that have financed large numbers of test cases include Jehovah's Witnesses, the American Civil Liberties Union (ACLU), and the National Association for the Advancement of

Colored People (NAACP). Because of changes in the Supreme Court's rules governing lawsuits, it is much easier for controversial laws to be tested in the courts than in the 1960's.

—*Kenneth M. Holland*

See also Appellate practice; Constitution, U.S.; Litigation; Public interest law; Supreme Court, U.S.

TESTIMONY

Evidence provided by witnesses in legal cases that is given under oath either orally or in the form of affidavits or depositions

Testimony is critical because it provides support for arguments and positions advocated by either side in a legal proceeding. Although testimony can loosely be defined as evidence, it is distinguishable from evidence derived from writings or other sources. For evidence to be testimony, a witness must speak under oath to a judge or tribunal.

Testimony is a component in three aspects of the legal process: grand jury hearings, preliminary hearings, and trials. A grand jury consists of a body of citizens who determine whether probable cause exists that a crime has been committed. In order to make that determination, they hear testimony from witnesses presented by the state, or prosecution. If they determine that probable cause exists, they return an indictment against the defendant. In a preliminary hearing, a judge hears testimony from prosecution witnesses and makes a decision as to whether or not an individual should be held for trial. In a criminal or civil trial, witnesses are questioned through direct and cross-examination and a judge or jury listens to the testimony in order to reach a verdict. In all three instances, witnesses take oaths in which they swear or affirm to tell the truth.

Testimony in a grand jury is usually secret and is not used in later trials. However, testimony in a preliminary hearing is preserved for later use, either by a court reporter or tape recorder. The testimony provided in a preliminary hearing might be used in a trial to refresh a witness's memory or to demonstrate inconsistencies in the testimony. The testimony in a preliminary hearing may also be used at trial if a witness dies or becomes unavailable to testify.

The prosecution in a criminal case and the plaintiff in a civil case present their testimony first because they have the burden of proof. Testimony is provided in brief question-answer format; witnesses usually do not tell their stories in a continuous narrative. In direct examination, the attorneys question the witnesses that support their side of a case. Typically, the questions are open-ended in order for the witnesses to elaborate on their testimony, thus presenting a strong case. In cross-examination, the attorneys question the witnesses on the opposing side. The attorney may attempt to obtain testimony by using closed-ended or leading questions so that the witness does not have a chance to elaborate on answers. During closing arguments, attorneys make convincing arguments and provide reasons for the jurors or judge to return a verdict in their favor. They draw on the testimony of witnesses to help support their arguments.

—Ann Burnett

See also Affidavits; Confessions; Cross-examination; Depositions; Evidence, rules of; Grand juries; Immunity from prosecution; Perjury; Preliminary hearings; Self-incrimination, privilege against; Subpoena power; Trial transcripts; Trials; Witnesses; Witnesses, confrontation of; Witnesses, expert.

THREE-STRIKES LAWS

Laws mandating more severe prison sentences for three-time offenders

Sometimes referred to as recidivist statutes, three-strikes laws impose more severe penalties on offenders who have multiple felony convictions than on those without multiple convictions. Life imprisonment is often the more severe penalty. The idea behind this type of legislation is to remove three-time offenders from society, as prior rehabilitative efforts evidently have not succeeded.

New York was the first jurisdiction in the country to have such legislation. At the present time, virtually all jurisdictions have some provision that either requires or permits increased sentences for persons with a prior conviction or convictions.

Approximately half of all jurisdictions authorize life sentences for persons convicted of a felony for the third or fourth time. In the event of third felony convictions, Illinois classifies persons as "habitual criminals" and authorizes a life sentence if all three felonies involved force or the threat of force. In Texas a first-degree felony conviction subsequent to a prior felony conviction is punished by a sentence of life imprisonment or fifteen to ninety-nine years. A third felony conviction receives a sentence of life imprisonment or twenty-five to ninety-nine years.

Texas also has a recidivist statute for misdemeanors. If an individual has a prior misdemeanor or felony conviction, a subsequent misdemeanor conviction could result in a sentence of as much as one year. Massachusetts has a more general and somewhat less severe statute for habitual criminals. Anyone who has been twice convicted of crime and sentenced to prison shall, upon conviction of a felony, be punished for that felony by imprisonment for the maximum term provided by law. That is, a habitual criminal in Massachusetts receives the maximum penalty for a felony, such as five, ten, or twenty years, rather than life imprisonment, as is common in approximately half of all jurisdictions. Jurisdictions generally include in their counting of felonies those for which convictions occurred in other jurisdictions (including at the federal level). New York and other jurisdictions include in the count convictions for misdemeanors in other jurisdictions that would have been felonies in their own jurisdictions. Notably, the crime of escape from prison is usually excluded from the count.

Questions have arisen as to whether three-strikes laws violate due process, the protection offered by the Eighth Amendment to the U.S. Constitution against cruel and unusual punishment, and double jeopardy provisions. The laws do not grant prosecutors unbridled discretion in determining who should be sentenced to life imprisonment and do not require imposition of life imprisonment while foreclosing consideration of mitigating factors. Thus, it has been concluded that three-strikes laws violate no constitutional rights, because they do no more than describe circumstances under which increased punishment may be imposed.

—*Dana P. McDermott*

See also Convictions; Criminal records; Cruel and unusual punishment; Double jeopardy; Due process of law; Felonies; Incapacitation; Judges; Parole; Sentencing.

Torts

Any "wrongful acts" that are actionable in civil courts for which damages can be recovered; legal wrongs that are not covered by contract law

Tort actions cover a wide variety of behaviors and represent a significant portion of the cases in civil court. There was original no general principle of tort liability in English common law, but the king's court allowed the recovery of damages for various types of trespass that resulted in injury. The law of torts evolved from a common-law tradition making it possible to recover damages in civil court for a wrongful act. The connection of torts with wrongful acts has the potential to be confusing; there is no implication of criminality or moral delinquency in the use of the term "wrongful." The concepts of tort and crime differ in many ways. Nevertheless, many common-law criminal acts are actionable as torts. Assault, for example, is both a common-law crime and actionable as a tort.

In a tort case, the defendant incurs liability when his or her action or failure to act causes a breach of a legal duty and results in a foreseeable injury or harm to a legally recognized right of a plaintiff. Not every injury or harm is considered a tort (thereby being actionable). There is no liability for the inevitable accident or an event considered an act of God.

A tradition in Anglo-American law is that the government cannot be sued without giving its permission. In a 1907 decision upholding sovereign immunity, Justice Oliver Wendell Holmes, Jr., held that "there can be no legal right as against the authority that makes the law on which the right depends." The U.S. Congress passed the Tort Claims Act in 1946, authorizing the U.S. district courts to adjudicate liability for all tort claims of injury or harm resulting from the acts or failure to act of the federal govern-

(continued on page 656)

ELEMENTS OF COMMON TORTS

Traditional Intentional Torts

Tort	Elements
Assault	Intentional creation of a situation giving plaintiff reason to fear imminent battery
Conversion	Intentional exercise of dominion or control over personal property sufficiently serious to amount to permanent deprivation or destruction of property
False imprisonment	Intentional confinement that is unlawful and of which the plaintiff is aware
Intentional infliction of emotional distress	Intentional or reckless conduct that is extreme and outrageous and that causes severe emotional distress
Trespass to chattels	Intentional harm to, interference with, or use or possession of another's personal property
Trespass to land	Intentional entry into, or physical invasion of, land of another

Other Intentional Torts

Tort	Elements
Abuse of process	Defendant makes otherwise legitimate use of legal process for an improper purpose or to accomplish an objective not authorized by the process
Defamation	Defendant made defamatory statement of and concerning the plaintiff, published the statement to others, and damaged plaintiff. In order to satisfy First Amendment free speech concerns, in cases involving matters of public concern and public officials or figures, plaintiffs also must prove that the statement is actually false and that the defendant made the statement with knowledge of its falsity or in reckless disregard of the truth (actual malice)

Tort	Elements
Fraud	Misrepresentation of a material fact by defendant; knowledge by defendant that the representation is false; defendant intended to induce plaintiff to act or refrain from acting in reliance on misrepresentation; plaintiff actually relied on the misrepresentation; plaintiff's reliance was reasonable; there was actual damage to plaintiff
Malicious prosecution	Defendant initiated prior legal proceeding against plaintiff; prior proceeding terminated in plaintiff's favor; there was absence of probable cause for prior proceeding; defendant acted with malice or improper purpose in initiating prior proceeding; there were damages to plaintiff

Negligence

Tort	Elements
Negligence	Existence of a legal duty; defendant breached legal duty; defendant's breach was the cause of plaintiff's injuries; there are no policy reasons to preclude liability (proximate cause); plaintiff suffered actual damages

Strict Liability

Tort	Elements
Animals	Liability for trespass by livestock; harm results from a wild animal's dangerous propensity that is characteristic of the animal or known to the owner; harm results from a domestic animal's dangerous propensity that is abnormal to that class of animal and of which owner had knowledge
Abnormally dangerous activities	Activity that involves a high degree of risk; resulting harm is likely to be great; defendant cannot avoid the harm by exercising care; the activity is not a matter of common usage; the activity is not appropriate to the location; the activity's value to the community is outweighed by the risks

(continued)

ELEMENTS OF COMMON TORTS (CONTINUED)

Product Liability

Tort	Elements
Defectiveness	Negligence; implied warranty of merchantability; strict liability in tort
Representations	Intentional misrepresentation; negligent misrepresentation; strict liability for public misrepresentation; express warranty; implied warranty of fitness for a particular purpose

ment's employees, officers, and agencies. It directed the courts, furthermore, to hold the federal government as responsible as a private individual, in the same circumstances and to the same degree.

In tort law, the standard by which actions are judged is the action's (or failure to act's) reasonableness in the circumstances. The remedy for a tort claim is generally a monetary award for damages. In a case of wrongful death, the monetary damages may be the present value of all future income that the individual would have earned had the person lived a normal life expectancy. The determination of such a value usually requires the services of a professional economist as an expert witness. In the case of a nuisance, an injunction may be the proper remedy.

The law of torts permits any and all parties to be held liable. The liability is held to be vicarious liability, and even the plaintiff may be wholly or partially responsible for the injury. In cases in which the plaintiff is held partially responsible, a proportional reduction in any damage award may be made to the degree that the plaintiff is held responsible.

See also Civil rights and liberties; Commercial litigation; Common law; Damages; Felonies; Liability, civil and criminal; Long-arm statutes; Misdemeanors.

TRIAL PUBLICITY

Information about a trial that is disseminated through the print or broadcast media

Issues regarding trial publicity emerge from two opposing principles: the right of the accused to a fair trial and the constitutional imperative that court proceedings be public. The two concerns conflict when trial publicity threatens to bias the outcome of a trial.

Traditionally, tacit professional limitations were imposed on attorneys, restricting the information they could reveal to the news media. By the late twentieth century the potential for instantaneous, in-depth trial coverage by electronic media made trial publicity a broader social issue involving the whole judicial system, the public's right to know, and the professional conduct of journalists. The result is freer movement of information to the public and less accountability for any one party or institution.

The principle of publicity was key to the development of modern mass democracies in Europe and America. It was through the publicizing of the private affairs of kings and other ruling authorities that a public sphere of discourse developed. Consequently, most modern constitutions call for conducting the affairs of state in public. The Sixth Amendment to the U.S. Constitution states that "the accused shall enjoy the right to a speedy and public trial." This ensures that justice will be carried out under the watchful eye of other private citizens.

In the eighteenth and nineteenth centuries the right to a public trial meant that private citizens and print journalists could attend court proceedings. In the twentieth century access was sometimes extended to radio and television broadcasters as well. However, the U.S. Supreme Court has been reluctant to grant to broadcast journalists the access given to citizens and print journalists. The Supreme Court takes the position that broadcast technology adversely affects court proceedings.

In some cases the individual's right to privacy takes precedence over the public's right to know. In certain states an attorney can move to close the courtroom. If the attorney shows good cause the judge may remove spectators from the courtroom for part or all of the proceedings. This is most often done in cases involving juveniles, adoptions, or rape. Judges may also clear the courtroom if witnesses must provide embarrassing evidence, usually in cases involving sexual assault.

Typically, trial publicity is limited to coverage of a crime, the police investigation, and regular reports on courtroom testimony. In the majority of trials, publicity is not a problem. If a judge believes that trial publicity may bias the proceedings, a gag order can be issued restricting what parties in the trial may say to journalists. A judge may also sequester a jury by cutting off their access to news broadcasts and newspapers and by restricting them to their hotel rooms and court facilities. However, it is rare for gag orders to be enforced or for a jury to be sequestered.

If excessive local publicity presents a problem, a judge may also call for a change of venue by moving the trial to an area in which the pool of potential jurors is less exposed to news coverage of the case in question.

—Thomas J. Roach

See also Change of venue; Constitution, U.S.; Death row attorneys; Gag orders; Juries; Jury sequestration; Public interest law; Trial transcripts; Trials.

TRIAL TRANSCRIPTS

Official records of trial proceedings that are used chiefly by appellate courts in evaluating whether any errors occurred in trial courts

A trial consists in the main of statements made by lawyers and the judge and of the questions asked of witnesses and the answers given by them. A court reporter normally records these matters as they are spoken and produces a formal trial transcript. With the benefit of special training and equipment, court reporters can produce a verbatim record of the words spoken in a proceeding.

Sometimes the transcript of the trial is used during the trial itself. For example, a lawyer cross-examining a witness might wish to confront the witness with statements made during direct examination. In these cases, the lawyer requests that the court reporter produce a transcript of the witness's testimony so that the lawyer can present it to the witness and question the witness about it.

More commonly, however, the trial transcript is a key portion of the material considered by an appellate court when a case is appealed. On appeal, the appellate court does not conduct a trial again and hear the testimony of witnesses and the arguments of lawyers. Instead, the appellate court reviews what happened in the trial court to determine whether legal errors were made. The appellate court reviews the record of the trial, which includes the trial transcript, the evidence offered by the parties, and any official court documents filed with the trial court. Of these items, the trial transcript is normally the most important source for the appellate court to determine what happened during the trial.

Although the court reporter does not charge the parties in the case for transcribing the proceedings, the reporter does charge for making a formal transcript. This charge can be quite substantial, especially in cases that last for extended periods of time. The party wishing to appeal a case must normally shoulder the cost of having a transcript prepared, because the appellate court generally does not consider an appeal without a record (including the transcript) of the trial.

In at least some cases the U.S. Supreme Court has found that due process of law requires that indigent persons not be denied access to courts simply because they lack the financial resources to pay for a trial transcript. In *Griffin v. Illinois* (1956), for example, the Supreme Court determined that a state must furnish a free trial transcript for indigent criminal defendants if the transcript is necessary for appellate review. Similarly, in *M.L.B. v. S.L.J.* (1996) the Court ruled as unconstitutional a state law that prevented a parent from appealing the termination of parental rights to a child unless the parent paid for a record of the termination proceedings. In *M.L.B.* these costs amounted to $2,352.36.

—Timothy L. Hall

See also Appeal; Appellate practice; Court reporters; Criminal records; Depositions; Discovery; Evidence, rules of; Testimony; Trial publicity; Trials; Witnesses.

TRIALS

Courtroom proceedings involving presentation of evidence and arguments by lawyers to a judge or jury that are used to seek the truth and arrive at verdicts in civil and criminal cases

The outcomes of civil and criminal cases in the American legal system are determined by the actions of lawyers representing opposing sides. When opposing attorneys cannot negotiate agreements to end legal cases, called "settlements" in civil cases and "plea bargains" in criminal cases, the legal system provides a procedure for a judge or jury to decide the relevant facts, apply the appropriate laws, and issue a decision. This truth-seeking procedure is called a trial.

Origins and Modern Forms

U.S. trials have their origins in English traditions. Prior to the thirteenth century the guilt of criminal suspects in England was determined by making them undergo physical ordeals. For example, they were forced to lift red-hot irons, were placed into boiling water, or thrown into ponds with their hands and feet tied. People assumed that if persons were killed or injured during such physical trials, God was showing that they were guilty. When Pope Innocent III (1160-1216) forbade the clergy in 1215 to endorse the results of such ordeals, legalistic trials began to develop as a means of discovering facts and determining guilt. Groups of citizens were called upon to serve on juries that decided whether accused persons were guilty of crimes.

Trials are very time-consuming. Lawyers frequently spend weeks or months preparing for trial. They must interview potential witnesses, examine relevant documents and physical evidence, and plan a strategy for presenting evidence and arguments. Trials are also very expensive because they absorb so much of a lawyer's time and may involve the hiring of investigators and expert witnesses.

After both sides have prepared their cases, a trial takes place in a courtroom. A trial constitutes the ultimate truth-seeking process in an adversarial legal system. Lawyers for each side attempt to persuade the decision maker, whether the judge or jury, that their clients should prevail. Opposing lawyers must follow detailed rules about the kinds of evidence and arguments they may present in court. Each side's opening arguments present an overview of the case. Then each side presents its evidence and attempts to point out the weaknesses in the other side's evidence. Witnesses are questioned by the opposing attorneys. Each side may also present physical evidence, such as weapons or documents relevant to the case. Expert witnesses may also be called to the stand, such as psychiatrists or scientists who have special knowledge relevant to the case. Presentation of evidence is followed by closing arguments in which the opposing attorneys attempt to persuade the judge or jury to issue a verdict favorable to their side.

Judge and Jury

The judge supervises the trial to make sure that the rules of evidence and procedure are followed. In a jury trial the judge also supervises the selection of jurors, instructs the jurors on what information they may consider in reaching a decision, or verdict, and informs them about the relevant law that they must apply in their deliberations.

In reaching a verdict, jurors are sent to a private room to discuss the facts and the law involved in the case. No one else is allowed in the room and no one is allowed to listen to jurors' deliberations. Jurors elect their own foreperson to guide their discussions. They must continue to meet, sometimes for days, until they either reach a verdict or convince the judge to declare a mistrial when they are hopelessly deadlocked. When a mistrial is declared, either because the jury is deadlocked or because one of the opposing sides in the case violated a procedural rule, a new trial takes place in front of a new jury, unless the prosecutor drops the charges in a criminal case or the plaintiff decides to drop a civil lawsuit.

Trial verdicts may be appealed to a higher court only when one side claims that the trial judge made an error in enforcing rules of evidence and court procedure. Appellate courts are not permitted to disagree with a trial verdict or with the trial judge and jury's determination of the facts. Appellate courts can merely order a new trial if a significant error by a trial judge violated court procedures or led to a misapplication of the appropriate law. Because appellate courts have only limited authority to reverse the decisions of trial judges and jurors, trials are especially important procedures for determining the outcomes of legal cases.

Trials are relatively infrequent in both criminal and civil cases. In most jurisdictions, typically only 10 percent of cases are resolved through trials. Most cases end prior to trial through a settlement agreement in civil cases and plea bargaining in criminal cases. Although trials are unusual, they are extremely important. Trials often occur in the most difficult or serious cases when the two sides cannot reach an agreement. Thus, most cases concerning the death penalty are decided through trials rather than plea bargains. Trials also have an impact on cases resolved through settlements and plea bargains. When the attorneys for each side meet to discuss a settlement or plea bargain, their discussions are based on their predictions about how the case is likely to turn out if it goes to trial. If a criminal defense attorney believes that a jury will convict a defendant at trial because the prosecution's evidence is strong, the defense attorney may seek a plea bargain to avoid the maximum possible punishment. Similarly, if attorneys in a civil case believe that the evidence favors the opposition, they will likely cooperate in reaching settlement agreements that avoid the worst possible outcomes for their clients. The anticipated expense of carrying cases to trial may also lead to settlements in civil cases. Thus, trials or the perspective of trials guides or determines the outcomes of most legal cases.

Jury Trials

In criminal cases the Sixth Amendment to the U.S. Constitution guarantees the right to trial by jury, but this right only applies when a defendant faces "serious" charges, which are defined as those for which the possible punishment is more than six months in jail or prison. In reality, people may face the possibility of serving years in prison without having a jury trial, because the U.S. Supreme Court ruled in *Lewis v. United States* (1996) that there is no right to a jury trial for people charged with multiple nonserious offenses, even when they face the possibility of several separate six-month sentences consecutively. The right to a jury in criminal cases does not depend on the total possible sentence. Rather, it depends on whether a defendant is charged with a crime which by itself can incur a sentence longer than six months' imprisonment.

There is no general constitutional right to jury trials in civil cases, which are lawsuits involving disputes among individuals, corporations, government agencies, and other entities not involved in the prosecution of crimes. The Seventh Amendment to the U.S. Constitution entitles persons to civil jury trials in certain cases in federal court, but the vast majority of civil cases concern contracts, torts, real estate, and other matters handled by state courts. Thus, the opportunity to have a jury trial in a civil case depends on the state or federal statute under which lawsuits are initiated. For some types of civil cases statutes specify that trials shall be held before a judge without a jury.

Jury trials provide citizens with the opportunity to serve as decision makers in the legal process. Jury service is an important civic responsibility. When called upon to serve on a jury, a citizen is asked to make important decisions about how laws should be applied and about when criminal punishment should be imposed, depriving persons of life and liberty. Potential jurors are usually called to court from voter registration lists, driver's license roles, and other records available to the government. The attorneys for both sides in a case are permitted to request that specific individuals be excluded from the jury if there is reason to believe that they may be unable to be objective in deciding the case. Each side is also permitted to exclude a limited number of potential jurors for strategic reasons without providing a reason for these exclusions.

Some critics believe that citizen jurors are not capable of understanding complex legal issues. Others believe that jurors often decide cases based on their own emotions and prejudices rather than on the facts. As a result, some have proposed that jury trials be reformed, so that jurors are given clearer instructions and permitted to take notes and ask questions during trial. These suggestions are intended to help jurors collect and understand information more effectively before they are called upon to issue a verdict.

Bench Trials

Only about half of all trials are jury trials. The rest are trials before a judge, which are called bench trials. In some civil cases, state and federal statutes permit only bench trials. Attorneys make strategic decisions to request bench trials. They may seek a bench trial if a case is so controversial, such as a notorious sex crime case, that they fear jurors will be unduly influenced by their emotions. Attorneys may also seek a bench trial if they believe that a particular judge will understand or sympathize with their arguments. Attorneys may also seek a bench trial if they believe juries' decisions are so unpredictable that it is not worth putting their client's fate in the hands of citizens randomly drawn from the community.

In a bench trial, the judge may be less concerned about strictly enforcing rules of evidence. If a jury hears or sees improper evidence, its decision may be affected. If a judge hears improper evidence, the judge recognizes the need to exclude it from consideration in reaching a verdict.

Civil and Criminal Trials

The constitutional right to jury trials in serious criminal cases distinguishes such cases from civil cases in which no such right exists. The standard of proof required for verdicts also differs in civil and criminal cases. In civil cases, verdicts typically must be supported by only "a preponderance of evidence"—in other words, by the doctrine that it is more likely than not that the plaintiff should prevail. By contrast, in criminal cases guilt must be proven "beyond a reasonable doubt." Depending on the applicable state or federal law, civil trial juries may be smaller than criminal trial juries. For example, federal courts use six-member juries for civil cases and twelve-member juries for criminal cases. Additionally, the relevant rules of evidence and procedure often differ in criminal and civil cases, with stricter rules typically applying in criminal cases because criminal defendants enjoy various constitutional rights that are not applicable to litigants in civil cases.

—*Christopher E. Smith*

Suggested Readings

Details of trials and pretrial processes are presented in Frank Miller, Robert Dawson, George Dix, and Raymond Parnas, *Prosecution and Adjudication* (4th ed. Westbury, N.Y.: Foundation Press, 1991). A comparison of civil and criminal trials in different jurisdictions is presented in a report entitled *On Trial: The Length of Civil and Criminal Trials* (Williamsburg, Va.: National Center for State Courts, 1988). Two comprehensive reference works on trials are Christopher E. Smith's *Courts and Trials: A Reference Handbook* (Santa Barbara, Calif.: ABC-CLIO, 2003) and *Covering the Courts: Free Press, Fair Trials, and Journalistic Performance*, edited by Robert Giles and Robert W. Snyder (New Brunswick, N.J.: Transaction

Publishers, 1999). A critical assessment of trials in the judicial system can be found in William T. Pizzi's *Trials Without Truth: Why Our System of Criminal Trials Has Become an Expensive Failure and What We Need to Do to Rebuild It* (New York: New York University Press, 1999).

See also Acquittal; Adversary system; Bailiffs; Change of venue; Convictions; Court calendar; Court costs; Court reporters; Court types; Courts-martial; Double jeopardy; Judges; Juries; Litigation; Mistrials; Officers of the court; Pleas; Prosecutors; Reasonable doubt; Sentencing; Speedy trial requirement; Trial publicity; Trial transcripts; Verdicts; Witnesses.

UNAUTHORIZED PRACTICE OF LAW

Practice of law by a person lacking a law license in the relevant jurisdiction or the filing or preparation of court pleadings or other activities on behalf of a client by an unlicensed person

The practice of law is a profession consisting of attorneys licensed by state authorities. A person is licensed by law in the jurisdiction in which he or she practices. Most states permit a lawyer licensed in one jurisdiction to make a special appearance in another state's court. However, a license must be obtained if that person is to hold himself or herself out as a lawyer in that state. As the practice of law has become nationalized, many attorneys hold memberships in several state bars.

A few states have reciprocity agreements that permit members of another state's bar to receive membership upon application. Vermont requires licensed lawyers of another state to complete a six-month internship with a Vermont attorney or pass the Vermont bar examination to qualify for membership in that state. Most states require that applicants to the bar pass a written bar examination, meet a moral character requirement, and have graduated from an accredited law school.

Law is a regulated profession to protect the public against persons who hold themselves out to the public as lawyers but who lack the training to competently perform legal work. The public interest requires that those persons rendering legal advice have competence. To protect this public interest, it is necessary to investigate complaints of the unauthorized practice of law. The highest court in most states appoints committees to investigate and punish the unauthorized practice of law. Unlicensed persons who hold themselves out to the public as lawyers may be punished by criminal and civil sanctions depending on the activities in which they have engaged.

Lawyers may employ the services of paraprofessionals and delegate functions to them as long as the work they perform is supervised by a licensed member of the bar. Lawyers may provide professional advice and instructions to nonlawyers whose work requires knowledge of the law, such as claims adjusters or employees of financial institutions. Licensed lawyers may not assist a person who is not a member of the bar in the performance of activity that constitutes the unauthorized practice of law. A lawyer aids in the unauthorized practice of law by delegating key duties to such persons as real estate brokers. An attorney, for example, may not knowingly delegate to a broker the legal responsibility of answering legal questions. Similarly, a lawyer may not allow any person who has been suspended from the practice of law to have a presence in an office in which the practice of law is conducted by the lawyer. Solicitation by a lawyer not admitted to practice law is a form of unauthorized practice of law.

—*Michael L. Rustad*

See also American Bar Association; Attorney-client relationship; Attorney types; Bar associations; Bar examinations and licensing of lawyers; Law schools.

UNETHICAL CONDUCT OF ATTORNEYS

Inappropriate behavior by attorneys that may be punished by the bar associations or supreme courts in the states in which the attorneys practice law

In the United States admission to the practice of law and oversight of attorney conduct are matters supervised generally by the supreme courts of each state. In most states the supreme court remains the final authority in regulating admissions and attorney conduct, although the court may rely in part on the assistance of state bar associations. In practice, however, complaints concerning the conduct of lawyers should normally be directed to the state or local bar association, which generally plays the most important role in the initial investigation of and decisions concerning complaints.

Sanctions against attorneys for unethical conduct should be distinguished from other means of redress for inappropriate attorney behavior. The chief alternative avenues for such redress are criminal proceedings and civil lawsuits. Attorneys who violate the law in connection with their legal practice can find themselves subject to criminal sanctions. Similarly, attorneys who violate legal obligations owed to clients and other third parties can be sued for legal malpractice or a variety of other legal claims.

Varieties of Sanctions

The sanctions available to disciplinary authorities who regulate the conduct of lawyers vary from private reprimands to disbarment. For a relatively minor infraction disciplinary authorities may simply censure an attorney privately, informing him or her of the bar's verdict and warning against repeating the infraction. This private reprimand remains in the attorney's file, however, and might have a bearing on the severity of sanctions in future cases should further transgressions occur. For more serious cases, disciplinary authorities may move to a public reprimand, which informs other lawyers of the offending lawyer's ethical misconduct, generally by mentioning it in a legal publication such as the state bar association's monthly periodical. The next level of sanction is a suspension from the practice of law for some period of time, generally ranging from three months to five years. Finally, disciplinary authorities deal with the most severe ethical lapses by disbarring the offending attorney. Disbarment strips the attorney of the right to practice law in the state in question. In some cases, attorneys so disbarred may seek reinstatement to the bar after a period of time, normally specified in the original disbarment order. Reinstatement depends on whether the attorney demonstrates that the offending conduct is not likely to be repeated.

In the late twentieth century the traditional sanctions of reprimand, suspension, and disbarment were supplemented with other sanctions designed to educate offending lawyers. For example, disciplinary authorities sometimes dismiss complaints against lawyers for relatively minor infractions if the lawyers agree to attend a continuing legal education program on the subject of attorney ethics. Sometimes the right to undertake the practice of law again after a suspension or disbarment is linked to this kind of requirement. In addition, disciplinary authorities may occasionally make readmission to the bar after disbarment contingent on an erring lawyer's passing all or part of the state bar examination.

Ethical Rules

Beginning early in the twentieth century national and state bar associations attempted to set forth principles of legal ethics that would guide the conduct of lawyers and provide a basis for disciplining wayward attorneys. In 1983 the American Bar Association (ABA) proposed a set of ethical rules called the Model Rules of Professional Conduct. Since the ABA does not itself have authority to establish standards for legal ethics in each state, the Model Rules were simply a uniform collection of ethical principles proposed for adoption by the various state supreme courts. In fact, most states subsequently enacted some version of the Model Rules as their own, although many states modified them in some respects. A few states still operate under a predecessor set of ethics rules proposed by the ABA in the 1970's called the Model Code of Professional Responsibility.

Rules of legal ethics, whether the Model Rules or the older Model Code, attempt to set forth ethical principles to guide lawyers in dealing with the various ethical problems that occur in the practice of law. They define the various obligations that lawyers owe their clients, the courts, and third parties. Violation of these rules, which touch on matters as various as the kinds of fees lawyers may charge and their obligation to disclose the misconduct of their fellow lawyers, is the chief basis for sanctions against lawyers.

Sanctions for Other Types of Unethical Conduct

In the main lawyers receive sanctions for unethical conduct committed in their role as attorneys. Occasionally, however, disciplinary authorities sanction lawyers for ethical infractions that are not committed in the context of legal practice. For example, a lawyer might be sanctioned after being convicted of embezzlement or tax evasion. Lawyers may also be sanctioned for unethical business conduct, even if the conduct does not occur in connection with their practice of law.

The modern view—reflected, for example, in the ABA's Model Rules of Professional Conduct—is that lawyers should be disciplined only for conduct outside the scope of their practice under certain circumstances. According to the ABA's Model Rules, some kinds of illegal or unethical conduct may not reflect adversely on lawyers' fitness to practice law. Thus, even though private moral infractions, such as adultery, might be a crime in particular jurisdictions, this infraction does not necessarily mean that an attorney who engages in this conduct lacks the characteristics necessary to practice law. On the other hand, criminal offenses involving violence, dishonesty, or interference with the administration of justice would reflect adversely on a lawyer's fitness to practice law.

—*Timothy L. Hall*

Suggested Readings

Among the many books cataloging the unethical practices of lawyers and suggesting possible remedies are Deborah L. Rhode's *In the Interests of Justice: Reforming the Legal Profession* (New York: Oxford University Press, 2001), Jethro K. Lieberman's *Crisis at the Bar: Lawyers' Unethical Ethics and What to Do About It* (New York: W. W. Norton, 1978), Donald E. DeKieffer's *How Lawyers Screw Their Clients: And What You Can Do About It* (New York: Barricade Books, 1995), and David W. Marston's *Malice Aforethought: How Lawyers Use Our Secret Rules to Get Rich, Get Sex, Get Even . . . And Get Away With It* (New York: W. Morrow, 1991). The late twentieth century witnessed a spate of books seeking to divine the roots of ethical failure in the legal profession. These include *Betrayed Profession: Lawyering at the End of the Twentieth Century* by Sol M. Linowitz with Martin Mayer (New York: Charles Scribner's Sons, 1994), and Anthony T. Kronman's *The Lost Lawyer: Failing Ideals of the Legal Profession* (Cambridge, Mass.: Harvard University Press, 1993). The many authoritative works on ethics in the legal professions include *Ethical Standards in the Public Sector: A Guide for Government Lawyers, Clients, and Public Officials*, edited by Patricia E. Salkin (Chicago: Section of State and Local Government Law, American Bar Association, 1999); *Ethics for Adversaries: The Morality of Roles in Public and Professional Life*, by Arthur Isak Applbaum (Princeton, N.J.: Princeton University Press, 1999); *The Practice of Justice: A Theory of Lawyers' Ethics*, by William H. Simon (Cambridge, Mass.: Harvard University Press, 1998); and *Ethics in Practice: Lawyers' Roles, Responsibilities, and Regulation*, edited by Deborah L. Rhode (New York: Oxford University Press, 2000).

See also Adversary system; American Bar Association; Attorney-client relationship; Attorney confidentiality; Attorney fees; Attorney trust accounts; Attorneys as fiduciaries; Bar associations; Effective counsel; Evidence, rules of; Family law practice; Grievance committees for attorney discipline; Judicial conduct code; Model Rules of Professional Conduct; Personal injury attorneys; Pro bono legal work; Solicitation of legal clients.

UNIFORM LAWS

National movement to establish uniform state laws that aims to eliminate differences that impede legal dealings among the states

The uniform law movement began when the Alabama State Bar Association recognized in 1881 that significant but unnecessary legal problems were created by wide variations in state laws involving interstate transactions or the movement of persons from one state to another. For example, wills that were valid in one state might have been invalid in another and sellers might have required different forms of contracts depending on where buyers lived.

Creating Uniform Laws

In 1889 the American Bar Association (ABA) decided to work for "uniformity of the laws" in the forty-four states. Within a year the New York legislature authorized the governor of New York to appoint three commissioners to explore the best way to effect uniformity of law among states, and the American Bar Association endorsed New York's action. The result was the first meeting of the Conference of State Boards of Commissioners on Promoting Uniformity of Law in the United States in 1892. By 1912 every state had appointed uniform law commissioners to what was thereafter known as the National Conference of Commissioners on Uniform State Laws. The U.S. Virgin Islands was the last jurisdiction to join, appointing its first commission in 1988.

The National Conference is a nonprofit, unincorporated association composed of state commissions on uniform laws from each state, the District of Columbia, the Commonwealth of Puerto Rico, and the U.S. Virgin Islands. Each jurisdiction determines its methods of appointment and the number of commissioners. Most commissioners are appointed by the governors of their respective states or by the state legislatures. The one requirement for the more than three hundred uniform law commissioners is that they be members of the bar in their jurisdictions. Some commissioners serve as state legislators while most are practitioners and some are judges and law professors. They serve for specific terms and receive no compensation for their work with the National Conference. The National Conference is largely funded by state appropriations. Expenses are apportioned among the states by means of an assessment based on population size. However, the research and drafting expertise employed by the Conference is donated by its commissioners. Commissioners devote thousands of hours—amounting in some cases to millions of dollars worth of time—to the development of uniform acts.

Work of the National Conference

The state commissions come together as the National Conference for the purpose of studying and reviewing the laws of the states to determine which areas of the law should be uniform. The commissioners then draft and propose for enactment specific statutes in areas of the law in which uniformity among the states is desirable. The National Conference can only suggest; no proposed statute is effective until a state legislature adopts it.

California's state capitol, in which the laws of the state are enacted. (Digital Stock)

Since its founding, the National Conference has drafted more than two hundred uniform statutes on numerous subjects and in various fields of law, setting a uniform pattern for these subjects across the country. Uniform acts include the Uniform Probate Code, which protects the property of deceased persons; the Uniform Partnership Act, which is the basic law for a common form of doing business; and the Uniform Enforcement of Foreign Judgments Act, which ensures that court decisions in one state are recognized in another. In 1940 the National Conference turned to one of its most important efforts: offering comprehensive legal solutions to major commercial problems, resulting in the Uniform Commercial Code (UCC). The Uniform Commercial Code governs transactions involving the sale, lease, or financing of goods; negotiable instruments such as checks, promissory notes, and other methods of making payment; and letters of credit and transactions in securities. In short, the Code regulates matters essential to the economic development and well-being of the United States.

How Uniform Laws Are Developed

A uniform law takes at least several years to develop. The process starts with a committee of the National Conference that investigates each proposed act and then reports to the Executive Committee of the Conference as to whether the subject warrants a draft uniform law. If the Executive Committee approves the proposal, a drafting committee of commissioners is appointed. Drafting committees meet throughout the year. Tentative drafts are not submitted to the entire National Conference until they have received extensive committee consideration. Drafting committees are assisted in their work by reporters, experts on the subject at hand who are usually appointed from academia, advisors from the American Bar Association, and observers from interested groups and organizations. Advisors and observers test the proposed statutes' workability under concrete circumstances so that they may aid the committees in drafting realistic, as opposed to theoretical, statutory rules. The process involves formulating a uniform consensus from collective experience on a national scale.

Draft acts are then submitted for initial debate to the entire National Conference at annual meetings. Each act must be considered section by section at not less than two annual meetings by all commissioners sitting as a Committee of the Whole. Once the Committee of the Whole approves an act, the act's final test is a vote by the jurisdictions in the National Conference. A majority of the jurisdictions present and no less than twenty jurisdictions must approve acts before they can be officially adopted as Uniform Acts.

At that point, a Uniform Act is officially promulgated for consideration by the states, the District of Columbia, Puerto Rico, and the U.S. Virgin Islands. Legislatures are urged to adopt Uniform Acts as written in order to "promote uniformity in law among the several states." Since each act has benefited from the extensive input by commissioners from each jurisdiction and often by suggestions from interested organizations or groups from different parts of the country, further tailoring is seldom necessary or desirable to accommodate the particular circumstances of individual states. The process by which Uniform Acts are proposed, drafted, and ultimately promulgated is designed to produce statutes that can be enacted without local variations.

When the drafting of such acts is completed, the commissioners are obligated to advocate their adoption in their home states. Normal resistance to anything "new" makes this a hard part of commissioners' job. However, the result is workable modern state law that helps keep the federal system alive.

The Importance of Uniform Laws

Uniform state laws simplify the legal life of businesses and individuals by providing rules and procedures that are consistent from state to state. Representing state governments and the legal profession, the National Conference of Commissioners on Uniform State Laws is a genuine confederation of state interests. It has sought to bring uniformity to the divergent legal traditions of fifty-three sovereign jurisdictions and has done so with significant success—so much success, in fact, that federal agencies have adopted proposals of the National Conference for federal regulations. Moreover, an executive branch white paper and the U.S. Congress have cited, and relied on, the work of the National Conference.

—*Fred H. Miller*

Suggested Readings

The definitive work on the National Conference of Commissioners on Uniform State Laws is by Walter Armstrong, *A Centennial History of the National Conference of Commissioners on Uniform State Laws* (St. Paul, Minn.: West Publishing, 1991). Various uniform laws, such as the Uniform Commercial Code, are discussed in the American Bar Association's *Family Legal Guide* (Times Books, 1994).

See also Annotated codes; Breach of contract; Commercial litigation; Louisiana law; Model Penal Code; Probate; Statutes; United States Code.

UNITED STATES CODE

Official collection of federal statutes in force that are edited to eliminate duplication and arranged under appropriate headings

The U.S. Code provides easy access to federal legislation which has been "codified"—that is, assembled and presented in a uniform format. Before 1926, when Congress authorized preparation of the U.S. Code, federal laws were added as they appeared to the Revised Statutes of 1875. This agglomeration of legislation was difficult to use, because laws were often redundant and their relevance often unclear. The first U.S. Code rearranged the laws in force in 1926 under fifty titles and published them in four volumes; subsequently these were updated annually with a cumulative supplement. Every six years, the federal government publishes a new edition of the code following the same format, and the number of volumes continues to grow. Another official collection of federal legislation, the *United States Code Annotated* (the USCA), is similarly structured. It contains, in addition to the texts of federal laws, notes on state and federal judicial decisions applying individual laws, together with cross-references to other sections of the code, historical annotations, and library references.

The laws enacted by Congress are also collected in a chronological arrangement; issued annually, this arrangement is known as the United States Statutes at Large. The U.S. Statutes at Large are indexed but are not arranged by subject matter. Congress numbers the volumes of the Statutes at Large, which also contain amendments to the Constitution and presidential proclamations.

See also Annotated codes; Model Penal Code; Statutes; Uniform laws.

VERDICTS

Formal decisions or findings made by juries upon matters of fact submitted to them for deliberation and determination

In legal cases the court interprets the applicable law associated with a given case and explains the law to the jury. Based on the presented evidence the jury must determine the facts in the case and make a proper application of the law relating to those facts to arrive at a verdict. In general, the jury's verdict must be unanimous, but many states have modified the condition of unanimity, particularly in civil cases, so that the verdict can be rendered by a designated majority of the jury.

Verdicts may be either general or specific. A general verdict is that in which the jury pronounces "guilty" or "not guilty" and thus decides whether the plaintiff or the defendant wins the case. A general verdict is the verdict most often rendered in criminal cases. Moreover, in criminal cases the verdict must generally be unanimous and must be returned by the jury to the judge in open court. This verdict is based on every material fact submitted for the consideration of the jury. The court may also submit to the jury appropriate forms for a general verdict and, in some cases, a list of written questions concerning one or more of the relevant issues to the case that must be answered in the process of determining the verdict.

When the jury is asked by the court to answer specific questions of fact but leaves any decisions based on the law to the court, it is called a special verdict. The court often requires that the jury return a special verdict in the form of a special written finding upon each issue of fact, and the court determines if the defendant is guilty or not based on those answers. Civil cases may be decided by either a general or a special verdict.

When the verdict is presented in court, the defendant and all the jury members must be present. In most jurisdictions, the plaintiff or the defendant has the right to have the jury polled. If polled, each jury member is asked if the stated verdict is the one he or she favored. The verdict will not stand if the required number of jurors does not answer this question in the affirmative.

When the evidence conclusively dictates a clear verdict in favor of one of the litigants, the judge has the authority in many states to direct the jury to render a verdict in favor of either the plaintiff or the defendant. If it is evident to the court that a verdict is against the weight of the evidence, the court may order a new trial. However, in criminal cases, a verdict of acquittal is conclusive upon the prosecution (the state) so that the defendant will not be subjected to double jeopardy. However, in the event that the jury cannot reach a verdict, the defendant may be tried again.

—*Alvin K. Benson*

See also Acquittal; Appeal; Convictions; Courts-martial; Defendants; Directed verdicts; Dismissal; Double jeopardy; Harmless errors; Juries; Jury nullification; Mistrials; Reasonable doubt; Sentencing; Testimony; Trials.

WITNESSES

Persons whose testimony under oath or affirmation is received as evidence in courts or in depositions

The common law required that lay witnesses must speak only what they know first-hand and testify only as to facts. That is, they could not offer opinions, make inferences, or draw conclusions. The rule requiring first-hand personal knowledge has been preserved by the Federal Rules of Evidence (FRE). Because the meaning of the key terms "fact" and "opinion" is often unclear, the FRE have also liberalized the admissibility of lay opinions. Lay opinions are allowed whenever they would be helpful, provided that they are rationally based on the witness's perceptions. The latter requirement simply means that the witness must have first-hand (personal) knowledge of the matter at issue. Thus, witnesses are allowed to say that a person was (or appeared to be) angry, kidding, dying, strong, sober, or drunk. Speed may be estimated, even sometimes in such terms as fast or slow. Other examples include, "It was a sturdy fence" and "The apple was rotten."

The requirement of first-hand knowledge should not be confused with the hearsay rule. If a witness states, "Jack shot Mary" but knows this only from others, the witness violates the first-hand personal knowledge rule. If the same witness in the same circumstances testifies that "Joe told me Jack shot Mary," the first-hand rule is not violated but the hearsay rule may be violated. Hearsay rules govern the admissibility of a declarant's out-of-court statements. Accordingly, hearsay may be recounted in court pursuant to an exception or exemption; in such instances, the lack of first-hand knowledge would affect the weight rather than the admissibility of the witness's testimony.

Incompetency or Disqualification of Witnesses

A competent witness is one who testifies to what he or she has seen, heard, or otherwise observed. Trial courts recognize two kinds of witness incompetencies, which result in automatic disqualification: the lack of personal knowledge and the failure to take the oath or affirmation regarding telling the truth.

In the past witnesses have been ruled incompetent because they have a personal interest in the case, past criminal convictions, drug or alcohol intoxication or addiction, a marital relationship with one of the involved parties, or mental incapacity. Moreover, persons who are too young may be disqualified as witnesses. Such matters are mainly deemed factors to consider for whatever they are worth in the realms of relevance and credibility.

Persons who are to be offered as witnesses are often subjected to a special series of questions (often outside the presence of the jury) to ascertain foundational facts. This series of questions is to determine whether prospective witnesses understand the duty to

---

Hearsay, Nonhearsay, and Exceptions

Examples of hearsay:
- A witness testifies that her friend told her that he thinks the defendant committed the crime
- A witness testifies that his uncle saw the plaintiff run a red light.

Examples of Nonhearsay or Exceptions:
- A witness testifies that she thinks the defendant committed the crime.
- A witness testifies that he saw the plaintiff run a red light.
- While in jail the defendant tells his cellmate that he committed the crime, and at trial the cellmate testifies that the defendant confessed to him.

tell the truth, can distinguish fact from fantasy, and have the ability to communicate meaningfully with the jury. Children over six years old are rarely found to be incompetent. While state laws may differ, the FRE generally treat children, at least in principle, no different from other witnesses. These rules allow for the exclusion of child witnesses only for compelling reasons, which must be something other than mere age.

Witness Preparation and Sequestration

There are almost no formal limits on bona fide efforts to prepare a prospective witness for taking the witness stand. Thus, in preparing to testify, a witness may review documents, recordings, notes, and other pieces of documentation. The witness may also be rehearsed by attorneys but not prompted to tell an untruth.

In most jurisdictions there is a process called "sequestration," whereby witnesses may be prevented from listening to other testimony in the case. Questions have arisen as to whether this bars trial witnesses from reading transcripts, attending depositions, listening to oral reports of what transpired at hearings, or watching televised portions of trials. The Oklahoma bombing trials of the late 1990's raised the question as to whether families of the deceased victims were permitted to view the trial if they planned to give "victim impact" statements at the death-penalty sentencing phase. The trial judge, upheld by the court of appeals, concluded that they could not. The U.S. Congress then legislated, specifically with retroactive effect, that such witnesses in such cases could view the trials.

Additionally, the FRE exempts from sequestration witnesses who are parties, the designated representatives of organizations that are parties, or essential persons, such as experts needed at counsel's table to assist the attorneys. This rule also requires the judge to enter a sequestration order upon an attorney's request or upon the judge's own motion. The judge's order serves to clarify the scope of witness sequestration in a particular case.

Procedure for Examining Witnesses

The basic pattern of trials after jury selection and the opening statements of counsel is that the plaintiffs presents their cases through witnesses, documents, and other evidence. Then the defendants present their cases, which may consist of both denying facts asserted in the plaintiffs' cases and establishing affirmative defenses. A witness presented at either phase will normally be examined directly by the attorney presenting the witness, by the attorney from the opposing side during cross-examination, by the proponent to redirect examination and repair the damage caused during cross-examination, and finally by the opposing attorney in a second cross-examination to repair the damage of the proponent. In the absence of an exercise of the judge's discretion, repair is the only acceptable purpose of the last two sequences. Furthermore, repair may be severely limited or disallowed completely by the judge when the contribution of additional examination would be minimal. Further redirects and recrosses are always possible if necessary.

The order of presentation of witnesses in both civil and criminal trials is basically the same. The most significant difference is that the U.S. Constitution's Fifth Amendment privilege against self-incrimination prohibits the prosecution from calling criminal defendants to the stand as witnesses. In civil trials the plaintiff's lawyers often call defendants before other witnesses.

On direct examination attorneys usually must ask for and get yes-no or short answers. However, many jurisdictions give the judge discretion to permit extended narratives to the extent that they help develop the witness's testimony. Leading questions, those that suggest the answer, are generally improper on direct examination, with exceptions for forgetful, older, young, hostile, or adverse witnesses. In the case of forgetful, older, or young witnesses, leading questions serve a valid function in refreshing their memory or directing their attention. When lawyers call hostile or adverse witnesses to the stand, the danger that the witness will consciously or unconsciously acquiesce to the examiner's version of the truth is minimal, and leading questions are thus allowed. When witnesses are hostile to the examiner, the need for forcing them to answer the lawyer's questions is greater than the danger that leading questions present.

In common-law jurisdictions there are restrictions not only on leading questions but also on those deemed argumentative, misleading, compound, or otherwise multifaceted. The FRE treat these matters by reposing power in the judge to supervise witness examinations. Specifically, the FRE exhorts the judge to take reasonable measures to promote effectiveness and efficiency in ascertaining the truth and to protect witnesses from harassment or undue embarrassment.

There are two views as to the permissible scope of cross-examinations. The restrictive rule confines the cross-examiner to matters within the scope of direct examination. The wide-open rule allows any material issue in the case to be explored. The federal rules adopt the restrictive rule but allow the judge to make exceptions. Convenience of witnesses and trial efficiency often dictate that the judge exercise discretion regarding the proper scope of a witness's cross-examination.

Witnesses' Character and Credibility

By introducing personal testimony about a witness's character, it is possible to judge whether the witness has testified accurately, lied, or made a mistake; whether a person did or did not commit rape; whether a person was or was not careful; or whether a person turned a corner in an automobile in a particular way. However, such character-type propensity evidence is sometimes prejudicial, misleading, too time-consuming, or unfair. Accordingly, there is a general ban on the use of character-type propensity evidence unless it fits special rules for special exceptions. The exceptions are many.

It must be shown that reputation or character witnesses are familiar with the reputation of the person about whom they are testifying. Thus, in the case of reputation testimony, courts normally require that the witness and the subject have lived or done business in reasonable proximity to each other for a substantial period in the comparatively recent past. Also, the reputation reported must be the subject's reputation in the relevant community and relatively current.

A prerequisite for the admissibility of personal opinions about another's propensities is that the person providing personal opinions had some substantial recent contact or relationship with the other person that would furnish a reasonable basis for a current opinion. Weaknesses in these foundational elements affect the weight rather than the admissibility of character-type propensity evidence. Rules of impeachment govern the efforts to test the opposing witnesses' credibility.

Everyone's Duty to Testify

Two kinds of witnesses may appear at a trial or deposition: ordinary lay witnesses or expert witnesses. A properly subpoenaed witness who fails to show up at the time and date specified is subject to arrest. Except for the reimbursement of costs of coming to court, ordinary witnesses may not be paid to testify. Because of the truth-seeking function of the court, parties and other witnesses can be compelled to give testimony, even if it is damaging to themselves or others. Accordingly, a person normally cannot prevent another person from disclosing confidences, secrets, or other matters. However, privileges are a narrow exception to these general rules. The privileges for confidential communications in the attorney-client, physician-patient, psychotherapist-patient, and husband-wife contexts are examples of such exceptions. Privileges operate to exclude relevant evidence in the name of some other social objective. Most true privileges are designed to promote certain kinds of relationships and particularly to promote confidential communications within these socially desirable relationships.

—W. Dene Eddings Andrews

Suggested Readings

Elaborate treatments of judicial procedural matters that discuss witnesses include Paul Bergman and Sara J. Berman-Barnett's *Represent Yourself in Court: How to Prepare and Try a Winning Case* (2d ed. Berkeley Calif.: Nolo Press, 1998) and Paul Bergman's *Trial Advocacy in a Nutshell* (3d ed. St. Paul, Minn.: West Publishing, 1995). Both of these easy-to-read, helpful, and inexpensive paperbacks review the fundamentals of direct examinations and cross-examinations through numerous examples. *Bender's Forms of Discovery* (New York: Matthew-Bender; regularly updated) is a ten-volume treatise with sample questions for numerous kinds of cases, including product liability, employment discrimination, slip-and-fall, automobile accident, and breach of contract cases. This and similar lawyer "practice guides" are often available in the reference sections of public libraries. For a quick summary of the procedural rules involved in civil lawsuits, see Mary Kay Kane's *Civil Procedure in a Nutshell* (St. Paul, Minn.: West Publishing, 1996) and *Fundamentals of Litigation for Paralegals,* by Thomas Mauet and Marlene Maerowitz (3d ed. Boston: Little Brown, 1998). *Transcript Exercises for Learning Evidence,* by Paul Bergman (St. Paul, Minn.: West Publishing, 1992) contains various questions, answers, and judicial rulings from a variety of civil and criminal cases. This book is helpful for understanding the legal propriety of common objections. For discussions of the evidence rules on which common objections are based, see *Casenotes Law Outlines: Evidence*, by Kenneth Graham (Santa Monica, Calif.: Casenotes, 1996), and *Evidence: State and Federal Rules in a Nutshell*, by Paul F. Rothstein, Myrna Raeder, and David Crump (3d ed. St. Paul, Minn.: West Publishing, 1997). Recent studies of expert witnesses include *Expert Witnessing: Explaining and Understanding Science*, edited by Carl Meyer (Boca Raton, Fla.: CRC Press, 1999); *Applying Statistics in the Courtroom: A New Approach for Attorneys and Expert Witnesses* by Phillip I. Good (Boca Raton, Fla.: CRC Press, 2001); and *The Art and Science of Expert Witnessing: The Definitve Guide for Attorneys and Experts* by Olen R. Brown and Debra Karr (Leawood, Kans.: Cypress Publishing, 2002).

See also Cross-examination; Depositions; Objection; Perjury; Subpoena power; Testimony; Trial transcripts; Trials; Witnesses, confrontation of; Witnesses, expert.

WITNESSES, CONFRONTATION OF

Right, guaranteed by the U.S. Constitution's Sixth Amendment, of criminal defendants to have the witnesses against them testify in open court, face to face with them and the fact-finder, and to cross-examine those witnesses

The Sixth Amendment's confrontation clause fosters reliability and fairness in federal and state prosecutions. It allows criminal defendants to confront witnesses against them in open court, under oath or affirmation, face to face, and to cross-examine these witnesses. The scope of its protections, which benefit criminal defendants, has been defined by Supreme Court decisions citing history, reason, and practicality.

Normally, words may not be reported by others or in writing—that is, the witness must appear—and may be cross-examined under the full panoply of courtroom safeguards. However, the defendants' entitlements are qualified. For example, the separate, long-standing evidentiary rule against hearsay has numerous exceptions permitting second-hand or reported evidence, most of which, if they are deemed "firmly rooted" (rational and historically traditional), the Court has gradually been incorporating into the confrontation clause as in *White v. Illinois* (1992) and *Bourjailly v. United States* (1987). Thus, excited utterances, statements to physicians, coconspirator statements during and furthering the conspiracy, and the like can be reported, though the person who spoke them is not at trial to be confronted. These sorts of statements are presumed to be especially reliable and necessary. In *Idaho v. Wright* (1990), the Court ruled that some second-hand statements could be allowed if special facts demonstrated their reliability and necessity. In *Ohio v. Roberts* (1980), the Court ruled that sometimes the litigators must demonstrate the unavailability of the witness for appearance at trial before second-hand statements could be admitted as evidence.

Once witnesses *are* produced at trial, defendants' opportunity to cross-examine them may similarly be confined within reasonable limits. In *Montana v. Egelhoff* (1996), the Court ruled that, for example, the judge may apply normal exclusionary evidence rules, recognize privileges, or prohibit unduly prejudicial, harassing, time-consuming, or misleading questioning. If a witness becomes ill or dies after giving testimony but before full cross-examination, the testimony might still be allowed to stand. In *Maryland v. Craig* (1990), the Court determined that if a specific child-witness will suffer trauma from confronting his or her accused molester, the child may testify on one-way closed-circuit television, despite some infringement of the face-to-face requirement, provided there is full opportunity to put questions to the witness and all can see the screen.

Thus, the rights conferred by the confrontation clause are not absolute but are qualified by countervailing concerns and may amount merely to a strong preference.

—*Paul F. Rothstein*

See also Cross-examination; Objection; Perjury; Testimony; Trials; Witnesses; Witnesses, expert.

WITNESSES, EXPERT

Persons with specialized knowledge who testify as objective witnesses in court

Generally speaking, witnesses are expected to provide testimony concerning only the facts of a case; they are not allowed to give personal opinions or their own interpretations of the facts. Expert witnesses are the exception; their task is specifically to provide opinions and interpretations concerning matters on which they have special training.

While there is no particular degree or set of credentials that qualify persons as expert witnesses, there are three criteria that are considered before allowing persons to offer opinion as part of their testimony. First, the topic under examination must be something that is not considered to be common knowledge—that is, it must be something about which a typical jury would not be knowledgeable. Such topics include, but are not limited to, specialized knowledge about medicine, firearms, engineering, psychology, or computer programming. Second, expert witness must be able to provide documentation of their expertise in the form of an advanced degree, professional certification, or proof of completion of specialized training that is officially recognized in their field.

The third criterion is that the testimony of expert witnesses must be "relevant" and "valid"—that is, such witnesses must confine their opinions to the specifics of the case and to interpretations that are supported by science and other practitioners in the field. This criterion is often difficult to put into practice, partly because judges are often not able to assess the validity of opinions in fields other than law and partly because even experts may disagree on controversial subjects. The result is that a particular opinion may be considered acceptable and admissible in one court at one time but not in another court at another time.

Until 1993 the most commonly cited precedent for the admissibility of expert testimony was the 1923 case of *Frye v. United States*. In that case the court, in ruling on the admissibility of the results of a polygraph test, decided that expert opinion was only admissible if the scientific principle upon which it was based was "sufficiently established to have gained general acceptance in the particular field in which it belongs." In this case, the expert's testimony was not allowed. However, in the 1993 case of *Daubert v. Merrell Dow* the U.S. Supreme Court ruled on appeal that the "Frye test" was too strict. The intended effect of the judgment in *Daubert v. Merrell Dow* was to allow opinions based on newer, "cutting edge" research and technology to be heard in court, thereby allowing the legal system to keep pace with the rapid changes in science. An unavoidable, perhaps negative, consequence is that both expert testimony and judicial decisions regarding expert testimony are now less consistent than in the past. Particularly controversial areas include the domains of psychiatry, as in assessments of personal injury, violence-proneness, and insanity; eyewitness memory, especially in cases involving child witnesses and so-called "false memory"; and statistical probability, as in cases involving deoxyribonucleic acid (DNA) "fingerprinting" and class-action suits claiming discrimination or criminal negligence.

—Linda Mealey

See also Adversary system; Cross-examination; Evidence, rules of; Litigation expenses; Medical examiners; Testimony; Trials; Witnesses; Witnesses, confrontation of.

GLOSSARY

Note: Terms printed in SMALL CAPS are also the subjects of essays in the main text.

Abstention: Decision by a federal court to refuse to consider a matter more properly addressed to a state court.

Abuse of discretion: Standard used by an appellate court to reverse actions of a lower court that are clearly erroneous.

Abuse of process: Improper use of a legal action after it has been filed.

Accessory: Person who assists in the commission of a crime in some secondary role.

Accomplice liability: Liability for intentionally assisting another in the commission of a crime.

Accused: Person charged with having committed a crime.

ACQUITTAL: Declaration at the conclusion of a trial that a criminal defendant is innocent.

Actionable: Providing grounds for a lawsuit.

ADVERSARY SYSTEM: System in which opposing parties rather than judges have chief responsibility for presenting evidence necessary to resolve a case.

Adverse possession: Means of acquiring title to property by occupying it openly for a lengthy period of time.

AFFIDAVIT: Sworn, written statement.

Affirmative defense: Specific defense against a claim other than a general denial of the facts contained in the charge—for example, self-defense as a defense to the charge of murder.

AGE OF MAJORITY: Age when a person is old enough to enter into a contract.

Aggravation: Circumstances of a crime that increase its seriousness in the view of the law.

Alias: Another name by which a person is known.

Alimony and maintenance: Payments that an individual is obligated to make to a former spouse for support.

Ambulance chaser: Lawyer or person working with a lawyer who attempts to contact an accident victim shortly after an accident for the purpose of representing the victim in a lawsuit.

American Association of Law Schools: Professional association of law schools in the United States.

AMERICAN BAR ASSOCIATION: Largest national association of lawyers.

American Civil Liberties Union (ACLU): See appendix on legal assistance organizations.

American Inns of Court: Organization of attorneys, judges, law professors, and law students dedicated to the improvement of the legal profession.

Amicus curiae **BRIEF:** Brief filed with a court by persons or organizations who are not parties to a case but are interested in the matter.

AMNESTY: Pardon granted to persons guilty of a political crime.

ANNOTATED CODES: Copies of statutes organized by topic, accompanied by brief descriptions of cases referring to the statutes.

ANNULMENT: Declaration that a transaction, most commonly a marriage, was never valid.

APPEAL: Request made to a higher court to review the decision of a lower court.

Appellant: Person who appeals a decision of one court to a higher court.

Appellee: Person whose victory in a lower court is appealed to a higher one by an appellant.

ARBITRATION: Submission of a dispute to a neutral third party with the agreement that this party's decision of the dispute will be binding.

ARRAIGNMENT: Point in criminal proceeding when a person accused of a crime is brought before a court to be informed of the charges and to enter a plea.

ARREST: To take a person into custody for the purpose of bringing the person to court on criminal charges.

Assessment: Determination of property's value for the purpose of taxation.

Assignment of error: Points made by a party appealing a case that specify errors made in a lower court.

ATTACHMENT: Legal procedure for taking possession of property as security for an anticipated judgment.

Attempt: Effort to commit a crime that may be punished even if the crime is not carried out.

Attorney trust account: Separate bank accounts maintained by attorneys for client funds.

Bail: Money or other property given to obtain the release from custody of a criminal defendant and to ensure that the defendant will subsequently appear in court.

Bail bond: Agreement by one party to procure the release of a criminal defendant specifying that the party will pay the bail amount should the defendant fail to appear in court.

Bailiff: Person who keeps order in a courtroom.

Bankruptcy: Legal proceeding that allows a person to obtain release from debts.

Bar association: Professional organization of attorneys established to support the practice of law, legal issues, and the interests of their members.

Bar examinations: Comprehensive tests of legal knowledge given to persons desiring to become lawyers.

Bench warrant: Order issued by a court in session for the immediate arrest of a person for the purpose of allowing matters at bar to continue without a lengthy delay

Beyond a reasonable doubt: Degree of certainty required to convict a person accused of a crime.

Bill of attainder: Unconstitutional legislative action that singles out persons or groups for punishment without a trial.

Bill of Rights, U.S.: First ten amendments to the U.S. Constitution, which safeguard various individual liberties.

Billable hours: Hours an attorney spends working on a client's matter, for which the attorney bills an agreed upon hourly rate.

Black's Law Dictionary: Foremost American dictionary of legal terms.

Bond: Instrument issued by a government or company promising to pay a certain rate of interest for a loan to a person who has loaned the government or company money.

Breach of the peace: Criminal disturbance of public order.

Brief: Concise statement of the facts and arguments in a case or a short summary of a matter.

Burden of proof: Duty to prove a particular issue in a case.

Capital crime: Crime punishable by death.

Capital punishment: Punishment by death.

Case law: Law derived from the decisions of courts rather than from the actions of legislatures.

Cause of action: Grounds for bringing a claim against another party.

Certiorari, WRIT OF: Most commonly an application to the U.S. Supreme Court seeking review of a lower court decision.

CHAIN OF CUSTODY: Account by one who offers physical evidence of the possession of the evidence from the moment it is discovered until it is offered in court.

Chambers: Private office of a judge.

Chancery court: Court that decides issues on general grounds of fairness rather than on precise rules of law.

CHANGE OF VENUE: Transfer of the location of a lawsuit.

Circuit court: Court with jurisdiction over several districts or counties.

Circumstantial evidence: Secondary evidence from which a primary issue may be inferred.

Citation: Order issued by a court or law-enforcement officer requiring a person to appear in court.

Cite: To order someone to appear in court; to refer to legal authority in support of one's argument.

CIVIL ACTION: Action brought for the redress of a wrong suffered by an individual or entity, as opposed to a criminal proceeding.

CIVIL LAW: Law relating to noncriminal matters; law deliberately implemented by a nation or state, as opposed to natural law.

Civil service: Employment in some branch of government other than the military.

CLASS ACTION: Legal action brought on behalf of many individuals with a common interest by one or more representative plaintiffs.

Clemency: Reduction of a criminal sentence by the leniency of an executive official.

CLERKS OF THE COURT: Court officials who maintain court records and files.

Code of Professional Responsibility: Rules of legal ethics effective in many states from the early 1970's to the mid-1980's.

Collateral estoppel: Judicial doctrine providing that the resolution of issues litigated by parties in one case will thereafter be binding on them if raised in another case.

Collusion: Secret agreement to commit fraud.

COMMON LAW: Law based on judicial decisions rather than legislative enactments.

Common-law marriage: Agreement that is illegal in many states between a man and woman to live as husband and wife without participating in a formal ceremony or obtaining a marriage license.

Comparative negligence: Doctrine comparing the negligence of a defendant and a plaintiff in a negligence action that allows the plaintiff to recover for damages that may be attributable to the defendant, even if the plaintiff was also partially negligent.

Compensatory damages: Damages that remedy an injury suffered, as opposed to punitive or nominal damages.

Competency: Capacity to understand and to act rationally.

Compulsory process: Right of a person charged with a crime to summon witnesses to court on his or her behalf.

Concurrent jurisdiction: Authority of two or more courts to hear the same case.

Concurring opinion: Judicial opinion in a case that agrees with the result reached by other judges but has different reasons for agreeing with this result.

Confession: Admission of guilt.

Consent decree: Court decree based on the agreement of the parties to a case.

Consequential damages: Damages not immediately caused by a loss but flowing secondarily from it, such as lost profits of a business destroyed by a flood.

Conspiracy: Agreement among two or more parties to commit a criminal act.

Contempt of court: Disobedience of a court order, or conduct that disrupts court proceedings or undermines the dignity of a court.

Contingency fees: Fee payable to a lawyer only if the lawyer achieves a successful result in a case.

Continuance: Delay of court proceedings until some future date.

Conviction: Final determination of guilt in a criminal proceeding, whether based on a trial or a guilty plea.

Coroner: Public official charged with investigating the circumstances of violent or suspicious deaths.

Corporal punishment: Physical punishment.

Corporate general counsel: Attorney, often an employee of a corporation, who handles general legal affairs of the corporation.

Corporations: Entities created by law and treated as having identities distinct from the identities of their shareholders.

Corpus delicti: Body or substance of a crime, such as the corpse of a murder victim.

Counterclaim: Claim made by a defendant in a lawsuit against a plaintiff.

COURT-AWARDED FEES: Attorneys fees provided to a prevailing party by law and assigned by a court.

COURT COSTS: Expenses, excluding attorneys fees, of a lawsuit.

COURT-MARTIAL: Proceeding to decide matters relating to the conduct of military personnel.

COURT REPORTER: Person who transcribes testimony in court proceedings.

Crime of passion: Crime committed under the influence of strong emotion.

Criminal intent: Guilty or wrongful purpose.

Cross-claim: Claim made by a party against another party on the same side of a lawsuit.

CROSS-EXAMINATION: Questioning of a witness called on behalf of an opponent in a court or other legal proceeding.

CRUEL AND UNUSUAL PUNISHMENT: Punishment forbidden by the Eighth Amendment to the U.S. Constitution that is disproportionate to a crime or otherwise excessive.

Culpable: Worthy of blame.

DAMAGES: Monetary compensation awarded in a lawsuit to an injured party.

De minimus: Trivial or unimportant.

Death certificate: Official document declaring that an individual has died.

DEATH ROW ATTORNEYS: Attorneys who represent criminal defendants sentenced to death in appeals of their convictions.

DECLARATORY JUDGMENT: Court order stating the rights and liabilities of parties or rendering an opinion without otherwise awarding relief.

Default: Failure to perform some legal duty.

Default judgment: Judgment entered against a defendant in a civil case who fails to respond to a lawsuit.

DEFENDANT: Person sued in a civil case or accused of having committed a crime in a criminal case.

Deficiency judgment: Judgment entered against a debtor for the amount of a debt still owing after a lender has used the debtor's collateral to reduce the debt partially.

Deportation: Forced removal of a person from a country by government order.

DEPOSITION: Recorded questioning of a witness under oath prior to a trial.

Derivative action: Lawsuit brought by a shareholder to enforce a claim or right of the corporation.

Dictum: Language in a judicial opinion that is not necessary to the decision.

Dilatory tactics: Attempts to delay or frustrate the progress of a legal proceeding.

DIPLOMATIC IMMUNITY: Freedom of diplomatic personnel from prosecution for crimes in the country in which they are posted.

Direct examination: Examination of a witness by the party who called the witness.

DIRECTED VERDICT: Verdict rendered by a judge in favor of a criminal defendant or against a party in a civil action who has failed to present sufficient evidence to justify letting a jury determine a case.

DISCOVERY: Procedures for allowing parties to a court case to discover relevant information prior to the trial.

Discrimination: Treating persons or matters differently when no reasonable grounds exist for doing so.

DISMISSAL: Discontinuation of a case.

Disorderly conduct: Conduct that disturbs the peace.

Disposition: Transferring of something to the care of another; the final settlement of a legal issue.

Dissenting opinion: Opinion written by one or more judges who disagree with the result reached by a majority of judges in a case.

DISTRICT ATTORNEY: Prosecuting attorney who represents the government within a particular judicial district.

DIVERSITY JURISDICTION: Authority of the federal courts to resolve disputes among citizens of different states or among citizens and aliens when certain conditions prevail.

Divorce: Termination of the marriage relationship.

Docket: Brief record of the proceedings in a case; also, the calendar of cases to be heard in a court.

Doctor of jurisprudence: Basic graduate degree necessary to practice law in the United States.

Domicile: Permanent home or residence.

DOUBLE JEOPARDY: Second prosecution for the same offense.

DUE PROCESS: Fair and orderly treatment by law.

Duress: Use of threats or other exercises of power to force one to act against his or her will.

Eminent domain: Power of government to take property with just compensation for public purposes.

En banc: Determination of a case by all of the judges of a particular court.

Enjoin: To command that something be done or not done.

EQUAL PROTECTION OF THE LAW: Constitutional requirement that persons similarly situated be accorded the same treatment.

EQUITABLE REMEDIES: Remedies granted by courts using their equity jurisdiction as opposed to their legal jurisdiction.

Equity: Legal principles and procedures that emphasize the resolution of disputes according to general principles of fairness; also, the value of property minus any debts owed against it.

Eviction: Forcing of a tenant to surrender possession of property.

Ex parte: Communication with only one side of a lawsuit.

EXCLUSIONARY RULE: Rule that prevents the use of evidence in a criminal trial that was obtained illegally.

EXECUTION OF JUDGMENT: Enforcement of a judgment rendered by a court, normally by seizing and selling property of a person against whom the judgment has been entered.

EXECUTOR: Person appointed by a now-deceased person to handle the directives in a will.

Exemplary damages: Punitive damages; damages in excess of those needed to compensate an injury.

FELONY: Serious crime, as distinguished from a misdemeanor.

FORECLOSURE: Termination of a party's property rights, generally by the holder of a mortgage.

Forum non conveniens: Doctrine that allows a court to decline to hear a case if a court in a more convenient location can do so.

Fraud: Intentional misrepresentation or distortion of facts.

GAG ORDER: Court order preventing parties, attorneys, and others from discussing matters related to a case.

GARNISHMENT: Legal procedure used to seize money or wages of a party owing a debt or against whom a claim has been made.

GRAND JURY: Group of citizens appointed to investigate possible crimes and to determine whether criminal indictments should be brought.

Habeas corpus: Application to a court to consider whether a person in custody is being held lawfully.

HEARING: Legal proceeding other than a trial in which evidence is taken or legal arguments presented for a court to make some determination.

Hung jury: Jury that cannot reach a verdict.

IMMUNITY: Freedom from having to fulfill some legal duty or from prosecution for a crime.

Impanel: To select a jury.

Impeach: To discredit or accuse of wrongdoing.

In forma pauperis: To proceed as a pauper—that is, to proceed without having to pay normal legal costs.

Inalienable: Incapable of being transferred or given away.

INCAPACITATION: Rationale of punishment that seeks to control crime by rendering criminals unable, or less able, to commit further crimes.

Incorrigible: Not capable of reform.

Incriminate: To provide evidence that would implicate someone in having committed a crime.

Incumbrance: Mortgage, lien, or other claim against property.

INDEMNITY: Agreement for one party to take on another's obligation or liability.

INDICTMENT: Accusation made by a grand jury that an individual has committed a crime.

Indigent: Poor.

Information: Accusation by a public official that an individual has committed a crime, used in many states as a counterpart to a grand jury indictment.

INJUNCTION: Order by a court for someone to do or not do something.

INQUEST: Official investigation of whether a crime has occurred, especially in connection with a death.

Insolvency: Inability to pay debts as they become due.

JD: Doctor of jurisprudence; the basic graduate degree necessary to practice law in the United States.

JOINT AND SEVERAL LIABILITY: Liability that allows an injured person to sue one or all the persons who contributed to the injury.

Judgment proof: Lacking assets that might be seized to satisfy a judgment.

Judicial review: Authority of courts to review the constitutionality of legislative and executive actions.

Jurisdiction: Authority of a court to hear and decide a particular case.

Jurisprudence: Legal philosophy.

Jury: Body of people assembled to give an impartial verdict in a civil or legal trial.

Jury nullification: Verdict rendered by a jury in disregard of the law.

Jury sequestration: Confinement of a jury during a trial or jury deliberations to prevent jury members from being influenced by contact with others.

Juvenile delinquent: Minor who has committed a crime.

Law School Admission Test (LSAT): Standardized test used by law schools to measure qualifications of potential law students.

Leading question: Question asked during the examination of a witness that suggests the answer desired.

Legalese: Technical legal language.

Lesser included offense: Crime whose elements are necessarily proven by proof that a more serious crime has been committed.

Libel: Written defamation of one's character or reputation.

License: Right to do something that one would not otherwise be entitled to do.

Lien: Interest in property to secure payment or performance of an obligation.

Litigation: Lawsuit, or a contest in court to enforce a right or to seek a remedy.

Living will: Written statement expressing a person's desire not to be kept alive by artificial means in the event of a serious illness or accident.

LLM: Master of laws, a graduate legal degree beyond the basic JD, or doctor of jurisprudence, degree.

Long-arm statute: Law that allows a court in one state to exercise jurisdiction over a defendant in another state.

Magistrate: Judicial official with authority to decide preliminary matters or minor cases.

Malpractice: Misconduct by a professional such as an attorney or a physician.

Mandamus: Court order commanding some public official, court, or corporation to take certain action.

Maritime law: Law relating to the sea.

MARTIAL LAW: Control of civilians by a military authority.

MEDIATION: Referral of a dispute to an objective third person, who attempts to help disputing parties reach a compromise.

MEDICAL EXAMINER: Physician employed by a municipal government who is certified to conduct autopsies to determine causes of death.

Minor: Person who has not reached the legal age of adulthood.

MIRANDA RIGHTS: Rights of criminal defendants when arrested.

MISDEMEANOR: Minor crime punishable by a fine or less than one year of imprisonment.

MISTRIAL: Termination of a trial because of misconduct or other unusual occurrence.

Mitigating circumstances:

Mitigation of damages: Requirement that an injured person take reasonable steps to minimize the degree of injury.

Modus operandi: Way an action or crime is carried out.

Motion: Request for some action directed to a court.

Naturalization: Granting of citizenship rights to a foreigner.

NEGLIGENCE: Unintentional failure to act with reasonable care.

Nolo contendere **PLEA:** Plea of a criminal defendant that neither denies nor admits guilt.

Nominal damages: Small or inconsequential damages awarded to a party who has been wronged but has suffered no actual damages.

NOTARY PUBLIC: Person authorized by law to certify the signing of documents under oath.

OBJECTION: Challenge to testimony or other evidence offered in court.

OBSTRUCTION OF JUSTICE: Crime of interfering with the administration of justice such as by influencing a witness.

OPINION: Written statement by a judge or court summarizing facts, issues raised, and justification for the resolution of a case.

Ordinance: Law adopted by a local political body such as a city council.

Original jurisdiction: Authority of a court to make the initial determination of a particular issue, in contrast to appellate jurisdiction.

Overrule: To deny an objection in a case; to overturn the legal authority of a prior case.

Paralegal: Nonlawyer with legal skills who works under the supervision of an attorney.

PARDONING POWER: Power of a president or governor to exempt a person accused of a crime from punishment.

PAROLE: Early release of a prisoner.

Penal code: Collection of state or federal laws defining types of criminal conduct.

Peremptory challenge: Lawyer's objection to the seating of a particular person on a jury that need not be supported by specific reasons.

PERJURY: False statement under oath.

Personal property: Property other than real estate; things that are movable.

PERSONAL RECOGNIZANCE: Pretrial release of criminal defendant without bail on the basis of the defendant's promise to appear for trial.

Plain error rule: Rule allowing an appellate court to reverse a trial court proceeding even if the person appealing did not complain about the error at trial.

Plain view doctrine: Rule allowing law-enforcement personnel to seize items in plain view without a search warrant.

Plaintiff: One who brings a civil action.

PLEA: Response of a criminal defendant to an indictment.

PLEA BARGAIN: Agreement between a prosecutor and a criminal defendant disposing of a criminal matter.

Pleadings: Documents filed by parties to a suit containing their claims and defenses regarding the suit.

Polling a jury: Asking each individual member of a jury whether he or she agrees with the jury verdict.

Polygraph: Machine used to conduct a lie detector test.

Positive law: Law created or enacted by an appropriate authority, in contrast to natural law.

Possession: Control of property.

Post mortem: Investigation after a death.

Power of attorney: Document granting one person authority to act on behalf of another.

PRECEDENT: Case law that guides subsequent legal decisions.

Preemption: Constitutional doctrine that allows federal laws on a subject to override inconsistent state laws.

PRELIMINARY HEARING: Hearing used in cases not involving a grand jury indictment to determine whether there is probable cause to believe that an accused person has committed a crime.

Preliminary injunction: Order entered by a court at the beginning of a case to maintain the status quo during a trial.

Preponderance of the evidence: Sufficient evidence to suggest that it is more likely than not that an asserted claim is true.

PRESUMPTION OF INNOCENCE: Requirement that government affirmatively prove that an individual has committed a crime.

Pretrial conference: Conference between a judge and parties to a lawsuit after a case has been filed for the purpose of planning discovery and discussing the possibility of a settlement.

***Prima facie* case:** True or valid on first view; evidence sufficient to prevail in a case absent some response from an opponent.

PRIVILEGED COMMUNICATIONS: Communications that may not be admitted into evidence in a judicial proceeding without the consent of the parties to the communications.

PRO BONO LEGAL WORK: Legal services provided by legal professionals at no charge.

Pro se: To represent oneself in a proceeding as opposed to being represented by an attorney.

PROBABLE CAUSE: Reasonable grounds for believing that an accused person has committed a crime.

PROBATE: Legal proceeding to establish whether a will is valid.

PROBATION: Early release of a criminal from prison.

Process: Legal procedure used by a court to obtain power over a particular person or property, such as a summons to appear in a case.

PROSECUTORS: Lawyers, such as district attorneys, who represent the government in cases against persons accused of crimes.

Proximate cause: Legal cause of an injury.

PUBLIC DEFENDER: Attorney appointed by government to defend a person accused of a crime who cannot afford to hire a lawyer.

PUNITIVE DAMAGES: Damages in excess of those needed to compensate an injury; also known as exemplary damages.

Real property: Land and structures or items permanently attached to it.

REASONABLE DOUBT: Standard of proof required in criminal cases; proof must be such as reasonably to preclude the possibility of innocence.

Recess: Temporary adjournment of legal proceedings.

Recidivism: Act of repeating a criminal offense.

Recusal: Disqualification of a judge from a legal case on the basis of objections of either party or at the judge's own request because of some prejudice or conflict of interest.

RELEASE: To abandon a claim.

Remand: Order returning a proceeding for further action to a court that had originally heard it.

Remittitur: Court order reducing the amount of damages awarded by a jury.

Removal: Transfer of a case from one court to another, as from a state court to a federal court.

Repossession: Creditor's taking possession of collateral upon the debtor's failure to pay a debt.

Reprieve: To postpone the execution of a criminal sentence.

RESTITUTION: Legal remedy that seeks to restore property or money to the person from whom it was originally taken or obtained.

RESTRAINING ORDER, TEMPORARY: Court order requiring or preventing some action for a short period of time until a more complete evaluation of the matter may be made by the court.

RETAINER: Fee for legal services paid in advance.

REVERSIBLE ERROR: Significant error committed by a trial court justifying an appellate court to overrule the trial court's decision.

SEARCH WARRANT: Judicial order allowing law-enforcement personnel to enter and search a particular location.

Self-defense: Protection of one's person or property from attack by another.

SELF-INCRIMINATION: Testimony by an individual that tends to suggest that the individual has committed a crime.

SENTENCING: Pronouncing of punishment on a person convicted of having committed a crime.

Service of process: Delivery to a defendant of a complaint or other documents representing the filing of a lawsuit against the defendant.

Side bar: Discussions between a judge and attorneys in a case that cannot be heard by the jury or spectators.

SMALL-CLAIMS COURT: Civil court with the power to decide cases involving only small amounts of money.

Solicitor general: Lawyer appointed by the president of the United States to represent the United States in cases before the U.S. Supreme Court.

Sovereign immunity: Doctrine that prevents suits against government unless the government has previously authorized such suits.

Special verdict: Verdict in which a jury responds to specific issues in a case.

Specific performance: Remedy for breach of contract that requires a breaching party to perform the obligation required by the contract.

SPEEDY TRIAL REQUIREMENT: Right provided to criminal defendants by the Sixth Amendment to the U.S. Constitution guaranteeing that they be tried without excessive delay.

STANDING: Right of a particular person to assert a claim in court.

Stare decisis: Principle that courts should generally follow the decisions of previous cases.

STATUTE: Laws enacted by the legislative branch of government.

Statute of frauds: Legal requirement that certain contracts be in writing to be enforced.

STATUTE OF LIMITATION: Statute setting forth a period of time in which a lawsuit must be filed.

STRICT LIABILITY: Liability imposed without regard to whether one is at fault.

Subornation of perjury: Crime of inducing another to commit perjury.

Subpoena: Order for a witness to appear in court to testify.

Subpoena duces tecum: Order for a witness to appear in court and to present to the court specified documents relevant to a case.

Subrogation: Legal right of one party to step into the shoes of another party and to assert that other party's claim.

SUMMARY JUDGMENT: Judgment rendered by a court without a trial when the facts of a case are not in serious dispute.

SUMMONS: Notice to a defendant that a lawsuit has been filed against him or her and a specification of the time at which the defendant must answer the claim.

TEST CASE: Lawsuit brought to clarify or challenge some legal principle.

Testator: Person who dies leaving a will.

TESTIMONY: Statement made by a witness under oath in a legal proceeding.

THREE-STRIKES LAWS: Laws requiring severe prison sentence for repeat criminal offenders.

Title: Ownership of property.

TORT: Civil wrong committed by one party against another, excluding breaches of contract.

Treason: Rebellious action toward one's government.

TRIAL TRANSCRIPT: Official record of a legal proceeding.

Trustee: Person appointed to safeguard or manage another's property.

Trustee in bankruptcy: Person who assumes control of a debtor's property in a bankruptcy proceeding.

Vacate: To move out of property; also, to set aside or rescind a court order or decision.

Venire: List of those summoned for jury duty.

VERDICT: Decision of a jury in a trial.

Vested: Presently existing right to something that is not contingent on the occurrence of a future condition.

Vicarious liability: Liability of one party for another party's actions or omissions.

Void: Of no legal force.

Voir dire: Examination of potential jurors to determine their ability to serve on a jury or the preliminary examination of a witness to determine whether the witness is competent to testify.

Ward of the court: Person under the protection of the court, such as a child or a mentally infirm person.

Warrant: Order permitting an official to take some action, such as permitting law-enforcement personnel to arrest someone or search particular property.

White-collar crime: Nonviolent crimes committed by business or banking professionals.

Wills: Documents setting forth parties' desires as to the disposition of their property upon their deaths.

Wiretapping: Surreptitious monitoring of telephone conversations by law-enforcement officials.

WITNESS: Person who testifies to matters in a legal proceeding, whether orally or in writing.

WITNESS, EXPERT: Person who offers testimony in a legal proceeding based on specialized knowledge of a subject.

Workers' compensation: Statutory arrangement to pay a worker for an injury suffered on the job, whether or not the injury was the fault of the worker.

Writ: Court's written command to do something.

BIBLIOGRAPHY

Civil Rights and Civil Liberties

Amar, Akhil Reed, and Alan Hirsch. *For the People: What the Constitution Really Says About Your Rights*. New York: Free Press, 1998.

Bell, Jeannine. *Policing Hatred: Law Enforcement, Civil Rights, and Hate Crime*. New York: New York University Press, 2002.

Brill, Alida. *Nobody's Business: Paradoxes of Privacy*. Reading, Mass.: Addison-Wesley, 1990.

Cohen, William, and David J. Danelski. *Constitutional Law: Civil Liberty and Individual Rights*. New York: Foundation Press, 2002.

Cruit, Ronald L. *Intruder in Your Home: How to Defend Yourself Legally with a Firearm*. New York: Stein & Day, 1983.

Davis, Timothy, Kevin R. Johnson, and George A. Martínez, eds. *A Reader on Race, Civil Rights, and American Law: A Multiracial Approach*. Durham, N.C.: Carolina Academic Press, 2001.

Faux, Marian. *Roe v. Wade: The Untold Story of the Landmark Supreme Court Decision That Made Abortion Legal*. New York: Macmillan, 1988.

Friedman, Lawrence M. *American Law in the Twentieth Century*. New Haven, Conn.: Yale University Press, 2002.

Glasser, Ira. *Visions of Liberty: The Bill of Rights for All Americans*. New York: Arcade Publishing, 1991.

Levy, Leonard W., ed. *Encyclopedia of the American Constitution*. New York: Free Press, 1986.

Lewis, Thomas T., ed. *The Bill of Rights*. Pasadena, Calif.: Salem Press, 2002.

Lock, Shmuel. *Crime, Public Opinion, and Civil Liberties: The Tolerant Public*. Westport, Conn.: Praeger, 1999.

Meltzer, Milton. *The Bill of Rights: How We Got It and What It Means*. New York: Thomas Crowell, 1990.

Monk, Linda R. *The Bill of Rights: A User's Guide*. Alexandria, Va.: Close Up, 1991.

O'Brien, David M., ed. *The Lanahan Readings in Civil Rights and Civil Liberties*. Baltimore: Lanahan Publishers, 1999.

Schulhofer, Stephen J. *The Enemy Within: Intelligence Gathering, Law Enforcement, and Civil Liberties in the Wake of September 11*. New York: Century Foundation Press, 2002.

Consumer Law

Feinman, Jay M. *Law 101: Everything You Need to Know About the American Legal System*. New York: Oxford University Press, 2000.

Klein, David, Marymae E. Klein, and Douglas D. Walsh. *Getting Unscrewed and Staying That Way: The Sourcebook of Consumer Protection*. New York: Holt, 1993.

McGinn, Joseph C. *Personal Law: The Most Common Legal Problems and How to Solve Them*. Englewood Cliffs, N.J.: Prentice-Hall, 1982.

Taylor, Norman F., and Merrell G. Vannier. *Lemon Law: A Manual for Consumers*. Glendale, Calif.: Consumer Rights Center, 1991.

Courts and Judges

Abraham, Henry Julian. *The Judicial Process: An Introductory Analysis of the Courts of the United States, England, and France*. New York: Oxford University Press, 1998.

Alexander, S. L. *Covering the Courts: A Handbook for Journalists*. Lanham, Md.: University Press of America, 1999.

Benesh, Sara C. *The U.S. Court of Appeals and the Law of Confessions: Perspectives on the Hierarchy of Justice*. New York: LFB Scholarly Publishing, 2002.

Forer, Lois G. *Money and Justice: Who Owns the Courts?* New York: Norton, 1984.

Feeley, Malcolm M. *Court Reform on Trial: Why Simple Solutions Fail*. New York: Basic Books, 1983.

Finkel, Norman J. *Commonsense Justice: Jurors' Notions of the Law*. Cambridge, Mass.: Harvard University Press, 1995.

Giles, Robert, and Robert W. Snyder, eds. *Covering the Courts: Free Press, Fair Trials, and Journalistic Performance*. New Brunswick, N.J.: Transaction Publishers, 1999.

Hans, Valerie P., and Neil Vidmar. *Judging the Jury*. New York: Plenum Press, 1986.

Huber, Peter W. *Galileo's Revenge: Junk Science in the Courtroom*. New York: Basic Books, 1991.

Lewis, Thomas T., and Richard L. Wilson, eds. *Encyclopedia of the U.S. Supreme Court*. 3 vols. Pasadena, Calif.: Salem Press, 2000.

Nasheri, Hedieh. *Crime and Justice in the Age of Court TV*. New York: LFB Scholarly Publishing, 2002.

Neely, Richard. *The Politics of State Courts*. New York: Free Press, 1988.

O'Brien, David M. *What Process Is Due? Courts and Science-Policy Disputes.* New York: Russell Sage Foundation, 1987.

Rehnquist, William H. *The Supreme Court: How It Was, How It Is.* New York: Quill, 1987.

Rudy, Theresa. *Small Claims Court: Making Your Way Through the System—a Step-by-Step Guide.* Rev. ed. New York: Random House, 1990.

Sevilla, Charles M. *Disorder in the Court: Great Fractured Moments in Courtroom History.* New York: Norton, 1992.

Smith, Christopher E. *Courts and Trials: A Reference Handbook.* Santa Barbara, Calif.: ABC-CLIO, 2003.

Songer, Donald R., Reginald S. Sheehan, and Susan B. Haire. *Continuity and Change on the United States Courts of Appeals.* Ann Arbor: University of Michigan Press, 2000.

Spence, Gerry. *With Justice for None.* New York: Time Books, 1989.

Tribe, Laurence H. *God Save This Honorable Court: How the Choice of Supreme Court Justices Shapes Our History.* New York: Random House, 1985.

Criminal Law and Procedures

Abramson, Leslie. *The Defense Is Ready: Life in the Trenches of Criminal Law.* With Richard Flaste. New York: Simon and Schuster, 1997.

Baker, Liva. *Miranda: The Crime, the Law, the Politics.* New York: Atheneum, 1983.

Bazelon, David L. *Questioning Authority: Justice and Criminal Law.* New York: Knopf, 1988.

Bedau, Hugo Adam. *The Death Penalty in America.* 3d ed. New York: Oxford University Press, 1982.

_____, ed. *The Death Penalty in America: Current Controversies.* New York: Oxford University Press, 1997.

Bergman, Paul, and Sara J. Berman-Barrett. *The Criminal Law Handbook: Know Your Rights, Survive the System.* 5th ed. Berkeley, Calif.: Nolo Press, 2003.

Burnham, David. *Above the Law: Secret Deals, Political Fixes, and Other Misadventures of the U.S. Department of Justice.* New York: Scribner, 1996.

Champion, Dean J. *The Roxbury Dictionary of Criminal Justice: Key Terms and Major Court Cases.* Los Angeles: Roxbury, 1997.

Dershowitz, Alan M. *The Best Defense.* New York: Random House, 1982.

Dressler, Joshua, ed. *Encyclopedia of Crime and Justice.* New York: Macmillan Reference USA, 2002.

Elikann, Peter T. *The Tough-on-Crime Myth: Real Solutions to Cut Crime.* New York: Insight Books, 1996.

Estrich, Susan. *Getting Away with Murder: How Politics Is Destroying the Criminal Justice System.* Cambridge, Mass.: Harvard University Press, 1998.

_____. *With Justice for Some: Victims' Rights in Criminal Trials.* Reading, Mass.: Addison-Wesley, 1995.

Friedman, Lawrence M. *American Law in the Twenteith Century.* New Haven, Conn.: Yale University Press, 2002.

_____. *Crime and Punishment in American History.* New York: Basic Books, 1993.

Ginsburg, William L. *Victims' Rights: A Complete Guide to Crime Victim Compensation.* Clearwater, Fla: Sphinx, 1994.

Jacob, Herbert. *Crime and Justice in Urban America.* Englewood Cliffs, N.J.: Prentice-Hall, 1980.

Kennedy, Randall. *Race, Crime, and the Law.* New York: Pantheon Books, 1997.

Kopel, David B., and Paul H. Blackman. *No More Wacos: What's Wrong with Federal Law Enforcement and How to Fix It.* Amherst, N.Y.: Prometheus Books, 1997.

Kramer, Rita. *At a Tender Age: Violent Youth and Juvenile Justice.* New York: Henry Holt, 1988.

Lock, Shmuel. *Crime, Public Opinion, and Civil Liberties: The Tolerant Public.* Westport, Conn.: Praeger, 1999.

Nicolson, Donald, and Lois Bibbings, eds. *Feminist Perspectives on Criminal Law.* London: Cavendish, 2000.

Orth, John V. *Due Process of Law: A Brief History.* Lawrence, Kan.: University Press of Kansas, 2003.

Rothwax, Harold J. *Guilty: The Collapse of Criminal Justice.* New York: Random House, 1996.

Scheingold, Stuart A. *The Politics of Law and Order: Street Crime and Public Policy.* New York: Longman, 1984.

Uviller, H. Richard. *The Tilted Playing Field: Is Criminal Justice Unfair?* New Haven, Conn.: Yale University Press, 1999.

Wexler, Richard. *Wounded Innocents: The Real Victims of the War Against Child Abuse.* Buffalo, N.Y.: Prometheus Books, 1990.

White, Bertha Rothe. *The Crimes and Punishment Primer.* Dobbs Ferry, N.Y.: Oceana, 1986.

Winslade, William J., and Judith Wilson Ross. *The Insanity Plea: The Uses and Abuses of the Insanity Defense.* New York: Scribner's, 1983.

Family Law

Bove, Alexander A. *The Complete Book of Wills and Estates.* New York: H. Holt, 1989.

Brinig, Margaret F., Carl E. Schneider, and Lee E. Teitelbaum, eds., *Family Law in Action: A Reader.* Cincinnati: Anderson, 1999.

Cretney, Stephen. *Family Law in the Twentieth Century: A History.* New York: Oxford University Press, 2003.

Crotty, Patricia McGee. *Family Law in the United States: Changing Perspectives.* New York: Peter Lang, 1999.

Douglas, Gillian. *An Introduction to Family Law.* New York: Oxford University Press, 2001.

Fineman, Martha Albertson. *The Illusion of Equality: The Rhetoric and Reality of Divorce Reform.* Chicago: University of Chicago Press, 1991.

Fox, Greer Litton, and Michael L. Benson. *Families, Crime and Criminal Justice.* New York; Amsterdam: JAI, 2000.

Friedman, Gary J. *A Guide to Divorce Mediation: How to Reach a Fair, Legal Settlement at a Fraction of the Cost.* New York: Workman, 1993.

Gillis, Phyllis L. *Days Like This: A Tale of Divorce.* New York: McGraw-Hill, 1986.

Goldstein, Joseph, Anna Freud, Albert J. Solnit, and Sonja Goldstein. *In the Best Interests of the Child.* New York: Free Press, 1986.

Harwood, Norma. *A Woman's Legal Guide to Separation and Divorce in All Fifty States.* New York: Scribner's, 1985.

Horgan, Timothy J. *Winning Your Divorce: A Man's Survival Guide.* New York: Dutton, 1994.

Hughes, Theodore E., and David Klein. *A Family Guide to Wills, Funerals, and Probate: How to Protect Yourself and Your Survivors.* New York: Facts on File/Checkmark Books, 2001.

Kandel, Randy. *Family Law: Essential Terms and Concepts.* Gaithersburg, Md.: Aspen Law & Business, 2000.

Katz, Sanford N., John Eekelaar, and Mavis Maclean, eds. *Cross Currents: Family Law and Policy in the United States and England.* New York: Oxford University Press, 2000.

Ostberg, Kay. *Probate—Settling an Estate: A Step-by-Step Guide.* New York: Random House, 1990.

Schneider, Carl E., and Margaret F. Brinig. *An Invitation to Family Law: Principles, Process, and Perspectives.* St. Paul, Minn.: West Publishing, 2000.

Wadlington, Walter, and Raymond C. O'Brien. *Family Law in Perspective.* New York: Foundation Press, 2001.

_____, eds. *Family Law Statutes, International Conventions and Uniform Laws.* 2d ed. New York: Foundation Press, 2000.

Wallman, Lester, and Sharon McDonnell. *Cupid, Couples, and Contracts: A Guide to Living Together, Prenuptial Agreements, and Divorce.* New York: Master Media, 1994.

Wietzman, Lenore J. *The Marriage Contract: Spouses, Lovers, and the Law.* New York: Free Press, 1981.

Wilson, Carol Ann, and Edwin Schilling III. *The Survival Manual for Women in Divorce: One Hundred Eighty Two Questions and Answers.* Boulder, Colo.: Quantum Press, 1993.

Winner, Karen. *Divorced from Justice: The Abuse of Women and Children by Divorce Lawyers and Judges.* New York: ReganBooks, 1996.

General Legal Matters

Belli, Melvin M. *The Belli Files: Reflections on the Wayward Law.* Englewood Cliffs, N.J.: Prentice-Hall, 1983.

Christianson, Stephen G. *One Hundred Ways to Avoid Common Legal Pitfalls Without a Lawyer.* Secaucus, N.J.: Carol, 1992.

Fast, Julius, and Timothy Fast. *The Legal Atlas of the United States.* New York: Facts On File, 1997.

Friedman, Lawrence M. *American Law: An Introduction.* Rev. ed. New York: W. W. Norton, 1998.

_____. *American Law in the Twenteith Century.* New Haven, Conn.: Yale University Press, 2002.

Garry, Patrick M. *A Nation of Adversaries: How the Litigation Explosion Is Reshaping America.* New York: Plenum Press, 1997.

Haas, Carol. *Your Driving and the Law: A Crash Course in Traffic Tickets and Court, Auto Accidents and Insurance, and Vehicle-Related Lawsuits.* Bountiful, Utah: Horizon, 1991.

Helm, Alice K., ed. *The Family Legal Advisor: A Clear, Reliable, and Up-to-Date Guide to Your Rights and Remedies under the Law.* New York: Family Library, 1992.

THE U.S. LEGAL SYSTEM

Hill, Gerald N., and Kathleen Thompson Hill. *Real Life Dictionary of the Law: Taking the Mystery out of Legal Language*. Los Angeles: General, 1995.

Horder, Jeremy, ed. *Oxford Essays in Jurispudence. Fourth Series*. New York: Oxford University Press, 2000.

Howard, Philip K. *The Death of Common Sense: How Law Is Suffocating America*. New York: Random House, 1994.

Jordan, Cora. *Neighbor Law: Fences, Trees, Boundaries, and Noise*. 2d ed. Berkeley, Calif.: Nolo Press, 1994.

Lehman, Godfrey D. *We the Jury: The Impact of Jurors on Our Basic Freedoms*. Amherst, N.Y.: Prometheus Books, 1997.

Niles, Gayle L. *Woman's Counsel: A Legal Guide for Women*. Denver, Colo.: Arden Press, 1984.

Pringle, Peter. *Cornered: Big Tobacco at the Bar of Justice*. New York: H. Holt, 1998.

Sack, Steven Mitchell. *The Working Woman's Legal Survival Guide*. Paramus, N.J.: Prentice-Hall, 1998.

Schwartz, Bernard. *A Book of Legal Lists: The Best and Worst in American Law with One Hundred Court and Judge Trivia Questions*. New York: Oxford University Press, 1997.

History, Biography, and Famous Trials

Aaseng, Nathan. *The O. J. Simpson Trial: What It Shows Us About Our Legal System*. New York: Walker, 1996.

Baker, Liva. *Justice from Beacon Hill: The Life and Times of Oliver Wendell Holmes*. New York: Harper Collins, 1991.

Brandon, Craig. *The Electric Chair: An Unnatural American History*. Jefferson, N.C.: McFarland, 1999.

Bugliosi, Vincent. *No Island of Sanity—Paula Jones v. Bill Clinton: The Supreme Court on Trial*. New York: Ballantine, 1998.

Cretney, Stephen. *Family Law in the Twentieth Century: A History*. New York: Oxford University Press, 2003.

Deutsch, Linda, and Michael Fleeman. *Verdict: The Chronicle of the O. J. Simpson Trial*. Kansas City, Mo.: Andrews and McMeel, 1995.

Fisher, George. *Plea Bargaining's Triumph: A History of Plea Bargaining in America*. Stanford, Calif.: Stanford University Press, 2003.

Greenberg, Jack. *Crusaders in the Courts: How a Dedicated Band of Lawyers Fought for the Civil Rights Revolution*. New York: Basic Books, 1994.

Hall, Kermit. *The Magic Mirror: Law in American History.* New York: Oxford University Press, 1989.

Kessler, Ronald. *The Bureau: The Secret History of the FBI.* New York: St. Martin's Press, 2002.

Kluger, Richard. *Simple Justice: The History of Brown v. Board of Education and Black America's Struggle for Equality.* New York: Knopf, 1975.

Knight, Alfred. *The Life of the Law: The People and Cases That Have Shaped Our Society, from King Alfred to Rodney King.* New York: Crown, 1996.

Larson, Edward J. *Summer for the Gods: The Scopes Trial and America's Continuing Debate over Science and Religion.* New York: Basic Books, 1997.

Noel, F. Regis. *A History of the Bankruptcy Law.* New York: William S. Hein, 2002.

Novick, Sheldon M. *Honorable Justice: The Life of Oliver Wendell Holmes.* Boston: Little, Brown, 1989.

Orth, John V. *Due Process of Law: A Brief History.* Lawrence, Kan.: University Press of Kansas, 2003.

Paper, Lewis J. *Brandeis.* Englewood Cliffs, N.J.: Prentice-Hall, 1983.

Parrish, Michael. *For the People: Inside the Los Angeles District Attorney's Office, 1850-2000.* Santa Monica, Calif.: Angel City Press, 2001.

Rembar, Charles. *The Law of the Land: The Evolution of Our Legal System.* New York: Simon & Schuster, 1980.

Tushnet, Mark V. *Making Civil Rights Law: Thurgood Marshall and the Supreme Court, 1936-1961.* New York: Oxford University Press, 1994.

Urofsky, Melvin I. *Louis D. Brandeis and the Progressive Tradition.* Boston: Little, Brown, 1981.

Vile, John R., ed. *Great American Judges: An Encyclopedia.* 2 vols. Santa Barbara, Calif.: ABC-CLIO, 2003.

Walker, Samuel. *In Defense of American Liberties: A History of the ACLU.* New York: Oxford University Press, 1990.

Watkin, Thomas Glyn. *An Historical Introduction to Modern Civil Law.* Brookfield, Vt.: Ashgate/Dartmouth, 1999.

White, G. Edward. *Earl Warren: A Public Life.* New York: Oxford University Press, 1982.

Woodward, Bob, and Scott Armstrong. *The Brethren.* New York: Simon & Schuster, 1979.

Insurance and Personal Injury Law

Olson, Walter K. *The Litigation Explosion: What Happened When America Unleashed the Lawsuit.* New York: Truman Talley, 1991.

Sugarman, Stephen D. *Doing Away with Personal Injury Law: New Compensation Mechanisms for Victims, Consumers, and Business.* New York: Quorum Books, 1989.

Sunstein, Cass R., et al. *Punitive Damages: How Juries Decide.* Chicago: University of Chicago Press, 2002.

Law Enforcement

Axelrod, Alan, and Charles Phillips. *Cops, Crooks, and Criminologists: An International Biographical Dictionary of Law Enforcement.* With Kurt Kemper. New York: Facts On File, 1996.

Bell, Jeannine. *Policing Hatred: Law Enforcement, Civil Rights, and Hate Crime.* New York: New York University Press, 2002.

Bessel, Richard, and Clive Emsley, eds. *Patterns of Provocation: Police and Public Disorder.* New York: Berghahn Books, 2000.

Burns, Ronald G., and Charles E. Crawford. *Policing and Violence.* Upper Saddle River, N.J.: Prentice Hall, 2002.

Cohen, Paul, and Shari Cohen. *Careers in Law Enforcement and Security.* New York: Rosen, 1990.

Denenberg, Barry. *The True Story of J. Edgar Hoover and the FBI.* New York: Scholastic, 1992.

El-Ayouty, Yassin, Kevin J. Ford, and Mark Davies, eds. *Government Ethics and Law Enforcement Toward Global Guidelines.* Westport, Conn.: Praeger, 2000.

Ferguson, Tom. *Modern Law Enforcement Weapons and Tactics.* 2d ed. Northbrook, Ill.: DBI Books, 1991.

Fitzgerald, Terence J., ed. *Police in Society.* New York: H. W. Wilson, 2000.

Kenney, Dennis Jay, and and Robert P. McNamara, eds. *Police and Policing: Contemporary Issues.* Westport, Conn.: Praeger, 1999.

Kraska, Peter B. *Militarizing the American Criminal Justice System: The Changing Roles of the Armed Forces and the Police.* Boston: Northeastern University Press, 2001.

McGee, Jim, and Brian Duffy. *Main Justice: The Men and Women Who Enforce the Nation's Criminal Laws and Guard Its Liberties.* New York: Simon & Schuster, 1996.

Perlmutter, David D. *Policing the Media: Street Cops and Public Perceptions of Law Enforcement.* Thousand Oaks, Calif.: Sage Publications, 2000.

Philbin, Tom. *Cop Speak: The Lingo of Law Enforcement and Crime.* New York: J. Wiley, 1996.

Roth, Mitchel P. *Historical Dictionary of Law Enforcement.* Westport, Conn.: Greenwood Press, 2001.

Schulhofer, Stephen J. *The Enemy Within: Intelligence Gathering, Law Enforcement, and Civil Liberties in the Wake of September 11.* New York: Century Foundation Press, 2002.

Schwabe, William, et al. *Challenges and Choices for Crime-Fighting Technology: Federal Support of State and Local Law Enforcement.* Santa Monica, Calif.: Rand, 2001.

Skolnick, Jerome H., and James J. Fyfe. *Above the Law: Police and the Excessive Use of Force.* New York: Free Press, 1993.

Smith, Elizabeth Simpson. *Breakthrough: Women in Law Enforcement.* New York: Walker, 1982.

Thomas, Douglas, and Brian D. Loader, eds. *Cybercrime: Law Enforcement, Security, and Surveillance in the Information Age.* New York: Routledge, 2000.

Vann, Irvin B., and G. David Garson. *Crime Mapping: New Tools for Law Enforcement.* New York: Peter Lang, 2003.

Legal Education

Arnett, J. Robert, Arthur Coon, and Michael DiGeronimo. *From Here to Attorney: The Ultimate Guide to Excelling in Law School and Launching Your Legal Career.* Belmont, Calif.: Professional, 1993.

Arron, Deborah L. *What Can You Do with a Law Degree? A Lawyer's Guide to Career Alternatives Inside, Outside, and Around the Law.* Seattle: Niche Press, 1994.

Cooper, Cynthia L. *The Insider's Guide to the Top Fifteen Law Schools.* New York: Doubleday, 1990.

Deaver, Jeff. *The Complete Law School Companion: How to Excel at America's Most Demanding Post-Graduate Curriculum.* Rev. ed. New York: Wiley, 1992.

Hirshman, Linda. *A Woman's Guide to Law School.* New York: Penguin Books, 1999.

Kissam, Philip C. *The Discipline of Law Schools: The Making of Modern Lawyers.* Durham, N.C.: Carolina Academic Press, 2003.

Lermack, Paul. *How to Get into the Right Law School.* 2d ed. Lincolnwood, Ill.: VGM Career Horizons, 1997.

Miller, Robert H. *Law School Confidential: The Complete Law School Survival Guide: by Students, for Students.* New York: St. Martin's Griffin, 2000.

Morgan, Rick L., and Kurt Snyder. eds. *Official American Bar Association Guide to Approved Law Schools*. 3 vols. New York: Macmillan USA, 1998-2000.

Roth, George J. *Slaying the Law School Dragon: How to Survive—and Thrive—in First-Year Law School*. 2d ed. New York: Wiley, 1991.

Turow, Scott. *One L*. New York: Putnam, 1977.

Warner, Ralph E., Toni Ihara, and Barbara Kate Repa. *Twenty-nine Reasons Not to Go to Law School*. 4th ed. Berkeley, Calif.: Nolo Press, 1994.

Weaver, William G. *Peterson's Game Plan for Getting into Law School*. Princeton, N.J.: Peterson's, 2000.

Legal Practice

ABA Compendium of Professional Responsibility Rules and Standards. Chicago: Center for Professional Responsibility, American Bar Association, 2001.

Arron, Deborah L. *Running from the Law: Why Good Lawyers Are Getting out of the Legal Profession*. Berkeley, Calif.: Ten Speed Press, 1991.

Bartlett, Joseph W. *The Law Business: A Tired Monopoly*. Littleton, Colo.: Fred B. Rothman, 1982.

Couric, Emily. *The Trial Lawyers: The Nation's Top Litigators Tell How They Win*. New York: St. Martin's Press, 1988.

Deborah E. *Paralegal Practice and Procedure: A Practical Guide for the Legal Assistant*. 3d ed. Englewood Cliffs, N.J.: Prentice-Hall, 1994.

Friedman, Lawrence M. *American Law in the Twentieth Century*. New Haven, Conn.: Yale University Press, 2002.

Glendon, Mary Ann. *A Nation Under Lawyers: How the Crisis in the Legal Profession Is Transforming American Society*. New York: Farrar, Straus & Giroux, 1994.

Granfield, Robert. *Making Elite Lawyers: Visions of Law at Harvard and Beyond*. New York: Routledge, Chapman and Hall, 1992.

Grutman, Roy. *Lawyers and Thieves*. New York: Simon & Schuster, 1990.

Harnett, Bertram. *Law, Lawyers, and Laymen: Making Sense of the American Legal System*. San Diego: Harcourt Brace Jovanovich, 1984.

Lazega, Emmanuel. *The Collegial Phenomenon: The Social Mechanisms of Cooperation Among Peers in a Corporate Law Partnership*. New York: Oxford University Press, 2001.

Linowitz, Sol M. *Betrayed Profession: Lawyering at the End of the Twentieth Century.* With Martin Mayer. New York: Charles Scribner's Sons, 1994.

Margolick, David. *At the Bar: The Passions and Peccadilloes of American Lawyers.* New York: Simon & Schuster, 1995.

Marston, David W. *Malice Aforethought: How Lawyers Use Our Secret Rules to Get Rich, Get Sex, Get Even . . . And Get Away with It.* New York: W. Morrow, 1991.

Moll, Richard W. *The Lure of the Law and the Life Thereafter.* New York: Viking, 1990.

Munneke, Gary A. *Opportunities in Law Careers.* Lincolnwood, Ill.: VGM Career Horizons, 1994.

Nader, Ralph, and Wesley J. Smith. *No Contest: Corporate Lawyers and the Perversion of Justice in America.* New York: Random House, 1996.

Nossel, Suzanne, and Elizabeth Westfall. *Presumed Equal: What America's Top Women Lawyers Really Think About Their Firms.* Franklin Lakes, N.J.: Career Press, 1998.

Puccio, Thomas P. *In the Name of the Law: Confessions of a Trial Lawyer.* With Dan Collins. New York: W. W. Norton, 1995.

Ragano, Frank, and Selwyn Raab. *Mob Lawyer.* New York: Charles Scribner's Sons, 1994.

Rhode, Deborah L. *In the Interests of Justice: Reforming the Legal Profession.* New York: Oxford University Press, 2001.

Schwartz, Laurens R. *What You Aren't Supposed to Know About the Legal Profession: An Expose of Lawyers, Law Schools, Judges, and More.* New York: SPI Books, 1993.

Solomon, Neal E. *Transformation of the Corporate Law Firm.* Oakland, Calif.: Academic Ventures Press, 1998.

Stevens, Mark. *Power of Attorney: The Rise of the Giant Law Firms.* New York: McGraw-Hill, 1987.

Walsh, Francis, and Sheila V. Malkani, eds. *The Insider's Guide to Law Firms.* Boulder, Colo.: Mobius Press, 1997.

Legal Reference and Research

Black, Henry Campbell. *Black's Law Dictionary: Definitions of the Terms and Phrases of American and English Jurisprudence, Ancient and Modern.* 6th ed. St. Paul, Minn.: West Publishing, 1990.

Corbin, John. *Find the Law in the Library: A Guide to Legal Research.* Chicago: American Library Association, 1989.

Dressler, Joshua, ed. *Encyclopedia of Crime and Justice*. New York: Macmillan Reference USA, 2002.

Elias, Stephen. *Legal Research: How to Find and Understand the Law*. 5th ed. Berkeley, Calif.: Nolo Press, 1997.

Evans, James H. *Law on the Net*. Berkeley, Calif.: Nolo Press, 1995.

Garner, Bryan A. *A Dictionary of Modern Legal Usage*. 2d ed. New York: Oxford University Press, 1995.

Hall, Timothy L. *U.S. Laws, Acts, and Treaties*. Pasadena, Calif.: Salem Press, 2003.

Herskowitz, Suzan. *Legal Research Made Easy*. Clearwater, Fla: Sphinx, 1995.

Mellinkoff, David. *Dictionary of American Legal Usage*. St. Paul, Minn.: West Publishing, 1992.

Smith, Christopher E. *Courts and Trials: A Reference Handbook*. Santa Barbara, Calif.: ABC-CLIO, 2003.

Tomkovicz, James J. *The Right to the Assistance of Counsel: A Reference Guide to the United States Constitution*. Westport, Conn.: Greenwood Press, 2002.

Tax Law

Barlett, Donald L., and James B. Steele. *America: Who Really Pays the Taxes?* New York: Simon & Schuster, 1994.

Birnbaum, Jeffrey H., and Alan S. Murray. *Showdown at Gucci Gulch: Lawmakers, Lobbyists, and the Unlikely Triumph of Tax Reform*. New York: Random House, 1987.

Burnham, David. *A Law unto Itself: Power, Politics, and the IRS*. New York: Random House, 1989.

Schriebman, Robert S. *When You Can't Pay Your Taxes! How to Deal with the IRS*. Homewood, Ill.: Dow Jones-Irwin, 1986.

LEGAL ASSISTANCE
ORGANIZATIONS

A. Philip Randolph Educational Fund (APREF)
1444 I Street NW, No. 300
Washington, DC 20005
Founded in 1964, the APREF seeks to eliminate prejudice and discrimination from all areas of life, educate individuals and groups on their rights and responsibilities, defend human and civil rights, and assist in the employment and education of the underprivileged.

Alliance for Justice (AFJ)
11 Dupont Circle NW, 2nd Floor
Washington, DC 20036
Web site: http://www.afj.org/
The AFJ is a national association of environmental, civil rights, mental health, women's, children's, and consumer advocacy organizations. Since its inception in 1979, the Alliance has worked to advance the cause of justice for all Americans, strengthen the public interest community's ability to influence public policy, and foster the next generation of advocates.

American Association of University Women (AAUW) Legal Advocacy Fund
Department LAF.INT
1111 Sixteenth Street NW
Washington, DC 20036
Web site: http://www.aauw.org/laf/index.cfm
The nation's largest legal fund that focuses solely on sex discrimination in higher education, the AAUW Legal Advocacy Fund provides funding and support for women seeking judicial redress for sex discrimination. Since 1981 the AAUW Legal Advocacy Fund has helped students, faculty, and administrators in higher education challenge discriminatory practices involving sexual harassment, denial of tenure or promotion, and inequality in women's athletics programs.

American Association of Retired Persons (AARP)
601 East Street NW
Washington, DC 20049
Web site: http://www.aarp.org/
The AARP is a nonprofit, nonpartisan organization dedicated to helping older Americans achieve lives of independence, dignity, and purpose and assists retired persons with a variety of legal information.

American Citizens for Justice (ACJ)
P.O. Box 2735
Southfield, MI 48037-2735
The ACJ was founded in 1983 by Asian Pacific Americans and other individuals concerned with discrimination against ethnic groups. The ACJ works to combat and prevent racial intolerance, operates the Asian American Center for Justice, monitors legislation and law enforcement, works for civil rights in the areas of mental health, safety, health, and welfare, and promotes the teaching of Asian Pacific American history and culture.

American Civil Liberties Union (ACLU)
125 Broad Street, 18th Floor
New York, NY 10004
Web site: http://www.aclu.org/
Founded in 1920, the ACLU had 275,000 members and a staff of 125 in 1996. It champions the rights set forth in the Bill of Rights of the U.S. Constitution, such as freedom of speech, press, assembly, and religion; due process of law and fair trial; and equality before the law regardless of race, color, sexual orientation, national origin, political opinion, or religious belief. ACLU activities include litigation, advocacy, and public education. It sponsors litigation projects in such fields as women's rights, gay and lesbian rights, and children's rights.

American Prepaid Legal Services Institute (API)
541 North Fairbanks Court
Chicago, IL 60611
Web site: http://www.aplsi.org/
The API supports insurance companies, prepaid legal plan sponsors and administrators, lawyers, and law firms with a concept similar to that of health insurance. Consumers pay a fixed

premium in exchange for specified legal benefits that are used as needed.

Americans for Religious Liberty (ARL)

P.O. Box 6656

Silver Spring, MD 20916

Web site: http://www.arlinc.org/

Founded in 1982, the ARL comprises individuals dedicated to preserving religious, intellectual, and personal freedom, the constitutional principle of separation of church and state, democratic secular public education, reproductive rights, and the Jeffersonian-Madisonian ideal of a pluralistic secular democracy.

Anti-Defamation League (ADL)

823 United Nations Plaza

New York, NY 10017

Web site: http://www.adl.org/adl.asp

Founded in 1913, the ADL seeks to stop the defamation of Jewish people and to secure justice and fair treatment to all citizens. The ADL educates Americans about Israel, promotes better interfaith and intergroup relations, works against anti-Semitism, counteracts antidemocratic extremism, and strengthens democratic values and structures.

Asian American Center for Justice/American Citizens for Justice

P.O. Box 2735

Southfield, MI 48037-2735

Founded in 1983, this organization works to eliminate discrimination and violence against Asian Americans by offering legal consultation and education, monitoring violence against Asians, and assisting local and county governments in developing affirmative action plans for recruiting Asian Pacific Americans.

Asian American Legal Defense and Education Fund (AALDEF)

99 Hudson Street, 12th Floor

New York, NY 10013

Web site: http://www.aaldef.org/home.html

Founded in 1974, the AALDEF includes attorneys, legal workers, and members of the community who seek to employ legal and educational methods to attack critical problems in Asian American communities by providing bilingual legal counseling and representation for people who cannot obtain access to legal assistance. Its areas of concern include immigration, employment, voting rights, racially motivated violence against Asian Americans, environmental justice, and Japanese American redress.

Asian Law Alliance (ALA)
184 East Jackson Street
San Jose, CA 95112
Web site: http://www.asianlawalliance-ala.org/
    The ALA is a nonprofit United Way agency that provides law services for the Asian Community by informing citizens of their legal rights and responsibilities and by helping to prevent legal problems for immigrants that have lived in the United States for short and long periods of time.

Association for the Sexually Harassed (ASH)
860 Manatawna Avenue
Philadelphia, PA 19128-1113
    Founded in 1988, ASH includes employers, talk shows, attorneys, schools, victims of sexual harassment, and other interested organizations and individuals. It seeks to create national awareness of sexual harassment by providing experts for talk shows and mediation troubleshooting services to resolve sexual harassment problems between employees and employers. It also provides telephone counseling and consultation services.

Center for Constitutional Rights (CCR)
666 Broadway, 7th Floor
New York, NY 10012
Web site: http://www.ccr-ny.org/v2/home.asp
    Founded in 1966, the CCR is a legal and educational organization dedicated to advancing and protecting the rights guaranteed by the U.S. Constitution and the Universal Declaration of Civil Rights. The organization is committed to the creative use of law as a positive force for social change.

Center for the Advancement of the Covenant
San Francisco University Philosophy Department
1600 Holloway Avenue
San Francisco, CA 94132

Founded in 1992, this organization publicizes the United States ratification of the 1992 International Covenant on Civil and Political Rights and the rights it contains by organizing a network of nongovernmental organizations to work toward federal, state, and local government compliance with the Covenant.

Center for Democratic Renewal (CDR)
P.O. Box 50469
Atlanta, GA 30302
Web site: http://www.thecdr.org/

Founded in 1979, the CDR advocates federal prosecution of the Ku Klux Klan and other groups or individuals involved in racist violence by seeking to build public opposition to racist groups and their activities. The CDR assists victims of bigoted violence by working with trade unions, public officials, and religious, women's, civil rights, and grassroots organizations.

Children's Rights
404 Park Avenue South, 11th Floor
New York, NY 10016
Web site: http://www.childrensrights.org/index.htm

Founded in 1995 with a staff of fifteen to fight for the rights of poor children who are dependent on government systems. Formerly called the Children's Rights Project of the American Civil Liberties Union (ACLU).

Chinese for Affirmative Action (CAA)
17 Walter U. Lum Place
San Francisco, CA 94108
Web site: http://www.caasf.org/

Founded in 1969, the CAA includes individuals and corporations seeking equal opportunity for and the protection of the civil rights of Asian Americans. It works with the larger community to ensure fair treatment under the law in employment matters and has cooperated with state and local governmental agencies to help develop bilingual materials to aid Asian American job applicants. It also encourages the appointment and participation of Asian Americans on public boards and commissions.

Citizens Against Lawsuit Abuse (CALA)
10736 Jefferson Boulevard, No. 401
Culver City, CA 90230
Web site: http://www.cala.com/

CALA is a nonprofit, grassroots organization composed of Southern Californians dedicated to putting an end to lawsuit abuse. Their mission is to educate the public on the effects of lawsuit abuse in order to create a climate for reform of the U.S. civil justice system. It educates the public about the direct costs of lawsuit abuse to consumers, taxpayers, and the state of California; it stimulates debate on the issue of civil justice reform and its process; and it serves as a watchdog over interest groups and persons who abuse the system for personal financial gain.

Citizens' Commissions on Civil Rights (CCCR)
2000 M Street NW, Suite 400
Washington, DC 20036
Web site: http://www.cccr.org/

Founded in 1982, the CCCR is a bipartisan organization of former federal cabinet officials concerned with achieving equality of opportunity. Its objectives are to monitor the federal government's enforcement of laws barring discrimination on the basis of race, sex, religion, ethnic background, age, or handicap, foster understanding of civil rights issues, and formulate constructive policy recommendations.

Citizens for a Better America (CBA)
P.O. Box 356
Halifax, VA 24558

Founded in 1975, the CBA includes churches and individuals united to create a better America by strengthening individual rights and serves as a public advocacy organization that lobbies for civil rights and environmental legislation.

Citizens for Sensible Safeguards (CSS)
1742 Connecticut Avenue NW
Washington, DC 20009

Founded in 1995, the CSS involves a coalition of over 200 organizations concerned with environmental, educational, civil rights, disability, health, and social services issues and works to improve laws and safeguards that protect citizens.

Commission for Social Justice (CSJ)
219 East Street NE
Washington, DC 20002

Founded in 1979, the CSJ serves as the antidefamation arm of the Order of Sons of Italy in America and monitors businesses, schools, and the media to combat negative portrayals of Italian Americans.

Commission for Racial Justice (CRJ)
475 Riverside Drive, 16th Floor
New York, NY 10115

Founded in 1963, the CRJ is a racial justice agency representing the 1.7 million members of the United Church of Christ and promotes human rights programs and strategies to foster racial justice in African American, Third World, and other minority communities.

Cuban American Legal Defense and Education Fund (CALDEF)
2513 South Calhoun Street
Fort Wayne, IN 46807-1305

Founded in 1980, the CALDEF strives for equal treatment and opportunity for Cuban Americans and Hispanics in the fields of education, employment, housing, politics, and justice by discouraging negative stereotyping of Hispanics and works to educate the public about the plight of Cuban Americans and Latin Americans.

Death with Dignity Education Center (DDEC)
P.O. Box 1238
San Mateo, CA 94401-0816

Founded in 1994, the DDEC is a diverse group of people who believe in the inherent right of persons to make their own choices about heath care and the end of life. The organization informs and educates the public about physician aid in dying so that people can make informed decisions.

Department of Civil Rights, AFL-CIO
815 16th Street NW
Washington, DC 20006
Founded in 1955, this staff arm of the American Federation of Labor-Congress of Industrial Organizations serves as an official liaison to women's and civil rights organizations and government agencies working in the field of equal opportunity. It helps to implement state and federal laws and AFL-CIO civil rights policies.

First Amendment Foundation (FAF)
1313 West 8th Street, Suite 313
Los Angeles, CA 90017
Founded in 1986, the FAF seeks to protect the rights of free expression of individuals and organizations and disseminates educational information on the First Amendment to the U.S. Constitution.

First Amendment Press (FAP)
8129 North 35th Avenue, No. 134
Phoenix, AZ 85051-5892
Founded in 1993, the FAP provides information on citizen's rights and alleged government misconduct, offers legal advice and solutions, conducts investigations, and maintains a speakers bureau.

Freedom of Expression Foundation (FOEF)
5220 South Marina Pacifica
Long Beach, CA 90803
Founded in 1983, the FOEF includes corporations, foundations, broadcasters, and publishers whose purpose is to provide information to the U.S. Congress and the public concerning freedom of speech as guaranteed by the First Amendment to the U.S. Constitution.

Freedom to Advertise Coalition (FAC)
2550 M Street NW, Suite 500
Washington, DC 20037
Founded in 1988, the FAC includes members of the American Advertising Federation, the American Association of Advertising Agencies, the Association of National Advertisers, the Magazine Publishers of American, the Outdoor Advertising Association of

America, and the Point of Purchase Advertising Institute. These organizations have united to protect the rights of advertisers to "truthfully and nondeceptively advertise all legal products." The protection of the right of commercial free speech as guaranteed by the U.S. Constitution and opposition to proposed legislation that would ban or restrict tobacco, alcohol, and other legal product advertising are among its chief activities.

The Generation After (TGA)
P.O. Box 14, Homecrest Station
Brooklyn, NY 11229
Founded in 1979, the TGA includes individuals working to eradicate anti-Semitism by advocating human rights and social justice. Goals of the TGA are to accumulate and store data of neo-Nazi groups, such as their leaders names and addresses, to share such information with authorities to prevent violence that might be caused by such groups, and to monitor neo-Nazi newspapers in the United States.

Institute for First Amendment Studies (IFAS)
P.O. Box 589
Great Barrington, MA 01230
Founded in 1984, this organization of former members of fundamentalist churches and others is dedicated to the principle of the separation of church and state as provided for in the First Amendment to the U.S. Constitution. It monitors and reports on the activities of fundamentalist right-wing groups.

International Committee Against Racism (ICAR)
150 West 28th Street, Room 301
New York, NY 10001
Founded in 1973, the ICAR is dedicated to fighting against all forms of racism and to building a multiracial society by opposing racism in all its economic, social, institutional, and cultural forms by sponsoring on-the-job, community, college, and high-school workshops.

Judge David L. Bazelon Center for Mental Health Law
1101 15th Street NW, Suite 1212
Washington, DC 20005
Web site: http://www.bazelon.org/

Founded in 1972, this organization's purpose is to clarify, establish, and enforce the legal rights of people with mental and developmental disabilities by providing technical assistance and training to lawyers, consumers, providers of mental health and special education services, and policymakers at the federal, state, and local levels.

Lawyers' Committee for Civil Rights Under Law (LCCRUL)
1401 New York Avenue NW, Suite 400
Washington, DC 20005
Web site: http://www.lawyerscomm.org/
The LCCRUL operates through local communities of private lawyers to provide legal assistance to poor and minority groups living in urban areas in such fields as employment, voting rights, and housing discrimination.

Leadership Conference on Civil Rights (LCCR)
1629 K Street NW, Suite 1010
Washington, DC 20006
Web site: http://www.civilrights.org/about/lccr/index.html
Founded in 1950, the LCCR is a coalition of national organizations working to promote the passage of civil rights, social, and economic legislation. It also seeks the enforcement of laws already on the books.

Media Coalition/Americans for Constitutional Freedom (MC/ACF)
1221 Avenue of the Americas, 24th Floor
New York, NY 10020
Founded in 1973, the MC/ACF includes trade associations united to defend the First Amendment right to produce and distribute books, magazines, recordings, video games, and videotapes. This organization also monitors censorship legislation at the federal and state levels.

Mexican American Legal Defense and Education Fund (MALDEF)
634 South Spring Street, 11th Floor
Los Angeles, CA 90014
Web site: http://www.maldef.org/

MALDEF was founded in 1968 following decades of discrimination and the violation of the civil rights of Mexican Americans. Its mission is to protect and promote the rights of the more than twenty-six million Latinos living in the United States.

National Academy of Elder Law Attorneys (NAELA)

1604 North Country Club Road

Tucson, AZ 85716-3102

Web site: http://www.naela.com/

The NAELA supports practicing attorneys, law professors, and others interested in the provision of legal services to the elderly by providing technical expertise and education to the elderly and their families.

National Association for the Advancement of Colored People (NAACP)

4805 Mt. Hope Drive

Baltimore, MD 21215

Web site: http://www.naacp.org/

Founded in 1909, the NAACP includes persons of all races and religions who believe in the objectives and methods of the NAACP to achieve equal rights through the democratic process and to eliminate racial prejudice by removing racial discrimination in housing, employment, voting, schools, the courts, transportation, recreation, prisons, and business enterprises.

National Association to Protect Individual Rights (NAPIR)

5015 Gadsen

Fairfax, VA 22032-3411

Founded in 1991, the NAPIR conducts research on issues including information privacy and government budgeting and provides information to public officials and the press.

National Clearinghouse for Legal Services (NCLS)

205 W. Monroe

Chicago, IL 60606

The NCLS supports legal services attorneys and programs, private attorneys, law universities and libraries, court judges, and government organizations in providing information on case law with respect to issues related to poverty law and the consumer.

National Committee Against Repressive Legislation (NCARL)
1313 West 8th Street, Suite 313
Los Angeles, CA 90017
Founded in 1960, the NCARL promotes First Amendment Rights and opposes repressive laws and inquisitorial activities of government. Notable activities include reform of federal criminal laws and control of federal intelligence gathering agencies. The NCARL seeks to ban covert operations by the Central Intelligence Agency (CIA) and what the group feels is political spying and harassment by the Federal Bureau of Investigation (FBI).

National Institute for Citizen Education in the Law (NICEL)
711 G Street SE
Washington, DC 20003
The NICEL operates programs in law-related education in high schools and juvenile corrections settings to assist young people in becoming active, successful citizens.

National Legal Aid and Defender Association (NLADA)
1140 Connecticut Avenue NW, Suite 900
Washington, DC 20036
Web site: http://www.nlada.org/
The NLADA supports legal aid offices and public defender organizations representing indigent and individual members by providing technical and management assistance to local organizations offering legal services to poor persons involved with civil or criminal cases.

National Legal Center for the Medically Dependent and Disabled (NLCMDD)
1 South 6th Street
Terre Haute, IN 47808
The NLCMDD is a service organization working to defend the legal rights of indigent older and disabled persons in their quest for proper medical care.

National Resource Center for Consumers of Legal Services (NRCCLS)
6596 Main Street
P.O. Box 340
Gloucester, VA 23061

The NRCCLS supports legal programs in North America by serving as a clearinghouse while advising individuals and groups seeking to establish or evaluate legal service plans.

National Structured Settlements Trade Association (NSSTA)
1800 K Street NW, Suite 718
Washington, DC 20006
Web site: http://www.nssta.com/nssta/

The NSSTA supports structured settlement firms, life insurance companies, claims adjustors, attorneys, and other consultants involved in the tort process.

National Urban League (NUL)
120 Wall Street, 8th Floor
New York, NY 10005
Web site: http://www.nul.org/

Founded in 1910, the NUL is a voluntary nonpartisan community service agency of civic, professional, business, labor, and religious leaders with a staff of trained social workers and other professionals. The organization aims to eliminate racial segregation and discrimination in the United States and to achieve parity for African Americans and other minorities in every walk of American life.

People for the American Way (PFAW)
2000 M Street NW, Suite 400
Washington, DC 20036
Web site: http://www.pfaw.org/pfaw/general/

Founded in 1980, the PFAW is a nonpartisan constitutional liberties organization of religious, business, media, and labor figures committed to reaffirming the traditional American values of pluralism, diversity, and freedom of expression and religion.

Pretrial Services Resource Center (PSRC)
1010 Vermont Avenue NW, Suite 300
Washington, DC 20005
Web site: http://www.pretrial.org/

The PSRC provides criminal justice consulting services covering subjects such as data collection, jail overcrowding, and drug testing.

Southern Christian Leadership Conference (SCLC)
P.O. Box 89128
Atlanta, GA 30312
Web site: http://sclcnational.org/
Founded in 1957, the SCLC is a nonsectarian coordinating and service agency for local organizations seeking full citizenship rights, equality, and integration of African Americans in all walks of life in the United States. It subscribes to the philosophy of non-violence.

Southern Poverty Law Center (SPLC)
P.O. Box 2087
Montgomery, AL 36102
Web site: http://splcenter.org/
Founded in 1971, the SPLC seeks to protect and advance the legal and civil rights of poor people, regardless of race, through education and litigation. It does not accept fees from clients.

Southern Regional Council (SRC)
133 Carnegie Way NW, Suite 1030
Atlanta, GA 30303-1055
Web site: http://www.src.w1.com/
Founded in 1944, the SRC includes leaders in education, religion, business, labor, the community, and the professions interested in improving race relations and combating poverty in the South.

Trade Union Leadership Council (TULC)
8670 Grand River Avenue
Detroit, MI 48204
Web site: http://www.tulc.org/tulc/home
Founded in 1957, the TULC includes primarily African American trade unionists in Michigan who seek to eradicate injustices perpetrated upon people because of race, religion, sex, or national origin. It also seeks increased leadership and job opportunities for African Americans.

OTHER ORGANIZATIONS

United States Privacy Council (USPC)

P.O. Box 15060

Washington, DC 20003

The USPC is composed of individuals and groups committed to strengthening the right to privacy in the United States by working to protect medical, insurance, and employee records, update legislation—including the Fair Credit Reporting Act, the Privacy Act of 1974, and the Electronic Communications Privacy Act—and improve public access to governmental information.

Volunteer Lawyers for the Arts (VLA)

1 E. 53rd Street, 6th Floor

New York, NY 10022-4201

Web site: http://www.vlany.org/

The VLA provides free legal services to artists and art organizations in art-related legal matters. It works to familiarize the legal profession and the arts community with legal problems that confront artists and provides them with available solutions.

Voters Telecomm Watch (VTW)

115 Pacific, No. 3

Brooklyn, NY 11201

Founded in 1994, the VTW works to protect individual electronic freedom and privacy and promote civil liberties in telecommunications by monitoring bills, positions, and voting records of elected officials, informing and alerting the public, and recommending legislation.

Western Center on Law and Poverty (WCLP)

3701 Wilshire Boulevard, Suite 208

Los Angeles, CA 90010-2809

Web site: http://www.wclp.org

The WCLP provides legal counsel and representation to individuals and groups whose actions may effect change in institutions affecting the poor.

Workers' Defense League (WDL)
218 West 40th Street, Room 203-204
New York, NY 10018

Founded in 1936, the WDL is a labor-oriented human rights organization that provides counseling to workers on employment-related problems, conducts educational campaigns to defend and advance workers' rights, and maintains a speakers bureau.

LEGAL RESOURCES

The reality of legal research is that no single volume of books contains the whole law applicable to a particular person or circumstance. Rather, different governments and different branches within these governments create law, and the products of this multiple creative work are scattered across innumerable volumes. One of the professional skills of attorneys is the ability to navigate these multiple sources of legal authority, but interested laypersons may profit from understanding at least the broad contours of the legal terrain.

Primary Sources of the Law. The first major division of legal authority has to do with the divisions among federal, state, and local lawmaking authorities. Authorities at each of these levels create law, with the higher authority sometimes but not always displacing laws of the lower authority. For example, according to the supremacy clause of the U.S. Constitution, when the federal government creates laws inconsistent with those of state or local governments, the federal law prevails. However, federal laws frequently leave room for state and local laws on the same subject. As a consequence, a given situation may be subject to the law of one or all of these authorities, and legal researchers must be prepared to consult resources available for each.

The second division of legal authority is among the various branches within government. Laws or legal rules may have their genesis in the legislative, executive, or the judicial branches of federal, state, or local governments. Legislatures create law in the form of statutes, which are ultimately collected in codes. Executives, at least at the federal level, create law in the form of executive orders or administrative regulations. Judicial branches create law in the form of case opinions and rules governing legal practice and procedure. Moreover, courts routinely interpret other legal materials, such as constitutions or statutes, and these interpretations are of sufficient importance that their content may be included in legal volumes containing constitutions or statutes. For example, a very common version of federal statutes is referred to as the United States Code Annotated and consists not only of statutes collected in the form of a code but also of references to case opinions that interpret the various provisions of the code.

Level	Branch	Chief Source of Legal Authority
Federal	Legislative (Congress)	United States Code or United States Code Annotated.
Federal	Executive branch	Executive orders and regulations enacted by federal departments and agencies and collected in the Code of Federal Regulations.
Federal	Judicial	Opinions in cases decided at the district court, court of appeals, and Supreme Court levels and collected in multivolume sets known as the *Federal Supplement*, *Federal Reporter*, and the *United States Reports*, respectively.
State	Legislative	Each state has a code of laws similar to the United States Code Annotated. Such codes include, for example, the Annotated California Code and the Code of Virginia Annotated.
State	Executive	State governors and other executive officials may produce executive orders comparable to those of the U.S. president. In addition, state administrative agencies generally promulgate regulations on a variety of subjects entrusted to them by state law.
State	Judicial	States have one or more levels of courts that produce published judicial opinions on questions of law. These opinions are collected in one or more "reporters," as they are called. In addition, West Publishing in St. Paul, Minnesota, a leading publisher of legal materials, collects opinions decided by the courts of states in various regions of the country into regional reporters, such as the *Pacific Reporter*, which includes cases decided by California and other western states, and the *Southern Reporter*, which includes cases decided by Mississippi courts and the courts of other southern states.

Thus, a given legal problem may require that researchers consult legal authorities created by multiple branches of government within the federal, state, and local governmental systems. The accompanying table attempts to summarize the key sources of legal authority for federal and state governments. In addition to the sources listed, the highest source of law for both federal and state governments is the U.S. Constitution. A copy of the U.S. Constitution is available in the United States Code Annotated and also at a number of sites on the World Wide Web, discussed below. In addition, state governments are subject to the authority of their respective state constitutions. Local governments produce laws as well in the form of municipal or county ordinances, but these laws generally lack the broad spectrum of lawmaking power as exercised by federal and state governments. Such laws enacted at the local level are generally available in local government offices and sometimes in public libraries.

Finding Primary Legal Sources. Primary legal sources, such as the United States Code and the various federal and state judicial opinions, are generally available from three sources. First, all the materials discussed in the preceding table are published as multivolume hardback series. Some public libraries have copies of such items as the United States Code Annotated and the annotated code for the relevant state. To find a more complete collection of primary sources of the printed type, one must generally gain access to a law library. Local courthouses are generally the most likely place to find a law library with the resources described above.

Second, all the sources above, and many more, may be accessed remotely from the two leading computer databases of the law profession: Westlaw and Lexis. These databases charge a subscription fee and per usage fees and are thus financially out of the range of most individuals other than lawyers.

Third, and perhaps most important, many primary legal sources are available free of charge on the World Wide Web. Individuals may access these sites either through personal or job-related Internet connections or through Internet connections made available in many public libraries. The following section describes some of the legal resources available on the Internet.

Online Resources. The following list contains a variety of World Wide Web resources relating to the law. One of the realities of the World Wide Web is that information sites sometimes change their locations and sometimes cease to exist altogether. Thus, readers may find that some addresses no longer work. It is impossible to summarize the varieties of legal materials now available online briefly, but two kinds of Web sites will be of most assistance to those interested in researching the law: sites that serve as indexes to legal resources generally and sites devoted to particular legal topics. The first list below contains the World Wide Web addresses of several general legal information sites on the Web.

ABA Network
www.abanet.org
Web site maintained by the American Bar Association (ABA) providing a variety of legal information for both lawyers and the public.

American Law Resources On-Line
www.lawsource.com/also/
Extensive collection of legal resources.

CataLaw
www.catalaw.com
Searchable index of legal information.

Center for Information Law and Policy
www.law.vill.edu
Collection of legal Web resources maintained by the Villanova Law School.

FedLaw
www.thecre.com/fedlaw/default.htm
Web site maintained by the U.S. General Services Administration (GSA) devoted to legal resources useful to federal lawyers and employees.

Internet Law Library
www.lawguru.com/ilawlib
General information source for federal law.

Law Lists
www.lib.uchicago.edu/~llou/lawlists/info.html
Guide to electronic discussion groups concerning the law.

LawInfo Com
www.lawinfo.com
Referral site for lawyers and a variety of legal resources.

Legal Information Institute
www.law.cornell.edu
One of the Web's most exhaustive collections of legal materials maintained by the Cornell Law School.

Legal List
www.lcp.com
An outline of and introduction to legal resources on the Internet.

Library of Congress
lcweb.loc.gov
Indexes to the holdings of the Library of Congress, on-line exhibits, and a variety of resources, including some legal materials.

Thomas
thomas.loc.gov
Detailed information about federal legislation maintained by the Library of Congress.

World Wide Web Virtual Library: Law
www.law.indiana.edu/v-lib/
General Web resources indexed by the Indiana University School of Law, Bloomington.

GOVERNMENT AGENCIES AND OFFICES

The next category of Web sites includes those maintained by various governmental agencies and offices that are generally devoted to a particular legal topic. Governmental agencies and offices frequently make available to the public legal information relevant to their operations.

Agriculture Department
14th and Independence Avenue SW
Washington, DC 20250

(202) 720-2791
www.usda.gov/
Federal agency that supports agricultural production.

Bureau of Alcohol, Tobacco, and Firearms
650 Massachusetts Avenue NW
Washington, DC 20226
(202) 927-7777
www.atf.gov/
Collects taxes on and generally regulates alcohol, tobacco, and
  firearms.

Central Intelligence Agency
Central Intelligence Agency
Office of Public Affairs
Washington, DC 20505
(703) 482-0623
www.odci.gov/
Provides intelligence information on issues relating to national
  security and conducts counterintelligence operations.

Consumer Product Safety Commission
4330 East-West Highway
Bethesda, MD 20814-4408
(301) 504-6816
www.cpsc.gov/
Federal agency charged with protecting the public from unsafe
  products.

Customs and Border Protection
1300 Pennsylvania Avenue NW
Washington, DC 20229
(202) 354-1000
www.cbp.gov/
Assesses and collects duties on imported goods.

Education Department
600 Independence Avenue SW
Washington, DC 20202-0498

(800) USA-LEARN
www.ed.gov
Federal agency that supports education in the United States.

Environmental Protection Agency
Ariel Rios Building
1200 Pennsylvania Avenue NW
Washington, DC 20460
(202) 272-0167
www.epa.gov/
Federal agency with responsibility for administering environmental laws.

Equal Employment Opportunity Commission
1801 L Street NW
Washington, DC 20507
(202) 663-4900, (800) 669-4000
www.eeoc.gov/
Site operated by federal commission that enforces civil rights
laws relating to employment.

Federal Bureau of Investigation (FBI)
J. Edgar Hoover Building
935 Pennsylvania Avenue NW
Washington, DC 20535-0001
(202) 324-3000
www.fbi.gov/
Information on federal law enforcement.

Federal Trade Commission
CRC-240
Washington, DC 20580
(202) 382-4357
www.ftc.gov/
Agency that registers complaints about credit reporting agencies
and debt collection agencies and handles other issues relating
to credit.

Fish and Wildlife Service
C Street NW
Washington, DC 20240

(202) 208-5634
www.fws.gov/
Federal office with responsibility for conserving and enhancing
  fish and wildlife and their habitats.

Food and Drug Administration
5600 Fishers Lane
Rockville, MD 20857-0001
(888) 463-6332
www.fda.gov/
Federal agency with regulatory authority over food, cosmetics,
  and medicines.

Government Printing Office
732 North Capitol Street NW
Washington, DC 20401
(202) 512-1530, (888) 293-6498
www.gpoaccess.gov/
Site of the government office that prints, binds, and distributes
  the publications of the U.S. Congress and the executive departments and offices of the federal government.

Health and Human Services Department
200 Independence Avenue SW
Washington, DC 20201
(202) 619-0257, (877) 696-6775
www.os.dhhs.gov/
Principal federal agency with responsibility for protecting health
  of citizens and providing essential services, especially to those
  of limited means.

Housing and Urban Development Department
451 7th Street SW
Washington, DC 20410
(202) 708-1112
www.hud.gov/
Generally regulates housing matters in the United States.

Immigration and Naturalization Service
425 I Street NW
Washington, DC 20536

(202) 514-4316
www.bcis.gov
Source of information relating to becoming a U.S. citizen.

Internal Revenue Service
1111 Constitution Avenue NW
Washington, DC 20224
(800) 829-1040
www.irs.ustreas.gov/
Determines, assesses, and collects taxes in the United States.

Justice Department
950 Pennsylvania Avenue NW
Washington, DC 20530-0001
(202) 514-2001
www.usdoj.gov/
Chief arm of federal law enforcement.

Labor Department
200 Constitution Avenue NW
Washington, DC 20210
(202) 219-8211, (866) 487-2365
www.dol.gov/
Federal agency charged with enhancing job opportunities and ensuring the adequacy of workplaces.

National Park Service
1849 C Street NW
Washington, DC 20240
(202) 208-6843
www.nps.gov/
Federal office that regulates the use and preservation of national
parks.

**Occupational Safety and Health Administration (in the Labor
Department)**
200 Constitution Avenue NW
Washington, DC 20210
(800) 321-6742 (for emergencies only)
www.osha.gov/

Federal office with responsibility for preventing accidents and illnesses in the workplace.

Official Federal Government Web Sites (maintained by the Library of Congress)
lcweb.loc.gov/global/executive/fed.html
List of sites maintained by various federal agencies and offices.

Secret Service
1800 G Street N
Washington, DC 20223
(202) 435-5708
www.secretservice.gov
Protects the president of the United States and other public officials; investigates certain commercial crimes, including counterfeiting.

Securities and Exchange Commission
450 Fifth Street NW
Washington, DC 20549
(202) 942-7040
www.sec.gov/
Federal agency with responsibility for administering federal securities laws and protecting investors.

Social Security Administration
Office of Public Inquiries
Windsor Park Building
6401 Security Boulevard
Baltimore, MD 21235
(800) 772-1213
www.ssa.gov/
Federal office that administers the Social Security program.

State Department
2201 C Street NW
Washington, DC 20520
(202) 647-4000
www.state.gov/
Chief agency for the implementation of U.S. foreign policy.

Treasury Department
1500 Pennsylvania Avenue NW
Washington, DC 20220
(202) 622-2000
www.ustreas.gov/index.html
Federal agency that regulates currency, taxes, customs, and related matters.

White House
1600 Pennsylvania Aveue NW
Washington, DC 20500
(202) 456-1111, (202) 456-1414
www.whitehouse.gov/
Site providing a variety of information on the U.S. presidency.

LEGAL ORGANIZATIONS

Many nongovernmental organizations also provide information
to the public on particular legal topics. The following list includes
a number of such organizations.

ABA Center for Professional Responsibility
American Bar Association
541 North Fairbanks Court, 14th Floor
Chicago, IL 60611-3314
(312) 988-5305
Web site: www.abanet.org/cpr/home.html
Promotes the study and discussion of ethics relating to lawyers
and judges.

Alliance for Justice
11 Dupont Circle NW, 2nd Floor
Washington, DC 20036
(202) 822-6070
Web site: www.afj.org/
National association of environmental, civil rights, mental health,
women's, children's and consumer advocacy organizations.

American Bar Association
750 N. Lake Shore Drive
Chicago, IL 60611
(312) 988-5000
Web site: www.abanet.org/
National association of lawyers.

American Inns of Court
127 South Peyton Street, Suite 201
Alexandria, Virginia 22314
(703) 684-3590
Web site: www.innsofcourt.org/
Association of lawyers, judges, law teachers, and students dedi-
    cated to increasing professionalism in the practice of law.

Association of Trial Lawyers of America
1050 31st Street NW
Washington, DC 20007
(800) 424-2725, (202) 965-3500
Web site: www.atlanet.org/
Association of plaintiffs' lawyers and others devoted to the cause
    of injured persons and other victims.

Better Business Bureau
Council of Better Business Bureaus, Inc.
4200 Wilson Boulevard, Suite 800
Arlington, VA 22203-1838
(703) 276-0100
Web site: www.bbb.org/
Organization devoted to promoting fair and ethical business
    practices.

Conflict Resolution Center International
204 Thirty-seventh Street
Pittsburgh, PA 15201-1859
(412) 687-6210
Web site: www.conflictres.org/
Organization that promotes nonviolent dispute resolution.

Electronic Privacy Information Center
1718 Connecticut Avenue NW, Suite 200
Washington, DC 20009
(202) 483-1140
Web site: www.epic.org/
Public interest research institute devoted to issues of privacy.

False Claims Act Legal Center
1220 19th Street NW, Suite 501
Washington, DC 20036
(800) 873-2573, (202) 296-4826
Web site: www.taf.org/
Organization that promotes whistle-blowers' suits against individuals and entities that have defrauded the U.S. government.

National Crime Prevention Council
1000 Connecticut Avenue NW, 13th Floor
Washington, DC 20036
(202) 466-6272
Web site: www.ncpc.org/
National organization dedicated to crime prevention.

National Fraud Information Center
National Consumers League
1701 K Street NW, Suite 1200
Washington, DC 20006
(800) 876-7060
Web site: www.fraud.org/
Organization that assists consumers in obtaining advice about telephone solicitations and reporting possible telemarketing fraud to law-enforcement agencies.

National Lawyers Guild
143 Madison Avenue, 4th Floor
New York, NY 10016
(212) 679-5100
Web site: www.nlg.org/
National association of progressive lawyers.

National Organization for Victim Assistance
1730 Park Road NW
Washington, DC 20010
(202) 232-6682
Web site: www.try-nova.org
Nonprofit organization that seeks to further victims' rights.

National Paralegal Association
P.O. Box 406
Solebury, PA 18963
(215) 297-8333
Web site: www.nationalparalegal.org
Organization for paralegals and those interested in a paralegal
    career.

SELECTED RESEARCH CENTERS

The following is a list of selected centers devoted to research on
particular topics. Since the titles of the centers reflect the centers'
concentration, the list does not describe each organization. A few
centers have Web sites, which have been included when available.

ABA Center on Children and the Law
740 15th Street NW
Washington, DC 20005
(202) 662-1720
Web site: www.abanet.org/child

American Indian Law Center
P.O. Box 4456, Station A
Albuquerque, NM 87196
(505) 277-5462
Web site: http://lawschool.unm.edu/AILC

**Arizona State University Center for the Study of Law, Science,
    and Technology**
College of Law
McAllister & Orange Streets

P.O. Box 877906
Tempe, AZ 85287-7906
(480) 965-6181
Web site: www.law.asu.edu/Programs/Sci-Tech/

California Center for Judicial Education and Research
2000 Powell Street, 8th Floor
Emeryville, CA 94608
(510) 450-3601

Center for Dispute Settlement
1666 Connecticut Avenue NW, Suite 501
Washington, DC 20009-1039
(202) 265-9572
Web site: www.cdsusa.org/

Center for Information Technology and Privacy Law, John Marshal Law School
315 South Plymouth Court
Chicago, Illinois 60604
(312) 427-2737
Web site: www.jmls.edu/

Center for Law and Computers, Chicago-Kent College of Law
565 West Adams Street
Chicago, Illinois 60661-3691
(312) 906-5000
Web site: www.kentlaw.edu/clc

Center for Reproductive Rights
120 Wall Street
New York, NY 10005
(917) 637-3600
Web site: www.crlp.org/

Center for Women Policy Studies
1211 Connecticut Avenue NW, Suite 312
Washington, DC 20036
(202) 872-1770
Web site: www.centerwomenpolicy.org/

College of William and Mary Institute of Bill of Rights Law
Marshall-Wythe School of Law
P.O. Box 8795
Williamsburg, VA 23187-8795
(757) 221-3810
Web site: www.wm.edu/law/ibrl/

Columbia University Center for the Study of Human Rights
Columbia University Mail Code: 3365
420 West 118th Street, Room 1108 IAB
New York, NY 10027
(212) 854-2479
Web site: www.columbia.edu/cu/humanrights

Crime Control Institute and Crime Control Research Corporation
1063 Thomas Jefferson Street NW
Washington, DC 20007
(202) 337-2700

Florida State University Center for Employment Relations and Law
College of Law
Tallahassee, FL 32306
(904) 644-4287

Freedom Forum First Amendment Center
Vanderbilt University
1207 18th Avenue South
Nashville, TN 37212
(615) 727-1600
Web site: www.freedomforum.org

Georgetown University Anne Blaine Harrison Institute for Public Law
111 F Street NW, Suite 102
Washington, DC 20001-2075
(202) 662-9600
Web site: www.law.georgetown.edu/clinics/hi/

Harvard Legislative Research Bureau
Harvard Law School
Cambridge, MA 02138
(617) 495-4400

Judge David L. Bazelon Center for Mental Health Law
1101 15th Street NW, Suite 1212
Washington, DC 20005
(202) 467-5730
Web site: www.bazelon.org/

Loyola University of Chicago National Center for Freedom of Information Studies
820 North Michigan Avenue
Chicago, IL 60611
(312) 915-8662

Marine Law Institute, University of Maine School of Law
246 Deering Avenue
Portland, Maine 04102
(207) 780-4474
Web site: www.mli.usm.maine.edu/

Marquette University National Sports Law Institute
Sensenbrenner Hall
1103 West Wisconsin Avenue
Milwaukee, WS 53201
(414) 288-7090
Web site: http://law.marquette.edu/cgi-bin/site.pl

Meiklejohn Civil Liberties Institute
P.O. Box 673
Berkeley, CA 94701-0763
(510) 848-0599
Web site: www.sfsu.edu/~mclicfc/

N. Neal Pike Institute on Law and Disability, Boston University School of Law
765 Commonwealth Avenue
Boston, MA 02215
(617) 353-2904
Web site: www.bu.edu/law/pike/index.html

National Center for Juvenile Justice
710 Fifth Avenue, Suite 3000
Pittsburgh, PA 15219-3000
(412) 227-6950
Web site: http://ncjj.servehttp.com/NCJJWebsite/main.htm

National Center on Women and Family Law
799 Broadway, Room 402
New York, NY 10003
(212) 674-8200

National Council on Crime and Delinquency
1970 Broadway, Suite 500
Oakland, CA 94612
(510) 208-0500
Web site: www.nccd-crc.org/

National Immigration Law Center
3435 Wilshire Boulevard, Suite 2850
Los Angeles, CA 90010
(213) 639-3900
Web site: www.nilc.org/

National Women's Law Center
11 Dupont Circle NW, Suite 800
Washington, DC 20036
202-588-5180
Web site: http://www.nwlc.org/

Vermont Law School Environmental Law Center
P.O. Box 96
Chelsea Street
South Royalton, VT 05068
(888) 277-5985 ext. 1201
Web site: www.vermontlaw.edu/elc/index.cfm

—*Timothy L. Hall*

STATE BAR ASSOCIATIONS

Lawyers within each state and the District of Columbia are organized into a statewide association that serves the interests of its members, the public, and the administration of justice. In many states membership in this bar association is mandatory—that is, a lawyer wishing to practice law in the state must be a member of the bar. In other states membership in the association is purely voluntary.

Bar associations generally supervise several matters of interest to the public. First, the state bar association in the state in which a lawyer practices is normally responsible for the professional discipline of the lawyer. Members of the public who believe that an attorney has acted unethically may make a complaint to the state bar association. In response, the bar typically investigates complaints and, in appropriate cases, brings disciplinary proceedings against a lawyer. Second, most state bar associations assist the public by referring people needing legal assistance to particular lawyers. Third, state bar associations often provide some form of legal education to the general public in the form of public lectures, telephone hotlines, pamphlets, and other services.

Alabama
415 Dexter Avenue
Montgomery, AL 36104
Telephone: (334) 269-1515
Web site: http://www.alabar.org/

Alaska
550 W. 7th Avenue, Suite 1900
Anchorage, AK 99501
Telephone: (907) 272-7469
Web site: http://www.alaskabar.org/

Arizona
111 West Monroe, Suite 1800
Phoenix, AZ 85003-1742
Telephone: (602) 252-4804
Web site: http://www.azbar.org/

Arkansas
400 West Markham
Little Rock, AR 72201
Telephone: (501) 375-4606, (800) 609-5668
Web site: http://www.arkbar.com/

California
180 Howard Street
San Francisco, CA 94105
Telephone: (415) 538-2000
Web site: http://www.calbar.ca.gov/state/calbar/calbar_home.jsp

Colorado
1900 Grant Street, Suite 900
Denver, CO 80203
Telephone: (303) 860-1115
Web site: http://www.cobar.org/

Connecticut
30 Bank Street
New Britain, CT 06050-0350
Telephone: (860) 223-4400
Web site: http://www.ctbar.org/

Delaware
301 North Market Street
Wilmington, DE 19801
Telephone: (302) 658-5279
Web site: http://www.dsba.org/

District of Columbia
1250 H Street NW, 6th Floor
Washington, DC 20005-5937
Telephone: (202) 737-4700
Web site: http://www.dcbar.org/

Florida
651 E. Jefferson Street
Tallahassee, FL 32399-2300
Telephone: (850) 561-5600
Web site: http://www.flabar.org/

Georgia
104 Marietta Street NW, Suite 100
Atlanta, GA 30303
Telephone: (404) 527-8700, (800) 334-6865
Web site: http://www.gabar.org/

Hawaii
1132 Bishop Street, Suite 906
Honolulu, HI 96813
Telephone: (808) 537-1868
Web site: http://www.hsba.org/

Idaho
525 West Jefferson Street
P.O. Box 895
Boise, ID 83701
Telephone: (208) 334-4500
Web site: http://www2.state.id.us/isb/gen/isb_info.htm

Illinois
Illinois Bar Center
424 S. 2nd Street
Springfield, IL 62701
Telephone: (217) 525-1760
Web site: http://www.illinoisbar.org/

Indiana
Indiana Bar Center
230 E. Ohio Street, 4th Floor
Indianapolis, IN 46204-2199
Telephone: (317) 639-5465, (800) 266-2581
Web site: http://www.inbar.org/

Iowa
521 East Locust, 3rd Floor
Des Moines, IA 50309-1939
Telephone: (515) 243-3179
Web site: http://www.iowabar.org/main.nsf

Kansas
1200 SW Harrison Street
Topeka, KS 66612-1806
Telephone: (785) 234-5696
Web site: http://www.ksbar.org/

Kentucky
514 West Main Street
Frankfort, KY 40601-1883
Telephone: (502) 564-3795
Web site: http://www.kybar.org/

Louisiana
601 St. Charles Avenue
New Orleans, LA 70130-3404
Telephone: (504) 566-1600, (800) 421-5722
Web site: http://www.lsba.org/

Maine
124 State Street
P.O. Box 788
Augusta, ME 04332-0788
Telephone: (207) 622-7523
Web site: http://www.mainebar.org/

Maryland
520 W. Fayette Street
Baltimore, MD 21201
Telephone: (410) 685-7878, (800) 492-1964
Web site: http://www.msba.org/index.htm

Massachusetts
20 West Street
Boston, MA 02111
Telephone: (617) 338-0500
Web site: http://www.massbar.org

Michigan
Michael Franck Building
306 Townsend Street
Lansing, MI 48933-2083

Telephone: (800) 968-1442
Web site: http://www.michbar.org/

Minnesota
600 Nicollet Mall, Suite 380
Minneapolis, MN 55402
Telephone: (612) 333-1183, (800) 882-6722
Web site: http://www.mnbar.org/

Mississippi
643 North State Street
P.O. Box 2168
Jackson, MS 39225-2168
Telephone: (601) 948-4471
Web site: http://www.msbar.org/

Missouri
P.O. Box 119
Jefferson City, MO 65102-0119
Telephone: (573) 635-4128
Web site: http://www.mobar.org/

Montana
P.O. Box 577
Helena, MT 59624
Telephone: (406) 442-7660
Web site: http://www.montanabar.org/

Nebraska
635 S. 14th Street, 2nd Floor
P.O. Box 81809
Lincoln, NE 68501
Telephone: (402) 475-7091
Web site: http://www.nebar.com/

Nevada
600 E. Charleston Boulevard
Las Vegas, NV 89104
Telephone: (702) 382-2200
Web site: http://www.nvbar.org

New Hampshire
112 Pleasant Street
Concord, NH 03301
Telephone: (603) 224-6942
Web site: http://www.nhbar.org/

New Mexico
5121 Masthead NE
P.O. Box 92860
Albuquerque, NM 87199-2860
Telephone: (505) 797-6000
Web site: http://www.nmbar.org/

New Jersey
New Jersey Law Center
One Constitution Square
New Brunswick, NJ 08901-1520
Telephone: (732) 249-5000
Web site: http://www.njsba.com/

New York
One Elk Street
Albany, NY 12207
Telephone: (518) 463-3200
Web site: http://www.nysba.org/

North Carolina
P.O. Box 3688
Cary, NC 27519-3688
Telephone: (919) 677-0561, (800) 662-7407
Web site: http://ncbar.org/

North Dakota
515 1/2 East Broadway, Suite 101
P.O. Box 2136
Bismarck, ND 58501
Telephone: (701) 255-1404, (800) 472-2685
Web site: http://www.sband.org/

Ohio
1700 Lake Shore Drive
P.O. Box 16562
Columbus, OH 43204
Telephone: (614) 487-2050, (800) 282-6556
Web site: http://www.ohiobar.org/

Oklahoma
P.O. Box 53036
1901 N. Lincoln Boulevard
Oklahoma City, OK 73152-3036
Telephone: (405) 416-7000
Web site: http://www.okbar.org/

Oregon
5200 SW Meadows Road
P.O. Box 1689
Lake Oswego, OR 97035-0889
Telephone: (503) 620-0222
Web site: http://www.osbar.org/

Pennsylvania
100 South Street
P.O. Box 186
Harrisburg, PA 17108-0186
Telephone: (717) 238-6715
Web site: http://www.pabar.org/

Rhode Island
115 Cedar Street
Providence, RI 02903
Telephone: (401) 421-5740
Web site: http://www.ribar.com/

South Carolina
950 Taylor Street
Columbia, SC 29202
Telephone: (803) 799-6653
Web site: http://www.scbar.org/

South Dakota
222 East Capitol Avenue
Pierre, SD 57501-2596
Telephone: (605) 224-7554, (800) 952-2333
Web site: http://www.sdbar.org/

Tennessee
221 Fourth Avenue North, Suite 400
Nashville, TN 37219-2198
Telephone: (615) 383-7421
Web site: http://www.tba.org/index.html

Texas
1414 Colorado
Austin, TX 78701
Telephone: (512) 463-1463, (800) 204-2222
Web site: http://www.texasbar.com/

Utah
645 S. 200 East, #310
Salt Lake City, UT 84111
Telephone: (801) 531-9077
Web site: http://www.utahbar.org/

Vermont
35-37 Court Street
P.O. Box 100
Montpelier, VT 05601-0100
Telephone: (802) 223-2020
Web site: http://www.vtbar.org/

Virginia
707 E. Main Street, Suite 1500
Richmond, VA 23219-2800
Telephone: (804) 775-0500
Web site: http://www.vsb.org/

Washington
2101 Fourth Avenue, Suite 400
Seattle, WA 98121-2330
Telephone: (206) 443-9722, (800) 945-9722
Web site: http://www.wsba.org/

West Virginia
2006 Kanawha Boulevard East
Charleston, WV 25311-2204
Telephone: (304) 558-2456
Web site: http://www.wvbar.org/

Wisconsin
5302 Eastpark Boulevard
P.O. Box 7158
Madison, WI 53708-7158
Telephone: (608) 257-3838, (800) 728-7788
Web site: http://www.wisbar.org/index.html

Wyoming
500 Randall Avenue
Cheyenne, WY 82001
Telephone: (307) 632-9061
Web site: http://www.wyomingbar.org/

CATEGORIZED INDEX

COURT CASE INDEX

Subject Index